# Guide to Recordings

D0705345

| Composer | Title | | CD/ Track | Cassette Tape/No. |
|---|---|---|---|---|
| | | **Chapter** | | |
| Dufay | "Vasilissa, ergo gaude" | 4.1 | 1/25 | 1a/25 |
| | Gregorian chant, "Pange lingua," stanza 1 | 4.2 | 1/26 | 1a/26 |
| Josquin | *Missa pange lingua*, Kyrie eleison | 4.3 | 1/27 | 1b/1 |
| Josquin | *La Bernardina* | 4.4 | 1/28 | 1b/2 |
| Isaac | "Isbruck, ich muß dich lassen" | 4.5 | 1/29 | 1b/3 |
| Byrd | "Ave verum corpus" | 4.6 | 1/30 | 1b/4 |
| Monteverdi | "A un giro sol de' begli'occhi lucenti" | 4.7 | 1/31 | 1b/5 |
| Morley | "Now Is the Month of Maying" | 4.8 | 1/32 | 1b/6 |
| | **Chapter 5** | | | |
| Monteverdi | *Orfeo*, aria "Vi recorda" | 5.1 | 1/33 | 1b/7 |
| Monteverdi | *Orfeo*, recitative "Tu se' morta" | 5.1 | 1/34 | 1b/8 |
| Monteverdi | "Domine ad adiuvandum" | 5.2 | 1/35 | 1b/9 |
| Carissimi | *Jephte*, "Plorate filii Israel" | 5.3 | 1/36 | 1b/10 |
| Frescobaldi | Canzona "LaVincenti" | 5.4 | 1/37 | 1b/11 |
| D. Gaultier | *Rhétorique des dieux*, Gigue in G Major for lute | 5.5 | 1/38 | 1b/12 |
| Corelli | Sonata in A Major, Op. 4, No. 3 | 5.6 | 1/39 | 1b/13 |
| | **Chapter 6** | | | |
| Vivaldi | Violin Concerto in G Major, Op. 3, No. 3, movement 1 | 6.1 | 1/40 | 1b/14 |
| Couperin | *Leçons de ténèbres*, lesson 1, opening | 6.2 | 2/1 | 2a/1 |
| Bach | *Herz und Mund und Tat und Leben*, BWV 147, movement 6 | 6.3 | 2/2 | 2a/2 |
| Bach | *Brandenburg Concerto* No. 2, movement 1 | 6.4 | 2/3 | 2a/3 |
| Bach | Toccata and Fugue in D Minor, BWV 565 | 6.5 | 2/4 | 2a/4 |
| Handel | *Tamerlano*, "Se non mi vuol amar" | 6.6 | 2/5 | 2a/5 |
| Handel | *Messiah*, "Comfort Ye" | 6.7 | 2/6 | 2a/6 |
| Handel | *Messiah*, "Ev'ry Valley" | 6.7 | 2/7 | 2a/7 |
| Handel | *Messiah*, Hallelujah Chorus | 6.8 | 2/8 | 2b/1 |
| | **Chapter 7** | | | |
| Pergolesi | *La serva padrona*, "Sempre in contrasti" | 7.1 | 2/9 | 2b/2 |
| J. C. Bach | Symphony in D Major, Op. 18, No. 4, movement 3 | 7.2 | 2/10 | 2b/3 |

# The Art of Music

# The Art of Music

## An Introduction

**Bryan R. Simms**
*University of Southern California*

*HarperCollinsCollegePublishers*

Acquisitions Editor: Lisa Moore
Developmental Editor: Walt Jackson
Project Editor: Brigitte Pelner
Text and Cover Design: Dorothy Bungert
Cover Illustration: Jacob Rosinski
Photo Researcher: Rosemary Hunter
Production Administrators: Kathleen Donnelly and Valerie A. Sawyer
Compositor: York Graphic Services, Inc.
Printer and Binder: Von Hoffmann Press, Inc.
Cover Printer: The Lehigh Press, Inc.

For permission to use copyrighted material, grateful acknowledgment is made to the
copyright holders on pp. 519–520, which are hereby made part of this copyright page.

The Art of Music: An Introduction
Copyright © 1993 by Bryan R. Simms

All rights reserved. Printed in the United States of America. No part of this book may be
used or reproduced in any manner whatsoever without written permission, except in the
case of brief quotations embodied in critical articles and reviews. For information address
HarperCollins College Publishers, 10 East 53rd Street, New York, NY 10022.

Library of Congress Cataloging-in-Publication Data

Simms, Bryan R.
    The art of music: an introduction / Bryan R. Simms.
        p.    cm.
    Includes bibliographical references and index.
    ISBN 0-673-38916-2   (Student edition)
    ISBN 0-673-46826-7   (Instructor edition)
    1. Music appreciation.   I. Title.
MT90.S55 1992
780—dc20                                        92-16878
                                                CIP
                                                MN

92  93  94  95  9  8  7  6  5  4  3  2  1

# Contents in Brief

*v*

# Contents

Contents

**2.**
**Rhythm,**
**Form, and**
**Musical**
**Instruments**
**45**

## Movement II • Early Music  75

**3.**
**Music**
**in the**
**Medieval**
**World**
**77**

Contents

**4.
Music
in the
Age of
Humanism
111**

Contents

**5.**
**The Early**
**Baroque**
**Period,**
**1600–1700**
**143**

Contents

**6.
The Late
Baroque
Period,
1700–1750
175**

## MOVEMENT III • Music of Modern Times   211

**7.**
***Introduction
to the
Classical
Style
213***

Contents

## 8. Viennese Classicism 245

Contents

**9.**
**The Age of Expression: Music in the Early Nineteenth Century 287**

**10.
The Late
Romantic
Period,
1850–1900
321**

**11.
The
Rebellion
Against
Romanticism,
1900–1945
361**

## Contents

**12.
Music
in the
Age of
Anxiety,
1945
to the
Present
401**

Contents

# MOVEMENT IV • Jazz and Non-Western Music   431

**13.
Jazz
433**

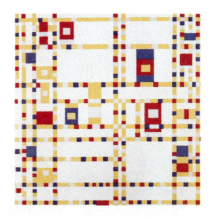

**14.
The
Music of
Selected
World
Cultures
467**

# Music Today

# Preface

This book is designed for basic courses in music and music history. It deals with music from both the European tradition and non-Western cultures. Throughout the book, four repeated points of emphasis help students to develop an appreciation for music and for its relation to art and culture.

## Points of Emphasis

The primary emphasis is on selected works of music. Students will learn how these pieces came to be composed and how they convey meaning. The works that were chosen represent the major styles and categories of music throughout history. They were also selected on the basis of their appeal to my students who have studied them. The selection of music is broad, including masterworks by such composers as Couperin, Denis Gaultier, Fauré, Nancarrow, and others often ignored in similar texts.

The principal musical selections are all contained on an accompanying set of six recordings, which are available as either cassette tapes or compact discs. These recordings should be obtained by all users of this book, since the discussion in the text relies on careful and repeated listening to the music. The recordings are made from outstanding, up-to-date performances, which, so far as possible, are historically accurate in choice of instruments and performing styles. Each musical selection in the recording package is numbered for easy reference to the text. "Recording 10.3," for example, is the third selection in Chapter 10. A synopsis of all of these musical selections, showing each one's identifying number, the CD/track, and cassette tape/number, is given inside the front and back covers of this book. The identifying numbers are also given in the discussions of the selections within the text itself as well as in the Listening Guides that are provided for virtually all of the musical works.

A second area of emphasis is to show music in its cultural context. The opening pictures and vignettes that begin each chapter and the discussions which immediately follow will help to establish the intellectual and historical setting in which this music was composed. Students will learn that music is a part of the culture in which it develops.

A third focal point in the book is to show, whenever possible, the relation of musical ideas in the past to those of the present. With this goal in mind, I have included in each chapter a discussion called "Music Today." Students will discover that many aspects of contemporary or recent musical culture have their origin in music of the past. I have also emphasized twentieth-century music in the text itself, devoting two chapters to it and also referring to modern innovations in the survey of musical elements at the beginning.

A fourth emphasized feature is the investigation of music of non-Western cultures. Learning about music throughout the world is especially important in any study of the art of music today. Students will learn of the increasingly close relationship between Western music and music outside of the European tradition.

## Organization

The organization of the book follows that of a symphony with a prelude and four movements. The prelude should be read by students first, as it deals with basic general information about listening to music and about the differences among the popular, folk, and classical styles. The prelude is an overview of music outside of the chronological material presented in the chapters.

At the heart of the book are four large parts, or "movements." Movement I (Chapters 1 and 2) surveys the elements of music and terminology. In covering this material, readers will need no previous musical training or knowledge of musical notation. The terms and concepts introduced here, however, are fundamental for the later discussions. I urge the users of this book to begin with Movement I, since a firm knowledge of basic terms, concepts, and listening strategies will be needed for all that follows.

Movement II (Chapters 3–6) deals with music of the European tradition from the Middle Ages through the baroque period. Movement III (Chapters 7–12) continues this tradition with music from the mid-eighteenth century through the twentieth. After the basic introduction of Movement I, a strictly chronological reading can be followed, or readers can leap to Movement III, beginning with music of the classical period and later returning to early music. This plan has the advantage of beginning with music of the age of Haydn, Mozart, Beethoven, and the romantics, with which students may be more familiar. Movement III is, in fact, written so that this nonchronological usage is possible.

Movement IV (Chapters 13 and 14) deals with the African-American heritage of jazz and with music of non-Western cultures. The final chapter investigates music of India, Japan, Africa, Indonesia, and native North Americans.

## Learning Aids

At the conclusion of each chapter, the reader will find a concise bibliography of books, all in English and all accessible to the nonspecialist. There are also suggestions for additional listening for readers whose interest has been stimulated and suggested topics for written essays or for general discussion.

The Appendix contains a brief lesson on reading musical notation. Although knowledge of musical notation is not necessary for studying this book, some instructors may want to use the Appendix to present the fundamentals of reading musical notation to their classes.

A glossary at the end of the book contains definitions of technical musical terms and obscure instruments. The first time any glossary word is defined in the text it appears in bold type.

## Available Supplements

The Study Guide that supplements this text serves as a review of each chapter and a means for students to prepare for examinations. It contains questions of different types on the materials of each chapter and on the works of music that have been analyzed. Using the guide is a way for students to extend their thinking about music and about the ideas they have encountered in the book.

The Instructor's Edition contains the complete text and provides scores (sheet music) of selected pieces discussed within. It also includes outlines regarding the discussion questions at the end of each chapter and practical teaching suggestions for lessons.

TestMaster, a Computerized Test Bank (IBM or Macintosh), is available to instructors. It contains a variety of questions in different formats for each chapter in the book. With TestMaster instructors can design their own examinations and quizzes. It is also available as a Print Test Bank in hard copy.

Grades, a grade-keeping software package for the IBM PC and compatibles, maintains data for up to 200 students, and is available to adopters.

In addition to the Recording Package of six compact discs or six cassette tapes already mentioned, qualified adopters of this book may obtain laserdiscs or videos of select operas and concerts identified in the text's Listening Guides. An attractive selection of compact discs or cassettes of works cited in the "Additional Listening" sections at the ends of chapters is also available to qualified adopters. For more information, please contact your local HarperCollins representative.

## Acknowledgments

I am deeply grateful to all who have assisted me with the writing of this book. My wife, Charlotte E. Erwin, read the entire manuscript and made many suggestions for its improvement. Leah Morrison and William Thomson, my colleagues at the University of Southern California, commented on parts of the book and offered valuable advice. Donald Crockett, Vicki Ray, and Larry Lash assisted in producing the recording package and musical examples. I gratefully acknowledge the suggestions made by colleagues at other universities who reviewed the manuscript: Thomas Bauman, University of Washington; Karen Bryan, Georgia State University; James Davis, Tallahassee Community College; Daniel Fairchild, University of Wisconsin; Richard Fisk, Los Angeles Pierce College; William George, San Jose

*Preface*

*State University; William Gudger, College of Georgia; Rudolph Kremer, University of North Carolina; Arthur Lewis, Illinois State University; Rey Longyear, University of Kentucky; Robert Mann, Austin State University; Raymond Moore, University of Georgia; Wayne Moore, Auburn University; Roy Nitzberg, Queens College; Michael Tusa, University of Texas; and Steven Winick, Georgia State University. The assistance and support of the editors at HarperCollins have been unstinting, especially that of Lisa Moore and Walt Jackson. Finally, my students in music classes at the University of Southern California have taught me a great deal by helping me to formulate ideas about explaining music.*

*Bryan R. Simms*

# The Art of Music

# Prelude

---

## The Art
## of Music

---

## Three Musicians

*Our curiosity about this painting by Pablo Picasso will probably be directed at first to the way that its images are formed, rather than to the element of music mentioned in its title, "Three Musicians." To be sure, the artist's technique is highly ingenious. By using flat, starkly colored shapes that fit together like a jigsaw puzzle, he has created several recognizable images. Within a darkly lit room there appear three figures engaged in a musical performance. The one on* the left is dressed in the loose white gown of Pierrot, a familiar clownlike character in traditional comedies and pantomimes. He plays what appears to be a woodwind instrument. In the middle is the brightly checkered outfit of the related clown Harlequin, who is playing a guitar. At the right is a bearded and hooded monk, a character type sometimes appearing in popular theater. He seems to be singing from the sheet music that he holds. A dog is lying on the floor to the left.

The painting has an exceedingly flat quality, almost as though the component pieces were made from colored paper that has been pasted on the canvas. Part of Harlequin's face resembles a wire mesh, thus increasing the resemblance of the picture to the technique of collage, which Picasso had essayed only a few years before 1921, when this picture was completed. Indeed, Picasso's organization and assembly of the painting is a virtuosic display of new artistic resources.

But what does the painting mean? Why are characters from traditional comedy enlisted? What is the role of music? We can give only tentative answers to such questions. The characters Pierrot and Harlequin recur in paintings throughout Picasso's long and diverse career. In an earlier picture, "Family of Saltimbanques," Picasso depicts himself as Harlequin, a sad and tragic figure destined by fate to wander about giving performances, but never achieving permanence or acceptance. Picasso, like his clown figures, must have sensed that his own destiny as an artist was to wander in isolation, *performing for a skeptical audience by whom he would never be fully understood.*

*Music—also a recurrent subject in Picasso's paintings—appears to be a symbol for art in general. It can be produced by comedians like Pierrot and Harlequin, by performers with instruments, or by a painter like Picasso himself. Picasso lines his three musicians up, across the very front edge of the canvas. Their eyes bear down on us, as though asking us to listen carefully to their song and to try to fathom its importance. It is truly an emotional appeal to meet them halfway and to become as engaged as they are in their art.*

Human beings have always performed and listened to music. From prehistory until the present, the vitality of music in human culture is evidence of a continuing need to communicate artistically and to share in the pleasure that music offers. But what does music of earlier times have to do with our own interests or our present concerns? The answer is: everything! The music that we listen to today and our entire understanding of it rest on the work of centuries of musicians and lovers of music, who have passed on to us a vigorous stock of ideas that shape our modern tastes and outlook. This book will seek to chronicle this development by looking closely at the diversity of music past and present.

To show how the past informs the present, let us examine ideas concerning music among the ancient Greeks. To begin with, the Greeks gave us the word for music—*mousiké*—or art of the Muses. Naming music collectively after these patronesses of the arts suggests its closeness in Greek culture to poetry, dance, and other forms of artistic expression. Indeed, the term *music* was sometimes used by ancient writers to designate intellectual activity in a general sense, although it also referred more specifically to the combination of sounds accompanying dance or poetic declamation. Music as a completely independent art of sound originated relatively late in Greek culture.

4

The Greeks developed ideas about the nature of music that have continued to shape our understanding of it to this day. The first of these is the notion that music can arouse emotions or even change the state of mind of the hearer. Both Plato and Aristotle comment on the marvelous effect of certain types of music on people's actions. Given these powers, music was invaluable in education, since it could be used to dispose young minds toward the good and the beautiful. "Education in music is most sovereign," wrote Plato in *The Republic,* "because more than anything else, rhythm and harmony find their way to the inmost soul and take strongest hold upon it, bringing with them and imparting grace."

The Greeks also believed that music represented a numerical organization in audible form. In *Timaeus,* Plato refined the preexisting idea that music reflected the mathematical scheme of the cosmos. By comparing the lengths of strings which, when plucked, produced musical tones, Plato and his contemporaries discovered that these lengths formed only simple numerical ratios in relation to each other, just as the universe itself was thought to consist of simple mixtures of fire, air, earth, and water. So strong was the perception that music rested on a science of numbers that it was studied throughout the Middle Ages as a mathematical discipline, within the "quadrivium" of learning that also included arithmetic, geometry, and astronomy.

*The great philosopher Aristotle (384–322 B.C.) was one of the most important early writers on music. His doctrines reflect the idealism of his teacher, Plato, but he also accepts music for its mundane values. This statue of Aristotle was copied by a Roman sculptor from a Greek original.*

Finally, the Greeks recognized that music could be a delightful and valuable form of entertainment. Although idealists such as Plato were little interested in music as a source of idle amusement, we can be sure that it had this use for many of his contemporaries. Aristotle explicitly approved of music as a leisure activity. In the *Politics,* he writes:

> For all harmless pleasures are not only suitable for the ultimate object but also for relaxation; and as it but rarely happens for men to reach

5

their ultimate object, whereas they often relax and pursue amusement not so much with some ulterior object but because of the pleasure of it, it would be serviceable to let them relax at intervals in the pleasures derived from music.[1]

The threefold Greek view of music as emotional or ethical stimulus, numerical organization, and as entertainment has resounded throughout history and still echoes in the present day. Music continues to evoke our emotions and to spur us to action. The twentieth-century composer Paul Hindemith reminds us of Plato in his belief that music is an ethical stimulus that we can convert into moral betterment:

> It is our own mind that brings about this conversion; music is but a catalytic agent to this end. The betterment of our soul must be our own achievement, although music is one of those factors which, like religious belief, creates in us most easily a state of willingness towards this betterment. In short, we have to be active; music, like humus in a garden soil, must be dug under in order to become fertile.[2]

Music in our own time is still interpreted by important composers and theoreticians as an art of numbers. The contemporary American composer Milton Babbitt, for example, has used set theory to guide his work. "Contemporary serious music," writes Babbitt,

> is a result of a half-century of revolution in musical thought, a revolution whose nature and consequences can be compared only with, and in many respects are closely analogous to, those of the midnineteenth-century revolution in mathematics and the twentieth-century revolution in theoretical physics.[3]

But we can also ignore, at least temporarily, these deeper understandings of music and relish it purely as the "harmless pleasure" of which Aristotle spoke. Music heard purely as a leisure activity, a means of relaxation, or a simple diversion is as valid for the classics as for popular music. It can be, in the words of the eighteenth-century critic Charles Burney, "an innocent luxury, unnecessary, indeed, to our existence, but a great improvement and gratification of the sense of hearing."

A proper understanding and enjoyment of music need not be limited to these ideas inherited from the ancients. From our own experience with music, we can add other ways in which we have found this art to be an important part of our lives. Some of these aspects of music surely have more importance than others, but their diversity suggests that music is, in the words of the eighteenth-century writer Joseph Riepel, "an inexhaustible sea." It is perhaps just this multiplicity of meanings that has given music its continuing vitality, which holds out to each era a significance that must be pondered anew.

## Listening to Music

Even though we may be aware of the power of music to communicate and to inspire, most of us today feel that we do not entirely "understand" music, especially classical music, and for this reason we may suspect that we do not fully enjoy or appreciate it. To be sure, classical music is not, for most people, a part of everyday culture, and this unfamiliarity may be the source of insecurity that many of us feel in its presence. How, then, can we remedy this situation and come to a better understanding and appreciation of music?

The most basic faculty leading to an understanding of classical music is *concentration*. All else depends on it. The importance of concentration makes classical music different from many other types of music. Some popular music, including much rock as well as background music, may be enjoyed and have an effect even if it is not the sole object of our attention. Classical music, on the contrary, demands our complete engagement, and a primary reason that listeners who are familiar with popular music have difficulty in understanding the classics is that total concentration is not customary in their approach to listening.

Another strategy for successful listening is to gain *familiarity* with as much great music as possible. For virtually all lovers of classical music, enjoyment and understanding increase as we hear more music and as we listen repeatedly to the masterworks. In this way we become familiar with their melodic and harmonic language, we learn to listen for favorite passages, and we become accustomed to certain styles. A lack of familiarity is a key reason why classical music, especially that of the twentieth century, is not more universally or more readily understood.

Another method by which we can enhance our enjoyment of music is to teach ourselves to recognize and to understand its *elements*. We should know a melody when we hear one and understand how it differs from harmony or rhythm. We should be able to differentiate the various textures of music. Gradually, we should be able to distinguish between musical styles and the distinctive musical parlance of major composers. Our appreciation of music will also be enhanced by our perseverance in listening, our willingness to open our ears to unfamiliar styles, and a curiosity about music of different cultures and historical eras.

A final and necessary requirement for a better understanding and enjoyment of music is *active involvement*. Classical music understandably seems remote and difficult to people who have never seriously played an instrument or sung or who rarely hear live musical performances. These activities are basic to an appreciation of music. It is never too late to take up a musical instrument or to learn to read music. Practice will, of course, be required, but time spent in this way will be repaid many times over.

Throughout history, amateur music making has been a delightful entertainment for people of all backgrounds and professions. It can pay social dividends, and it helps to cultivate an interest in and sensitivity to good music. Participation in singing groups is especially suitable for the amateur. The value of this activity is underscored by Paul Hindemith:

> Once you join an amateur group, you are a member of a great fraternity, whose purpose is the most dignified one you can imagine: to inspire one another and unite in building up a creation that is greater than one individual's deeds. Amateurs of this kind, when listening to music, will not be the stupid receivers, the targets of virtuosity, the idle gourmands of which our audiences predominantly consist.[4]

Attending concerts of classical music is a pleasant duty for all who love music. Recordings, even under the best of circumstances, miss important elements of music: richness of sound, contact with performers, an awareness of new insights into the masterpieces of music that are brought by sensitive artists, and an awareness that music is a living art. While learning about music, it is of the utmost importance to attend concerts and to make music.

While studying music, we should cultivate the habit of listening with concentration and exploring the constituent elements of music, all the while inquiring about the ideas or meanings that great works of music communicate to us. The rewards from this study will be a better understanding of our own emotional and artistic faculties and an increased sensitivity to the beautiful, wherever it may be encountered. It will also teach us a powerful lesson about the culture in which we live. If we learn about our culture solely from a history of political events or economic factors, we may neglect the more basic motivating forces among people. Art reveals this dimension of history, since it documents the inner life and emotion of humanity. Art—more than any other product of a society—reveals the essence of life.

## Attending Concerts

One of the most pleasurable aspects of studying music is making it the occasion for regular attendance at concerts of classical music and opera. This may be found so enjoyable that it will become a lifelong habit! All lovers of good music regularly go to concerts. Even the best of recorded performances cannot compare to the interest, sound quality, and drama that live music provides.

You can probably find listings of forthcoming concerts in a local or campus newspaper. Be as adventuresome as possible. Try to attend at least one performance of an opera, a symphony concert, an early music concert, a contemporary music concert, and a jazz concert in the near future. Tickets can normally be purchased at a box office or through ticket agencies, and phone orders are often possible. Don't forget to inquire about the availability of discounted tickets for students. Most concert organizations have special prices for students, especially if a concert is not sold out.

The more you know in advance about the music to be performed, the more enjoyable the concert will be. If you are about to attend an opera, it is especially important to read the story of the work beforehand (the text of an opera can usually be located in a recording of the work or in a music library). How you dress is up to you. Wear whatever you feel comfortable wearing. Even at formal concerts, one will see as many people in jeans as in tuxedos. The important thing is being there.

Some conventions of concert behavior may at first seem unusual. First is the necessity in a classical concert of maintaining absolute silence once the music has begun. This is perhaps different from a rock or pop concert. In order to concentrate on the music, it is crucial that there be no talking or whispering whatsoever, no rustling of candy wrappers or programs, and a minimum of coughing.

One final word of advice. All performers appreciate applause for a good performance. But applause, like other forms of noise, should be reserved until the right time. A good rule of thumb is this: Don't be the first to applaud, and don't applaud between movements of a longer work.

Concert conventions are designed to allow you to focus totally on the music. Once you have learned to immerse yourself in the experience, you will find there is nothing quite like it. Enjoy yourself!

# The Types of Music

Even by a casual hearing of music such as Beatles songs, African tribal chanting, Scottish folk ballads, or symphonies by Beethoven, we can immediately sense that the realm of music is divided into distinct provinces. All music is not the same: It does not all carry the same ideas, and it is not intended to be heard in the same way, even though it is all made from the same materials. At least four general types of music exist: artistic music (also called "classical" or "serious" music), popular music, folk music, and tribal or primitive music. Let us explore the ways in which these categories differ from one another.

**Popular music** consists of pieces that are relatively simple in construction and direct or immediate in effect. They are intended to entertain, divert, or stimulate a mass audience, and they do not demand study or total concentration to have their intended impact. They are composed and performed, by and large, by professional musicians. Most popular music involves singing. The words that are used normally deal with mundane subjects with which people are familiar, and their presence in the music facilitates our understanding of it.

Music of this description is relatively recent in origin, since its existence is tied to a large middle class with sufficient leisure time to seek entertainment. Popular music remained a minor phenomenon until the appearance of mass media (including radio, phonograph, and television) in the twentieth century. Currently, popular styles such as rock and country are central to the entertainment industry.

**Folk music** consists primarily of songs and dance tunes that are composed either by amateurs or by trained musicians. Because of their uncomplicated structure, simplicity of performance, and widely appealing sentiments, such pieces are taken over by a large segment of a society, passed on by an oral rather than by a written tradition, and performed and appreciated by a large number of people not trained in music. Many folk songs use simple rhymes intended for children; others contain more sophisticated, though nonetheless mundane, poetry.

Folk music may be of great antiquity, preserved, with many variants, over a span of centuries. It may also be recent in origin; in fact, many of the best-known American folk songs were composed in the twentieth century.

**Tribal music** shares many of the characteristics of folk music. Both consist of pieces that are passed on orally among amateur musicians, and both are heard and preserved by a large segment of the society in which they exist. Tribal music differs from folk music in that it exists in nonliterate cultures, where artistic music does not simultaneously exist. Tribal music is also much

*Georges Seurat's depiction of the* chahut—*a type of dance akin to the cancan— captures the gaiety of the Parisian music hall at the end of the nineteenth century. His painting technique, called* pointillism, *was highly original. Tiny dots of pure color were applied to the canvas, which, at a distance, seem to merge into recognizable images.*

more functional than either artistic or folk music, since it is normally encountered in the religious or social rituals of its culture rather than being intended purely for entertainment or spiritual development.

**Artistic music** is written by trained musicians in literate cultures. It is preserved primarily among the educated classes, and its intent is, at least in part, to move the emotions, to edify or inspire, or to produce spiritual betterment. Its value to society leads to its preservation (usually in a written form) and maintenance over long periods of time. It is this category of music with which this book will primarily deal, although our discussion will also lead us briefly into a consideration of folk and popular genres. Many types of music originated as popular or folk styles but have developed with classical tendencies. American jazz is an example. Classical music also exists outside of the European tradition, as, for example, in the art music of India and the Orient.

## BIBLIOGRAPHY

A provocative introduction to the art of music is contained in a series of books stemming from the Charles Eliot Norton Lectures at Harvard University. This distinguished lectureship is normally held by scholars in literature, but musicians are occasionally appointed, and the books that have resulted establish a high level of cogency and original thought. All are intended for the general student of music rather than for the specialist. The following books on music are among those that have arisen from the Norton Lectures:

Bernstein, Leonard. *The Unanswered Question: Six Talks at Harvard.* The Charles Eliot Norton Lectures, 1973. Cambridge, Mass.: Harvard University Press, 1976. Bernstein applies to music the theory of transformational grammar associated with the linguist Noam Chomsky.

Copland, Aaron. *Music and Imagination.* The Charles Eliot Norton Lectures, 1951–1952. Cambridge, Mass.: Harvard University Press, 1952. Copland investigates the powerful effect of music on the imaginative mind. He also deals authoritatively with the special role of the composer in America.

Hindemith, Paul. *A Composer's World: Horizons and Limitations.* The Charles Eliot Norton Lectures, 1949–1950. Garden City, N.Y.: Anchor/Doubleday, 1961. Hindemith's lectures are wide-ranging, touching on aspects of musical creativity, perception, performance, and education. He strongly asserts his belief in the ethical aspect of music and its demands on composers.

Sessions, Roger. *Questions About Music.* The Charles Eliot Norton Lectures, 1968–1969. New York: Norton, 1971. Sessions focuses on the importance of the "willing listener" and the characteristics of such willingness.

Stravinsky, Igor. *Poetics of Music in the Form of Six Lessons.* Translated by Arthur Knodel and Ingolf Dahl. Preface by Darius Milhaud. The Charles Eliot Norton Lectures, 1939–1940. New York: Vintage Books, 1947. Stravinsky's lectures were delivered in French. In them, he deals with the elements of music and with his own approach to composition. It is likely that the lectures were ghostwritten by Alexis Roland-Manuel and Pierre Souvchintsky, and they repeat opinions touched on by Stravinsky in his autobiographical *Chroniques de ma vie* (1935).

## NOTES

**1.** Aristotle, *Politics,* trans. H. Rackham (Cambridge, Mass.: Harvard University Press, 1944), p. 655.

**2.** Paul Hindemith, *A Composer's World* (Garden City, N.Y.: Anchor/Doubleday, 1961), p. 6.

**3.** Milton Babbitt, ''Who Cares If You Listen?'' *High Fidelity,* 8 (February 1958), 38.

**4.** Hindemith, *A Composer's World,* p. 253.

# *Movement*
# I

# The Elements
# of Music

**Music** is an organization of sounds and time capable of conveying meaning. What principles guide this organization? How do musical gestures express meaning? An exploration of these questions will lead us to a close study of the elements of music, a knowledge of which is basic to its enjoyment. Although we may be delighted and inspired by the exterior appearance of a sculpture, a more profound understanding of it will be gained by knowing how it is put together, how its parts relate to one another, and how its form helps to express its aesthetic content. So it is in hearing a piece of music. Our attention may at first be attracted by an external or general feature, but our full understanding and appreciation will begin only when we perceive its complete shape, differentiate its constituent parts, and understand how they work together to produce their effect.

We all have an intuitive idea of the parts of a musical work, since we have all at some time made music by singing, whistling, or playing an instrument. If we whistle a piece that we know by heart, we are immediately confronted by the element of *melody,* which consists of the tune of our piece. An aspect of melody of which we are also instinctively aware is *rhythm*, heard in the varying lengths of time that the notes are held. If our tune is accompanied by a guitar or a piano, these instruments are probably playing sounds called *harmonies* that make our melody more enjoyable to hear.

Our piece is clearly more elaborate if it is accompanied by an instrument than if we whistle it alone, and this difference in the outward quality of the work is called *texture*. The tune obviously has a different effect depending on whether it is whistled, sung, or played on an instrument; we apply the term *medium* to describe this distinction. Our piece, finally, has a certain *form*, depending on how and when its subsections recur.

A discussion of the constituent elements of music will help us to learn what to listen for in a piece of music, and we should be attentive to each of these parts and features and try to describe and compare them verbally. The first two chapters will also assist us in developing a basic vocabulary with which to discuss the musical masterworks introduced in later chapters.

# 1

## Melody and Its
## Presentation in Music

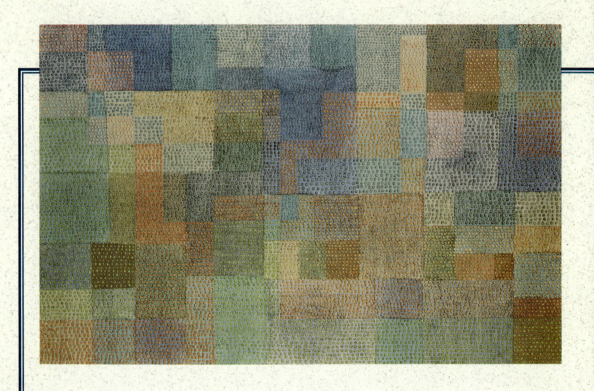

## Words and Music

*What do we see in this painting by Paul Klee? How can we describe its elements, subject, or meaning? These are not simple questions, since Klee's picture resists description in everyday terms. The painting contains no identifiable objects. It appears to consist instead only of intersecting squares and patches of color. But the picture is nonetheless expressive and meaningful, since it piques our curiosity and holds our interest. In order to describe it and to discover how it engages our attention, we need words to capture the elusive elements of the picture and to aid in explaining its ideas.*

The same need for an appropriate descriptive language will be felt when we encounter a piece of music. Like Klee's painting, music normally contains no concrete objects, only fleeting and immaterial sounds. How can we put into words what these sounds mean or how they relate to one another? The answers to such questions, in art as in music, can be found only after we command a vocabulary that will allow us to learn of and to communicate the principles of organization and expression in artistic works.

Klee, a Swiss painter who lived from 1879 to 1940, gives us a hint about the meaning of his painting by its one-word title: "Polyphony." This term comes from music. Polyphony is an element encountered in certain musical works, a way in which a composer can present certain types of ideas. A polyphony is created when several melodies are stated simultaneously. To an extent, these tunes keep their own identities. We could easily sing them one by one. But together, merged into a polyphony, they form an intricate fabric or texture by which their impact is magnified.

This simultaneity of dimensions is also apparent in Klee's painting. It consists of a complex, abstract vision made from interwoven lines and colors. The artist's inspiration for this textural quality probably came from music. Klee was himself a trained musician, well versed in musical concepts and terminology. He often found in the structure of music an analogy with his own concepts of visual organization.

In his writings and lectures on art, Klee spoke of the need for a painting to achieve a "polyphony" of simultaneous lines, tone values, and colors. He found it difficult to explain this simultaneity in words, so he resorted to the metaphor of music. In his lecture "On Modern Art" (1924), he describes simultaneity as the key to the drama of his paintings:

> The so-called spatial arts have long succeeded in expressing what the time-bound art of music has also gloriously achieved in the harmoniousness of polyphony: this phenomenon of many simultaneous dimensions, which helps to bring the drama to its climax.

Klee's discussion shows that a deeper understanding of art, whether it be abstract painting or music, demands from us a basic knowledge of rudiments and their terminology. Without the proper vocabulary, we will be deprived not only of the tools to communicate about music in a significant way, but also of the possibility of learning what to listen for in music. In Chapter 1 of this book, we begin to develop an understanding of how musical compositions are put together.

## A Checklist of Basic Musical Elements and Terms

### Melody

| | | |
|---|---|---|
| phrase | note (tone) | keynote (tonic) |
| motive | pitch | tonality |
| cadence | interval | key |
| rest | half step (semitone) | atonality |
| theme | whole step (whole tone) | scale (major, minor) |
| register | leap | mode |
| introduction | octave | period form |
| | | sequence |

### Harmony

| | | |
|---|---|---|
| accompaniment | consonance | triad |
| chord | dissonance | resolution |

### Texture

| | | |
|---|---|---|
| monophony | counterpoint | canon |
| homophony | broken chord | fugue |
| polyphony | round | subject |
| | | mass of sound |

"Supremacy to melody, the noblest element of music!" Most lovers of music can heartily agree with this declaration by the French composer Olivier Messiaen. We all tend to remember a piece of music by its tune. It is what usually first attracts our attention and what makes us want to return to a piece to hear it again. Given this overriding importance, we will want to know about the main features of a melody, how one is put together from more basic elements, and how it can be presented in an actual musical work. These are the subjects addressed in this chapter.

## Melody and Its Basic Materials

Let us begin our investigation of the nature of melody by listening to a passage from Mozart's Piano Concerto No. 21 (Recording 1.1). What is it about this music that makes it so eloquent and touching? What aspect of the work is most easily recalled, and what part of the music most directly captures its meaning? No doubt it is the melody, a dimension of music in which Mozart was supremely gifted.

A **melody** is a succession of musical tones that belong together and convey a distinctive musical thought. Using this definition, we can distinguish melodies from other musical phenomena. Imagine a succession of tones that are chosen and played randomly. These do not create a melody since the notes do not belong together in any musical context. Now listen to the succession of tones heard on Recording 1.2 (Figure 1.1). (Musical examples are provided for the benefit of those who read music. The ideas that they illustrate can also be understood by listening carefully to the recorded excerpts.) These notes do, in fact, seem to belong together, but we cannot consider them melodic since they are undistinctive: They are repetitive, formulaic, and unvaried. Clearly, they do not create a melody because they convey no distinctive musical idea.

**Figure 1.1**

Now listen again to Mozart's melody on Recording 1.1. After a brief introduction, the violins enunciate a series of tones that is both distinctive and coherent. It is the central focus of the music, and, in its great expressivity, it conveys the musical thought.

### The Components of Melody

What makes this and other melodies so powerful and important to musical expression? An answer can be found by comparing melodies to elements of verbal expression. Indeed, a melody within a musical composition is very similar to an important sentence in an essay or other written composition. Both melodies and sentences contain complete and distinctive thoughts, and both are comparable in structure. A sentence, like a melody, is readily divisible into smaller units of thought, called **phrases.** Consider the first sentence in Hamlet's soliloquy from Shakespeare's *Hamlet,* Act 3: "To be or not to be, that is the question." This famous line is divided at the comma into two units that are joined together in order to clarify their meaning. Mozart's melody falls, similarly, into several units or phrases, each marked off by a brief silence that is comparable to the division in Shakespeare's line. Such divisions into phrases make both the sentence and the melody easier to comprehend and to retain.

Both musical and verbal phrases are themselves divisible into still smaller, though nonetheless distinctive, fragmentary units. In music, these smallest distinctive patterns are called **motives.** They are decidedly incomplete in themselves, but they provide the composer with building blocks with which to construct larger compositions. Motives in a musical work often recur in subtle transformations to build up longer units of thought or even within what may seem to be different melodic ideas. In this way they promote unity and ease of comprehension.

In Shakespeare's play, a counterpart of the musical motive may be found in the very first line. As the play opens, the sentinel Barnardo, fearful after having seen ghostly apparitions, cries out, "Who's there?" Despite its brevity, this question is basic to the play. It is a motive that runs throughout the entire work, in which virtually every character seeks to establish identity.

Motives occur in melodies in a way that is not shared by good writing. A basic musical motive normally returns several times within a single melody, creating an intentional redundancy that is usually unnecessary in verbal expression. A melody from Franz Schubert's *Unfinished* Symphony (Recording 1.3; Figure 1.2) provides an example. The first two tones of the melody—the second lower than the first—create a basic motive that returns no less than six times within the space of a few seconds. The seeming redundancy of these repetitions is necessary in musical expression so that the listener may retain fleeting musical ideas. Musical comprehension would be difficult for most listeners without such repetitiveness.

**Figure 1.2**

Melodies, like sentences, are thus divisible into the smaller units of phrase and motive. Also like the sentence, a melody comes to a definite point of conclusion, a point at which its thought is completed. This end point is signaled in a sentence by the placement of a period; in music the end point is called a **cadence.** Composers have various ways to signal the arrival of a cadence. It may be followed by a momentary silence (in music called a **rest**), by a change of featured instruments or voices, or by a change of loudness. Sometimes the music will become slower as a cadence is approached. Cadences in music have varying degrees of strength. The final cadence of a work is the strongest of all, and others may be weak or temporary. Some cadences overlap the beginning of new musical phrases and are thus scarcely noticeable. But all melodies, in order to create distinctive thoughts, must have a point of conclusion.

Some melodies in a musical composition are **themes;** that is, they take on added importance by their recurrence at later points in the work. The first sentence of Hamlet's soliloquy is likewise a theme. In this speech, he tries to decide whether or not he should go on living: "To be or not to be, that is the question." The content of this sentence is the theme of the entire soliloquy, in which Hamlet weighs the advantages and disadvantages of life, only to leave the question in the end unanswered. The enjoyment and understanding of a piece of music usually demand that we learn to retain and recognize its principal themes. We can test ourselves for this level of understanding by trying to sing from memory one or more of the main themes of a work that we are studying. If this is not possible, we probably need to listen to the piece again.

### How Melodies Are Presented

When we examine actual compositions, we find that melodies occur with certain common characteristics and common features of presentation. Melodies, first of all, are normally encountered in a musical work accompanied by other sounds that are subsidiary in importance. Such accompanying events in music have the role of enhancing the melody, placing it against an intelligible and attractive backdrop. Let us turn again to the passage from Mozart's piano concerto heard in Recording 1.1. At the very beginning of this excerpt, we hear lower stringed instruments softly playing throbbing, repeated notes. Clearly, these tones are too undistinctive to be part of the melody; their role is instead to accompany the melody, which enters a few seconds later in the higher-sounding violins.

A melodic line, as in Mozart's concerto, is normally clear and distinguishable against the backdrop of the accompaniment. This prominence accorded the melody is appropriate to its overwhelming importance in musical expression. One way in which Mozart has made the melody stand out is to place it in a high **register.** Register in music refers to the relative highness or lowness of notes. If most of the notes of a melody are relatively high, we can say that the melody is in a high register. Notes in high registers are inherently clearer and more audible than those in lower registers, so it is these notes that are most often used to highlight a melodic line. But occasionally, in order to create special expressive effects, a composer may place a melody in a low register. An example is found in the melody on Recording 1.4.

Melodies are not ever-present in a musical work. They are periodically introduced or restated in alternation with passages in which distinct melody is temporarily absent. The nonmelodic areas of a composition may sometimes function as **introductions**—passages that call for our attention and set the stage for the entrance of the star performer, the melody. The first few seconds of the Mozart concerto on Recording 1.1, prior to the entrance of the melody, are devoted to an introduction. A composer dispenses melodies in a work much as a chef uses sugar in a recipe: Just the right amount is crucial. Too little will produce a work that is sterile and unpleasing; too much will result in a work that is sickish and overly rich.

## Musical Tones and Their Relationships

If we continue to disassemble a melody beyond the level of the fragmentary motive, we soon arrive at the atomic particle of the **note** (or **tone**). A single note in music has four essential characteristics: duration in time, sound quality, loudness, and **pitch.** We will focus now on this last characteristic and return to the other three shortly.

The pitch of a tone is the highness or lowness of its sound. Generally speaking, a single musical note has a single, steady pitch, not significantly changing in highness or lowness until a new note is sounded. How many different pitches can melodies contain? We might think that the number could be very high, even infinite, since there are infinite gradations in how high a tone can sound. But by an ancient tradition, only a relatively small number of pitches are usable in music, and these have fixed distances, called **intervals,** between them. The smallest interval in music is a **half step** (also called a **semitone**). If we were to place all of the available pitches in music in ascending order, we would find that each pitch was separated from its upper and lower neighbors by the same small interval of the half step. The next larger interval (equal in distance to two consecutive half steps) is the **whole step** (or **whole tone**).

Half and whole steps are fundamental melodic intervals since they are relatively easy to sing and flow naturally together. Some melodies that are intended to be simple and unpretentious move almost entirely by these two intervals. A theme from Ludwig van Beethoven's Symphony No. 9 (Recording 1.4; Figure 1.3) is an example. In this melody, the low stringed instruments of

**Figure 1.3**

the orchestra seem to glide from one note to the next, since virtually each note of the melody moves to the next note by a half or a whole step. Now sing the melody. Given its "stepwise" intervals, this will be found reasonably easy to do.

Most melodies, however, become tedious unless stepwise motion is occasionaly diversified by larger intervals. Any interval larger than a whole step is called a **leap.** Often, leaps or a series of leaps in one direction in a melody will then be filled in by stepwise motion in the opposite direction. The opening of Mozart's melody on Recording 1.1 is an example of this pleasing disposition of steps and leaps (see Figure 1.4).

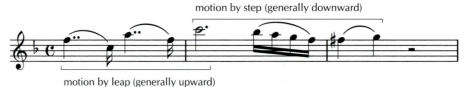

**Figure 1.4**

One large interval deserves special attention: the **octave.** If one note of a melody moves to the next note by leaping over exactly 12 half steps either up or down, the interval of the octave has been spanned. The two pitches making up an octave have a remarkable property: They sound almost identical in pitch, despite being far apart. Their pitches, indeed, seem to be equivalent, although not the same. Experiment with this important phenomenon by singing a note on any steady pitch. Now ask someone of the opposite sex to sing the "same" note. The note sung by the female voice, clearly the higher of the two despite sounding the same, will be an octave removed from that sung by the male voice.

The equivalence of pitches an octave apart introduces a powerful limiting factor in music. It reduces the number of "different," or nonequivalent, pitches to exactly 12. We can see why this is so by comparing pitches to the numbers 1 to 12 on the dial of a clock. The steady motion of notes progressing upward by half step is like the clock's hand moving around from 1 to 12. After 12 is reached, the numbers begin to repeat themselves, even though time has clearly continued to pass.

Musicians identify pitches by letter names. According to an old tradition, the letter A is assigned to a low pitch, B, C, and so forth to progressively higher ones. Since melodies are normally built from a mixture of half and whole steps, the intervals separating consecutive letters are also a mixture of these two intervals. The interval between B and C and between E and F is a half step, and all other consecutive letters are separated by a whole step. If we move up through the pitches from A to G, we might be tempted to name the next higher pitch H. But this note falls exactly an octave above A, so it too is called A, since its pitch is equivalent to the lower note.

We can visualize these relationships by studying the design of a piano keyboard, a segment of which is represented in Figure 1.5. The white keys sound notes that have letter names, beginning with A. The note above G is again A, since it is an octave above the lower A. We can now see why the octave (a word that refers to a unit of eight elements) was so named. In the succession of tones made from the repeating sequence A through G, the octave is reached as the eighth note from any starting point.

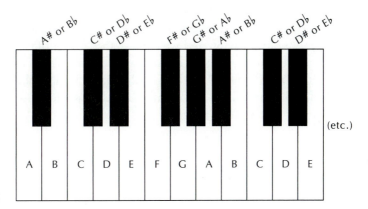

**Figure 1.5**

But an octave contains 12 different pitches, not just 8. Recall that an octave is, by definition, a leap that spans 12 half steps. So there must be other pitches available to the composer lying between some of the notes with letter names, specifically, between A and B, C and D, D and E, F and G, and G and A. These "in-between" notes are sounded by the black keys on a piano, and they are named using the signs or terms **sharp** and **flat.** The note between A and B, for example, is labeled A-sharp or B-flat. In modern notation, the symbol ♯ designates a sharp and the symbol ♭, a flat. The black notes are shown with these names in Figure 1.5. Further information on the identification of pitches and on musical notation is given in the Appendix to this book.

## Keynote

A fundamental property of virtually any well-known melody is its **keynote** (also called its **tonic**). The keynote is the one note (or its octave equivalents) that gives the melody its greatest sense of finality and completeness. Keynotes are often established in a melody by repetition or by placement at the beginning or end of phrases. The keynote is most predictably encountered at the end of the melody. If a melody did not conclude on its keynote, we would be left with a sense of incompleteness, a sense that a full cadence had not been reached and that the musical thought was not completely conveyed.

A keynote is clearly in evidence in "Victimae paschali laudes" ("Praises to the Easter Victim"), a melody sung on Easter in the Catholic church (Recording 1.5; Figure 1.6). The excerpt on the tape consists of the words and music to the first part of this piece. The melody falls naturally into five phrases, each of which except the third ends on the same note (D). This note is also the first note of the chant, it is the highest note (reached in phrase 3), and it is the note most often touched. For all of these reasons, we will hear the note D as a point of orientation and as a goal of the melodic motion. D is thus the keynote of the chant, and we can say that it identifies the **tonality** of this piece. In later music, tonality became a much more elaborate system of pitch organization than is found in this simple chant. In describing this more modern and familiar music, we normally say that a piece is in a certain tonality or **key** if that note is its tonic.

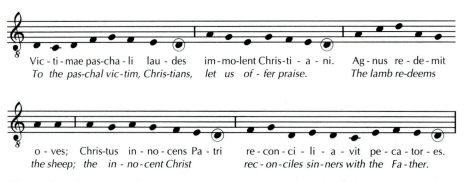

**Figure 1.6** *The keynote D is circled in its occurrences at the ends of phrases.*

A keynote provides the listener with a sense of orientation and greater ease of understanding. The twentieth-century composer Paul Hindemith has described tonality as a form of musical "gravity":

Tonality doubtless is a very subtle form of gravitation. . . . It suffices to sing in a chorus or a madrigal group to experience the strength of tonal gravitation: to sense how a synoptic tonal order has a healthy, refreshing effect on our moods.[1]

Our familiarity with melodies that assert keynotes makes it all the more difficult for us to understand music where a keynote is generally absent. Many works prior to the mid-seventeenth century lack a strong or consistent tonal focus, and much music of the twentieth century consciously avoids key in order to seek new possibilities for expression. Music of the latter type is often called **atonal.**

## Major and Minor Modes

If we rearrange the notes of a melody and place them into ascending order up from the keynote, we will have created the **scale** on which the melody is based. Scales are arrangements of the tones of a melody in ascending or descending order, usually begun and ended by the melody's keynote. Since they are closely related to works of music, scales are regularly practiced by musicians to facilitate their mastery of elaborate and difficult pieces.

The melody from Beethoven's Symphony No. 9 heard on Recording 1.4 will provide us with an example of the process by which a scale can be derived from a melody. Sing the melody several times until it is firmly in mind. Then sing its notes in ascending order up from the keynote, which is the final note of the excerpt. The scalewise rearrangement of tones is illustrated in Figure 1.7. It is typical of the calculated simplicity of this melody that its underlying scale does not span a complete octave but rather only the first five notes of the octave. For this reason, the melody is all the easier to sing and to retain.

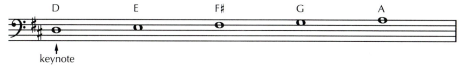

*Figure 1.7*

If we derive the scales from most other well-known melodies, we will discover the remarkable fact that virtually all of them are based on one of only two scale types, called **major** and **minor.** These two types differ in their **mode,** which refers to their precise sequence of half and whole steps that occurs as the notes progress upward from the keynotes. A single fixed order-

**29**

ing of half and whole steps is shared, for example, by all major scales. The distinctive pattern of this mode is shown at the right in Figure 1.8. Beethoven's melody is in the major mode, which is to say that it is based on a major scale. The ascending five-note scale of the melody (D-E-F♯-G-A) has exactly the order of half and whole steps common to the first five notes of all major scales.

The minor mode is more complicated, since it can exist in several different forms. For the sake of simplicity, let us examine only the first four intervals of an ascending minor scale, which are the same in all forms. This sequence of intervals is shown at the left in Figure 1.8. By comparing the two sides of the diagram, we see that the first five notes of the two scale types differ only in the third note above the keynote, which is lower in the minor scale than in the major.

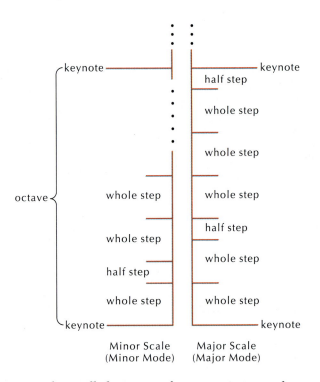

**Figure 1.8**

Minor Scale
(Minor Mode)

Major Scale
(Major Mode)

This seemingly small distinction between major and minor modes is vitally important to an understanding of music because mode is one of the most fundamental and universal of musical symbols. Music in the major mode tends to be affirmative, bright, positive, optimistic. Music in the minor mode often conveys the opposite sentiments: pessimism, anxiety, foreboding, mys-

---

## The Titles of Works of Classical Music

What does it mean when musicians refer to Beethoven's "Piano Sonata in D Minor" or Mozart's "Symphony in G Minor"? How are these pieces given their titles, and what do they mean?

Some musical works have "distinctive" titles (such as Prokofiev's *Peter and the Wolf* or Tchaikovsky's *Nutcracker*), since they use descriptive words or phrases that make them unique. But many titles refer only to categories of music, such as *symphony, sonata,* or *string quartet,* and a composer may have written many compositions of each type. In such cases, a title can refer to the chronological position of the piece. Beethoven's Symphony No. 1, for example, is the first piece that Beethoven composed within the category of the symphony.

It is also traditional to identify such works by their principal key and mode. If we refer to Beethoven's Symphony No. 1 in C Major, we help to identify this work not only by its chronological position within his symphonies but also by the keynote (C) and mode (major) of the opening of the work. Longer works of music remain in their opening key for only a brief time, but the opening key is normally the principal one for the work as a whole, and musicians regularly use it to identify the piece and to help to distinguish it from others of its type.

Another way to identify a piece is by its **opus number** (*opus* is the Latin word for "work"). These are also chronological designations (although often unreliable ones!) assigned by a publisher or by a composer to a new composition regardless of type. A final way is to refer to the number given to a composition in a standard catalog. The most famous of these is the catalog of Mozart's music by Ludwig von Köchel. The titles of Mozart's works are almost always followed by a "K" number, referring to Köchel's monumental list.

---

tery. Although we cannot always assume that these emotions are expressed by a certain mode, our ability to discriminate between major and minor will still provide us with an important capacity for more intelligent listening. Virtually all music that is commonly heard nowadays, whether popular or classical, will fall into one of these two modes.

### Melodic Forms

Melodies and themes may take on virtually unlimited numbers of moods and formal patterns, depending on the emotion that the composer wishes to convey and the ideas that he or she intends to express. But at certain times in the history of music, especially from roughly 1700 to 1900, standardized forms of melodic construction became widely used.

Among the most important of these patterns is **period form,** which is especially common in music of the late eighteenth and early nineteenth centuries. The works of Mozart, Haydn, Beethoven, and Schubert contain numerous examples. Melodies in period form are usually concise and symmetrical in phrasing, and they normally have a clear beginning, midpoint, and conclusion. A period melody is in two parts, both of the same length and both beginning similarly. The first half or phrase of the period (often called the *antecedent*) comes to a weak cadence, but not on its keynote. The second half or phrase (the *consequent*) comes to a full cadence on the keynote. We can compare a period melody to the famous command of John F. Kennedy: "Ask not what your country can do for you; ask what you can do for your country." The sentence is made from two related and symmetrical clauses, which, when put together, form a concise and striking thought. An example of period form is found in the slow movement of Beethoven's Piano Sonata in F Minor, Op. 2, No. 1 (Recording 1.6; Figure 1.9).

**Figure 1.9**

A very different type of melodic construction is characteristic of music in the first half of the eighteenth century. Rather than the symmetrical and repetitive phrases of period form, this earlier style stressed long and breathless melodies that were carried forward by a machinelike rhythm. The opening of J. S. Bach's Cantata No. 51, *Jauchzet Gott in allen Landen (Praise God in All Lands,* 1730), is an example (Recording 1.7). The trumpet states the primary melody, which consists of a continuous succession of motives, some repeated at different levels of pitch, and all pushed inexorably ahead by a motoric rhythm. The melody does not pause or breathe, and even at its cadence, its rhythmic energy passes without a break to the voice.

An important means by which melodies are constructed or expanded, found in all eras, is **sequence.** A sequence is a continuous and immediate repetition of a motive, moving to ever-higher or ever-lower levels of pitch. The beginning of a melody from Mozart's Symphony No. 29 (Recording 1.8)

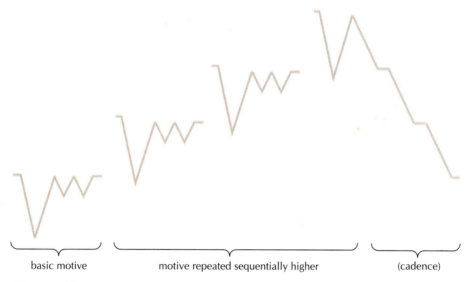

basic motive          motive repeated sequentially higher          (cadence)

**Figure 1.10**

is constructed almost entirely by sequence. The melody is stated by the violins, who begin with a short motive that is immediately repeated three times, each higher than the preceding. The fourth and final statement of the motive concludes by falling back to the keynote to form a cadence, which overlaps the beginning of a new melodic idea. The basic pattern of this sequence is illustrated in Figure 1.10.

## Harmony

We now turn our attention to the musical **accompaniment,** the stratum of a work that supports and enhances the melody. An accompaniment consists mainly of **chords,** which are musical sounds made from three or more different pitches. These notes are sounded all at the same time or rapidly in succession. The principles by which chords are made up and linked together are referred to as **harmony.**

If the melody in a musical work can be visualized as a line, then the chords that accompany it might be seen as pillarlike underpinnings, as shown in Figure 1.11. The nineteenth-century German composer Richard Wagner compared harmony to a vast sea on which melody was found in the cresting waves: "Tone itself is the primeval fluid element, and the immeasurable ex-

**33**

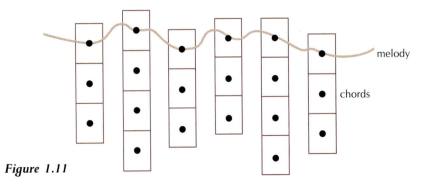

melody

chords

**Figure 1.11**

panse of this fluid is the sea of *harmony*. . . . A longing breeze arises, which agitates the placid surface in waves of melody, gracefully rising and falling."[2]

Although its role in music is primarily accompanimental, harmony all the same possesses a powerful capacity for expressiveness. For Wagner, one of the great masters of expressive harmony, this dimension was the source of pure emotion, color, and unbridled beauty in music. "The realm of harmony," he wrote, "is desiring, longing, raging, languishing."[3]

Just as melodies in modern Western music are rarely encountered without accompaniment, so too harmonies are only temporarily heard without melodies. Recording 1.9 contains a passage from Tchaikovsky's Symphony No. 5 (1888), music that will show the effect of harmonies devoid, at least briefly, of melody. At the beginning of this excerpt, the strings play solely a succession of chords. Their comforting and placid quality may well remind us of Wagner's assessment of the emotional potential of harmony, but their extended use without melody soon begins to make us restless. Finally, after almost one minute of pure harmony, our attention is all the more riveted on the entrance of the melody, which is stated here by the French horn. Since this is one of Tchaikovsky's most inspired melodies, it is likely that he extends the purely harmonic introduction in order to force our attention all the more on the melody when it finally arrives.

There are two categories of chords, and a distinction between them is important to our understanding of music. The more fundamental category involves **consonance;** the other, **dissonance.** Let us examine these two categories separately.

Consonant harmonies are by far the more familiar to our ears. Many listeners find them euphonious, or pleasant in sound, and such chords possess the greatest degree of stability. Due to this last quality, we will find consonant harmonies at the ends of musical works or at cadences. By a long-standing convention in music, consonant chords are limited to versions of the **triad,** a chord having three different pitches. Triads can be made by simultaneously playing alternate notes of a major scale. The first, third, and fifth notes of an ascending major scale, for example, render one type of triad; so too will the second, fourth, and sixth notes; and so forth. (The seventh, second, and fourth notes are an exception: Due to the intervals of the major scale, these notes do not form a consonant chord.)

Dissonant chords have the opposite effect of consonances. They are unstable rather than stable, and depending on the nature of the chords, dissonances may be found pungent, uneuphonious, perhaps even unpleasant. Why, then, do they exist in music? The sixteenth-century Italian theoretician Gioseffo Zarlino addressed this question with reasons that are still valid:

> Although dissonances are not pleasing in isolation, when they are properly placed . . . the ear not only endures them but derives great pleasure and delight from them. They are of double utility to the musician. . . . With their aid we may pass from one consonance to another. The second use is that a dissonance causes the consonance which follows it to sound more agreeable. The ear then grasps and appreciates the consonance with greater pleasure, just as light is more delightful to the sight after darkness, and the taste of sweets more delicious after something bitter.[4]

The dissonances that composers most often use are chords with four different pitches. In the abstract, we can construct them by the same process that we used to construct triads. By simultaneously playing four-note chords made up of every other note of an ascending major or minor scale, we can quickly reproduce some of the most familiar dissonances of music. Chords of this description are plainly unstable. We would not be satisfied with such sounds at the end of a work or at a cadence, since these chords need to move to triads to achieve a sense of completeness. Such a motion from a dissonance to a consonance is called a **resolution,** and the movement involved is interpreted by many listeners as producing a release of tension.

In the twentieth century, harmony has undergone a far-reaching change. Most of the major composers of serious music and some jazz musicians have ceased to consider dissonant chords merely as subsidiary in importance or effect to consonant triads. They have used dissonances, instead, as independent and stable sounds, appropriate at cadences or anywhere in a work and not in need of resolution to triads. They have allowed these chords to take on direct expressive or coloristic meaning, apart from melody, and they have availed themselves of a greatly expanded number of dissonant

*Like painters throughout the ages, Edgar Degas was inspired by performing artists, such as the musicians and dancers that he depicts in his* Orchestra of the Paris Opera *(1869). But here Degas takes us behind the scenes, shining his spotlight not on the dancers on stage but on the instrumentalists of an orchestra accustomed to working in obscurity.*

combinations. Composers in this century use virtually any combination of tones, even chords containing all 12 notes.

This expanded harmonic practice makes great demands, to be sure, on the understanding of the listener, since it runs contrary to virtually all of our past musical experience. But it has also introduced a new constructive dimension in music that parallels the innovative techniques of modern painting and literature. It permits the communication of ideas and emotions hitherto found only rarely in music.

## Musical Texture

A melody accompanied by a harmonic progression creates a familiar and pleasing quality of sound. As we can see in its graphic representation in Figure 1.11, such a composition is made up from two distinct strata: The primary layer is the melody, and a secondary stratum is formed by the underlying chords. The relationship and interaction of such musical strata create a **texture,** a quality that is basic to the shape and expressive content of the music.

The term *texture* is used, in general, to describe the surface quality of a material. The term refers more specifically to the characteristic patterns of weaving in cloth, or the ways that threads interlace. The image of a texture of woven fabric is appropriate to music. As we have already seen, a work of music is normally made up of several threadlike layers all heard at the same time and all coordinated or interlaced to create a connected and intelligible sound.

### Monophony, Homophony, and Polyphony

There are three basic textures in Western music: **monophony, homophony,** and **polyphony** (this last also called **counterpoint**). Monophony is a texture consisting solely, as the term itself suggests, of one melodic line, devoid of accompaniment. Works of this type are especially common in ancient music. Homophony is a texture consisting of an accompanied melodic line. It is by far the most familiar texture, since it occurs in virtually all popular music and in most classical works of the eighteenth and nineteenth centuries. Polyphony, or counterpoint, is a texture consisting of two or more distinct, simultaneous melodic lines, to which accompanimental strands may or may not be added. Polyphony was the dominant texture in Western art music from the thirteenth to the early eighteenth centuries, and it is also found in works of the twentieth century and in music of some non-Western cultures.

Since monophony is the most rudimentary texture, let us begin our discussion with this category. In a monophonic work or passage, there exists only a single melodic line. Music of this type is inherently simple, perhaps even austere. It is encountered in the ancient melodies of the Christian church and, in passing, in music of modern times. The Gregorian chant "Victimae paschali laudes" (Recording 1.5), used earlier to illustrate the phenomenon of keynote, also exemplifies a monophonic texture. The work consists solely of a melodic line (on this recording sung by a solo voice or in unison by a chorus of men). The texture ensures that it will have clarity and simplicity, although the melody itself is nonetheless expressive and beautifully crafted.

Artistic music composed after the late Middle Ages uses monophonic texture only rarely. But even the temporary use of such an austere texture can have striking expressive power, as in the passage from Beethoven's Ninth Symphony already heard in Recording 1.4. The melody in this excerpt is presented monophonically, as it is intoned by the bass instruments of the orchestra all playing in unison or in octaves without accompaniment. The texture suggests feelings of simplicity and naïveté, as though these instruments represent a congregation of the faithful, spontaneously raising their voices in a hymn.

Homophony is the texture most prevalent in music of all types. In works with a homophonic texture, there exists a melodic line plus an accompaniment made up of chords and other sounds intended to enhance or to clarify the principal melody. The beginning of Beethoven's song "In questa tomba oscura" ("In This Dark Tomb," Recording 1.10) is an example of a purely homophonic texture. The melody is stated by the voice, and the piano is devoted solely to playing blocklike accompanimental chords. The texture is simple, clear, and square-cut, which helps to communicate the somber idea of the words of the song: "In this dark tomb let me rest. When I was living, ungrateful one, you should have thought of me." Beethoven's texture expresses the poem's lifelessness, which is also suggested by the stately and even rhythms of the accompaniment.

Most music, however, is not so strictly or purely devoted to any one texture. Even in Beethoven's song, we would soon tire of the uniformity of the accompaniment. Most composers constantly vary the texture of their music, mixing the basic types and finding ways to diversify each of them.

A homophonic texture can be diversified in several ways. Perhaps the most common is to sound the accompanimental chords not, as in Beethoven's song, as blocklike simultaneities but by playing the notes of the chords in rapid succession, as so-called **broken chords.** Mozart uses this more ani-

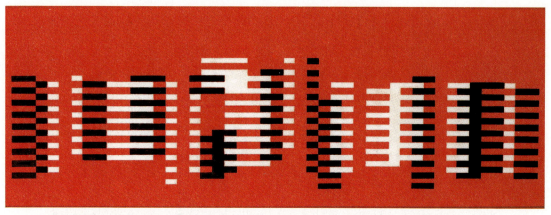

*Josef Albers's* **Fugue** *(1925) represents that musical texture by interlocking and parallel lines. Fugue is, as Albers's painting suggests, a type of polyphony in which several distinctive lines or strata of music are heard simultaneously.*

mated type of homophony at the beginning of his Piano Sonata in B-flat Major, K. 333 (Recording 1.11). The melody is heard in a high register. Beneath it, the harmonies are played one note at a time. But how can we be sure that this is a homophonic texture consisting of a single melody with accompaniment rather than a polyphonic one consisting of two distinct melodies played simultaneously? The answer has to do with the nature of melody. The lower stratum of this sonata is not melodically distinctive: It is rhythmically unvaried, it is repetitive in its recurring shapes, and it lacks a rhetorical quality by which musical ideas are directly intelligible.

Polyphony, or counterpoint, is inherently a more complicated texture than either homophony or monophony. Music of this type presents two or more melodic lines simultaneously, and listening to it is comparable to following several simultaneous conversations on different but related topics. In the music we will study, we will find two categories of polyphony: *imitative* and *free.* Imitative polyphony is a texture in which a single melody is stated in two or more strata in succession. In other words, an imitative texture usually begins with the monophonic presentation of a melody; a few seconds later, as the first line continues, the original melody is restated in a second line or stratum. Later still, as the first two lines continue, the melody may be stated again in a third stratum, and so forth.

A common example of an imitative texture is the song "Row, Row, Row Your Boat." One singer enters with the melody; a few moments later, a second singer enters with the same melody, while the first continues. Other

*Figure 1.12*

singers can enter later still, each a few moments after the previous singer has entered. This type of piece is called a **round** because the music can continue indefinitely by having the singers return to the beginning once they have completed a statement of the entire melody.

In "Row, Row, Row Your Boat," each singer exactly duplicates the entire melody, from beginning to end, of the first singer (only slightly later than the first). This type of imitative polyphony is called **canon.** A schematic representation of a canon is shown in Figure 1.12. The looping line represents a melody, which is sung or played by three different performers, each beginning slightly after the preceding one. Since each performer has the same melody from beginning to end, the piece is a canon. In this diagram, there are three lines, but the number can vary.

Other pieces of imitative polyphony are not so strict in their imitation. Often the imitation of the initial melody will extend only for a few notes and then become nonimitative. Such a passage is called a **fugue,** illustrated in Figure 1.13. Here the top line is at first imitated by the other lines, as in a

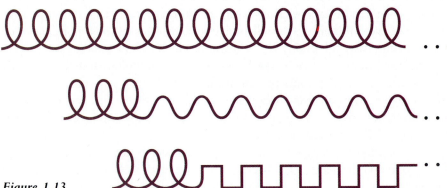

*Figure 1.13*

## Music Today

### Edgard Varèse: The Poet of Sound

Can noise be a part of music? The fact that it can is shown by recordings of rock groups such as the Beatles, Velvet Underground, and Tangerine Dream, in which electronic noise appears as an expressive backdrop. In modern jazz the playing of saxophonists such as John Coltrane and Albert Ayler often creates "sheets of sound" that are akin to noise. So too in modern art music. Composers including György Ligeti and Krzysztof Penderecki have used noiselike masses of sounds to communicate their ideas.

Regardless of their different styles and approaches, all of these musicians are indebted in their resourceful uses of sound to a remarkable pioneer of modern music, Edgard Varèse (1883–1965). People who knew him usually recall Varèse's crusty personality and his devotion to innovation in all aspects of music. Composition for Varèse was a constant struggle against the notion that music was limited by convention. In a lecture at Princeton University in 1959, he described his career as a "fight for the liberation of sound and for my right to make music with any sound and all sounds."*

Born and educated in Paris, Varèse immigrated to the United States in 1915. Although all of his early music was lost or destroyed, he quickly came to prominence in avant-garde musical circles in America with a series of compositions in which melodies, lines, and accompaniments were submerged into masses of sound. He wrote:

> When new instruments will allow me to write music as I conceive it, . . . the movement of sound masses, of shifting planes, will be clearly perceived. When these sound masses collide, the phenomena of penetration or repulsion will seem to occur. Certain transmutations taking place on certain planes will seem to be projected onto other planes, moving at different speeds and at different angles.†

His *Ionisation* (1931) was the first major piece of music solely for percussion ensemble, whose sound spectra are further enhanced by the addition of two wailing sirens. Always interested in new musical instruments, Varèse eagerly embraced electronic sources of sound when they became available. His *Poème électronique*, written for the Brussels World's Fair in 1958, was for many people the first inkling that an engaging piece of music could be intended for the medium of tape and employ primarily synthetic sounds. "To me," Varèse explained, "working with electronic music is composing with living sound."

*Edgard Varèse, "The Liberation of Sound," *Perspectives of New Music* 5 (1966–1967), 14.
†Ibid., p. 11.

canon. But unlike canon, the second and third lines cease to imitate the leading line after a few notes. The three lines then go their own ways independently.

As an example of fugal imitative polyphony, listen to the beginning of Contrapunctus No. 1 from J. S. Bach's *Art of the Fugue* (Recording 1.12). *Art of the Fugue* is a monumental cycle of fugues and canons that Bach composed late in his life. He did not leave instructions regarding the exact instruments that were to play them. The performance on Recording 1.12 uses brass instruments, whose differences in sound help the listener to distinguish the four different strata into which the texture is divided. A French horn begins the fugue by playing a short melody (called the **subject** of the fugue). A few seconds after this melody begins, it is repeated by a trumpet in a higher register, while the French horn continues. A few seconds later, a tuba enters with the subject, and later still, the trombone states the melody. Note also that after these instruments imitate the opening phrase of the melody, their imitation ceases, and they continue with their own distinct melodic material. For this reason, the passage is a fugue rather than a canon.

Polyphony that is not imitative may be termed "free," since, in this type of music, several entirely different melodies are heard at the same time. Guillaume Dufay's fifteenth-century song "Hélas mon deuil" ("Alas My Grief," Recording 1.13) is freely polyphonic. Its texture consists of three lines, two sung by voices and the third played by an instrument, and each of the three is melodic in character. Two voices sing the same words, which begin "Alas my grief, with this I died, felled by harsh refusal," and the third is played by a forerunner of the trombone called the **sackbut.**

### Innovations in Texture in Modern Music

In the twentieth century, some composers have sought alternatives to the three basic textures of traditional music. Their experiments are evidence of the greater importance of sound per se—divorced from melody, harmony, and rhythm—as a structural or expressive element in a musical composition. Such experiments were especially important among American avant-garde composers of the first half of the century, and their initiatives gained momentum after 1950 among composers of electronic music.

The use of a **mass of sound** as the basic element of a composition is central to this stylistic movement. In a work of this type, the composer deploys instruments (including electronic devices) and voices to create sound masses that do not contain traditional melody, accompaniment, or harmony. Each mass is characterized only by a texture determined largely by color and loudness, and the form of the entire composition is usually determined by the ways that such textures change, evolve, or interact. These textural masses may be created by the agglomeration of many minute polyphonic lines,

*Henri Matisse's image of Icarus illustrated his volume* **Jazz** *(Paris: Tériade, 1947). Icarus was a figure from Greek mythology who perished when he flew too close to the sun. Matisse's depiction may seem remote to the liveliness of jazz, but the picture's deep and resonant colors and fluid rhythms of flight capture a musical essence. "Colors must react on one another," wrote Matisse in* **Jazz.** *"Otherwise you have cacophony. Jazz is rhythm and meaning."*

chords, or pitches, but the individual motives and chords that make up the mass will not be heard distinctly. The mass as a whole is the indivisible element of the composition.

The beginning of György Ligeti's ingenious *Lux aeterna (Eternal Light),* heard on Recording 1.14, shows the haunting expressivity that such music can achieve. The piece is written for 16 voices. Their first sound mass is created as each voice softly enters on a single pitch, indistinctly singing the word "Lux." Then, as the voices gradually sing other pitches and words, the sound mass evolves in its color and loudness. Never do we perceive the familiar elements—melodies, counterpoint, rhythms—of a traditional piece of music for chorus. The work is instead expressive on a new level as it suggests the ever-changing eternal light mentioned in its title.

## BIBLIOGRAPHY

Additional definitions of musical terms can be obtained in *The New Harvard Dictionary of Music,* ed. Don Michael Randel. Cambridge, Mass.: Harvard University Press, 1986. Most books on melody and harmony require a knowledge of the rudiments of musical notation and theory. The following selections should be accessible to most readers.

Clough, John, and Joyce Conley. *Scales, Intervals, Keys, Triads, Rhythm, and Meter.* New York: Norton, 1983. An elementary study of musical rudiments and notation.

Copland, Aaron. *What to Listen For in Music.* New York: Mentor, 1967. This is a comprehensive and unusually articulate treatment, intended for the layperson. Among other subjects, it deals with melody, harmony, and texture.

Forte, Allen. *Tonal Harmony in Concept and Practice.* Second edition. New York: Holt, Rinehart and Winston, 1974. This is a standard textbook on harmony, intended for undergraduate music majors.

Toch, Ernst. *The Shaping Forces in Music: An Inquiry into the Nature of Harmony, Melody, Counterpoint, Form.* New York: Dover, 1977. Toch's discussion is intended for readers already possessing a knowledge of music.

## NOTES

1. Paul Hindemith, *A Composer's World* (Garden City, N.Y.: Anchor/Doubleday, 1961), pp. 64–65.
2. Richard Wagner, selected and annotated by Oliver Strunk, in *Source Readings in Music History* (New York: Norton, 1965), p. 144.
3. Ibid., p. 147.
4. Gioseffo Zarlino, *The Art of Counterpoint* (1558), trans. Guy A. Marco and Claude V. Palisca (New Haven, Conn.: Yale University Press, 1968), p. 53.

# 2

# Rhythm, Form, and Musical Instruments

*The characters in Joan Miró's painting "Rhythmic Personages"*
*(1934) seem to have been caught in a madly earnest dance, frozen in*
*time. Their bodies are made up from outrageously distorted body*

parts and from plastic, organic shapes. They light up in brightly alluring colors, as though trying to attract similar creatures of the opposite sex in a determined mating dance.

The Catalan artist Miró began his career as a painter in the cubist vein of his friend Pablo Picasso. His fertile imagination soon led him in numerous innovative directions. In the 1920s his pictures took on surrealistic qualities, although the flat shapes defined by outline and by pure color continued to betray his cubist background. Later still, Miró was one of the first European painters to work in the medium of collage, by which a surface is covered with everyday objects in addition to paint.

How should we interpret this painting and its implicit actions? One approach is to ponder its hidden symbolism and meaning. We may well laugh at the ludicrous figures, since Miró has quite plainly made them absurd and ridiculous in their childish pomposity. The artist, like Paul Klee in the painting that opened Chapter 1, helps us to understand the picture by using a musical term in the title. The humanlike shapes are "rhythmic," we are told. This term implies that the whimsical figures that we see are not to be thought of as static or decorative. They are instead in motion. Rhythm, in its broadest meaning, refers to the sense of movement in music. Inevitably, it suggests a relationship between bodily movement and musical sounds. The element of rhythm is nowhere more apparent and forceful than in music for the dance. Here the motion and pulse *of a piece of music are explicitly shared with the gestures of dancers.*

*In Chapter 2 we continue a discussion of the elements of music and its basic terminology. It is appropriate that we should begin with rhythm, since this element is basic to our innate sense and understanding of music.*

## A Checklist of Basic Elements and Terms

### Rhythm

| | |
|---|---|
| value | beat |
| tempo | rubato |
| meter | |

### Form

| | |
|---|---|
| movement | sonata form |
| strophic form | binary form |
| ternary form | finale |
| rondo form | genre |
| variations form | |

### Instruments

timbre (tone color)     overtones
voices: soprano, alto, tenor, bass
stringed instruments: violin, viola, cello, bass
woodwind instruments: flute, oboe, bassoon, clarinet, saxophone
brass instruments: French horn, trumpet, trombone, tuba
percussion instruments: timpani, drums, mallet instruments
keyboard instruments: piano, harpsichord, organ
plucked instruments: guitar, harp, lute
electronic instrument: synthesizer
medium
chamber music

In Chapter 1, we explored the nature of melody and its manner of presentation. In this chapter, we shall continue to survey vital elements of music, beginning with rhythm. **Rhythm** refers to the sense of movement in music. We then turn to a discussion of form and explore the patterns by which longer musical compositions are constructed. Finally, we shall investigate musical instruments, the means whereby abstract principles of musical organization are converted into an art of sound.

## Rhythm and the Temporal Dimension of Music

Melodies are musical shapes that a composer draws in a two-dimensional space. The notes of a melody occupy the dimension of pitch as they move up and down; they move through a horizontal dimension, that of time, as they unfold from one moment to the next. We focus now on this second domain in order to explore the ways in which music creates patterns in time.

The organization of time through music is a powerful and primary expressive tool. Indeed, many people have speculated that rhythm is the most primitive and basic musical impulse, observable in dance, drumming, or any regular bodily movement. The American composer Roger Sessions finds a prototype for musical rhythm in breathing, the basic process of life:

> It seems to me clear indeed that the basic rhythmic fact is not the fact simply of alternation, but of a specific type of alternation with which we are familiar from the first movement of our existence as separate beings. We celebrate that event by drawing a breath, which is required of us if existence is to be realized. The drawing of the breath is an act of cumulation, of tension which is then released by the alternative act of exhalation.[1]

Despite its importance, the temporal dimension of music has not produced a terminology that is precise or that is universally accepted among either musicians or musical scholars. This circumstance may well stem from the complex and elusive nature of time itself. In this chapter, definitions will be put forward that derive from the general usage of today's musicians.

### Rhythm and Beat

Nowhere in the study of music is the impreciseness of terms more acute than with regard to *rhythm*. The word is used by musicians in a multiplicity of ways. In general, it can refer to virtually any aspect of the duration of notes, their similarities and differences in length, their accented or unaccented qualities, or configurations made by their onsets or "attacks." Musicians also use the term in a more specific sense to describe a pattern that is created in a particular work by the lengths of time that notes are held (called **values**) or lengths of time between attacks.

Let us listen to a passage from George Frideric Handel's *Messiah,* "He Shall Feed His Flock" (Recording 2.1), in which we will hear a simple rhythm. The melody in this music is first presented by the orchestra, then repeated, with some changes, by the voice. At first, the melodic tones alternate between two values, one longer than the other. If we represent the shorter duration by a **U** and the longer one by a dash, we will have depicted the rhythm of the passage, that is, its pattern of durational values. Figure 2.1 contains such a representation for the first two brief melodic phrases. The

**50**

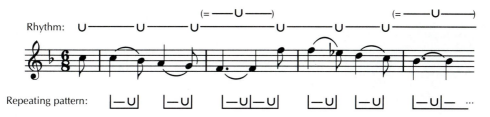

**Figure 2.1**

note that ends each of the two phrases is held longer than any of the other values, so it is depicted by an elongated dash.

From this diagram, it is clear that Handel's rhythm is based on a *repeating pattern* of long and short notes. The pattern itself is extremely simple. After an initial short value, it consists of a single long note followed by a single short one (the patterns are marked off by brackets at the bottom of Figure 2.1). This pattern is nearly synonymous with the rhythm itself, except occasionally when several consecutive values are consolidated into a longer note or when a normal value is broken up into several shorter ones. The long note that ends each of the initial phrases is an example of a consolidation: This long value is exactly equal to a normal long plus a normal short plus another normal long value (see Figure 2.1). Later in the melody, quicker rhythms are produced by subdividing the two basic values.

In virtually all music, rhythms are based on simple underlying repeated patterns. The pattern itself may be clearly heard, as in Handel's melody, or it may be obscured by many consolidations or subdivisions. The pattern that governs the rhythm of a melody also normally appears in the accompaniment, although it may occasionally have different consolidations and subdivisions.

An important relationship to be noted in the music of Recording 2.1 is that the short value is a simple fraction of the longer one. In this piece, for example, the shorter value is precisely one-half as long as the longer value. Musical rhythm depends on these simple numerical fractions and multiples. Rhythmic durations are fixed in their proportions, much as intervals between pitches are all multiples of the space of a semitone.

If we listen carefully to a simple rhythmic pattern, like the one from Handel's *Messiah,* we will hear a series of **beats.** These are regularly recurring, equally spaced pulses. Beat is intimately connected with rhythm but distinguishable from it. We can see this difference by watching performers who tap their feet to mark the beat while simultaneously singing or playing a rhythm. Beat is usually steady and regular—it divides the flow of time into equal

segments. Rhythm, by contrast, is usually uneven as it divides time into a mixture of long and short values. Beat is a basic measuring device in music: It allows the performer to gauge precisely when notes are to be sounded and released, and it allows a group of players to perform precisely together.

The crucial distinction between rhythm and beat can be learned by singing any well-known song and, at the same time, clapping the beat that is suggested by its rhythm. At first, it may be difficult to keep a regular beat, since there is a tendency for the clapping to duplicate the rhythm. But with practice, these two activities, which exist continually and simultaneously in the minds of all musical performers, can be mastered.

Music may temporarily dispense with beat in order to produce variety and an expressive suspension in the unfolding of time. Listen to the playing of Indian musicians on Recording 2.2. At the beginning of their piece, the musicians do not establish a regular beat. We react to this music with suspense and anticipation, which are dispelled when the ensemble at last merges into a clear pulse. Modern Western music makes only temporary use of passages without a recognizable beat; without one, music to Western ears usually seems directionless and difficult to understand.

## Tempo and Rubato

The speed of the beat in music is called **tempo** (Italian for "time"). Performers are usually apprised of the approximate tempo by verbal instructions, such as "slow," "moderate," or "fast." By convention, these

*Robert Delaunay ingeniously captured the idea of musical rhythm in this painting of 1934, called* **Endless Rhythm.** *Its semicircular shapes regularly wind their way about a vertical midpoint. In a similar manner, beats mark off regular spaces in the passage of musical time, creating the basis of rhythm.*

instructions are often written in Italian, since they began to be written into musical compositions in the seventeenth century, when Italian composers were especially prominent. These are some of the most important Italian tempo instructions:

| | | | |
|---|---|---|---|
| *Adagio* | slowly | *Allegro* | fast |
| *Andante* | moving (moderately slowly) | *Presto* | quickly |
| *Moderato* | moderately (fast) | *Vivace* | lively |

Some of these terms, such as *vivace,* suggest not only a tempo but also a mood or style of playing, in this case fast, sprightly, and bright. Since the early nineteenth century, musicians have also made use of a mechanical device called a *metronome,* which clicks regularly to mark a beat at some predetermined speed. Although many musical works from the nineteenth and twentieth centuries are provided with precise metronome markings, musicians often insist that variations in tempo must always be allowed, depending on differing modes of interpretation and differing circumstances of performance.

A temporary slowing or speeding of the beat is called **rubato** (from the Italian verb *rubare,* "to steal"). This effect is normally added by the performer—it is an aspect of tasteful playing that adds suppleness and diversity to the music and is often used to underline the end of a phrase or the approach of a cadence. In a passage played rubato, the performer "steals" time by slowing the beat; later, the stolen time may be repaid by temporarily speeding the beat. The piano music of Frédéric Chopin is usually played with rubato. Listen to the opening of Chopin's Waltz in A♭ Major (Recording 2.3). Sing the melody and clap the beat. This exercise will make clear the constant slowing and speeding of the beat, by which the performer seems to make the music breathe.

## Meter

The beats in a work of music form a continuum of pulses, which is organized and differentiated by the phenomenon of **meter.** The effect of meter in music is to break up the continuum of beats by collecting them into groups. If, for example, every third beat in a piece is emphasized and if rhythmic values, harmonies, or melodic motives recur every third beat, a meter has been established. Meter normally breaks up the flow of beats into regularly recurring groups of twos, threes, or fours.

A passage from Franz Joseph Haydn's Symphony No. 102 in B♭ Major (Recording 2.4) will illustrate the phenomenon of meter and ways by which a composer can establish metric groups. Listen first to the melody, which is stated by the violins and clearly establishes the beat. Then concentrate on the playing of the rest of the orchestra. At the very beginning of the music, its role is to provide harmonies and, even more important, to establish unmistakably the meter. After a single preliminary beat in the melody (called an *upbeat* or *pickup*), the orchestra plays loudly and crisply only every third beat (see Figure 2.2). In this way, they emphatically establish an organization of the flow of beats into groups of threes that continues, although with less emphasis than at the beginning. Other, more subtle factors also help to establish the sense of meter. The melody itself is based on a sequence in which the basic motive is repeated at a higher pitch every third beat. The harmonies also tend to change at the beginning of three-beat groups.

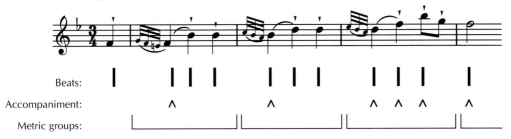

**Figure 2.2**

Since the meter of this music is based on recurring three-beat groups, we say that it is a *triple meter*. Music that uses meters having groups of two or four beats will be called *duple*. Certain types of music invariably fall into one of these two categories. Marches, for example, are always duple. Since marches were originally works intended to accompany walking by a group of people, duple meter is the natural outcome of returning to the same foot every second step. Most jazz and popular tunes are also in duple meters.

Triple meters are found in certain types of dance music, such as the minuet or the waltz (Haydn's music on Recording 2.4 is a minuet). If we watch a couple dancing a waltz, we will see a visual representation of triple meter, since similar movements recur every third step or beat. We can also see a visual representation of beat and meter by watching the hands of an orchestra or band conductor. Each movement of the hands marks a beat, and conductors organize these movements into recurrent patterns of two, three, four, or more beats, depending on the meter of the music that they are leading. A march in duple meter, in which every second beat is stressed, might be conducted with the recurrent pattern shown in Figure 2.3. A waltz, by contrast, needs a pattern in which there are three movements, as in Figure 2.4. Information on the notation of rhythm and meter is found in the Appendix.

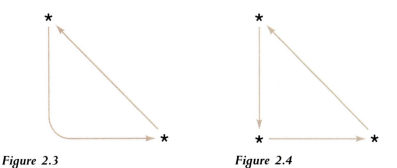

**Figure 2.3**                              **Figure 2.4**

# Form and Genre

Our survey of the elements of music has shown that the choices facing a composer in creating a work are by no means entirely free. In virtually every dimension of music, a composer must select materials from a limited number of options. In traditional music, for example, there are only 12 different notes, and these have fixed interval relations. The available metric patterns are few in number, and the traditional textures are limited. Indeed, most composers relish these restrictions. They offer guidance in the formulation of new works, just as a clearly understood vocabulary and grammar support and direct the work of a writer. The Russian-American composer Igor Stravinsky welcomed the concreteness of such limitations:

> The more art is controlled, limited, worked over, the more it is
> free . . . My freedom will be so much the greater and more
> meaningful the more narrowly I limit my field of action and the more
> I surround myself with obstacles. Whatever diminishes constraint
> diminishes strength.[2]

## Form

The constraints of which Stravinsky speaks are encountered in music nowhere more decidedly than in the realm of **form** (also called **structure**). Form in a work of music is created by a guiding plan or principle. Viewing a piece as a whole, we can see the formal plan at work by finding how the piece is divided into sections and by assessing their character and relationship to each other. For example, if we notice that a work has three major sections, each with its own themes and tempo, we have begun to perceive its form.

Virtually all long pieces, such as symphonies or string quartets, are broken down into several major subdivisions that are marked off from one another by complete pauses. During these major breaks, the music comes to a temporary end; musicians may retune their instruments, and people may be shown to their seats. When the music resumes, it will probably have a new tempo and character. These primary subdivisions are called **movements,** the number and general character of which establish the overall form of the entire composition.

A movement of a piece is comparable to a chapter of a novel or to an act of a play: It is a major subdivision after which a definite break in attention is possible, even invited. The break between movements of a musical work is an opportunity for reflection on the piece in general and on its expressive implications. It is not appropriate during this pause to applaud, because this would disrupt the mood that the music has created. The movements of a piece usually have different tempos (hence the origin of the term *movement*) as well as differences in character. A short piece may be complete in one move- ment, but longer works are usually divided into several. The last movement of a multimovement instrumental composition is called the **finale** (pronounced "fi-NAH-lee"). Occasionally, two or more movements are played without a pause between them, in which case a change of tempo alerts us to the beginning of the new subdivision.

It is also important for us to be aware of the form that exists within a single movement or within a work in only one movement. Form in this more localized dimension is created by a plan that dictates repetitions among sec- tions. Here we lose our analogy with literature. An act of a play or a chapter of a novel may well fall into several sections, but these almost never repeat one another. Musical movements, on the contrary, are usually constructed using large sectional repetitions. These would be redundant in literature, but they are necessary to ensure musical comprehensibility.

A very common plan within a musical movement is to have three connected sections, each lasting a few minutes or less. Typically, the second section will be very different from the first, having a different melody and possibly a different keynote or mode. But the third section will duplicate the music of the first, creating a standardized pattern of repetition that promotes our understanding of the music. Musicians often summarize standard formal plans by letter schemes. The one just described, called **ternary form,** could be concisely represented by the letters A B A, which show both the threefold division of the movement into sections as well as the pattern by which sections are repeated.

Still using ternary form as an example of the standardized patterns that usually exist within a single movement, let us listen to Robert Schumann's song "Widmung" ("Dedication," Recording 2.5) in order to understand how a composer divides music into similar or contrasting sections. The poem of this song is by Friedrich Rückert, and it is in two stanzas:

*1. Du meine Seele, du mein Herz,*
   *Du meine Wonne, du mein Schmerz,*
   *Du meine Welt, in der ich lebe,*
   *Mein Himmel du, darein ich*
     *schwebe,*
   *O du mein Grab, in das hinab*
   *Ich ewig meinen Kummer gab'!*

*2. Du bist die Ruh', du bist der*
     *Frieden,*
   *Du bist der Himmel mir beschieden,*
   *Daß du mich liebst, macht*
     *mich mir wert,*
   *Dein Blick hat mich vor mir*
     *verklärt,*
   *Du hebst mich liebend über*
     *mich,*
   *Mein guter Geist, mein bess'res ich!*

*1.* You my soul, you my heart,
   You my joy, you my pain,
   You my world in which I live,
   My heaven you, in which I
     float,
   O you my grave, in which
   I forever cast my sorrows.

*2.* You are my calm, you are my
     peace,
   You are heaven given to me;
   That you love me makes me
     valuable to myself,
   Your gaze transfigures me in
     my own sight,
   You raise me lovingly beyond
     myself;
   My good spirit, my better self!

The tone of the two stanzas is very different. The first contains a series of exclamations, each more emotional than the preceding. The second stanza, by contrast, is contemplative, as the poet seeks to understand and interpret the role in his own life played by the beloved. Schumann captures this difference of tone by writing music for the second stanza that is very different from that for the first. These two musical sections differ in melody, keynote, texture, and rhythm. For the ending, however, Schumann creates a scheme independent of the textual form: He repeats the first stanza, together with its original music. Rückert's poem does not suggest such a repetition, but Schumann has chosen to make it conform to a standardized musical plan. The A B A ternary song that he creates is musically satisfying in its symmetry and, by adopting a conventional formal pattern, all the easier for the listener to follow.

Ternary form is only one of at least six patterns commonly encountered in musical movements or pieces existing in a single movement. In **strophic form,** an opening section of music is repeated a number of times.

It can be represented by the letters A A . . . A. In **binary form** there are two sections of music, each immediately repeated (A A B B). **Rondo form** is characterized by the return of an initial passage separated by contrasting material (A B A C . . . A). **Variations form** begins with a theme followed by several paraphrases (A $A_1$ $A_2$ . . . ). **Sonata form** was originally derived from binary form but later developed into a more sophisticated plan. All of these movement forms will be encountered in musical works in later chapters, where they will be described in more detail.

## Genre

In any historical era, many musical works share the same overall form, instrumentation, and general character. Haydn, for example, wrote over 100 pieces for orchestra having four movements, of which the first is fast, the second slow, the third dancelike, and the fourth a quick conclusion. Mozart wrote numerous works having the very same description, as did Beethoven, Johann Vanhal, Karl von Dittersdorf, and other masters of the eighteenth and nineteenth centuries. We are correct in assuming that these composers had in mind a preexistent norm or type of composition in these pieces, which governed their basic concepts. Any such type or category is called a **genre** (French for "type").

A genre is akin to a musical form, but it is a considerably broader concept. Whereas form describes the internal relation of sections within a composition, genre tells us more about the outward character and purpose of a piece. A genre implies not only an overall form but also a customary **medium** (that is, a specific group of instruments or voices), and, often, the general character, nature of the text, and purpose for which the music is intended. Like conventional forms, genres provide preexistent constraints that composers accept to guide them in the creation of coherent works.

In the survey of music literature contained in the following chapters, it will be important to know the medium and overall form associated with a given genre in a given era. Some genres, such as the concerto, have exhibited remarkable historical consistency. A work of this type, whether composed in the eighteenth, nineteenth, or twentieth century, usually has three movements and calls for instrumental soloists accompanied by orchestra. Other genres have undergone extensive redefinition from one era to the next. The sonata is an example. From an ensemble piece in the early 1700s, it soon evolved into a work usually intended for a soloist, most often a pianist.

In the twentieth century, the stability of genres has, to a large extent, disappeared. Works called "symphonies," for example, have not always adopted the form or medium traditionally associated with this type of music. This dissolution of genre is one of the primary reasons why much twentieth-century music is difficult to understand. At the same time, it has allowed composers a new flexibility of expression.

## Musical Timbre, Instruments, and Media

The musical elements that we have encountered so far—including melody, harmony, rhythm, and meter—are in large part abstractions. They may exist in the form of musical notations, or they may be viewed simply as formal or theoretical ideas. For these entities to be made into concrete works of sound, they must be interpreted and realized by musical instruments and voices.

The instruments of music have a long and distinguished history through which they evolved to their modern forms. New instruments have appeared periodically and continue to do so. By comparing the various instruments, old and new, we will find that similarities of construction or manner of use suggest groupings into families. Still, each of the major instruments maintains distinctive features. We shall begin our exploration of the instruments of music by describing their individual characteristics while also touching on their history, construction, and manner of use.

### Timbre

**Timbre** (or **tone color**) is the distinctive quality of sound produced by an instrument or a voice. If a trumpet plays a note at the same pitch and loudness as a piano, we have no difficulty distinguishing between the two because they have clearly different timbres.

The distinctive tone color of an instrument is created by the physical nature of the sound it produces. A tone produced by virtually any musical instrument consists of numerous simultaneous frequencies, of which the lowest is the most audible. It is interpreted by our ears as the sole pitch or **fundamental.** For most instruments, the higher frequencies are related to the fundamental as **harmonics,** meaning that they are all simple multiples of it. If a trombonist, for example, plays a pitch whose fundamental vibrates at 200 cycles per second (cps), that tone will also contain the frequencies of 400 cps, 600 cps, and so forth. The audibility of the higher frequencies (called **overtones** or **partial frequencies**) contributes to the distinctive tone color of the trombone. The flute, played softly in the low register, for example, contains few audible overtones; the clarinet tone contains partial frequencies with significant energy only in odd-numbered overtones (specifically, the fundamental, which is counted as the first partial; the third partial; fifth partial; and so forth). Bell or gong tones have predominantly nonharmonic partial frequencies since these higher frequencies are not related to a lowest frequency as simple integral multiples. For this reason, bells or gongs usually lack an apparent fundamental pitch.

In addition to overtone structure, the tone color of an instrument or a voice is distinguished by the characteristics of its attack, the body of its tone, and its ending (or "decay").

## The Human Voice

For many musicians, the human voice is the most perfect musical instrument. When properly trained, it has beauty of tone, expressive nuance, power, and delicacy. It has the unique capability of expressing meaning by words at the same time as it conveys musical ideas. It is no wonder, then, that many instrumentalists try to imitate the musical and expressive techniques of singers.

Voices are traditionally divided into categories by register. A high male voice is called a **tenor;** a low male voice, a **bass.** A high female voice is called a **soprano;** the low female voice is called an **alto** (or **contralto**). The ranges of most untrained voices fall between these extremes: The male voice between the tenor and bass range is called a **baritone;** the female equivalent is the **mezzo-soprano.** Other categories exist in order to describe the quality of a voice. The "lyric" tenor or soprano is a light and melodious voice; a "coloratura" soprano is capable of singing in a very high register, typically with great agility. The "heroic" tenor specializes in music requiring great power, intensity, and endurance.

## Instruments of the Orchestra

The modern **orchestra** has been in existence from the late seventeenth century. Its size and exact constitution have evolved considerably since that time, but its overall features have remained relatively constant. The orchestra may have as many as four primary subdivisions: strings, woodwinds, brass, and percussion. Composers may use these four separately or in varying combinations, or some sections may be omitted altogether.

For most composers, the choice of a specific instrument to entrust with an important melody, or the exact constitution of the orchestra at large, is an important decision that affects the way a work is perceived. The art of distributing musical ideas to specific instruments, called **orchestration,** is intended not only to give the orchestra its best possible sound but also to communicate distinctly the content of a work. The American composer Elliott Carter has emphasized the expressive power of each orchestral instrument:

> To compose for the orchestra, as far as I am concerned, is to deal practically with the instruments, writing idiomatic passages for them, and, particularly, to compose music whose very structure and character is related to the instruments that play it. The entrance, register, sound of an oboe or a solo viola must be a matter of formal and expressive signification for the whole piece.[3]

In most orchestras, the *string section* is fundamental, since it is entrusted with most of the important melodic material. There are four instruments in this subdivision: violins, violas, cellos (or violoncellos), and basses. These four (see Figure 2.5) are all closely related. They differ from one another primarily in size and, accordingly, in the register in which they play (the smaller the instrument, the higher the register). Each of the instruments is made from wood and provided with four gut or wire strings. These are made to sound by

**Figure 2.5** *From left to right: viola, bass, cello, violin.*

**Pablo Picasso often chose musical instruments as subjects for artworks in the cubist style. In this charcoal drawing of 1912, he depicts a violin that is literally taken apart and presented as a collection of planar and geometric designs.**

plucking (called **pizzicato**) or, more typically, by a horsehair bow that is drawn over the strings. The sound produced by the vibrating string is amplified as the vibrations pass through the body of the instrument. The player raises the pitch of a string by pressing it down with fingers of the left hand against the neck or "fingerboard." If the finger is shaken as it is pressed down, the tone will take on greater warmth and resonance in an effect called **vibrato.**

The penetrating sound and technical flexibility of the violin make it a leading solo instrument. So great is its prominence in the orchestra that the principal violinist (called the **concertmaster**) occupies a role of leadership second only to the conductor. The proportions of the viola make it somewhat less agile and less brilliant in sound than the violin and, accordingly, less appropriate as a solo instrument. The cello, played resting on the floor and propped between the player's knees, rivals the violin in its agility, its noble and powerful sound, and its great dynamic and pitch range, so that it often emerges as a soloist. The bass (also called the "double bass" or "string bass") is played by a musician standing or seated on a stool. Due to its somewhat unwieldy proportions and its lack of resonance and tonal focus, the instrument is rarely used as a soloist.

The *woodwind section* of the orchestra is confusingly named, since its members are not always made from wood. The primary instruments of this subdivision of the orchestra are flutes, oboes, clarinets, and bassoons (see Figure 2.6). For each of these, the breath of the performer creates sound waves within the tubing of the instrument. This tubing is perforated by finger holes, whereby the performer changes notes. The range of the woodwind instruments can be extended upward by increasing air pressure or by using special keys that allow the instrument to sound overtones rather than fundamental pitches. This process, which is also basic to playing the brass instruments, is called *overblowing*.

The modern orchestral flute comes in several sizes. The smallest is the diminutive piccolo, characterized by its high and sometimes shrill sound. The regular flute is usually made from precious metal and provided with an elaborate key mechanism to facilitate closing the finger holes. The oboe and bassoon are members of a single subfamily of instruments since they are closely similar in construction and manner of use. One end of these instruments has a double reed (two layers of cane or other reed material) over which the player blows to generate a sound. The double reed construction and conical shape of the wooden tubing give the instruments their distinctively nasal tone. The clarinet is a relative newcomer to the standard orchestra. Although it appeared in the late seventeenth century, when it was closely

*Figure 2.6* *From left to right: flute, clarinet, oboe, bassoon.*

related to a forerunner called the *chalumeau,* it was not universally included in the orchestra until the end of the eighteenth century. The clarinet is normally made from a short wooden tube; the player blows into one end over a mouthpiece equipped with a single reed.

The *brass section* within the orchestra consists of the French horn (or, more simply, "horn"), trumpet, trombone, and tuba. These instruments have much in common: They are all made from a metal tube that is coiled to give them a compact shape. One end of the tube flares into a pronounced "bell," and the other end is provided with a cup-shaped mouthpiece into which the player blows. Air in the tube is made to vibrate by the buzzing of the player's lips.

Pitches on a brass instrument are changed by two means: by altering the length of the tube (accomplished by valves or by movement of a slide) and by increasing wind pressure in order to sound overtones. The tubing of some brass instruments, such as the tuba and the French horn, is predominantly conical in shape, which gives these instruments a mellow and rounded sound. Others, such as the trombone and the trumpet, have predominantly cylindrical tubing, giving them penetrating tones. The basic brass instruments are illustrated in Figure 2.7.

*Percussion* instruments are those whose sounds are created by striking or shaking. A fully developed percussion section appeared in the orchestra in the nineteenth century, although such instruments were occasionally used earlier for exotic effects. The sole percussion instrument that appeared regularly in the orchestra from its earliest history is the kettledrum (also called timpani). The modern percussionist must be equipped with many instruments, which we can group into four categories: drums; mallet instruments; metallic, unpitched instruments; and non-Western or "exotic" instruments. Some of the most important of them are illustrated in Figure 2.8.

**Figure 2.7** *From left to right: tuba, trombone, trumpet, French horn.*

**Figure 2.8** *From left to right: gong, xylophone, cymbals, snare drum.*

### Keyboard and Plucked Instruments

The principal instruments sounded by means of a keyboard are the piano, harpsichord, and organ (Figure 2.9). Indeed, these are among the most important instruments in the entire history of music. They are independently capable of realizing an entire work, including both melody and accompaniment. They may also function as purely accompanimental instruments or components of larger ensembles.

The piano has been the preeminent keyboard instrument since the late eighteenth century. Early pianos, by makers such as the Italian Bartolommeo Cristofori (1655–1731), were versions of the harpsichord that, unlike the true harpsichord, could sound either loudly or softly depending on the force exerted on the keys. The Italian words for "soft" (*piano*) and "loud" (*forte*) were used to designate this experimental instrument. The older terms *pianoforte* or *fortepiano* were subsequently shortened to *piano*, although **fortepiano** is currently used to refer to a piano of the eighteenth or early nineteenth century or a copy of such an instrument.

The modern piano may have a flat, winglike shape (a grand piano), or it may be upright. The keys control hammers that are thrown against strings, making them sound. Their tone is amplified by the nearby soundboard and by other elements of the instrument's body. Pedals control the damping of the string or the loudness of the tone, and they can often produce other effects as well.

The **harpsichord** is the historical predecessor of the piano, and it enjoyed its greatest vogue in the sixteenth, seventeenth, and eighteenth centuries. Its shape generally resembles that of a small grand piano, but its mechanism is very different. When a key is depressed on a harpsichord, a string is plucked. The resonance of the sound is not changed by the force exerted on the keys. In the small, wood-framed harpsichord, the strings are under much lower tension than in the modern piano, so its sound is more delicate. Harpsichord playing has undergone a revival in the twentieth century, and many modern composers continue to write for this instrument.

The tones of a pipe organ are produced by wind blown into pipes, rather than by the vibrations of a string. The organ is by far the oldest of the keyboard instruments, having been known among the ancient Greeks and Romans. Organs with few pipes may be simple and portable and appropriate to use in the home. In the present day, however, they are usually encountered only in churches in much more elaborate and permanent installations.

A typical organ consists of several divisions, each connected to a separate group of pipes and each operated by a separate keyboard. Usually, two or

**66**

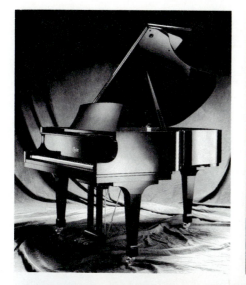

***Figure 2.9*** *Piano (top left), harpsichord (top right), organ (bottom).*

more keyboards are worked by the hands, and another, called a *pedalboard,* is played by the feet. Electronic organs imitate the tone of acoustic organs, but their sounds are made by loudspeakers rather than by pipes.

**Figure 2.10** *Guitar (top), lute (bottom), harp (right).*

The plucked instruments, like the keyboard instruments, allow a single musician to realize a complete musical texture. These stringed instruments are often played by both amateurs and trained musicians, and they are encountered in popular, folk, and artistic music. The principal plucked instruments are the guitar, harp, and lute (Figure 2.10), although many other related instruments are found in the folk music of various regions of the world.

The guitar is characterized by its relatively flat back, four to six strings, and fingerboard frets (ridges on which the player's fingers can stop the strings). It is a very ancient instrument, which has been increasingly associated with Iberian musicians. Its construction is similar to numerous folk instruments, including the banjo and the ukulele. In recent times, it has been imitated by the electric guitar—an instrument having little in common with the refined and quiet authentic guitar.

The strings of the harp are attached to two sides of a triangular frame, and the instrument is normally played with the fingers. Harps are very ancient and of great diversity in construction. The elaborate concert harp emerged in the nineteenth century as a regular member of the orchestra as well as a solo instrument. This harp has 47 strings and a pedal mechanism that allows the performer to move the pitch of all of the strings up one or two semitones.

The lute is related to the guitar, although the two are differentiated by several technical features. The body of the lute has a rounded back, and most of the strings are laid out in adjacent pairs called *courses.* The instrument attained its greatest importance in the sixteenth and seventeenth centuries, and it has also experienced a revival in the recent twentieth century. Lutes were first brought to Europe from the Middle East, and the related 'ud remains a popular instrument throughout the Arabic world.

## Electronic Instruments

The strikingly new musical instruments of the twentieth century are electronic devices capable of generating and manipulating sound. These have a history extending to the early years of the century, although they have played a major role in musical culture only since about 1950. At that time, some composers in Europe and America began to use electronic signals generated by oscillators as the starting points of works of music. These signals were modulated and edited, then reconstituted in musical form on the medium of tape.

In the 1960s the creation of electronic music was greatly advanced by the appearance of **synthesizers.** These devices typically contained several modules, each of which created or acted on an electronic signal. Some modules functioned as oscillators, producing a signal that could be converted to sound by a loudspeaker; other modules amplified the signal, filtered it, created a distinctive envelope, or otherwise changed it. These early synthesizers made electronic composition much quicker and simpler by allowing the composer to hear in real time the results of the electronic manipulations.

The application to music of computer hardware, software, and digital circuitry has produced astonishing results since the 1980s. Digital electronic music synthesizers are now capable of assisting people with or without training in music in the composition, performance, recording, and notation of works in all styles. The impact of these devices has been felt especially in commercial music, most of all in composing and recording for film and

## Musical Instruments for the Twenty-first Century

In 1985, sales of the piano, heretofore the most popular musical instrument, were outstripped by sales of electronic keyboards. These are probably the best-known types of digital music synthesizers, devices that in more sophisticated versions have, in less than a decade, revolutionized commercial music.

Synthesizers can range from simple keyboards to computerized music centers capable of imitating an entire orchestra. A composer can encode his or her ideas and hear them "performed" at the same time. The more sophisticated synthesizers produce electronically generated sounds or recall recorded sounds of human voices or instruments that have been "sampled" and stored. These sounds can then be edited or manipulated at the will of the composer-operator and reconstituted as an entire musical composition.

The musical results of this new technology are known to virtually everyone, especially in the form of music for radio commercials (known as "jingles"), television background music, or film sound tracks. The music to the motion picture *Chariots of Fire* was created by the composer Vangelis without the involvement of a single instrumentalist; other movies and television shows, including *Out of Bounds, Beverly Hills Cop II,* and *Miami Vice,* have their music composed and "performed" by a single person with the help of the synthesizer. Other sound tracks achieve realism by combining a few acoustic instruments or voices in a "foreground score," which is fleshed out by a synthesized background.

Synthesizers are also basic to the work of the modern pop or rock singer. Stevie Wonder and Michael Jackson regularly use synthesizers, especially in recordings, but also in live concerts, to increase the flexibility and sonority of their music.

Will the synthesizer eventually leave its mark on classical music? Since the 1950s, composers of serious music have used the synthesizer to create dynamic soundscapes. But the synthesizer has had little impact to date on traditional classical music. Certainly, the synthesizer could quickly and economically realize and record a symphony by Beethoven. Mahler's *Symphony of a Thousand* could easily

television. Most digital synthesizers use traditional keyboards, but the computer keyboard can be programmed as a control device just as well.

Synthesizers marketed under trade names such as Synclavier and Emulator have the capacity for *sampling,* recording and storing the sounds of live instruments and subsequently using these sounds to imitate familiar media. The results are technically impressive, but they do not completely duplicate the sound quality of live performance. Their use in commercial music is increasingly to support and to flesh out recordings or performances in which live performers also play a role. Unquestionably, the computer and digital synthesis will play an ever-larger role in music in the future.

be recorded by a single operator. But would the music be as satisfying as when performed by an orchestra of live musicians, each with their own personality and insight?

For most connoisseurs of classical music, the answer is emphatically no. For the time being, the synthesizer will exert its impact primarily in the realm of popular or commercial music, where the quality of sound and details of expression are not so crucial as they are to the classics.

## Media

The term *medium* will be used in this book to describe the group of instruments and voices that are called for in a specific composition. If a composer calls, for example, for tenor voice and piano in a work, these constitute the work's medium. The orchestra is another example of a medium, although its exact constitution may vary from one work or historical era to the next.

Medium in music is closely tied to expressive content. Beethoven, for example, used the symphony orchestra for a certain type of music and for

*In this serigraph called* **Orchestra Chairs** *(1951), Ben Shahn used the flat linear shapes of cubism to depict a scene familiar to all orchestral musicians. The music is now silenced, the rehearsal space is empty, and the music stands and chairs remain behind in a forlorn jumble.*

works conveying a certain message—one that was often different from the content of his string quartets or piano works.

Throughout the history of music, composers have returned time and again to certain media, making them conventional elements in the language of music. The *orchestra,* whose constitution was just outlined, is one such group. The *band* (sometimes called a *wind ensemble*) consists primarily of woodwinds, brass, and percussion. Its forceful resonance makes it appropriate for outdoor or marching use, although bands are concert media as well. The *chorus* is another typical large medium. Choruses can be made up of all men, all women, children, or combinations of the three. A *mixed chorus* normally sings four lines of music: The highest is sung in unison by the sopranos, the next lower line by altos, the next lower by tenors, and the lowest line by the basses. Mixed choruses may or may not be accompanied by instruments.

Music for small numbers of instruments in which only one player performs a line is called **chamber music.** Some of the most familiar and important chamber media consist of two violins, a viola, and a cello (a *string quartet*); violin, cello, and piano (a *piano trio*), or one melodic instrument accompanied by piano. Chamber music for woodwinds and brass has become increasingly important in the twentieth century. A *woodwind quintet* normally consists of flute, oboe, clarinet, bassoon, and horn; a *brass quintet* is usually made up of two trumpets, a trombone, a horn, and a tuba (or a second trombone).

## BIBLIOGRAPHY

Baines, Anthony. *Musical Instruments Through the Ages*. New edition. New York: Walker, 1975.

Cone, Edward. *Musical Form and Musical Performance*. New York: Norton, 1968. This volume is primarily for the experienced musician.

Green, Douglass M. *Form in Tonal Music*. Second edition. New York: Holt, Rinehart and Winston, 1979.

Marcuse, Sibyl. *Music Instruments: A Comprehensive Dictionary*. New York: Norton, 1975.

*The New Grove Dictionary of Musical Instruments*. New York: Grove Dictionaries, 1984.

Sachs, Curt. *Rhythm and Tempo: A Study in Music History*. New York: Norton, 1953.

## NOTES

1. Roger Sessions, *The Musical Experience of Composer, Performer, Listener* (Princeton, N.J.: Princeton University Press, 1950), p. 12.
2. Igor Stravinsky, *Poetics of Music,* trans. Arthur Knodel and Ingolf Dahl (New York: Vintage Books, 1947), pp. 66–68.
3. Elliott Carter, "The Orchestral Composer's Point of View," in *The Composer's Point of View,* ed. Robert S. Hines (Norman: University of Oklahoma Press, 1970), p. 49.

# Early Music

Most people are familiar with artworks created in the Middle Ages and the Renaissance. Gothic cathedrals, sculptures by Michelangelo, and paintings by Leonardo da Vinci are well known to most of us, as are masterpieces of medieval literature, such as Chaucer's *Canterbury Tales*. But relatively few people have heard a piece of music composed during these same periods. This is because performances of classical music nowadays are overwhelmingly devoted to works composed in the eighteenth and nineteenth centuries, with an occasional foray into the twentieth century. Music from before 1700 is rarely heard in concert.

But a treasure trove of inspired music from early times most assuredly exists, waiting to be discovered by inquisitive listeners. And it is music that is by any standard of comparison the equal of more familiar music in its power to communicate, to move, and to delight. Why, then, is it relatively ignored? The answer has to do perhaps with our lack of familiarity with its components. Its scales are somewhat different from the major and minor scales that we are accustomed to hearing; its degree of focus on a keynote is sometimes different from what we, perhaps unconsciously, have come to expect; and its genres, forms, and media are regrettably unfamiliar. Music, more than any of its sister arts, has been susceptible to the establishment of a canon of classics that now dominates the concert world. A relatively small group of composers and works, as great as they are, have diverted the attention of musicians and listeners alike away from masterworks of an earlier era.

Fortunately, since about 1970 the balance between earlier and later music has begun to be restored. Recordings by first-rate performers have shown that the works of Machaut, Josquin des Prez, Monteverdi, and their contemporaries cannot be permanently ignored or passed off as historical curiosities. This music is as vibrant today as it was in its own time.

The works that we shall encounter in Chapters 3 through 6 create, to be sure, the background to later masterpieces. But this music is not in any sense primitive. It should be approached with the same attention to detail, the same concentration, and the same repeated listening that is demanded by a symphony by Beethoven or an opera aria by Verdi. We will not be disappointed by its power to move and to delight us, and by studying it we will come to understand much more fully the foundations of the Western musical tradition.

# 3

*Music in the*
*Medieval World*

## Music and Everyday Life

*It is a warm spring day. People from the village temporarily suspend their work in the gardens or the tending of flocks of sheep in order to indulge in a moment of diversion and conviviality. One of them is skilled in playing the bagpipes, and to his merry tune the villagers gather to perform a round dance.*

*Scenes such as this must have been common in the Middle Ages, for they are often captured by artists of the day. The painter of this manuscript illumination has shown the village merrymakers true to life. They wear the simple clothing of working people, which some have adorned with greenery as befits the season of spring. They perform a dance around a blooming tree, much as their ancestors had done each spring since antiquity.*

*But the artist is also intent on placing the merriment of his fellow people into a religious context. An angel above the gathering proclaims the message of the birth of Christ. "Glory to God in the highest and peace on earth to men of good will," read the Latin words of the angel. Shepherds on the right side of the picture carefully point to his proclamation. These Latin words were chanted during the Middle Ages in the Christian service of worship, and they have their origin in the biblical account of the Nativity.*

*The artist does not appear to have been bothered by the incongruity of joining the image of a spring dance to a Christmas message. Both seasons, after all, suggest birth and renewal. More important than* this common theme, however, is his depiction of the closeness of everyday and sacred matters. This congruency was found everywhere in medieval art and society. Indeed, the painting suggests a new context for the joy of music and dance. No longer are these activities to be mere revelry, but, instead, an expression of exuberance over basic Christian beliefs.

Miniature illumination of manuscripts was one of the leading genres of painting among French and Flemish artists of the late Middle Ages. Some of the most dazzling examples of the miniaturist's art are to be found in prayer books commissioned for aristocratic patrons. This diminutive painting was entered into a "book of hours," a prayer book so named because the prayers and services of worship that it contained are intended for certain times of day and for certain seasons of the year. This book was prepared in the late fifteenth century for a French count, Charles d'Angoulême. It is richly provided with scenes portraying everyday life and suggestions of the close relationship between music and the church.

As we will see in Chapter 3, music of high artistry during the Middle Ages was almost exclusively associated with the church. To be sure, a robust music also existed elsewhere. For the common men and women of the medieval period, as for us today, music was an art that brought people together and provided them with a source of great pleasure. "What can music do?" asked the medieval scholar Isidore of Seville in his early medieval Etymologies:

> Music moves the feelings and changes the emotions . . . .
> Music soothes the mind to endure toil, and the modulation of the voice consoles the weariness of each labor.

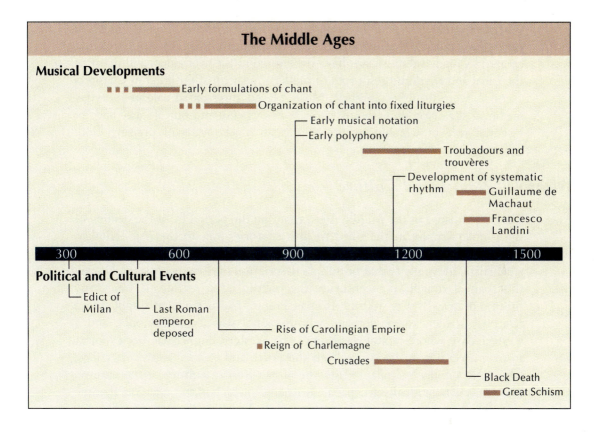

**The Middle Ages**

**Musical Developments**

- Early formulations of chant
- Organization of chant into fixed liturgies
- Early musical notation
- Early polyphony
- Troubadours and trouvères
- Development of systematic rhythm
- Guillaume de Machaut
- Francesco Landini

300    600    900    1200    1500

**Political and Cultural Events**

- Edict of Milan
- Last Roman emperor deposed
- Rise of Carolingian Empire
- Reign of Charlemagne
- Crusades
- Black Death
- Great Schism

In a book on counterpoint completed in 1477, Johannes Tinctoris, a musician and priest living in Italy, looked back disdainfully on music of the past. "It is a matter of great surprise," he remarked, "that there is no composition written over forty years ago which is thought by the learned as worthy of performance." Tinctoris's slighting view of music before his own time was typical of fifteenth-century Italian writers, who often dismissed all culture of preceding centuries as the product of a "dark age." Tinctoris and his contemporaries looked back to the highly developed civilization of ancient Greece and Rome to find in arts and letters the equal of their own times. Between these two cultural peaks stretched a long and seemingly bleak expanse that they termed the "Middle Ages."

We are now aware that Tinctoris's view was, at best, shortsighted. To be sure, the Middle Ages encompassed times of great hardship and cultural deprivation, but it was also the period when the foundations of modern Western civilization were established and its institutions significantly advanced. It was an especially important period for music. During medieval times, basic musical textures such as counterpoint were invented. Genres first created by medieval musicians have lived on in music ever since, and many of the tonal and rhythmic resources of modern music, just outlined in Chapters 1 and 2, were firmly established. Music played an essential role in everyday medieval life. Not only did it provide entertainment, but it also had an essential role in worship, where it was an ideal means of praising God.

## Medieval Politics and Culture

The vast expanse of the Middle Ages, covering the period from the decline of the Roman Empire in the third to fifth centuries A.D. to the rise of Italian humanism in the early to mid-fifteenth century, embraces so many political and artistic movements that no simple description of them is possible. During this span of roughly ten centuries, the political map of Europe was many times redrawn. By A.D. 500 the Roman Empire had permanently split into a relatively stable eastern domain, whose capital was Constantinople, and a western part, whose capital was Rome. The Western Empire had been subject to over a century of invasions from the north and east by Germanic tribes, who were rapidly assimilated into the Greco-Roman culture of the empire. These invaders gradually accepted Christianity, which in the year 313 became an officially tolerated religion in the realm. The last Roman emperor was deposed in 476. The pattern of settlement of Germanic tribes in Europe soon formed the basis for modern political and national divisions: Franks and Burgundians settled in France; Ostrogoths prevailed in Italy, Visigoths in Spain, and Alamans and Saxons in Germany.

In the eighth and early ninth centuries, the glory of the Roman Empire was in part recaptured by a powerful dynasty of Frankish kings, the greatest of whom was Charlemagne (768–814). Frankish military prowess and political skill led to the creation of an empire that encompassed all of Europe except for Spain, England, and southern Italy. The Carolingians, as they are called, bolstered their empire by a strong alliance with the popes in Rome, and Christianity afforded them a powerful means of unification and cultural stimulus. Charlemagne's reign witnessed a flowering of literacy, learning, and artistic accomplishment that had no precedent since the decline of ancient Rome. So great was the synthesis of cultures in the Carolingian Empire that it was during its existence that the first enduring body of Western artistic music, Gregorian chant, was firmly established. An example of this music will be studied shortly.

The post-Carolingian centuries were marked by a steady breakup of the empire, which was further fragmented by invasions of Vikings from the north and Muslims from the east and south. A measure of international unity under the banner of Christianity was regained in the late eleventh century, as knights and noblemen from all European lands converged on the Muslim East in the first Crusade. This military campaign, initiated by Pope Urban II in 1095, was a reaction to expansion by tribes of Muslim Turks. When the Byzantine emperor appealed for help from the West, the response was a massive invasion of the eastern shores of the Mediterranean. Jerusalem was captured and pillaged, and new states controlled by Europeans were established throughout the lands bordering the eastern Mediterranean.

But by the middle of the twelfth century, many of these areas had returned to Muslim control. In 1147 a second Crusade was launched, which had none of the success of the first. A third effort in 1189 was also a failure, despite the participation of the idealistic king of England, Richard Coeur de Lion ("the Lion-Hearted"). Later Crusades were directed at various targets, including the Christian Byzantine Empire itself, which was defeated by Western armies in 1204.

For the art of music, the Crusades were of great importance. The Crusaders brought back with them many musical instruments from Arab lands that became a permanent part of Western musical culture. They also encountered styles of singing and musical genres that were influential on future developments, and their booty included manuscripts containing records of the musical culture of ancient Greece.

The Crusades were made possible by two of the strongest institutions of the Middle Ages: the social system known as feudalism and the Christian church. From Carolingian times on, feudalism formed the basis of the European social structure. It was a diverse system of allegiances wedded to a rigid hierarchy of social classes, with royalty at the top and nobility, landowners, peasants, and serfs arranged in descending order of importance. Land was often given as a "fief" by a member of a higher class in return for homage, service, and some form of payment by a vassal. Few among the peasantry were landowners. Peasants usually worked instead on the land of an overlord or used land leased to them in return for payment in kind and for other services.

The Christian church was the most powerful political and cultural force throughout the Middle Ages. For most of this time, it was the only effective means of political and social unification, allowing all European peoples to share in a common culture. In the early years of the church, several powerful bishops emerged as leaders, but the bishop of Rome, called the pope, soon became head. The relation of the popes to secular life and politics was immensely varied but always important. Similarly, the church was the essential stimulus to art and education throughout the Middle Ages.

The work of monastic orders was also crucial. Early in the Middle Ages, monks of the Benedictine order functioned as missionaries of Christian doctrine and papal authority. They established an approach to communal living and rules of behavior and organization that were widely imitated, and their monasteries were centers for the preservation of knowledge and artistic endeavor. The monastic movement increased as the Middle Ages evolved, eventually witnessing the emergence of orders, such as the Franciscans, whose members did not live in isolated communities but rather mingled directly with people from all walks of life.

Education was always closely associated with the work of monasteries, without which literacy would perhaps have completely died out in Europe. The copying of manuscripts was an especially valuable undertaking of monks, which helped to preserve the cultural record of the West. As cities grew in the late Middle Ages, universities emerged. The basic curriculum at these institutions consisted of the "seven liberal arts," which placed music in the company of mathematical disciplines. Students could subsequently advance to professional studies in law, theology, or medicine.

Despite the harshness of life brought about by foreign invasions, warfare, and plagues, the fine arts flourished in medieval times. Poetic genres included the epic *chansons de geste,* which recorded heroic deeds, and the romance, a long narrative poem with a lyric character, often based on themes of courtly love. Painting in the Middle Ages, before the first stirrings of the Renaissance style in the fourteenth century, was much influenced by Byzantine art.

Medieval architecture reached inspiring heights of originality in the romanesque and gothic styles. Romanesque architecture, like medieval painting, copied aspects of ancient Roman and earlier Byzantine buildings. It appeared most spectacularly in churches in France, Germany, and Italy of the eleventh and twelfth centuries, and it is characterized by rounded arches and massive vaulting; the imposing elevation of thick, load-bearing walls; and one or two imposing towers at the entrances. The Basilica of Sainte-Madeleine in the Burgundian village of Vézelay (page 85) is one of the great remaining examples of the romanesque style. The nave and narthex of this church, completed by the middle of the twelfth century, are fine examples of romanesque architecture, although the choir and aspects of the exterior, completed later, are influenced by the early gothic style.

Gothic architecture, which dominated church building all over Europe for the remainder of the Middle Ages, displays a flamboyance and an emo-

*The romanesque nave of this magnificent church, the Basilica of Sainte-Madeleine in the French town of Vézelay, was built in the twelfth century. Its romanesque style is recognizable in the massive overall proportions of the church, the regularity of thick piers and columns along the sides of the nave, and the large semicircular vaults that span the nave and create an inspiring sense of interior volume.*

*This cathedral in Chartres, France, completed in the early thirteenth century, is a dazzling example of gothic architecture. Here the massive heaviness of romanesque churches is exploded into structures of elegance, lightness, and fantasy. The nave of the Chartres Cathedral is very much higher and wider than the Basilica in Vézelay (left). The walls of the Chartres Cathedral are punctuated by windows that admit streams of light and color, creating an exuberance that was also shared by church music of the thirteenth century.*

tionalism that reflect contemporary developments in theology and literature. One of its great examples is the Cathedral of Notre Dame in Chartres, built in a relatively brief period in the late twelfth and early thirteenth centuries. Its nave and choir (see above) reveal the distinctive features of the style: a surging verticality, the lines of which continue in the form of skeletal vault ribs merging in pointed arches, walls that are pierced by massive windows, and a general lightness and sense of fantasy that make romanesque buildings appear stodgily earthbound in comparison. Outside of the gothic cathedral, along its external and rear walls, distinctive flying buttresses support the high walls and allow them to be perforated by gorgeous stained-glass windows.

Romanesque and gothic churches are inspiring examples of medieval artistic expression and powerful reminders of the central role played by the church throughout medieval times. As we turn our attention to music of the Middle Ages, we will be reminded of the fundamental part played by the Christian church. Until well along in the medieval period, the only music that was preserved in written form was music intended for use in the church, where its function was both to glorify God and to spread Christian teachings.

# Music in the Medieval Christian Church

Although music existed outside of the church throughout the Middle Ages, before the twelfth century it was not preserved in a way that allows it now to be reconstructed or studied. Within the church, however, music played so fundamental a role that by the year 900, a means was devised for its preservation in written form. A relatively precise system for writing down melodies was a distinctive by-product of Western culture. Called *notation,* it allowed music to undergo a continual stylistic evolution that has proved unique to the European tradition. By the eleventh century, notation had been refined to the point that church melodies could be distributed and maintained uniformly in services of worship throughout Europe. Many of these tunes continue to be used in both Catholic and Protestant services of worship today.

## Chant

We begin our study of medieval music with a melody, or **chant,** sung during the Middle Ages in the Catholic church on Easter Sunday (Recording 3.1). Its words, "Alleluia. Pascha nostrum immolatus est Christus" ("Hallelujah. Christ the Paschal Lamb is sacrificed for us"), refer to events celebrated by Christians on this holiday. After listening to this piece, describe its constituent elements; then analyze the stylistic features that give the music its distinctive beauty.

In what respects is this piece similar to modern music, and in what way does it lack features that we have now come to expect? We are probably first aware of the music's unusual texture, which is purely monophonic. It consists solely of one melodic line, devoid of harmony or polyphony. All extant Western music prior to the eleventh century is similarly monophonic, in a texture that allows the words to be clearly heard even in a spacious church or cathedral.

The melody itself, however, is very sophisticated in its construction and artistry. Unlike many earlier chants, "Alleluia. Pascha nostrum" clearly establishes a keynote. The note G is the central tone, being the first one sung and appearing at each major cadence. If we arrange the notes of the melody ascending stepwise from G, however, we find that its scale is not exactly major or minor. In fact, chants use modes that are forerunners of major and minor and lend the melodies a distinctively antique sound.

The form of this chant is close to the ternary prototype. Initially, the music follows the division of the text into two sections. The first of these is devoted to the word "Alleluia," whose final syllable is dramatically extended by a melodic phrase called a **jubilus.** This initial part of the chant is begun by a soloist who sings the word "Alleluia"; he is then joined by a chorus of men, all singing in unison, who repeat what the soloist has just sung and add the jubilus to it. The second group of words, "Pascha nostrum immolatus est Christus," is sung on this recording entirely by the chorus, although in the Middle Ages it is likely that a soloist would have alternated with chorus. On the final word, "Christus," the music deviates from the form of the text, since here a shortened version of the music of the first part reappears, thereby creating a ternary form. In the Listening Guide that follows, this overall musical form is represented by letters in the left column, A B A′ (the prime sign added to the second A indicates that this music is slightly modified in comparison to its first appearance).

The rhythm of "Alleluia. Pascha nostrum" is decidedly different from what we have come to expect in music, since it has no regular beat or meter. Even now, there is no agreement about the rhythmic style in which chant should be performed. It is likely that in the early Middle Ages, chants were sung with some type of rhythmic differentiation in note lengths. But, if so, the principles guiding rhythm were not preserved or explained, either in written treatises or in early musical notation. By the late Middle Ages, chant was considered devoid of systematic rhythm and hence called *cantus planus,* or **plainsong.** Nowadays chants are usually sung with a free rhythm in which the stresses of the Latin words are reflected in note values. On the performance in Recording 3.1, the singers invent a free rhythm for their own use.

If we listen repeatedly to other examples of medieval chant (see the recommendations for additional listening at the end of this chapter), we will find that they have remarkably different styles. Some appear simple and subdued to the point of austerity, while others are nothing short of flamboyant. "Alleluia. Pascha nostrum" is one of the latter type, not surprising since it contains the word of praise *Hallelujah* and since it is sung on the joyous occasion of Easter. The range of the melody is, by chant standards, unusually wide, soaring repeatedly in the second part into a high register. The music of both sections is prolonged by **melismas,** melodic phrases that are sung

*Gregorian chants were first written down, in a primitive form of notation, in the ninth century. This page from a ninth-century manuscript, copied in Saint-Gall, Switzerland, contains words that were chanted in the Christian service of worship during the Christmas season.*

to a single syllable and give the music its pronounced ornateness. Clearly, this work is intended for well-trained singers.

Medieval church melodies like "Alleluia. Pascha nostrum" are commonly called **Gregorian chants,** taking their name from Pope Gregory I (c. 540–604). Legend has it that Gregory himself was their author, possibly receiving them from God. This idea is unlikely, given their great number and diversity, although it is probable that Pope Gregory supported the use of chant in the early church. It is now known that the sources of the chants were diverse: Some probably came from Jewish synagogue practices, others from secular tunes, still others were devised by individual (although now largely anonymous) singers. Many chants were probably assembled by several generations of singers from preexistent or stock phrases. The processes by which chants were created and put into use took place continuously in the early centuries, reaching a relatively fixed state during the Carolingian period. Some genres of chant, however, continued to be composed to the end of the Middle Ages. Given its symmetrical ternary form and the distinct presence of a keynote, "Alleluia. Pascha nostrum" has the character of a work by a composer active around the year 800. Typical of most chants, the identity of the composer is unknown.

*Listening Guide*

**Gregorian chant, "Alleluia. Pascha nostrum" (for Easter Sunday).**
Recording 3.1

**A**     0.00     A soloist begins with an upward-moving, fanfarelike figure on the word "Alleluia":

This music is then repeated by the chorus, leading to the long melisma called the jubilus (beginning at 0.13).

**B**  0.44  The second section (on the words "Pascha nostrum immolatus est Christus") continues an elaboration on an up-and-down motive already heard in music A:

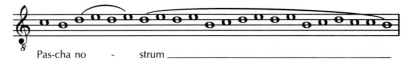

Pas-cha no - strum _____

The melody then soars into a high register, finally falling downward to the keynote G on the word "est."

**A′**  1.34  Music for the last word ("Christus"), sung by the chorus, is a shortened restatement of music A.

## The Role of Chant in the Liturgy

There are numerous services of worship (collectively called the *liturgy*) in the Catholic church, of which the most important is the **Mass.** The words of the Mass consist of prayers and excerpts from the Bible, concluding with a reenactment of the Last Supper of Jesus. The Mass is the only service in which the laity participate, and possibly for this reason, music has an especially vital part in it. Until the time of the Second Vatican Council, which ended in 1965, almost all words of the Mass were sung, either by the celebrant or by a choir. Some of this singing was musically uninteresting, since it consisted of little more than recitation on one or a few tones. The remaining singing consisted of the ancient and highly artistic melodies of Gregorian chant.

The words of some types of chants, such as "Alleluia. Pascha nostrum," change each day, since their content is appropriate to only one occasion. These chants and their words are hence called the **proper.** Other texts are unchangingly present in every Mass, so they form the **ordinary.** The Mass has importance to music not only because it contains chant melodies of great beauty but also because its words—especially those of the ordinary—have been used by generations of composers as starting points for original compositions. Bach's great B-minor Mass, Beethoven's *Missa solemnis,* and Mozart's *Coronation Mass* are only a few of the many masterworks whose texts are drawn from this service of worship.

## *Embellishments of Chant and Early Polyphony*

Since the elements of the liturgy were held by the church to be unchangeable, medieval musicians from the Carolingian period onward were forced to look within existing musical works for an outlet for artistic expression. Fortunately, the church took a tolerant view of such expansion from within, in the form of embellishments of, interpolations in, or additions to the established texts and music of the liturgy. Medieval writers had a comparable outlet in the widespread practice of adding commentaries and explanations to existing sacred texts.

From the ninth century to the end of the Middle Ages, chants from Christian worship were continually inflated by the insertion of new phrases of text and music. These interpolated materials are now called **tropes,** and the process of troping proved to be one of the most important channels for the creation of new music and literature in the late medieval period. This practice reveals an attitude on the part of the medieval musician different from the modern one. A piece of music such as chant must have seemed to the medieval singer to be a work in progress rather than something complete in itself. It could be embellished, even rewritten, in order to express new artistic ideas.

Unquestionably, the most important outcome of the practice of liturgical embellishment during the late Middle Ages was the birth of polyphony. This new texture was an outgrowth of monophonic chant, created when one or more singers added new melodic lines simultaneously to the singing of a preexistent chant. The importance of this innovation can scarcely be overstated. It quickly led to a type of musical discourse that was essentially different from that of any other culture, and it laid the foundation for the development of modern harmony and counterpoint.

Polyphony had its origins in a new method of performing chant. Singers in church choirs, at some point prior to the year 900, probably in Frankish lands, discovered that an enriched sonority could be obtained if some of them sang the chant a fixed interval above or below the others. This improvisatory practice apparently became widespread by the year 900, for about then it was described in several musical manuals. By about 1100 the new way of singing chant was taking a new and exciting direction. No longer were the added lines strictly in parallel with the chant line; they were beginning to gain independence from the preexistent melody and thus to create a truly polyphonic texture.

The polyphonic idiom took on a new degree of sophistication by the late twelfth and early thirteenth centuries in Paris in the work of musicians associated with the Cathedral of Notre Dame. Paris at this time was just becoming the major cultural and economic center that it is today. A university would be founded there in the early thirteenth century, and the magnificent gothic Cathedral of Notre Dame was constructed between 1163 and about 1250. The singer-composers connected with the cathedral were evidently in touch with experiments in polyphony elsewhere in France, and they reshaped these earlier initiatives into a coherent style.

The Parisian musicians worked at first in a genre that they called **organum,** which consisted of polyphonic embellishments of portions of existing chant. Their new polyphonic textures, however, posed a problem for the singers, who could no longer move together in unison, as they had done when singing the chant in a simple manner. In organum they were required to sing different melodies that had to be precisely coordinated. So the Notre Dame composers also developed a system of rhythm, which allowed for an accurate coordination of polyphonic lines, and a system of notation that could record the duration of tones. These innovations formed the basis for our modern system of rhythm.

Although organum was the earliest genre of polyphonic music, the Notre Dame composers also devised other polyphonic types, of which the **motet** has proved by far the most durable. This type of music, like organum, had its origins as an embellishment of chant. To the newly composed lines in certain types of organum a text was added, hence the term *motet* (from the French *mot,* "word"). These texts were probably at first Latin poetry that was relevant to the service at which the source chant was used. But the new genre quickly detached itself from its parent chant, indeed, from the liturgy itself. Motet texts in the vernacular were also used, often with a decidedly secular content, suggesting that they were intended for entertainment rather than for religious purposes.

## Songs of the Troubadours and Trouvères

Only in the twelfth century did music outside of the church take on an importance and a coherence that led to its preservation in written form. Beginning at this time or slightly before, musicians began to write down **songs,** that is, melodic settings of secular poetry. At first these pieces contained Latin words, but in the twelfth century there arose in southwestern France a brilliant movement of songwriting using vernacular poetry. This was the work of the **troubadours,** who created the first important body of secular music in Western history.

The troubadours were originally amateur poets and tunesmiths from the nobility. Their subject was courtly love, which they celebrated with great artifice and refinement. In their poems, women were portrayed as objects of an intense, often agonizing admiration to whom exaggerated expressions of gallant courtesy were due. The language of troubadour poetry was that of southern France, which is now called either the *langue d'oc* (*oc* was the word for "yes") or Provençal.

Fewer than 300 melodies of the troubadours have been preserved, and only in a primitive form that sheds but a dim light on how they were performed. Their overall structure, like that of their poetry, is strophic. Their musical style resembles Gregorian chant: They are preserved only as vocal melodies, with no accompaniment, and their notation has no decipherable information about rhythm. The melodies are based on the same antiquated modes as chant, and their style is generally simple, with occasional ornamental melismas.

The refined art of the troubadour was not long destined to remain isolated in the courts of southwestern France. The professional troubadours and the itinerant performers called *jongleurs* quickly introduced their art to other European regions. In German lands there arose a related movement of so-called *Minnesänger* ("singers of love"), and songs of courtly love on the Provençal model also spread to Spain, Portugal, and Italy. But the most fertile ground for growth of the art of the troubadour was in northern France, whose language was the forefather of modern French. The poet-composers of courtly love in this region were called **trouvères,** the equivalent in French to the Provençal term *troubadour.*

The trouvère repertory of poetry and song is very closely related to its Provençal antecedent, and it flourished in the north from about 1150 until 1300. The existing literary repertory of trouvère poems is about the same size as that of the troubadours, but many more melodies—some 1,700—are preserved. Regrettably, these were notated with the same limited means as the troubadour songs. Are they sung with instrumental accompaniment? Do they use a system of rhythm? These and other basic questions of style and performance remain largely unanswered.

An especially romantic figure in the trouvère movement was Richard Coeur de Lion (1157–1199). In 1189 he succeeded his father, Henry II, as king of England and ruler of the entire western half of France, which his father had solidified as crown lands. In addition to his love of song, he was also an ardent Crusader who led his troops into the Holy Land in 1190. On his return, he was taken prisoner in Austria and held for ransom, which was eventually paid by his English subjects.

According to a pleasant but no doubt apocryphal legend, King Richard was discovered during his imprisonment by a vassal and fellow trouvère, Blondel de Nesle. Blondel is said to have wandered throughout Europe, singing a melody known only to himself and to his lord. When he happened by the castle of Dürnstein (now in Austria), he heard Richard sing back a phrase of his song, and thus the king was found and later ransomed.

King Richard is the author of two extant songs, including "Ja nus hons pris" (Recording 3.2). The poem (see the translation in the Listening Guide) clearly stems from his time of imprisonment, which took place between 1192 and 1194, while he waited impatiently to be ransomed. The poem has eight stanzas, of which only the first two are heard on the performance in Recording 3.2. The final line of text and music in each stanza is the same, thus a **refrain,** whose presence is a typical feature of the mature trouvère repertory.

Only the pitches of the melody are preserved, and these to a single stanza that was repeated for all ensuing stanzas. The rhythm that is heard on the recording, the simple harp accompaniment, and the instrumental prelude and interlude between stanzas are all modern hypothetical attempts at reconstruction, although they are historically plausible and musically sensitive. The melody is exceedingly simple. It flows suavely in a basically stepwise motion over a range that would be easily sung by the amateur performer. It is also very repetitive, as the third and fourth lines of the stanza repeat the music of lines 1 and 2 and the fifth line is but a variation of the first line.

### Richard Coeur de Lion, "Ja nus hons pris" (c. 1194)
Recording 3.2

*1. Ja nus hons pris ne dira sa raison*
*Adroitement; s'ensi com dolans non.*
*Mais par confort puet il faire*
    *chançon.*
*Mout ai d'amis, mas povre sont li*
    *don.*
*Honte en avront, se por ma reançon*

*Sui ces deus yvers pris!*

*1.* A prisoner cannot plead his case
    cleverly, only sadly.
But he can take comfort in a
    song.
I have many friends, but small
    are their means.
Shame on them if, on account of
    my ransom,
I must remain a prisoner for
    these two winters!

2. *Ce sevent bien mi honme et mi baron,*
   *Englois, Normant, Poitevin et Gascon,*

   *Que je n'avoie si povre compaignon,*
   *Cui je laissasse por avoir en prison.*
   *Je nel di pas por nule retraçon*
   *Mais encor sui je pris!*

2. They know it well, my men and barons
   From England, Normandy, Poitou, and Gascony,
   that I have no friend so poor as to be left in prison.
   I don't say this out of spite, but I am still in prison!

A (stanza 1)   0.00   The melodies of the six lines of the stanza have the musical form *ababa'c,* of which the first is

Note that the accompaniment and rhythm are entirely modern reconstructions, as are the harp prelude and interlude between stanzas.

A (stanza 2)   1.26   The music of the first stanza is repeated.

## Music of the Fourteenth Century

The fourteenth century was a period of profound anxiety for most Europeans. A serious economic depression and a decrease in farm production caused great uncertainty that led in some regions to social turmoil. By mid-century, all of Europe came into the clutches of the Black Death, a disastrous epidemic of bubonic plague. The disease spread quickly from rodents to humans, given the unsanitary conditions in which most people lived. Exactly how many died from the plague is uncertain, but estimates range from one-third to three-fourths of the entire European population.

The Catholic church, hitherto the most stable and positive cultural force in Europe, was locked in a disruptive internal dispute. Early in the century, the French-born Pope Clement V moved the papacy from Rome to the city of Avignon in southern France, where it remained until 1376. From the following year until 1417 there were two rival popes, one in Rome and the other in Avignon, producing what has been termed the Great Schism. The energies and attention of the church were diverted not only by this split and by the bitter rivalries that it produced but also by a general waning of its influence in the face of increasingly powerful monarchies.

It is remarkable that the art of music in the fourteenth century underwent no decline. In fact, it appears to have flourished. During this century, we encounter the earliest major composers known to us by name, whose reputations extended far and wide in their own day. Their works achieved unprecedented artistic and technical sophistication. The genres and media of music multiplied continuously, and the regions where music flourished seemed broader than ever before.

## Instrumental Music

You may be surprised by the lack of any mention to this point of instrumental music. In fact, throughout the Middle Ages, instrumental music is an enigma, since there are very few works conclusively intended for instruments and virtually no precise indications of their role. From iconographic evidence and from some medieval writings, we can be certain that musical instruments of many different types were important elements in musical culture in the Middle Ages. But what music did they play? Existing manuscripts give very little definitive information. Evidently, instrumental music was adequately passed on orally, without the need for written notation. The lack of written music also suggests that instrumentalists did not perform independent "compositions" so much as they improvised, played transcriptions of vocal pieces, or provided a flexible and ever-changing enhancement to vocal music. Lines of music that were written down without words suggest instrumental performance, but it is likely that the precise medium by which any piece of music was realized was flexible.

Some of the instruments known to exist in Europe in the fourteenth century or before are shown in Figure 3.1. Among the wind group are flutes (both transverse and end-blown), bagpipes, oboelike **shawms,** and metal trumpets. Bowed stringed instruments include the **rebec,** vielle, and hurdygurdy, and plucked stringed instruments include the lute, psaltery, and harp. The percussion family was represented by various drums and bells. Many of these instruments were brought to Europe from Arabic lands, either during the Crusades or via Moorish Spain.

Perhaps the earliest musical genre associated with instruments was the **estampie.** This word and its cognates were used in the Middle Ages to designate a genre of poetry and, in the early fourteenth century, to label a few

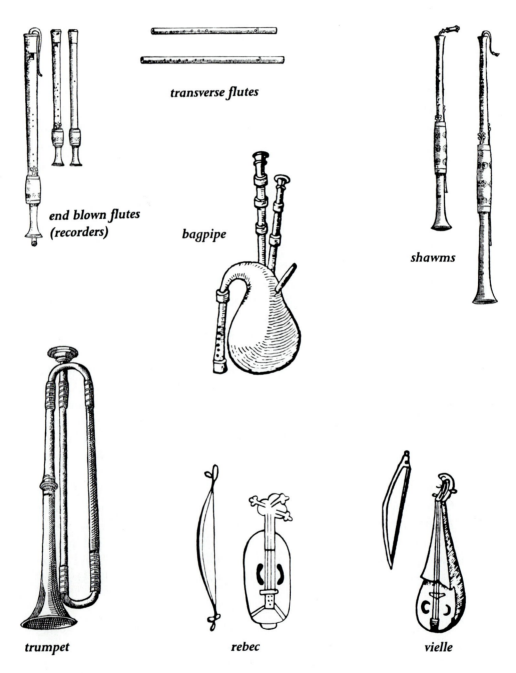

transverse flutes

end blown flutes
(recorders)

bagpipe

shawms

trumpet

rebec

vielle

**Figure 3.1** *Medieval musical instruments.*

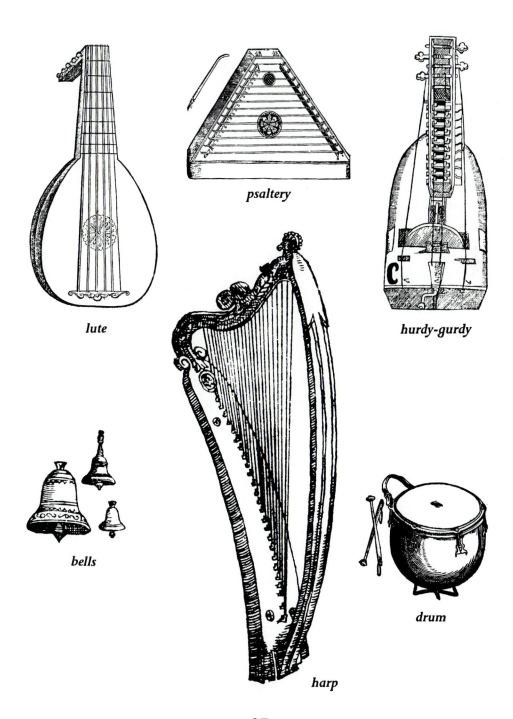

lute

psaltery

hurdy-gurdy

bells

harp

drum

simple pieces of textless music. The word itself (compare *stamp*) suggests a dance step, an activity that was no doubt accompanied by instruments. The Sixth Royal Estampie (Recording 3.3) is one of a group of eight related compositions preserved in a medieval collection of trouvère songs called the *Chansonnier du Roy* (The King's Songbook). These pieces may have originated at the French royal court around the year 1300. They are shown in the songbook solely as melodies without accompaniment, but it is possible that other instruments may have improvised harmonies. There is no indication of what instrument was to play the melody; indeed, it cannot even be said absolutely that the pieces were conceived as instrumental compositions.

The form of the Sixth Royal Estampie consists of four short melodic phrases, each immediately repeated with a new ending. The endings of both the first statement of a phrase and its repeat are identical in all four phrases. In the performance on Recording 3.3, the melody is played by a rebec, an instrument related to the Arabic **rabab,** which was brought to Europe during the Crusades. It is a distant cousin of the violin, although it had fewer strings. The accompaniment, which is entirely hypothetical, is provided by a plucked instrument called a citole. The music has a lively, dancelike character and is of simple construction.

*Listening Guide*

**Sixth Royal Estampie (c. 1300), from the *Chansonnier du Roy***
Recording 3.3

**A**    0.00    The music opens with a melody encompassing only a few different notes:

**B**    0.14    This phrase, like phrases C and D, is also repeated, whereupon its ending is the same as the ending of A when it was repeated.

**C**    0.30    The pattern of repetition with the endings of A continues.

**D**    0.48    The pattern of the earlier phrases continues.

## *Guillaume de Machaut (c. 1300–1377)*

In Guillaume de Machaut, we encounter the first of a line of geniuses whose works dominate the course of Western music from his day to our own. He is the first composer who left a carefully recorded and preserved corpus of music of breadth and great stylistic originality, music that was internationally known and admired in his own day and continues to be an inspiration to composers and audiences today.

His date of birth is not known, but it was probably close to the year 1300. The circumstances of his musical education are likewise obscure. But thanks to his own partly autobiographical poetic writings, we are relatively well informed about his later career. He made his living as a musician in what may be termed the patronage system; that is, he worked in the private service of several noble patrons of the arts and of the church, composing music partly from his own genius and partly at the command of his employers. This pattern of service was duplicated by most great composers from this time through that of Joseph Haydn in the late eighteenth century.

Machaut's first important patron was King John of Bohemia, whom he served as musician, writer, and poet. After John's death in 1346, Machaut's services were sought by several other French aristocrats. He was also appointed a canon of the cathedral in Reims, near his place of birth, probably after taking minor orders of the church. In return for a generous salary, he assisted in music making at the cathedral, and he lived primarily in Reims after John's death. He died there in 1377.

Not only was Machaut the greatest musician of his day, but he was also the most important French poet of the fourteenth century. His writings include lyric poetry in the style of trouvère verse, much of which he set to music in a new polyphonic song style. He

*In this manuscript illumination from the fourteenth century, the composer Machaut is shown at the far right. The figures in the painting are otherwise allegorical. The lady with the crown is Nature, who urges Machaut to continue to compose poems of love. She introduces him to her three children, Sense, Rhetoric, and Music, all of whom will guide and inspire Machaut in the poetic art.*

also wrote poetic narratives called *dits* (pronounced "DEE") and a valuable didactic narrative poem called the *Remède de fortune* (*Fortune's Remedy*, c. 1345). This work deals with the subjects of love and fortune, and it also contains information about medieval music and instructive examples of composition. We shall return momentarily to one of the musical works that Machaut incorporated into the *Remède.*

Despite his appointment to the clergy, Machaut seems to have led a decidedly worldly existence. From his poetic writings we know that he enjoyed sports and nature, and from his love poems and letters to a young lady named Péronne d'Armentières, we can be assured that he was not insensitive to the pleasures of the flesh. In the Middle Ages more than today, the life of the spirit was never far removed from the mundane. Machaut's exquisite poetry praising women's beauty could just as well be interpreted as praise of the immaculate beauty of the Virgin Mary.

Part of Machaut's oeuvre as a composer was, by the fourteenth century, antiquated in style. Like his trouvère predecessors, he composed monophonic settings of poetry on chivalrous themes. He also wrote 23 motets. This genre had undergone radical changes in style from its origin among Notre Dame musicians of the early thirteenth century. In Machaut's hands, the motet was secular music that typically consisted of three polyphonic lines. The top two carried different French poems that, oddly, were sung at the same time. The lowest line was slower in rhythmic motion, and its melody was borrowed from a fragment of Gregorian chant. This line was probably played on an instrument since it carried no text, and it exhibited a repetitive scheme that is now called **isorhythm.** It will be explained and illustrated in Chapter 4 in a discussion of an early motet by Guillaume Dufay.

In addition to the traditional genres of trouvère song and motet, Machaut also turned his attention toward the creation of new musical types and styles, which were destined to be embraced by generations of composers after his time. He was the first to compose a cyclelike setting of the major texts of the ordinary of the Mass. Machaut also went beyond the trouvères' simple approach to composing songs. In place of their rudimentary tunes, he created songs in polyphonic textures of great complexity, songs with an artfulness that equaled the refinement of his own lyric poetry. In these works Machaut turned to three poetic genres—the **ballade, rondeau,** and **virelai**—which had exceedingly intricate patterns of repetition. Such poetry would certainly have been daunting to the musical imagination of a lesser composer, but in Machaut's hands it became a stimulus to works of magnificent beauty. The ballade, rondeau, and virelai forms of poetry have certain features in common. All have refrains returning either at the end of successive stanzas, as in the ballade and virelai, or within a single stanza, as in the rondeau. All deal with themes of courtly love, with a refinement of language worthy of the trouvères.

Machaut's favorite texture in his polyphonic songs consisted of three lines, of which only one carried a text. Unlike the motet, which incorporated a line from chant, all lines of the songs were newly composed. Their notation recorded pitches and rhythms, but other choices that the performers must make, including tempo, dynamic level, and nuances, were not recorded. Since the lower lines have no text and move at a relatively slow pace, it may be assumed that these parts were performed on some unspecified instruments. In recent years, however, evidence has been put forward suggesting that even these lower lines were sometimes sung, as is done on the performance of the song "Dame, de qui toute ma joie vient" ("Lady, from whom comes all my joy") on Recording 3.4.

This song, from the *Remède de fortune,* will illustrate the poetic and musical form of the ballade. Typically, the poem has three stanzas, of eight lines each. The final line is repeated as a refrain at the end of each stanza. The words (see the Listening Guide) are a precious and characteristically overblown encomium to a lady by an admirer whose passion is sustained solely by the hope of catching sight of her. The music, like the poetry, is strophic in form. Within each stanza, the eight lines of text are set to music by only two phrases (*a* and *b*), in this manner:

| musical phrase: | *a* | *a* | *b* |
|---|---|---|---|
| stanza lines: | 1–2 | 3–4 | 5–8 |

The conclusion of music *b,* which sets the eighth line of the stanza, is a refrain that recurs in all stanzas. Furthermore, music *a* has a slightly different ending the second time that it is heard (with lines 3 and 4), and the conclusion of this second ending returns at the very end of music *b.* Clearly, then, Machaut has followed a strict poetic and musical plan, but the music that he writes is in no way studied or formulaic but rather filled with fantasy and apparent unpredictability.

Our attention is perhaps first attracted in this work to its remarkable rhythmic vitality, marked by syncopations and angularities that occasionally merge into sustained chords. The general harmonic content of the piece is decidedly dissonant, but when the voices reach a main cadence (at the end of music *a* and *b*), they come to rest on the notes B♭ and F, which are sounded simultaneously. This cadential sound, so different from the modern triad, clearly possessed a sense of stability and rest for the fourteenth-century musician. Some of the weaker, internal cadences do, in fact, settle on triads, which have a remarkable pungency and richness in comparison to their dissonant surroundings.

### Listening Guide

**Guillaume de Machaut, ballade, "Dame, de qui toute ma joie vient."**
Recording 3.4

*1. Dame, de qui toute ma joie vient,*

   *je ne vous puis trop amer, ne chierir,*

   *n'assés loer, si com il apartient,*
   *servir, doubter, honnourer, n'obeir.*

   *Car le gracieus espoir, douce dame,*
     *que j'ay de vous veoir,*
   *me fais cent fois plus de bien et de joie,*
   *qu'en cent mille ans desservir ne porroie.*

*2. Cils dous espoirs en vie me soustient*
   *et me norrist en amoureus désir,*
   *et dedens moy met tout ce qui couvient*
   *pour conforter mon cuer et resjoir;*
   *n'il ne s'en part main ne soir,*

   *einsois me fait doucement recevoir*

   *plus des dous biens qu'Amours au siens ottroie*
   *qu'en cent mille ans desservir ne porroie.*

*3. Et quant Espoir qui en mon cuer se tient*
   *fait dedens moy si grant joie venir,*

   *lonteins de vous, ma dame, s'il avient*

   *que vo biauté voie que moult désir,*

   *ma joie, si com j'espoir,*

1. Lady, from whom comes all my joy,
   I cannot love nor cherish you too much
nor praise, as you should be,
nor serve, fear, honor, nor obey you.
Because my precious hope, dear Lady, of seeing you,
is for me a hundred times better and more joyful,
than I could deserve in a hundred thousand years.

2. This sweet hope sustains my life

   and feeds my amorous desire,
and endows my breast with strength
to comfort and restore my heart.
It does not leave me day or night;
rather, it makes me sweetly receive
more of those sweet gifts that Love offers her servants
than I could deserve in a hundred thousand years.

3. And when Hope, which dwells in my heart,
produces within me such great joy
when I am far from you, my Lady, then if I should
see your beauty, which I so desire,
my joy, just as my hope,

| | | |
|---|---|---|
| | *ymaginer, penser ne concevoir* | could not be imagined, thought, or conceived |
| | *ne porroit nuls, car trop plus en aroie* | by anyone, because I would have more |
| | *qu'en cent mille ans desservir ne porroie.* | than I could deserve in a hundred thousand years. |

**A** (stanza 1)     0.00     The music within any one stanza has the form *aab.* The texture consists of four lines, of which the higher two move with greater animation than the others. The performance on this recording uses vocalists on all four, rather than a mixture of voices and instruments. Thanks especially to the virtuosity of their singing, the results are musically satisfying.

**A** (stanza 2)     1.47     The music of the first stanza is repeated to new words.

**A** (stanza 3)     3.34     The music is once again repeated.

## Francesco Landini (d. 1397)

French musicians dominated European music from the twelfth century until the end of the Middle Ages. But after about 1350, an important group of Italian composers of polyphonic songs began to rival the dominance of the French. Given the prominence of the church in Italy, it is surprising that their music is so overwhelmingly secular, devoted almost exclusively to songs of courtly love. These Italian composers focused on three poetic genres, each with fixed forms akin to their French counterparts. The **ballata,** for example, is identical in form to the French virelai, and its name suggests that it once functioned as a dance song. It has from one to three stanzas, each of which is divided into four groups of lines. The first group is identical in poetic structure to the fourth group, and these are separated by two other similar line groups between. The first line group is repeated at the end of the poem, and possibly also between each stanza, as a refrain.

The most important of a large number of composers active in Italy in the fourteenth century is Francesco Landini. Blind from childhood, he gained renown as an organist, and he performed at the Church of San Lorenzo in Florence for most of his adult life. Like his great contemporary Machaut, Landini was also a celebrated poet who wrote most of the verses that he set

## Music Today

### David Munrow and the Early-Music Phenomenon

The performance of medieval music was long considered an activity that could appeal only to a small audience. It seemed arcane, specialized, and perhaps academic in comparison to the performance of classical and romantic works. But in the 1960s this attitude changed dramatically, first in England, then in America and, indeed, around the world. The popular discovery of early music has proved one of the most important developments in the perform-

ing musical arts of the entire twentieth century. It was catalyzed by a group of outstanding virtuosi who devoted themselves to this literature, rather than to a more normal specialization in music of modern times, and by the enlightened leadership and musical vision of a few individuals.

Among these figures, David Munrow (1942–1976) was pivotal. He was born in Birmingham, England, and studied English at Cambridge. While teaching in South America, he began to collect and perform on early European instruments, becoming proficient on the flute and the recorder. Having returned to London, he performed with an early-music group called Musica Reservata, led by Michael Morrow. This ensemble was just beginning to attract a large following, not just among antiquarian specialists but from the musical public at large.

In 1968 Munrow founded his own ensemble, called the Early Music Consort. Their success was nothing short of phenomenal. In the

to music, and, also like Machaut, this poetry uses the refined and artificial devices of troubadour verse.

The music by Landini that has survived consists entirely of songs, with a clear emphasis on the ballata form. His songs of this type have a texture consisting of either two or three simultaneous lines, and his approach to mixing voices and instruments was highly varied. Some of his songs, like "Cara mie donna" (discussed momentarily), contain only a single voice accompanied by instruments, and others are entirely vocal without independent accompaniment. Still others are vocal duets with a single instrumental line.

"Cara mie donna" (Recording 3.5) is a typical example of Landini's treatment of the ballata form. It is performed by only one singer with two additional lines that carry no text. Works copied in this way suggest that the wordless lines were played by instruments, as is the case in the performance in Recording 3.5, but they do not rule out other authentic or tasteful modes

eight years of their existence, they made more than 20 acclaimed recordings, performed in concert throughout the world, and delved as well into educational programs, even offering their skills to contemporary composers.

Munrow's style combined personal exuberance and magnetism with musical taste and high technical standards. He became a respected authority and writer on ancient instruments and performing practices, but he was always on guard against traditional assumptions about his subject. His own style had something of Morrow's brash excitement and iconoclasm, leavened by a great lyrical sense and technical polish.

Certainly Munrow was not solely responsible for the early-music phenomenon. His success was based on the work of many predecessors, including Morrow and Noah Greenberg of the New York Pro Musica. But Munrow's open-minded approach to early music, his ability to make the music seem new and vital, and his great success in challenging, on both musical and scholarly grounds, long-held assumptions about this repertory made him central to the emergence of early music as a serious rival to the modern repertory. He also inspired members of his consort, including the conductor and harpsichordist Christopher Hogwood and lutenist James Tyler, to continue his work in their own distinctive ways.

Following Munrow's untimely death in 1976, Robert Donington wrote:

I do not believe our notions of the earliest of available great music will ever quite be the same again. We know now that while some of it really is refined (and the Early Music Consort has not lacked refinement in the proper places), some of it is of a potency— well, to fill the Albert Hall. That knowledge is a measure of what we owe so largely to David Munrow.*

*Robert Donington, "Tributes to David Munrow," *Early Music* 4 (1976), 380.

of performance. The poem, in only one stanza, speaks of the tortures of unrequited love. Its first and fourth line groups each have four lines; the middle two groups have two lines each.

Landini accommodates this poetic structure by composing two phrases of music: The first sets groups 1 and 4, and the second, the middle two groups. At the end, the text and music of the first group are repeated as a refrain. The music itself is very different from that of Machaut. Our attention is drawn primarily to the suave vocal melody, which has a natural lyricism and few of the sharp rhythmic edges, lively interplay of lines, and biting dissonances of the French master. Landini's melodic line is made primarily from stepwise motion, and its rhythm is, by and large, simple and regular. The texture is far less complicated than in Machaut. To be sure, both composers use polyphony, but in Landini's ballata the nonvocal lines have a secondary, almost accompanimental role.

**Listening Guide**

## Francesco Landini, ballata, "Cara mie donna."
Recording 3.5

**1.** *Cara mie donna, i'vivo oma' contenta*
*Ch'anzi mi vo' sofrir la mie gran*
*doglia*
*Che con tuo piena voglia*

*Cercar grati, al disio che mi*
*tormenta.*

**2.** *Come degio da te gratia volere*
*Di quel piacer che turba la tuo*
*mente.*

**3.** *Che pur che tu me 'l die nol posso*
*avere,*
*Po' che con pena l'animo 'l consente.*

**4.** *Però ch'i' t'amo sì perfectamente*
*Che come che del dono i' mi sia vago*
*Poco nel cor m'apaga,*
*Pensando ch'appagata te non senta.*

**1.** Dear lady, I live contented
despite suffering a great pain,

which has your complete
approval,
and seeking solace from my
torment.

**2.** I look for that pleasure from you
although it troubles your mind.

**3.** But I cannot have it in any other
way,
unless you give it to me.

**4.** But I love you so perfectly
that, though I desire the gift,
my heart takes no pleasure
knowing that it is not given
freely.

**A** (line group 1)   0.00   The melody is sung by a tenor, and the other lines are taken by
the loud and nasal shawm (a predecessor of the oboe) and by a
quiet-sounding sackbut (a predecessor of the trombone). The melody begins

Ca - - - - - - - - ra

**B** (line group 2)   0.51   The melody continues in an ornate fashion, with cadences prepared by lengthy melismas.

**B** (line group 3)   1.28   Music *B* is repeated to new words.

**A** (line group 4)   2.07   Music *A* is repeated to new words.

**A** (line group 1)   2.57   The work is concluded by a refrain consisting of the words and
music of *A*.

## TOPICS FOR DISCUSSION AND WRITING

**1.** Compare the music of Machaut's "Dame, de qui toute ma joie vient" and Landini's "Cara mie donna." Begin with an assessment of the poetry of the two works, seeking similarities and differences in tone, content, and form. Does the music of either piece significantly express poetic content? Take into consideration texture, rhythm, harmony, and aspects of melody.

**2.** The early gothic style of architecture came into existence at about the time that composers began to embellish chant with polyphonic textures. Do similar artistic or spiritual impulses seem to underlie this type of architecture and late medieval music? Find aspects of Machaut's ballade "Dame, de qui toute ma joie vient" that have analogies in the image of gothic cathedrals such as the one in Chartres depicted on page 85.

**3.** Since the chant "Alleluia. Pascha nostrum" was composed over 1,000 years ago, can we conclude that it is a primitive work of music? In what ways does it exhibit a high degree of artistry and sophistication? What ideas or emotions does it convey, and how does it accomplish this task?

**4.** Compare the vocal melody of the trouvère song "Ja nus hons pris" (ignoring, so far as possible, the harp accompaniment to the song) to the chant "Alleluia. Pascha nostrum." Focus on mode, rhythm, range, and the use of melismas to achieve ornateness. What might account for the differences and similarities in style?

## ADDITIONAL LISTENING

The selections on these recordings, both enjoyable and informative, give a fuller understanding of the music of the Middle Ages.

### Chant

*Gregorianischer Choral.* Benedictine Monastery Maria Einsiedeln. Archiv 2533131.

### Landini

*Ecco la primavera: Florentine Music of the 14th Century.* Early Music Consort. Decca-Argo ZRG 642.

### Machaut

*Mass.* Hilliard Ensemble. Hyperion CDA 66358.

*Remède de fortune.* Machaut Ensemble of Paris. Adès ACD 14077-2.

Songs: *The Art of Courtly Love.* Early Music Consort. Seraphim SIC 6092; *The Mirror of Narcissus.* Gothic Voices. Hyperion CDA 66087.

### Miscellaneous

*The Gothic Era.* Early Music Consort of London. DGG ARC 415292-2.

*The Instruments of the Middle Ages and Renaissance.* Musica Reservata. Vanguard VSD 71219-20.

*A Medieval Christmas.* Boston Camerata. Elektra/Nonesuch 71315-2.

*Voices of the Middle Ages.* Capella Antiqua Munich. Elektra/Nonesuch H-71171.

## Organum

*Ars antiqua: Organum, Motette, Conductus.* Capella Antiqua Munich. Teldec SAWT 9530-31 B.

## Troubadour and Trouvère

*Chansons der Troubadours.* Studio der frühen Musik. Teldec SAWT 9567-B.

*Chansons der Trouvères.* Studio der frühen Musik. Teldec DAWT 9630-A.

*Medieval Music and Songs of the Troubadours.* Musica Reservata. Everest 3270.

*Songs of Love and War: Music of the Crusades.* Early Music Consort of London. Decca-Argo ZRG 673.

## BIBLIOGRAPHY

### Background to the Medieval Period

Henderson, George. *Gothic.* Harmondsworth, England: Penguin, 1967.

Hollister, C. Warren. *Medieval Europe: A Short History.* Fifth edition. New York: Wiley, 1982.

Huizinga, J. *The Waning of the Middle Ages.* Garden City, N.Y.: Doubleday, 1954.

Knowles, David. *The Evolution of Medieval Thought.* New York: Random House, 1962.

Pevsner, Nikolaus. *An Outline of European Architecture.* Harmondsworth, England: Penguin, 1943.

Southern, R. W. *The Making of the Middle Ages.* New Haven, Conn.: Yale University Press, 1953.

Simson, Otto Georg von. *The Gothic Cathedral.* Second edition. revised. Princeton, N.J.: Princeton University Press, 1974.

Tuchman, Barbara. *A Distant Mirror: The Calamitous Fourteenth Century.* New York: Knopf, 1978.

Werner, Eric. *The Sacred Bridge: The Interdependence of Liturgy and Music in Synagogue and Church During the First Millennium.* New York: Columbia University Press, 1959.

Winston, Richard. *Charlemagne.* New York: Random House, 1954.

### Musical Studies

Apel, Willi. *Gregorian Chant.* Bloomington: Indiana University Press, 1958.

Crocker, Richard. *A History of Musical Style.* New York: McGraw-Hill, 1966. Chapters 1–5 deal clearly and authoritatively with medieval music.

Fischer, Kurt von. "On the Technique, Origin, and Evolution of Italian Trecento Music." *Musical Quarterly* 47 (1961), 41–57.

Hoppin, Richard H. *Medieval Music*. The Norton Introduction to Music History. New York: Norton, 1978.

Reaney, Gilbert. *Guillaume de Machaut*. Oxford Studies of Composers, volume 9. London: Oxford University Press, 1971.

Seay, Albert. *Music in the Medieval World*. Second edition. Englewood Cliffs, N.J.: Prentice Hall, 1975.

Van der Werf, Hendrik. *The Chansons of the Troubadours and Trouvères*. Utrecht, Netherlands: Oosthoek, 1972.

Wright, Craig. *Music and Ceremony at Notre Dame de Paris, 500–1550*. Cambridge: Cambridge University Press, 1989.

# 4

---

*Music in the*
*Age of Humanism*

---

## A Joyful Noise Unto the Lord

In the Renaissance as in the Middle Ages, the main location for artistic music remained the church. But the solemn tones of Gregorian chant and the experimental idiom of organum had by then given way to a remarkably elaborate music making by choirs of voices and diverse instruments. Music was heard daily in large churches and cathedrals throughout the Christian world, especially in the service of Mass, the only service regularly attended by the laity.

An especially festive celebration of Mass is depicted in this late-sixteenth-century engraving, based on a painting by the Dutch artist Jan van der Straet (1523–1605). It shows a magnificent procession of altar boys bearing candles and incense. They approach the altar, where the celebrant is officiating. Two groups of musicians gather around large music stands and books at the left and upper right, from which vantage points they play and sing to accompany the procession. Near the book at the left is a singer with his hand up, suggesting that he is conducting the other musicians.

Pictures such as this have much to tell us about the way that music was performed in earlier periods of music history. We notice, first of all, that all of the singers and instrumentalists are men and boys. Only much later were women admitted as performers in church. Written music was obviously quite rare, even though by 1590, when this engraving was made, music printing had long been in existence. Only two music books were on hand, and these were placed high up so as to be seen by as many performers as possible. The singer standing in the back at the lower left must use a magnifying glass to read his part.

The instruments consist of several cornetts and sackbuts. The former are seen in the front row of musicians at the left. These are curved wooden instruments played like a trumpet, but having finger holes like a woodwind instrument. They produce an airy though penetrating sound. Sackbuts, which are seen in several different sizes, are closely similar to their modern counterparts, the trombones. Since *the instrumentalists appear to be reading from the same music as the singers, we can assume that they only reinforced the voices, rather than having independent lines. Another important feature is the division of the musicians into two widely separate groups. This produces an effect called* cori spezzati *("split choirs"), which was popular in sixteenth-century church music. Throughout this century, the division of choirs was a practice particularly associated with the city of Venice. But it was also used in northern European churches, and this scene was, in all likelihood, based on a Mass given in a church in the Netherlands.*

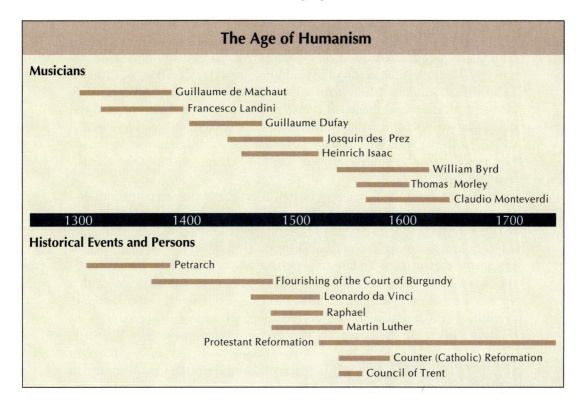

During the early fifteenth century in the cities of northern Italy, there occurred a reorientation in the arts, literature, and philosophy of such scope and importance as to be recognized by later observers as a renaissance. This term, which denotes rebirth and renewal, refers to a primary feature of the new artistic and philosophical outlook: its active study and vigorous reinterpretation of the culture of ancient Greece and Rome. An attempt to regain aspects of ancient civilizations was, at the time, called *humanism*. This was an appropriate word, since the emphasis then, as in classical antiquity, was on the power of the human spirit rather than on the otherworldly concerns that dominated the interests of medieval artists and intellectuals.

The principal forefather of Italian humanism was the poet Petrarch (1304–1374). His writings were inspired by ancient authors, including Virgil, Ovid, Horace, and, most of all, Cicero. But Petrarch was not satisfied with simply imitating the ancients. He aimed instead to make these earlier writers relevant to his own age by recapturing their celebration of intellectual freedom and their keen insight into the human condition.

**115**

Petrarch's objective of a creative emulation of the ancients was continued by artists and writers in Florence early in the fifteenth century. Among the most representative was Leone Battista Alberti (1404–1472). Like Petrarch, Alberti used his study of classical culture—in Alberti's case, Roman architectural antiquities and theory—to launch a new architectural style imbued with the spirit of ancient Rome. Alberti also left behind practical and theoretical works in many different disciplines, including literature, music, and social theory. Indeed, Alberti's many and varied accomplishments made him a model for the "universal man," an ideal characteristic of the Renaissance period.

The sculpture and painting of Italian artists of the later fifteenth and early sixteenth centuries, including the works of Leonardo da Vinci (1452–1519), Raphael (1483–1520), and Michelangelo (1475–1564), soared to great heights of inspiration and technical perfection. So diverse were their accomplishments that it is misleading to generalize about their style. But it can be said that they all shared a common emphasis on human figures, drawn with a realism that not only captures their outward shape but also reveals their inner psychology. In the religious paintings of Raphael, such as *Madonna with the Goldfinch* (page 117), the figures are depicted with a pristine beauty, harmony,

and clarity that is also encountered in sixteenth-century sacred vocal music. In the statuary of Michelangelo, this serenity is usually displaced by passionate emotion. His immense *Moses* (at the left) depicts the erupting fury of this leader of the Israelites, directed at his sinful people. But like Raphael, Michelangelo finds in the human figure a medium sufficient to make his artistic message clear.

*The religious statues of Michelangelo (1475–1564) are imbued with a very different spirit from the religious images of his contemporary Raphael. Michelangelo's statue of Moses (c. 1515), larger than life, depicts a furious energy that is scarcely containable in the man's powerful body. Moses' wrath is directed at his people, who have fallen into sinful ways during his period of absence to receive the Law.*

*The Italian painter Raphael (1483–1520) specialized in depictions of the Madonna. His* **Madonna with the Goldfinch** *is an early example, completed in 1506 while the artist resided in Florence. As in his other Madonna paintings, Raphael strives here for a highly idealized image of the Virgin Mary, conveying a sense of perfection, beauty, and repose.*

The humanist revolution of the fifteenth century was slow in making an impact on the course of musical style. After all, the exact nature of Greek and Roman music was virtually unknown to artists or scholars of this time, except in theoretical writings, which seemed to ignore musical practice in favor of mathematical discussions. Greek and Roman writings on music had an influence on musical practice only in the 1570s, when they led to experiments that produced the genre of opera. But in general, the designation of the fifteenth and sixteenth centuries as a renaissance is a misnomer in the history of music, although it is nonetheless widely used.

There is, all the same, much that sets the fifteenth and sixteenth centuries apart as a distinct stylistic period. Music during this time departed from the sharp dissonances and rhythmic angularities of Machaut and settled instead on a harmonic language based on the triad. A standardized texture in church music emerged, consisting of four vocal lines, each bearing the same text and each made equal in importance by the use of imitative counterpoint. In this standard texture and medium, no independent instrumental or accompanimental parts are required. Also in the Renaissance period there emerged a body of instrumental music having its own distinctive properties, and new genres of vocal music such as the Mass and the madrigal were born.

The rise and flourishing of centers of musical activity during the Renaissance in general reflect political and economic factors. Close relations existed in the early 1400s among England, parts of France, and the duchy of Burgundy, and these alliances are mirrored in the transmission of new musical ideas among artists living in these three regions. The economic and intellectual power of northern Italy led to an immigration of leading northern musicians and, in the sixteenth century, to the rise of an indigenous Italian school of composition. The immense wealth and military might of Spain in the sixteenth century stimulated music in that land.

Music of the Renaissance was also shaped by the Reformation, certainly the most potent historical and cultural movement of the sixteenth century. This attack on Catholic orthodoxy was begun early in the century by the German monk Martin Luther (1483–1546), who used his pulpit and the new invention of printing to spread criticism of the papacy, to challenge long-standing beliefs of the church, and to question the very role of the church and its ministry in the spiritual life of the faithful. Luther's Protestantism was eagerly embraced by many Germans from all walks of life, leading to a permanent sectarian division of German states. Luther's movement was imitated by the followers of John Calvin in France and Switzerland, and it also provided the stimulus for the Anglican Reformation in which papal authority in England was entirely set aside.

For music, the Reformation had a major and lasting impact. Luther's encouragement of congregational singing led to the creation of a body of hymns, called **chorales.** Their tunes and words came to be quoted by generations of composers in their music for Lutheran services of worship. We will return to a discussion of these hymns in Chapter 6, in connection with the music of J. S. Bach. As the rigid makeup of the Catholic Mass was partly displaced in Lutheran services of worship, the way was opened for new genres of church music, which began to flourish in Protestant regions early in the baroque period.

The Catholic church was by no means deaf to the protest that led to the Reformation. The sixteenth century was indeed a period of reform within the church as well, leading to the so-called Counter-Reformation. A series of councils were convened to clarify church doctrines. The Council of Trent, which met sporadically from 1545 until 1563, dealt with music in the services of worship, urging greater clarity in the treatment of words and an end to the introduction of secular musical elements into liturgical music. The church also supported the increased involvement of the laity in religious matters. During the 1500s, Italy and other countries were swept by popular revivalist movements, and composers were quick to provide new types of music for these circumstances.

# Music of the Early and Mid-Fifteenth Century

It is ironic that Italy, which so dominated the visual arts in the fifteenth century, produced no major composers until much later in the Renaissance. Virtually all of the leading musicians born in that century came instead from northern France or the Netherlands, regions that in those years were part of the duchy of Burgundy. Courtly life in Burgundy in the fifteenth century was known for its lavish formalities, in which music played an important role. A banquet celebrated by Burgundy's Order of the Golden Fleece in Lille in 1454, described by the chronicler Mathieu d'Escouchy, provided the opportunity for extravagant, if not preposterous, courtly ceremony, including a unique contribution of musicians. On one banqueting table, writes Mathieu, was a model church, complete with bells, organs, and choristers. On another table rested a pie in which 28 musicians were hidden.

> First, as soon as the company had appeared and were seated at the tables, from inside the church . . . a bell rang out loudly. After this bell was stilled, three little children and a tenor began to sing a sweet

song from within the church. What it was I do not know, but it seemed to me to be a proper blessing for the meal. After those in the church had done their duty, out of the pie, which was the first course on the long table, came a shepherd who played a bagpipe very nicely.[1]

The wealth and artistic brilliance of Italy also created many opportunities for musicians. Throughout the entire Renaissance, the courts of northern Italy and the Vatican attracted leading northern composers to participate, usually as singers and composers, in their musical enterprises. After establishing their reputations, the emigrant northern musicians often returned to French-speaking lands to enjoy the fruits of their success.

The career of Guillaume Dufay is typical of a group of leading fifteenth-century composers that also includes Gilles Binchois (c. 1400–1460), Johannes Ockeghem (c. 1425–1495), and Antoine Busnois (c. 1430–1492). Although the circumstances of Dufay's early years are unknown, it is likely that he was born around the year 1400 near the city of Cambrai in northern France. He was educated at the choir school of the Cambrai Cathedral, after which he emigrated to Italy to work as a singer and composer for the court of the Malatesta family, who ruled the region surrounding Rimini. Later he was employed as a singer and composer in the prestigious papal choir in Rome. Dufay then returned to Cambrai, where he was a canon in the musical service of the cathedral until his death in 1474.

Like virtually all fifteenth-century composers, Dufay specialized in three musical genres. Two of them—the polyphonic song and motet—are familiar from the age of Machaut. The third, a type of choral composition based on words from the ordinary of the Mass, was essayed by Machaut, but it was established as a major genre only during the early Renaissance period. Dufay's songs are based on the same general conception as those of Machaut. The highest line is the most melodious and rhythmically the most animated, while two or three additional lines—probably played on instruments—add a lively accompaniment. The verses are generally in French, using the fixed forms of lyric poetry of the preceding century, and their subjects continue to deal with courtly love.

Dufay's compositions for the Mass are entirely different from the Mass music that was described in Chapter 3. Dufay did not seek a simple polyphonic elaboration on the traditional chants of the Mass, like the medieval composers of organum. Instead, he wrote new music for voices and instruments that entirely replaced the singing of some of the traditional chant melodies, although, of necessity, the official words of the Mass had to be preserved. When composing his music for the Mass, Dufay chose texts from the ordinary, words that were pronounced in every celebration of this service. The use of words from the ordinary allowed his compositions to be performed at any celebration of Mass.

Dufay's Masses show his innovative musical thinking, but his motets most firmly establish the continuity of his art with that of the age of Machaut. The motet in his time was normally a piece in one section, based on a Latin text, sacred or secular. Some of Dufay's early examples continued the fourteenth-century practice of presenting different texts simultaneously. After his era, composers came to prefer sacred words over secular ones, drawing them from the liturgy or from the Bible (especially from the Psalms). Increasingly in the fifteenth century, the Mass and the motet shared a similar musical style.

Dufay's motet "Vasilissa, ergo gaude" (Recording 4.1) is one of his earliest surviving compositions, and it exemplifies his mingling of the antiquated style of Machaut with more modern ideas. It was composed during Dufay's years of service to the Malatesta family, specifically, to celebrate the wedding in 1420 of Cleophe de' Malatesta to the Byzantine prince Theodore Paleologus. The anonymous Latin text, in three six-line stanzas, fulsomely praises the bride, the bridegroom, and their noble families.

Musically, this motet is in one section with an introduction. It has the same rhythmic energy and angularity as Machaut's ballade "Dame, de qui toute ma joie vient" (see Chapter 3) but a much sweeter harmonic sound, without the pungent dissonances of fourteenth-century music. Indeed, most chords in the Dufay work are triads. At principal cadences, however, Dufay returns to a sonority characteristic of a fourteenth-century composer: a two-note chord having a distinctively hollow sound.

A prominent stylistic feature of Dufay's "Vasilissa" that became basic to music of the later Renaissance is imitation. Recall from Chapter 1 that **imitative polyphony** is a texture in which a melody is stated successively in different lines. The opening passage of the motet contains a clear example. Here, the leading voice sings a melody that is precisely replicated, beginning a few seconds later, by the second voice. Such strict and continuous imitation creates what is called *canon.*

After the introductory canon in two lines, the texture expands to four parts. In manuscripts that preserve this work, only the two upper lines, which are more melodious and quicker in motion, are provided with words. Although there is no record of how Dufay intended voices and instruments to be used, the way the manuscripts were copied suggests that the two top lines were to be sung and the bottom two played on some instruments. As with the Machaut ballade examined in Chapter 3, other performing media might also

**Guillaume Dufay, "Vasilissa, ergo gaude," 1420**
Recording 4.1

| | |
|---|---|
| *1.* *Vasilissa, ergo gaude,* | *1.* Rejoice, O Queen, |
| *Quia es digna omni laude,* | for you are worthy of all praise, |
| *Cleophe, clara gestis* | Cleophe, famed by the deeds |
| *A tuis de Maletestis,* | of your family, the Malatestas, |
| *In Italia principibus* | princes of Italy, |
| *Magnis et nobilibus!* | great and noble! |
| | |
| *2.* *Ex tuo viro clarior,* | *2.* Through your even more famous husband, |
| *Quia cunctis est nobilior.* | who is more noble than all. |
| *Romanorum est despotus,* | He is despot of the Romans, |
| *Quem colit mundus totus.* | and adored by all the world. |
| *In porphyro est genitus,* | He was born in purple, |
| *A Deo missus coelitus.* | sent by God in heaven. |
| | |
| *3.* *Juvenili aetate polles* | *3.* Your youth sparkles |
| *Et formositate volens,* | with kindness and beauty, |
| *Multum genio fecunda* | you are much gifted |
| *Et utraque lingua facunda,* | and eloquent in either tongue. |
| *Ac clarior es virtutibus* | These virtues make you more worthy |
| *Quam aliis his omnibus.* | than all others. |

| | | |
|---|---|---|
| **Introduction** | 0.00 | Two voices sing the first two lines of text in canon. |
| **Motet proper** | 0.40 | The remainder of the text is set for four lines, of which the lower two were probably intended for instruments. The cantus firmus is used in the lowest line. Its melody is drawn from a chant from a special Mass honoring virgins, hence appropriate as a prenuptial gift to the Malatesta daughter. Beginning at 1.47, the rhythmic scheme of each line is repeated. |

legitimately be employed, since flexibility in the use of voices and instruments was still the order of the day. On the performance on Recording 4.1, the two upper lines are sung by countertenors (male voices singing in the range of female voices); these are doubled by the violinlike rebec and organ, while the lower two lines are played on a trombone and a large shawm called a *bombard.*

When composing "Vasilissa," Dufay made use of two very powerful structural elements. One of these, called **cantus firmus,** influenced the building of the work's magnificent polyphonic texture. The other, called *isorhythm,* aided in the formulation of its rhythm. *Cantus firmus* can be freely translated as "basic melody." When Dufay began a new motet or Mass, his first task was usually to select a preexistent melody to be quoted in the new work and to form its structural basis. In Dufay's day, as in the Middle Ages, there was no expectation that an artistic work should be entirely original. Composers evidently found it more challenging to begin with some preexisting foundation, on which they could build a new musical edifice. In this motet, Dufay selected his basic melody from the tune of a Gregorian chant, although in other pieces a line from a song or from virtually any other source might also serve. He then gave the cantus firmus a proper rhythm, and new lines were finally composed to be sung above and below it.

Isorhythm is a way of creating the rhythm within a line of music by constantly repeating a pattern of durational values. In "Vasilissa," the rhythms in each of the four lines are constructed in this way, although isorhythm was normally applied only to the line bearing the cantus firmus. Beginning after the introduction (0.40) and continuing to the middle of the work at 1.47, each of the lines establishes a sequence of rhythmic values. These are then exactly repeated to different pitches for the remainder of that line. Isorhythmic construction was a holdover from the age of Machaut, during which a love for hidden patterns and secret meaning was pronounced in all of the arts. Its use quickly died out after the early fifteenth century.

## Music at the Time of Josquin des Prez

Music in the final decades of the fifteenth century and the early years of the sixteenth reached a new level of refinement and power, just as the same period witnessed the inspired artistry of Michelangelo, Raphael, and Leonardo da Vinci. Leading musicians of this time, often called the High Renaissance, retained certain traditions while also developing the innovative tendencies of the generation of Dufay. The genres of Mass, motet, and song continued to predominate, but antiquated features of Dufay's music, such as isorhythm, intricate rhythms, and freely used dissonant harmonies, disappeared. Composers achieved a new and increasingly uniform style in which a single text was heard in all lines. The triad became the fundamental harmonic sonority, imitative polyphony became the primary texture, and melodic lines lines more and more reflected the meaning and rhythm of their words.

## *Josquin des Prez*

The leading musical figure at this time was Josquin des Prez (c. 1440–1521), certainly one of the great geniuses in all of music. Josquin's life followed the pattern established in Dufay's time. He was born in northern France, in lands claimed by the duke of Burgundy, and he received his training at a nearby cathedral choir school. There is evidence that he was, in some sense, a student of Johannes Ockeghem. He then traveled to Italy, where he worked as a singer and composer in Milan, Rome, and Ferrara. He returned—an internationally known and celebrated figure—to northern France, where he died in 1521. The esteem in which he was held by his contemporaries is revealed in this commentary of 1567 by Cosimo Bartoli:

*This woodcut from the early seventeenth century is the only reliable depiction of the composer Josquin des Prez. Although it was executed almost a century after the composer's death, the illustration was probably made from an earlier painting, now lost.*

> Josquin, Ockeghem's pupil, may be said to have been, in music, a prodigy of nature, as our Michelangelo Buonarroti has been in architecture, painting, and sculpture. For, as there has not thus far been anybody who in his compositions approaches Josquin, so Michelangelo, among all those who have been active in these his arts, is still alone and without a peer. Both one and the other have opened the eyes of all those who delight in these arts or are to delight in them in the future.[2]

In Josquin's music we will indeed find the same mastery of materials and powerful expression of emotions that distinguish the art of his great contemporary Michelangelo. Josquin, like Dufay, favored the genres of song, motet, and Mass, but he went beyond his predecessors in the composition of instrumental pieces. The songs are exceedingly diverse in style and language. Some are settings of Italian poetry in a simple chordal texture. Most are French verse, but these tend to avoid the fixed forms of the preceding century. The motets, numbering about 100, use Latin words drawn from services of worship, from the Bible, or from other religious poetry. These pieces exhibit differing styles and constructive principles.

Josquin's 18 Masses contain some of his greatest music. As in the Masses by Dufay, these pieces have five movements, corresponding to the five major texts of the Mass ordinary. Also like Dufay's Masses, most of Josquin's are constructed on some cantus firmus, or basic preexistent melody, that the composer drew from chant, popular songs, or earlier polyphonic works. The ways in which these preexistent melodies were used are diverse. Some works resemble Dufay's motet "Vasilissa," in which the basic melody is presented in an inner line in relatively long note values. In Josquin's later music, a new principle of construction emerged that led to a much freer use of basic melodies. In these later pieces, a composition was no longer built outward by progressively adding lines above and below the preexistent cantus firmus. Instead, all lines were apparently composed at once; each has equal melodic and rhythmic interest, and the lines are usually interrelated by imitation.

We can observe this new compositional approach in Josquin's celebrated *Missa pange lingua ("Pange lingua" Mass)*. "Pange lingua" is the title of the preexistent basic melody, which Josquin chose from Gregorian chant. Let us first examine this melodic source. "Pange lingua" was an especially popular chant, in strophic form, used on the Feast of Corpus Christi. This is the occasion when the church recognizes the importance of Holy Communion. On Recording 4.2 we hear the first of its six stanzas. The words are appropriate to the feast, and the music consists of six different phrases, each corresponding to a new line of poetry within a stanza:

| | |
|---|---|
| *Pange lingua gloriosi* | Sing, O my tongue, of the mystery |
| *Corporis mysterium,* | of the glorious body |
| *Sanguinisque pretiosi,* | and precious blood, |
| *Quem in mundi pretium* | shed for the ransom of the world, |
| *Fructus ventris generosi* | fruit of a noble womb, |
| *Rex effudit gentium.* | by the King of Nations. |

Josquin did not simply lay out the basic melody in a single inner line, as Dufay had done in "Vasilissa." Instead, he used its phrases, one after the other, as subjects in a succession of concise fugues. The first movement of the Mass, the Kyrie Eleison (Recording 4.3), shows how this is done. The movement is divided into three large sections, following the three lines that make up the text: "Kyrie eleison" ("Lord have mercy upon us"), "Christe eleison" ("Christ have mercy upon us"), and "Kyrie eleison." These principal sections are each ended by a strong cadence. The three sections are then subdivided into two subsections each, although the juncture between them is bridged over by dovetailing in the various musical lines, and there is no strong sense of cadence.

**Listening Guide**

**Josquin des Prez,** *Missa pange lingua,* **Kyrie Eleison (c. 1515)**
Recording 4.3

| | |
|---|---|
| *Kyrie eleison, kyrie eleison, kyrie eleison.* | Lord have mercy upon us. . . . |
| *Christe eleison, Christe eleison, Christe eleison.* | Christ have mercy upon us. . . . |
| *Kyrie eleison, kyrie eleison, kyrie eleison.* | Lord have mercy upon us. . . . |

**Kyrie 1**  0.00  The music consists of two fugal subsections, each based on a paraphrase of a section of the chant "Pange lingua." The texture consists of four lines, each of which is sung to the same words, and the simultaneous use of instruments (not heard on this recording) was probably an option.

**Christe**  0.44  Two new imitative passages are constructed on the third and fourth phrases of the chant. The cadence of this section is especially ingenious and beautiful: The upper two voices reach a cadence only to have the lower two continue in deliberate motion, as though a meditative afterthought.

**Kyrie 2**  2.02  The text is the same as in the first section, but the music is new. The final two phrases of the chant provide the basis for two additional fugal passages.

Josquin then makes each of the six subsections into a fugue (see Chapter 1), in which the fugal subject is one of the six phrases of the chant. But a chant melody cannot, by itself, be a good fugal subject, since it has no rhythm. For this reason Josquin had to paraphrase the chant, giving it a lilting rhythm and adding notes to lengthen its short-winded phrases into a more supple contour. The process of paraphrase is illustrated in Figure 4.1, in which Josquin's reformulation is placed below the first phrase of the original chant. The paraphrased chant then becomes the subject of a fugue: It is stated alone in one line and imitated successively by all of the other lines. When the next subsection is reached, a new fugue is constructed on a new subject derived from the chant.

**Figure 4.1** *Notes marked with an asterisk duplicate those in the chant.*

The form and superstructure of Josquin's Mass are highly rational, but, as in masterpieces of Renaissance architecture, the listener or observer is little aware of a strict plan. Josquin leads our attention instead to external features: the ravishing sound of the harmonies, the beauty of the melodies, the clarity of the words, and the infectiously lilting rhythms. Josquin was indeed a master of sound; it was his chief expressive material. His polyphonic textures never become heavy or tedious as he constantly varies the number of voices. Dissonant chords pungently season the sonority, and he resorts at the final cadence to a traditional two-note sonority (here E-B), leaving the listener with this haunting vestige of earlier music.

Josquin lived shortly before the period when instrumental music, for the first time, achieved a distinct identity and became an important compositional medium. In his day, instrumental music was still mainly improvised or based on vocal transcriptions. It is not known whether the charming piece "La Bernardina" (Recording 4.4) was conceived by Josquin as a short song or as an independent instrumental work. Although no source preserves the piece with words, it appears in early prints in the company of songs or song transcriptions. If it is originally an instrumental work, the title probably refers to some dedicatee or patron.

Lacking any specific instructions about instrumentation, "La Bernardina" can legitimately be played by virtually any group of three instruments. On the performance on Recording 4.4, we hear three rebecs. The music is lively in rhythm and spirit. It consists of several sections of differing textures, although these are run together without pause. The opening section is a three-part fugue, which at 0.16 gives way to a passage in which the upper two instruments toss a short motive back and forth. Chains of melodic sequences are heard in the outer voices at 0.36, leading to a concluding passage in which the three lines intertwine in free polyphony.

*Lines from the first edition (1504) of Josquin's "La Bernardina." The printer was the Venetian Ottaviano dei Petrucci, the first important printer of music. Petrucci often printed works by Josquin, evidence of the composer's widespread popularity.*

"La Bernardina" was contained in one of the earliest musical publications, the work of the Venetian printer Ottaviano dei Petrucci (1466–1539). Petrucci was the first printer of music to use movable type, which he first employed in a collection of French songs printed in 1501 under the title *Harmonice musices odhecaton (One Hundred Songs of Harmonic Music)*. His prints reveal great craftsmanship. His technique involved multiple impressions: First the staff lines were printed, then the notes, and finally all other words and signs. This painstaking process was soon superseded by the use of smaller pieces of type and a technique involving only a single impression. These later systems were more practical, but they did not produce printed pages that were nearly so handsome as Petrucci's. Portions of "La Bernardina," in Petrucci's first edition, are illustrated above.

## Heinrich Isaac and Other Contemporaries of Josquin

In music, as in the visual arts, the High Renaissance produced an unprecedented number of great masters. Leading composers of this time continued to stem, almost exclusively, from the lowlands of northern France and southern Belgium. Like Dufay and Josquin, most of them migrated to Italy to practice their art under the patronage of enlightened noblemen such as Lorenzo de' Medici in Florence, Galeazzo Sforza in Milan, and Hercules d'Este in Ferrara. They continued to concentrate on the genres of the Mass, motet, and various types of songs.

Heinrich Isaac (c. 1445–1517) was one of the greatest of Josquin's contemporaries. He was probably born and educated in the Netherlands, although no record of his early years survives. He was hired as a singer in Florence by Lorenzo de' Medici, and in 1497 he entered the service of the Holy Roman emperor, Maximilian I. Maximilian wished to have an artistic retinue that would match the dynamic expansion of his Hapsburg realm. Although chiefly located in Vienna, Maximilian's court often traveled. The emperor was especially fond of the mountain village of Innsbruck, where Isaac also periodically lived. The composer apparently had the freedom to travel, and he resided alternately in several Italian and German cities. He died in Florence in 1517.

Isaac's music is highly eclectic, as he absorbed the regional musical preferences of Italy and Germany into his Netherlandish background. In addition to Masses, he also composed an immense cycle of polyphonic settings of texts from the proper of the Mass called the *Choralis constantinus.* His songs are exceedingly diverse in style. Some are in French, resembling the songs of Josquin; others use the simple chordal harmonies preferred in Italian secular music. Most of his songs on German texts observe the regional preference for placement of the main melody in an inner voice, around which other voices and instruments weave a polyphonic texture.

"Isbruck, ich muß dich lassen" ("Innsbruck, I Must Leave You," Recording 4.5) is related to this German style, but with many idiosyncrasies typical of Isaac's eclecticism. The song and its poem are in two stanzas, in which the singers lament having to leave their beloved Innsbruck (see the translation in the Listening Guide). The primary melody is in the highest voice, although, in the German manner, one of the inner voices has a line that is also distinctly melodious. In this recording, these two principal melodies are sung, and two additional lines are played on instruments.

Everything in Isaac's setting of the words conforms to their heartfelt, folklike sentiment. The melody itself has the simple directness of a folk song,

## Listening Guide

### Heinrich Isaac, "Isbruck, ich muß dich lassen."
Recording 4.5

*1. Isbruck, ich muß dich lassen,*
*Ich fahr dahin mein Straßen*
*in fremde Land dahin.*
*Mein Freud ist mir genommen,*
*Die ich nit weiß bekommen,*
*Wo ich im Elend bin.*

*1. Innsbruck, I must leave you.*
*I go forth on my way*
*into foreign lands.*
*My joy is gone,*
*which I shall not regain,*
*where I go in misery.*

*2. Mein Trost ob allen Weiben,*
*Dein tu ich ewig bleiben,*
*Stet treu der Ehren fromm.*
*Nun muß dich Gott bewahren,*
*In aller Tugend sparen,*
*Bis daß ich wieder komm'.*

*2. My consolation among all women,*
*with you will I always remain,*
*ever true in devout honor.*
*Now God must keep you,*
*save you in all virtue,*
*until I return.*

**A (stanza 1)**    0.00    The melody of this work is truly memorable in its simple tunefulness. It begins

Is - bruck, ich muß dich las - sen,

The plain directness of this tune is enhanced by its simple accompaniment, the many cadences, and the repetition of lines and musical phrases. On the recording, two of the four lines are sung, and recorders, organ, and stringed instruments provide the accompaniment.

**A (stanza 2)**    0.55    The music of the first stanza is repeated with new words.

and the harmonic style of Isaac's setting avoids the intricate polyphony so congenial to the Netherlander in favor of simple homophony. The melodic phrases are clearly divided from one another, making the poem all the easier to grasp, and the strong sense of keynote lends the song coherence and accessibility.

# Music of the Late Renaissance

Composers of the age of Josquin des Prez transformed music from its essentially medieval shape into a new and diverse art form. Although they were sensitive to national or regional differences in style, they forged a basic musical idiom—a common practice—that was equally applicable to song, motet, Mass, or developing instrumental genres. Such music consisted of three to five simultaneous lines (four lines was the most typical), combined in a texture of imitative polyphony. The emphasis on counterpoint served to integrate all lines: All shared an equal degree of rhythmic motion and melodic interest and all carried a text (optionally doubled by instruments). Josquin and his contemporaries also intensified the relation of music to words. They smoothed out rhythmic motion so that it would better approximate how the words were pronounced, making them easier to understand when sung. And they began to find musical turns of phrase that could capture and express the meaning or emotional content of their poetry.

The unified style of the age of Josquin was extended and refined by composers for the remainder of the Renaissance period, especially in the genres of Mass and motet. But the mid- and late sixteenth century was also a time of innovation. The concern for expression of a text, itself spurred on in Italy by humanistic ideas, was greatly expanded and intensified, even to the point of creating new genres in which text and music existed in near symbiosis. Instrumental music took on new importance. After about 1525, there emerged many genres and styles specifically associated with instruments. In fact, the history of instrumental music as a distinct medium begins at about this time.

Humanistic studies of ancient music at last made a major impact on musical style during the late sixteenth century. New ways of singing and new types of accompaniment were essayed in an attempt to revive the emotional power of ancient music, and these experiments ultimately led to the creation of the genre of opera. Finally, the center of musical activity moved decisively to Italy. Even early in the Renaissance, music was supported by Italian patrons as nowhere else, but the music itself had a distinctly French accent. In the late sixteenth century, the leading composers themselves, figures such as Claudio Monteverdi, Giovanni Gabrieli, and Giovanni Pierluigi da Palestrina, were Italian by birth and were trained and employed at home. Italy by 1600 had established a hegemony over music that would endure in Europe for nearly 200 years.

### Sacred Music

In the genres of the Mass and the motet, the main types of sacred music at this time, the common practice of the High Renaissance was accepted and refined by a younger generation of musicians. Among their leaders were Giovanni Pierluigi da Palestrina (c. 1525–1594), Orlande de Lassus (1532–1594), and William Byrd (1543–1623).

*Portrait of William Byrd, engraved by N. Haym.*

After establishing a reputation as a singer and composer, Palestrina was called to Rome in 1551 by Pope Julius III to lead the music at St. Peter's. He stayed in Rome for the remainder of his life, holding many different positions. Palestrina's work, including over 100 Masses, 375 motets, and other settings of liturgical texts, was overwhelmingly devoted to music for the church. These works are remarkable for their serenity, balance, and careful treatment of the words. As much as any composer of his day, Palestrina willingly conformed to the directives of the Council of Trent, which demanded a clearer audibility of the words in music for the church.

Orlande de Lassus was one of the last northern musicians to acquire fame in Italy. He was born in the Belgian city of Mons but moved (some say that he was kidnapped) as a child to Italy. His prodigious talent led to his appointment as musical director at Saint John Lateran in Rome at the young age of 21. Three years later, he joined the staff of the duke of Bavaria and moved permanently to Munich. Lassus composed an enormous quantity of music: more than 500 motets, 50 Masses, and numerous songs based on Italian, French, and German poetry. His music is eclectic in style, but, in general, he tends to bypass Palestrina's serenity and calm in favor of a dramatic and highly expressive idiom.

Lassus's versatility and eclecticism were duplicated, perhaps even exceeded, by the English master William Byrd. After a stint as organist and choirmaster at Lincoln Cathedral, Byrd in 1570 joined the musical staff of the Chapel Royal in London, where he served Queen Elizabeth and, following her death in 1603, King James I. Byrd was a devout Catholic at a time when the overt practice of Catholicism in England was illegal. The beauty of his music, however, apparently overcame sectarian concerns, and he enjoyed the continuing admiration of English people from all walks of life. He composed music for the Catholic liturgy—even brazenly had it published—although he also wrote much-admired music for Anglican services. He was one of the great composers for harpsichord and for instrumental ensembles as well as a master of secular vocal music.

Byrd's *Gradualia,* published in two volumes in 1605 and 1607, is a cycle of some 100 motetlike pieces for both the ordinary and the proper of the Mass for major feasts of the church year. It contains some of his greatest music, indeed, some of the greatest of the entire Renaissance. "Ave verum corpus" ("Hail True Body," Recording 4.6) was intended to be used in the service of the Benediction of the Blessed Sacrament, which in Byrd's day followed Mass on the Feast of Corpus Christi. Byrd's setting is for four lines without independent instrumental parts. The music recaptures the balance and serenity of Palestrina's style, and—something new—it is composed without the use of any preexistent musical material.

An understanding of Byrd's motets must begin with the Latin words, which served him as a guide in the formation of melodic and rhythmic design and inspired him with the idea his music embodies. He spoke of the power of the word in the dedication to the 1605 volume of the *Gradualia:*

> There is a certain hidden power, as I learnt by experience, in the thoughts underlying the words themselves; so that, as one meditates upon the sacred words and constantly and seriously considers them, the right notes, in some inexplicable manner, suggest themselves quite spontaneously.

The words thus become for Byrd what the cantus firmus was for an earlier Renaissance composer: a point of origin and a guide in the construction of an original work. Rhythm in the melodic lines carefully follows a pronunciation of the words, and only a few syllables are extended by melismas. The division of the text into units of thought is meticulously duplicated by the placement of cadences in the music, and the texture remains basically homophonic, giving it a translucence in which the audibility of the words is never obscured. And in the subtlest of ways, the sense of the words—an acclamation to the crucified body of Jesus that mixes suffering and hope—is embodied and expressed by the music. Fleeting, bittersweet dissonances project words such as "miserere" ("have mercy"), and a delicate imitative passage on a downward-moving line depicts the text, "unde fluxit sanguine" ("there flowed waves of blood").

*Music Today*

## The Choir of King's College, Cambridge

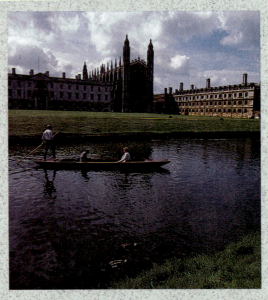

"The best people want to sing in the King's choir." This conclusion by the English musicologist Stanley Sadie explains in short order the excellence of the King's College Choir, long admired by lovers of music the world around. Founded in the fifteenth century by King Henry VI, King's College of Cambridge University has as the centerpiece of its campus a beautiful and intricate late gothic chapel. The interior of this much-admired building, completed in the early sixteenth century, is noted for the fantastic fan vaulting that completely covers its long ceiling. The acoustics of the chapel are lively and resonant, perfectly suited to the astringent sound of a choir of men and boys.

Since the fifteenth century, the choir has been resident in the chapel except for a brief period during the Reformation. Its reputation has never been greater than in the decades following World War II, when its precision of technique, purity of intonation, and light and flexible tone became its trademarks. During these years, the choir achieved worldwide esteem by touring and making recordings, such as that of Byrd's "Ave verum corpus" heard on Recording 4.6.

The choir consists of about 30 men and boys, which is a typical configuration for English choirs. Most of the music they sing was conceived for an all-male ensemble, which also lends it a distinctive sound. The choir is divided into four groups, based on voice ranges. The group with the highest voices consists of 16 boys, ages 9 to about 13, all outstanding musicians. They are selected from children attending the King's College School. The other three groups are made up of young adults attending King's College. Two consist of singers using natural male voices and a third by men who sing in falsetto, higher than in the normal male voice range. The result is a blend of sounds possessing great flexibility, color, and clarity. Membership in the choir is prestigious, though very demanding. In addition to daily rehearsals, frequent tours, and recording sessions, the choir sings evensong five days each week, plus two services on Sundays. Their most famous performance is on Christmas Eve, in the service of Lessons and Carols. Here, appropriate biblical readings alternate with the singing of Christmas music.

The Choir of King's College rose to its present level of artistry and renown under the leadership of Sir David Willcocks, who served as organist and choirmaster of the college chapel from 1957 until 1974. Under his successors, Philip Ledger and Stephen Cleobury, the choir has continued its outstanding tradition of musicianship.

**Listening Guide**

**William Byrd, "Ave verum corpus," from *Gradualia* (1607)**
Recording 4.6

| | |
|---|---|
| *Ave verum corpus,* | Hail true body, |
| *natum de Maria virgine:* | born of the Virgin Mary. |
| *Vere passum, immolatum in cruce pro* | You who truly suffered and were |
| *homine,* | sacrificed on the cross for mankind, |
| | |
| *Cujus latus perforatum unde fluxit* | You whose side was pierced and |
| *sanguine:* | whose blood flowed in waves, |
| *Esto nobis praegustatum in mortis,* | May we have tasted of you when |
| *examine.* | we face death. |
| *O dulcis, O pie, O Jesu, Fili Mariae,* | O sweet, holy Jesus, son of Mary, |
| *miserere mei. Amen.* | have mercy upon me. Amen. |

**A**    0.00    The first section is predominantly homophonic in texture and very subdued in emotion. It is divided into many short phrases, each ended by a clear cadence, in order to clarify the text. These phrases are held together by the central keynote of G.

**B**    1.53    The last line of text begins with a new texture, in which the highest line is answered by the other three.

**B**    2.57    The text and music of passage B are repeated, leading to a conclusive "Amen."

## The Italian Madrigal

Whereas composers of Masses and motets remained faithful, by and large, to traditional Renaissance styles, a new direction in Italian music was begun about 1530 with the rise of the **madrigal.** This new musical type was inspired by a revival of interest in the lyric poetry of Petrarch, whose verse was then widely read and imitated. The serious tone and refinement in Petrarch's writings seemed to call for a type of music that would avoid the naïveté and lightheartedness of earlier styles of Italian song and attain a gravity and loftiness of tone. The result was the madrigal.

A madrigal is normally a short work in one movement sung by a small group of vocalists including both men and women. It typically uses Italian poetry in a single stanza, and the music normally goes to considerable lengths to express the structure and inner content of the words. Since the earliest composers of madrigals were mainly northern musicians transplanted to Italy, the model for their works of this type can be found in motets and French songs, in which, by the time of Josquin, the relation of word and tone had already become intense and intimate.

The composition of madrigals quickly became widespread. They were sung by amateurs as well as by professional musicians at court, and the demand for them is reflected in the large number of printed collections that appeared in Italy during the sixteenth century. Leading composers included Jacques Arcadelt (c. 1505–1568), Luca Marenzio (1553–1599), Cipriano de Rore (c. 1516–1565), and, later, Carlo Gesualdo (c. 1560–1613) and Claudio Monteverdi (1567–1643). Numerous musical styles emerged. Some madrigalists maintained the serious tone that characterized the early examples of the genre, while others wrote madrigals in a light and happy spirit. Some cultivated a dramatic idiom that relished the unexpected, while others wrote simple recitational pieces. But an underlying common ground was the intimacy between text and music. Marenzio, for example, specialized in a graphic correlation of single words and music. A word such as *valley* might typically have been set to music with a melodic figure whose contour sketched the shape of a valley. This direct method of relating the text to the music is now called **word painting,** and an example of it is often termed a **madrigalism.** Other madrigal composers were content to allow the text to be unmistakably heard and projected by limiting the music to a type of declamation. Still others, such as Rore, sought a more abstract depiction of the emotions contained in a poem—for example, by introducing expressive dissonances.

In the madrigals of Claudio Monteverdi, virtually all of these styles and techniques can be found. Monteverdi was born in Cremona. After completing his training, he entered the musical service of Duke Vincenzo Gonzaga in Mantua. In 1613, Monteverdi, then an internationally acclaimed composer of madrigals and opera, became the director of music at the Church of Saint Mark in Venice. After this time he turned his attention to music for the church, although he continued to compose madrigals. Monteverdi's life sits astride a major change of taste in music, which divides the Renaissance from the baroque period. So we will treat his music also in the next chapter. For now, let us focus on his early madrigals, which are among the greatest works of their type.

Most of Monteverdi's madrigals were published in eight collections printed between 1587 and 1638; a ninth was issued posthumously in 1651. Monteverdi was also the composer of lighter madrigalesque pieces that he called *canzonette* or *scherzi musicali* ("musical jokes"). "A un giro sol de' begl'occhi lucenti" ("At One Turn of Those Beautiful, Gleaming Eyes," Recording 4.7) comes from the fourth book of madrigals, published in 1603. Like all of the early madrigals, the pieces in this collection are for five voices, each with its own independent music, without instrumental accompaniment. The words are by Giovanni Battista Guarini, one of the leading madrigal poets of his day and a particular favorite of Monteverdi's.

The words are entirely characteristic of madrigalian verse. They form a short poem of only eight lines, in one stanza. The first four lines (see the translation in the Listening Guide) constitute a single unit of thought, as they describe elements of nature that have been transformed by a single glance from the beloved. The poet here seems to have had the madrigalian composer in mind, as he uses words such as *turn, gleaming, smiles,* and *quiet,* which are susceptible to word painting. In the fifth line the mood changes completely. At this point, the narrator of the poem begins to speak not descriptively but of his own turbulent emotions. In the last three lines the speaker concludes that the birth of the beloved has led directly to his own death. This poetry seems intended for musical use, with its suggestive diction, concise form, and clear exposition of ideas and emotions.

The music, typical of the madrigal genre, closely follows the sense of the text. Monteverdi treats the first four lines in a fairly traditional fashion: The music to each line is set off by a cadence, and our interest is drawn mainly to the succession of madrigalisms that graphically illustrate the meaning of single words. The "turn" of the beloved's eyes is depicted by turning figures in the two sopranos. Her "smile" is portrayed, in fact, as a widening grin, beginning with a florid motive in the low register that is progressively imitated in the upper lines. Next, the quiet sea is interpreted by a very slowly moving wavelike pattern in the higher voices, which suddenly is enlivened at the word "wind" *(venti).*

The sudden change of tone in the poem at the fifth line is made even more dramatic in the music. From a serene major triad on the note G, the music at 0.58 moves abruptly to a major triad on E, creating a sonorous jolt. Monteverdi runs the final three lines of the poem together, since they are clearly intended to be understood as a single unit. Here he selects a pair of voices to deliver a steady alternation of dissonance and consonance, all the while following a descending course. Vividly, the sentiments of the poem, and the bitterness of its narrator, are expressed by the music.

**Claudio Monteverdi, "A un giro sol de' begl'occhi lucenti," from *Il quarto libro de madrigali* (1603)**
Recording 4.7

| | |
|---|---|
| *A un giro sol de' begl'occhi lucenti* | At one turn of those beautiful, gleaming eyes |
| *ride l'aria d'intorno,* | the air around me smiles, |
| *e'l mar s'acqueta e i venti,* | and the sea and winds grow quiet, |
| *e si fa il ciel d'un altro lume adorno.* | and the sky is adorned by a new light. |
| *Sol io le luci ho lagrimose e meste.* | Only I have eyes that are sad and tearful. |
| *Certo quando nasceste,* | Certainly, when you were born, |
| *così crudel e ria* | so cruel and evil, |
| *nacque la morte mia.* | my death was also born. |

**A** (lines 1–4)    0.00    The music consists of a succession of word paintings with little concern for unity among subsections. The bass line provides coherence by functioning as a slow-moving accompaniment.

**B** (line 5)    0.58    The key moves abruptly to E major to underscore the new subjective tone of the poem.

**C** (lines 6–8)    1.10    Monteverdi here leaves behind the traditional emphasis on word painting and seeks in its place an expression of the emotions underlying the words. He projects these by the prominent use of dissonant intervals within pairs of voices.

### The English Madrigal

At the same time that the leading Italian composers fostered the high art of the madrigal, others specialized in a lighter derivative of this genre. These lively and high-spirited works were designated by terms such as **canzona, canzonetta, villanesca,** and **balletto.** Different from the madrigal proper, they are normally settings of strophic texts, often exhibiting a purely homophonic texture. They are similar to the madrigal in their medium of three or more solo voices without obligatory accompaniment and occasional word paintings, but they have none of the true madrigal's lofty tone.

The lighter madrigalesque works by the 1580s became popular among English amateur musicians. In 1588 there appeared in London an anthology of Italian madrigals in English translation, *Musica transalpina*. An immense success, it served to stimulate native composers to try their hands at a similar sort of music. The leading composer was Thomas Morley (c. 1558–c. 1602). Morley had studied with William Byrd, who inspired his early efforts as a composer. Shortly after entering the musical service of Queen Elizabeth in 1592, Morley began to publish collections of works in the style of the light madrigal. These were directly based on Italian models, especially on the *balletti* of an Italian contemporary named Giovanni Gastoldi. Their great popularity inspired other younger English composers, including Thomas Weelkes and John Wilbye, to compose similar Italian imitations.

"Now Is the Month of Maying" (Recording 4.8) comes from Morley's *First Booke of Balletts to Five Voyces* (1595). The piece is often said to be a paraphrase of "Se ben mi c'ha bon tempo" by Orazio Vecchi, but although it shares the spirit and form of the Italian work, the two are not decisively related. As in the *canzonetti* and *balletti* of Vecchi and Gastoldi, Morley's balletto is strophic and predominantly homophonic, and both Morley and the Italians intersperse passages on nonsense words ("fa la la," for example) in each stanza.

**Listening Guide**

**Thomas Morley, "Now Is the Month of Maying," from the**
***First Booke of Balletts to Five Voyces***
Recording 4.8

| | | |
|---|---|---|
| **A** (stanza 1) | 0.00 | The music of each stanza is divided into halves, each of which is immediately repeated. The opening melody begins |

Now is the month of may-ing, When mer-ry lads are play-ing.

| | | |
|---|---|---|
| **A** (stanza 2) | 0.35 | The first stanza is repeated with new words. |
| **A** (stanza 3) | 1.05 | The music of the first stanza returns, again with new words. |

Morley's charming music perfectly captures the carefree spirit of the verse, whose meaning is made crystal clear by the direct rhythms and homophonic texture.

## TOPICS FOR DISCUSSION AND WRITING

**1.** Compare Byrd's motet "Ave verum corpus" with one or more of the Madonna paintings of Raphael, made during his residence in Florence from 1504 to 1508 (one example is seen on page 117). Take into consideration the spirit that reigns in both media, and point to specific aspects of style and construction that help to create this mood.

**2.** Compare and contrast Dufay's motet "Vasilissa, ergo gaude" with Machaut's song "Dame, de qui toute ma joie vient" (Recording 3.4). Focus especially on the works' textures, harmonic vocabularies, and rhythmic styles. How does Dufay's work represent a continuation of the language of Machaut, and in what ways does it look forward to new styles?

**3.** Study the Kyrie of Josquin's *Missa pange lingua* and, solely by ear, explore the ways in which phrases from the source hymn are paraphrased for use in the Mass. Sing a phrase of the hymn until it is clearly in mind; then sing the corresponding melody from the Mass. What processes does the composer use to transform one into the other?

**4.** Analyze Monteverdi's madrigal "A un giro" for the ways in which the composer expresses verbal structure and meaning in the music. Some of these techniques are touched on in the foregoing discussion of this piece. Continue to seek ways in which Monteverdi finds musical equivalents for his text. Focus on the poetic structure of the words, the meaning of single words, and the general emotion they convey.

## ADDITIONAL LISTENING

### Byrd

*Masses for 3, 4, and 5 Voices.* The Hilliard Ensemble. EMI, CDM 7634412.

*Pavans and Galliards.* Davitt Moroney, harpsichord. Harmonia Mundi, HMC 901241.42.

### Dufay

*Motets.* Pro Cantione Antiqua, London. Archiv, 2533291.

### Isaac

*The Bavarian Court Orchestra in the 16th Century.* Capella Antiqua München. Das alte Werk, SAWT 9431.

## Josquin des Prez

*Marien-Motetten*. Monteverdi-Chor Hamburg. Archiv, 2533110.

*Missa La sol fa re mi, Motets, Chansons, Instrumental Music*. Capella Antiqua München. ABC Records, AB-67017/2.

## Monteverdi

*Quarto libro dei madrigali*. The Consort of Musicke. L'Oiseau-lyre, 414148-2.

*Quinto libro dei madrigali*. The Consort of Musicke. L'Oiseau-lyre, 410291-2.

(Also see Chapter 5.)

## Morley

*Elizabethan and Jacobean Madrigals*. The Scholars. Enigma, K53529.

## Palestrina

*Missa Papae Marcelli*. The Tallis Scholars. Gimmel, CDGIM 339.

*Missa Assumpta Est Maria*. Choir of St. John's College, Cambridge. Argo, ZRG 690.

## BIBLIOGRAPHY

Abraham, Gerald, ed. *New Oxford History of Music, Volume 4: The Age of Humanism, 1540–1630*. London: Oxford University Press, 1968.

Arnold, Denis. *Monteverdi*. The Master Musicians. London: Dent, 1963.

Aston, Margaret. *The Fifteenth Century: The Prospect of Europe*. Orlando, Fla.: Harcourt Brace Jovanovich, 1968. A short cultural history.

Bergin, Thomas G. *Petrarch*. New York: Twayne, 1970. An authoritative and elegantly written short study.

Blume, Friedrich. *Renaissance and Baroque Music: A Comprehensive Survey*. Translated by M. D. Herder Norton. New York: Norton, 1967.

Brown, Howard M. *Music in the Renaissance*. Englewood Cliffs, N.J.: Prentice Hall, 1976.

Dickens, A. G. *The Age of Humanism and Reformation: Europe in the Fourteenth, Fifteenth, and Sixteenth Centuries*. Englewood Cliffs, N.J.: Prentice Hall, 1972.

Fallows, David. *Dufay*. London: Oxford University Press, 1982.

Kerman, Joseph. *The Masses and Motets of William Byrd*. Berkeley: University of California Press, 1981.

Kristeller, Paul O. *The Classics and Renaissance Thought*. Cambridge, Mass.: Harvard University Press, 1955.

Palisca, Claude. *Humanism in Italian Renaissance Musical Thought*. New Haven, Conn.: Yale University Press, 1985.

Panofsky, Erwin. *Renaissance and Renascences in Western Art*. New York: Harper & Row, 1969.

Reese, Gustave. *Music in the Renaissance.* Revised edition. New York: Norton, 1959. The standard, detailed reference source.

Stevens, Denis, ed. and trans. *The Letters of Claudio Monteverdi.* Cambridge: Cambridge University Press, 1980.

Tomlinson, Gary. *Monteverdi and the End of the Renaissance.* Berkeley: University of California Press, 1987.

Wittkower, Rudolf. *Architectural Principles in the Age of Humanism.* Fourth edition. London: Academy, 1973.

## NOTES

1. Mathieu d'Escouchy, quoted in Jeanne Marix, *Histoire de la musique et des musiciens de la cour de Bourgogne* (Geneva: Minkoff, 1972), p. 38.
2. Cosimo Bartoli, quoted in Gustave Reeve, *Music in the Renaissance,* rev. ed. (New York: Norton, 1959), pp. 259–260.

# 5

## *The Early Baroque Period,*
## *1600–1700*

## The Lion Hunt

*Peter Paul Rubens's massive depiction of a bloody encounter between hunters and lions unleashes all of the extravagant motion and passionate vigor that differentiate much of baroque artistic expression from the calm and serenity that ruled in the sixteenth century. This painting, commissioned by Sir John Digby, the English ambassador to Brussels, is highly idealized in conception. It shows six Berber tribesmen of North Africa, together with what appears to be a mounted European warrior in armor, waging hand-to-hand combat* with two enraged lions. The Berbers were known for their warlike fervor, but they have clearly met their match in the ferocious animals. The horseman in armor, on the contrary, is about to control the wild melee with a powerful thrust of his sword.

Several different themes are addressed by Rubens's painting. First among them is the ferocious hunt in which man engages animal on nearly equal terms, with man destined to be victorious. The scene also suggests warfare, for which hunting during this period was often a form of practice. All of the figures embody great heroism, lions and horses as well as men. A religious message is also conveyed as the armored figure, certainly a representative of Christianity, looms commandingly above the prostrate Muslims. This figure almost exactly duplicates an earlier depiction by Rubens of St. George slaying the dragon. The subjects addressed by the painting are all enhanced by its angular organization, which heightens its sense of tumult. We can easily understand how Rubens's riotous conceptions were judged by later critics as "baroque," a word that came to mean bizarre, irregular, or extravagant.

Peter Paul Rubens (1577–1640) led a life reminiscent of many leading Renaissance artists and musicians. He was born in Flanders, worked and acquired fame in Italy, and returned to the region of his birth in order to capitalize on his reputation. During his eight years in Italy, he served the Duke of Mantua, at the very time that Claudio Monteverdi was also in the service of this prince. The *powerful vigor of Rubens's paintings has its parallel in such colorful and dynamic works as Monteverdi's Vesper motets, discussed in this chapter. In these pieces, the pristine serenity of Renaissance church music, as conceived by a figure such as William Byrd, is superseded by a music whose motion and force call to mind the powerful canvases of Rubens.*

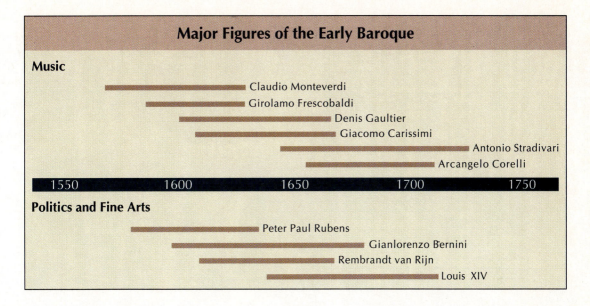

**Major Figures of the Early Baroque**

**Music**

Claudio Monteverdi
Girolamo Frescobaldi
Denis Gaultier
Giacomo Carissimi
Antonio Stradivari
Arcangelo Corelli

| 1550 | 1600 | 1650 | 1700 | 1750 |

**Politics and Fine Arts**

Peter Paul Rubens
Gianlorenzo Bernini
Rembrandt van Rijn
Louis XIV

Monteverdi's madrigals were symptomatic of a great flowering of musical culture that occurred in Italy toward the end of the sixteenth century. Especially in the large cities of northern Italy, music was performed with a skill that seemed better than ever before. Native composers such as Monteverdi and Palestrina achieved in their works a level of expressiveness and originality that promised to usher in a whole new era.

We now see the onset of a new period in music, called the baroque, around the year 1600. The term *baroque,* like many in music, is derived from art history, where it designates a style of painting, sculpture, and architecture seen especially in Italy in the early 1600s. Its elements are clearly evident in the paintings of Peter Paul Rubens (1577–1640). His painting *The Lion Hunt* (see the opening of this chapter) is a large panorama of ferocious motion, brutal energy, and calculated confusion. Clearly, Rubens had a far different artistic objective in such a painting from the serene religiosity of Raphael or the heroic self-control over passionate impulses implicit in Michelangelo's sculpture.

The largeness of scale of Rubens's studies of bodies in action is captured also in the architecture of Gianlorenzo Bernini (1598–1680). Virtually all of his major works are located in Rome, where he received lifelong support from a series of popes. In 1629 Bernini was appointed chief architect for the completion of the Basilica of Saint Peter, a project that had earlier occu-

**147**

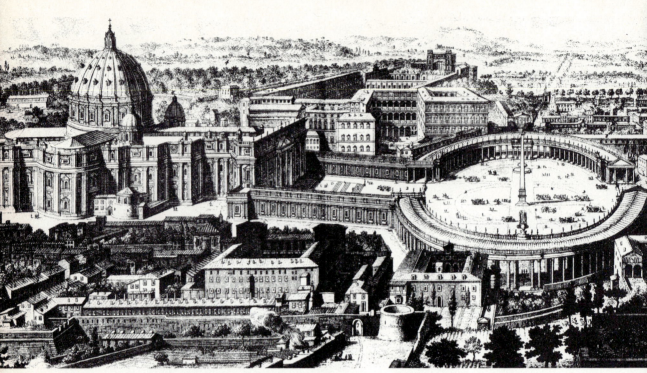

*Aerial view of the Basilica of Saint Peter in Rome. The piazza and collonade in front of the basilica are the work of Gianlorenzo Bernini.*

pied Michelangelo. In addition to creating many of the interior features of this great church, Bernini also designed the spectacular piazza in front of it (see above). Here a quadruple colonnade describes an ellipse that leads into wings connecting to and seemingly embracing the façade of the church. The design combines classical features, inherited by Bernini from Renaissance architecture, with fluid motion, vastness, and geometric shapes.

Bernini's designs were especially influential on seventeenth-century French architecture, as is evident in the Palace of Versailles and its surrounding gardens (page 149). These were begun in 1682, when Louis XIV moved his court to Versailles, and the architectural designs were executed by a staff led by Charles Le Brun, Jules Hardouin-Mansart, André Le Nôtre, and Louis Le Vau. From Bernini's idiom, the French architects adopted vastness of scale, geometric order, and classical detail. They tended, however, to displace Bernini's sculptural fluidity with a massiveness that suggested the absolute power of the French monarch. Nowhere is the bold dictum of Louis XIV, "L'état, c'est moi" ("I am the state"), more imposingly communicated than in the monumental conception of Versailles.

Music of the **baroque period,** which extends from about 1600 until the middle of the eighteenth century, shares many of the same qualities as these contemporary artworks. Baroque music can possess the same energy and dramatic color as a painting by Rubens, or it can, as in late baroque opera, take on the larger-than-life proportions of the Palace of Versailles. It can be as ornate as Bernini's interior designs for Saint Peter's and as searchingly emotional as a portrait by Rembrandt. Baroque music, to be sure, is not strictly unified in style. In fact, this was a period in which composers began to practice very different styles—not just to appeal to regional tastes, as in the Renaissance, but to express differing musical ideas.

Musical culture of the seventeenth century was inevitably influenced by political and social forces. During this century, the prestige and wealth of northern Italian courts began to ebb, and, as a consequence, Italy gradually had to share its preeminence in music with France and England and, in the eighteenth century, with the German states. The rise of France as a political and artistic force was an especially important historical phenomenon in the

*Aerial view of the Palace of Versailles, outside Paris. Only a small part of the gardens attached to the palace is seen in this photograph.*

seventeenth century. Under the rule of the "Sun King," Louis XIV (1638–1715), France became a model for the centralized nation-state. By the end of the century, France was the arbiter of taste throughout Europe. French was the language of cultured people across the Continent, and French artistic styles were an inspiration to artists of all nationalities. No longer did French composers feel compelled, as in the Renaissance, to immigrate to Italy. On the contrary, throughout the seventeenth century, leading Italian and German musicians, including Giovanni Battista Lulli and Johann Froberger, settled in Paris, where they were integrated into a flourishing native musical culture.

Early in the century, German-speaking lands were allied into a federation called the Holy Roman Empire, which for centuries had been led by Austrian kings of the Hapsburg family. The Thirty Years' War (1618–1648), however, caused great devastation to this realm and delayed its artistic development. The Thirty Years' War was a complicated struggle primarily concerned with the Hapsburgs' unsuccessful attempt to unify the empire under one king and under the Catholic faith. Only in the eighteenth century did musical culture in German lands begin to flourish, but then with a brilliance that would eventually outshine the Italians.

The seventeenth century was also the time when modern science and the scientific method were founded. The startling discoveries of Galileo, Kepler, and Newton, which at first seemed threatening to traditional philosophy and religious beliefs, by the end of the century became widely accepted and led to an international flowering of scientific and rational thought.

## Baroque Musical Style

The baroque period was the time when many important features of modern music were created. During this era, the modern orchestra was first assembled. Instruments, including those of the violin family, were brought virtually to their modern state of construction. The modern phenomenon of key evolved during the baroque period, as did basic genres of music including opera, oratorio, sonata, and concerto (all of which will be discussed presently). Given the essentially modern nature of baroque music, we will often hear it performed nowadays by musical organizations. But we rarely hear music before this period played in typical concert circumstances.

If we survey music by major composers written during this century and a half, our attention will probably first be drawn to its differences in style rather than to its similarities. The works of Monteverdi, J. S. Bach, and

François Couperin, for example, may seem to have little in common. But a closer look will reveal some striking correspondences. The texture of most baroque music, whether vocal or instrumental, almost always contains a stratum of accompanimental chords. Usually, a harpsichord, organ, or group of plucked instruments will be assigned to play this part. This accompanimental stratum is called the **basso continuo,** or **thorough bass,** and its presence is a distinctive feature of baroque music.

Another link that joins composers so disparate as Monteverdi, Bach, and Couperin is their overriding concern for intensity of expression, usually governed by ideas contained in a text. This orientation was anticipated by late Renaissance composers such as William Byrd and the Italian madrigalists, but in the baroque it became so central an objective that composers were willing to dispense with time-honored rules of composition in order to make their music directly express the emotional content of words. The closeness of music to the written or spoken word has never been greater than in baroque music, even during the nineteenth century, when a comparable musical rhetoric appeared.

Indeed, the principal artistic aim of baroque music was to move the emotions of the listener. In vocal music, this was accomplished by a coordinated use of word and tone, addressing mind and heart both. This objective is enunciated by the composer Giulio Caccini in the foreword to his songbook *Le nuove musiche* (*The New Music,* 1602). "The goal of music," Caccini wrote, "is to give delight and to move the affect of the soul."

Both a multiplication and a sharper definition of musical genres is another general feature of baroque music. In the Renaissance, as we have seen, the various genres tended to merge and lack distinctive features. The Mass resembled the motet in all but text, and instrumental pieces often resembled songs. Moreover, these musical types were not firmly linked to specific media. Josquin's "La Bernardina," for example, could be played by any instruments and probably also, if desired, adapted to a text and sung. In the baroque period, on the contrary, genres became increasingly distinct. By 1700, for instance, a **sonata** was a chamber instrumental work whose overall form and medium were, by convention, fairly well established.

The characteristic features of the baroque style were introduced by Italian composers of secular vocal music in the years just before 1600, and they only gradually spread to instrumental music and to music of the church. From their origins in Italy they were transported to all other European lands, where, by the late baroque period, Italian music constituted a universally accepted and admired artistic language.

# *I*talian Song and Opera in the Early Baroque Period

The beginnings of a distinctive baroque style are to be found in vocal music from the courts of northern Italy toward the end of the sixteenth century. The madrigal had earlier been the most important type of music in this milieu. But by the end of the century, its medium of four or five unaccompanied singers was losing out in popularity to works in which a solo singer could dazzle an audience with expressive nuances and vocal fireworks.

What did these solo performers sing? One important genre was the **aria.** In the sixteenth century, arias were songs for one singer, accompanied by lute or other instruments. They consisted of simple and well-known melodic lines and harmonic patterns on which a soloist could improvise. They were infrequently written down, since their underlying musical formulas were passed on orally and brought to life only by improvisation. Soloists also adapted older madrigals to suit their needs, simply by singing one line and playing the others, perhaps reduced to simple chords, on the lute.

A change of medium and texture is thus a major feature of the new style. Composers of the Renaissance favored ensembles singing four or five independent, contrapuntal lines. But by 1600 this type of sonority was becoming outdated and increasingly replaced by music in a predominantly homophonic texture, where one singer (or a few) was accompanied by instruments of a basso continuo. In the early years of the seventeenth century, hundreds of songs with instrumental accompaniment were composed in Italy. Ostensibly, these could be defined as arias or madrigals, depending on whether they were strophic or not, but they were so different in character from traditional sixteenth-century music that they are now usually designated by a new term, **monody.**

We can observe the emergence of the new soloistic medium in the madrigals of Monteverdi. Beginning with his *Fifth Book,* published in 1605, a basso continuo line is provided, which enables fewer than five singers to perform the works without sacrificing full harmonies. In later collections, the texture of his madrigals is even more radically altered, as these pieces begin to be composed expressly for few voices plus basso continuo.

A second characteristic of the new style, also found in Monteverdi's madrigals composed near the turn of the seventeenth century, is an intensified relationship of music and its text. The earlier madrigal composer typically searched for musical figures that could depict the meaning of single words. But Monteverdi chose verse that instead described powerful emotional states, and through a prominent use of dissonance, he perfected a musical language that could poignantly express these passions. So readily did Monteverdi break

**152**

the existing rules of counterpoint and harmony that he was accused of willful formlessness in composition. He defended himself against such charges by saying that his music stemmed from an entirely new compositional approach, a "second practice," to use his term. In the foreword to his *Fifth Book of Madrigals,* Monteverdi's brother Giulio explained this new approach: "My brother says that he does not compose his works at haphazard because, in this kind of music, it has been his intention to make the words the master of the harmony and not the servant."

Additional features of the early baroque style were the outcome of outright experiment. The laboratory was in Florence, which, despite political turbulence during the early sixteenth century, remained, under the ruling Medici family, a brilliant center of humanism and artistic activity. Throughout the Renaissance, Florentine citizens had participated in **academies,** clublike gatherings loosely based on the model of the ancient school of Plato, called the Academy. Their members gathered periodically to discuss a variety of issues, including those concerning the arts.

For the history of music, an academy called the Camerata, which met in the 1570s and 1580s at the palace of Count Giovanni Bardi, was especially important. One of its members was the singer and composer Giulio Caccini, who describes its activities with lavish praise:

> Indeed, in the times when the most virtuous "Camerata" of the most illustrious Signor Giovanni Bardi, Count of Vernio, flourished in Florence, and in it were assembled not only a great part of the nobility but also the first musicians and men of talent and poets and philosophers of the city, and I too frequently attended it, I can say that I learned more from their learned discussions than I learned from descant [the study of counterpoint] in over thirty years.[1]

Other recollections by Caccini indicate that the Camerata, in truly humanistic fashion, aimed at reviving the marvelous expressive effects of Greek music, as they were known through the writings of Plato and other ancient authors. Their method was to eliminate counterpoint in vocal music in favor of clear homophony. In this way, the words were made more audible. They also wrote melodies that were not so tuneful as to obscure the melodious qualities of the words when read aloud. Some of the songs in this new style, written by Caccini for use in the Camerata, he later published in *Le nuove musiche.* This volume contains songs in madrigal and aria forms for solo voice with lute accompaniment. The melodies are not especially tuneful but are infinitely sensitive to the rhythm of the words. The accompaniment is almost primitive in its simplicity and lack of any suggestion of counterpoint.

An even more ambitious experiment at reviving the musical ethos of ancient Greece occurred when the Florentine academicians applied their new musical idiom to the theater. Spurred on by their belief that Greek tragedy was entirely sung rather than spoken, they experimented in the 1590s with plays in which all of the words were delivered in singing. The result was a new genre later called **opera.** Their innovations were not as radical as might be suspected, since plays at this time were normally performed with the addition of music of various types. But the Florentines succeeded in devising a type of recitational singing by which dramatic lines could make a heightened impact on the listener.

The first opera for which all of the music survives is *Euridice* (1600). The play, written by the Florentine court poet Ottavio Rinuccini, deals with the Greek myth of Orpheus and his quest for his beloved Euridice. The music is primarily by the singer and composer Jacopo Peri. The opera contains types of music that would have been familiar to any theatergoer at the Medici court in 1600: choruses, strophic solo arias, and dance music. But for the most dramatic and emotional portions, Peri used a new melodic style, called **recitative** (pronounced "re-si-tah-TEEV"). This style even exceeded Caccini's monodies in its devotion to the expression of the words. The accompanimental instruments play long-held chords, above which the singer declaims the words in a style midway between speech and song.

Peri's operatic experiment was closely studied by Claudio Monteverdi, who used many of its innovative features in a related work, *Orfeo,* presented in 1607 at the court in Mantua. With *Orfeo,* opera leaves behind its experimental phase and becomes an established musical genre, destined to survive and flourish continuously to the present. The play, by the Mantuan poet Alessandro Striggio, is also a version of the legend of Orpheus (see the accompanying synopsis). This subject was much loved by humanistic writers of the period because it depicts the human spirit overcoming the forces of fate. Its appeal to musicians is also understandable, since Orpheus was himself a singer and instrumentalist whose art proves to be more powerful even than the gods. Striggio also emphasizes the force of the emotions, which seem to hold sway over men and women regardless of their noble qualities of mind.

The problems Monteverdi faced in creating music for Striggio's play would have been daunting to a lesser composer. The play was long and filled with diverse situations and conflicting emotions. Monteverdi solved these problems brilliantly by composing music in which several styles coexist. He then deftly added recurrent elements to unify the different parts into a coherent whole. The music of *Orfeo* is divided into sections, each devoted to one of four different media: solo voice with accompaniment, two voices with accom-

## *Synopsis*

**Alessandro Striggio and Claudio Monteverdi, *Orfeo* (1607), based on a Greek legend. The opera is divided into five acts.**

Orpheus has married Euridice, and he rejoices with his friends. A messenger arrives to inform the party that Euridice is dead, the victim of the bite of a snake. Orpheus sings a lament, "Tu se' morta" ("You are dead"), and then resolves not to be undone by fate. He boldly declares that he will fetch his bride back from the underworld.

To gain access to Hades, he relies on the power of his art by singing the boatman, Charon, to sleep. Orpheus then rows himself to the underworld. The inhabitants there are moved by his plight, and Pluto agrees to release Euridice. But a heavy condition is imposed: If Orpheus looks at his beloved before completing their journey back to earth, she will be lost to him forever. Orpheus' noble spirit is ultimately conquered by his passions: He gazes on her, and she is gone.

He returns bereft to his native land, where he loses himself in grief and self-pity, finally forswearing all other women. But his father, the god Apollo, descends on a cloud to impart wise counsel: Orpheus, he says, has foolishly become a slave to his passions. After all, earthly pleasures are fleeting. So Apollo brings Orpheus with him to heaven where he can gaze eternally on the likeness of Euridice in the sun and the stars.

paniment, chorus, or groups of instruments alone. The instrumental music is varied in form and function. Sometimes it accompanies dancing, or it may introduce or conclude a major portion of the opera (the composer called each such passage a **sinfonia**). Certain passages of instrumental music also bind together longer scenes by recurring as refrains (these are called **ritornelli**). The first edition of *Orfeo,* published in Venice in 1609, contains unusually detailed information about the instruments that the composer wished to have used. For melodic lines, he specified primarily violins, flutes, and brass instruments. The basso continuo was to be played in group fashion by harpsichords, harps, lutes, organs, and stringed instruments.

The choruses of *Orfeo* express the sentiments of groups of shepherds, nymphs, and infernal spirits. Musically, they are similar to madrigals, although they are more consistently homophonic. Like the instrumental ritornelli, choral sections frequently recur to bind together long scenes. We find in the vocal duets some of the greatest music of the entire opera. This texture was especially attractive to Monteverdi, who uses it also in many of his later madrigals.

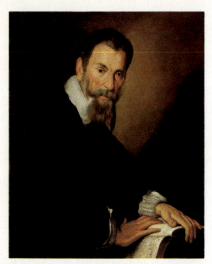

*Claudio Monteverdi in his old age, as recorded by the Venetian painter Bernardo Strozzi.*

The music for solo voices was sung by both men and women, although some of the leading female roles, such as that of Euridice, were originally performed by **castrati.** The practice of castrating boys to preserve the quality of sound and high pitch of their voices was prevalent mainly in Italy in the Renaissance. The castrato's popularity rose at the end of the sixteenth century along with the general interest in virtuosic solo singing. The extraordinary musical qualities of the best castrati attracted opera composers throughout the seventeenth and eighteenth centuries, so much so that baroque composers often wrote leading male roles for them as well, ignoring the seeming incongruity of a male part being sung by a high-pitched voice.

Monteverdi, like Peri before him, wrote two distinctly different types of music for solo voices: arias and recitatives. The recitatives have very little tune. Their accompaniment consists of sustained chords, and their rhythm is speechlike. Arias, by contrast, have a clearer melodic profile. They are tuneful, they have regular beat and rhythm, and the full-blown examples use strophic form. We shall encounter examples of these two idioms momentarily.

The second act of *Orfeo* illustrates how Monteverdi links his disparate musical resources into a powerfully unified shape. Act 2 of the play suggests a division into four sections, which Monteverdi follows in constructing the music. In the first, Orpheus, newly married, happily greets his friends. This part of the act is cast as a succession of arialike fragments, duets, and a chorus. Next, Orpheus recounts the emotions that he feels: He was earlier sad and grieved, but now he lives in joy. His narration consists of a poem in four stanzas, which Monteverdi treats as an aria (discussed in the Listening Guide).

The emotional high point of the act is next. Euridice's friend Sylvia arrives with the dire report that Euridice is dead. Orpheus at first despairs but then swears that he will overcome fate and bring her back to earth. Monteverdi sets these passionate words primarily as recitative (see the Listening Guide). The act ends with mourning by Orpheus' friends, in which the music, as in the first section, exhibits a succession of different styles: duets, recitative, refrain choruses, and instrumental sinfonie.

Monteverdi is clearly not content to allow the music merely to follow the words without achieving a coherence of its own. He uses refrains and focus on a single keynote to create musical unity. The key of the music throughout the lengthy act repeatedly returns to G or to closely related pitch centers. Refrains, whether instrumental ritornelli or recurrent choruses, effectively link the highly diverse musical styles. By these devices, Monteverdi overcomes the episodic nature of the text and presents us with a smoothly flowing, coherent musical drama.

On Recording 5.1 we hear two excerpts from Act 2, including all of Orpheus' aria and his lament in recitative style.

**Claudio Monteverdi, *Orfeo,* excerpts from Act 2**
Recording 5.1

### 1. Orpheus' aria

1. *Vi ricorda, o boschi ombrosi,*
   *de' miei lunghi aspri tormenti,*
   *quando i sassi ai miei lamenti*
   *respondean fatti pietosi?*

2. *Dite, allor non vi sembrai*
   *più d'ogn'altro sconsolato?*
   *or fortuna ha stil cangiato*
   *ed ha volto in festa i guai.*

3. *Vissi già mesto e dolente;*
   *or gioisco e quegli affanni*
   *che sofferti ho per tant'anni*
   *fan più caro il ben presente.*

1. Do you recall, O shady woods,
   my long and bitter torments,
   when the rocks, to my laments,
   answered pitifully?

2. Say, did I then not seem
   more disconsolate than any other?
   Now my luck has changed
   and my woes have become a feast.

3. Then I lived in sadness and misery;
   now I rejoice, and those miseries
   that I suffered for so many years
   make more precious my present
   good.

| | |
|---|---|
| **4.** *Sol per te, bella Euridice,* | **4.** Only for you, lovely Euridice, |
| *benedico il mio tormento;* | do I bless my torments; |
| *dopo il duol vi è più contento,* | after sadness, one is more content; |
| *dopo il mal vi è più felice.* | after pain, one is happier. |

**A** (stanza 1)   0.00   The first stanza is introduced by instrumental music (a ritornello), which is repeated after each of the ensuing stanzas. The vocal melody is very tuneful and dancelike in rhythm, and it is accompanied solely by the instruments of the basso continuo. The melody of the first line returns at the end of the stanza. It begins

Vi ri-cor-da   bos-chi om bro - si, Vi  ri-cor-da bos-chi om-bro - si

**A/A/A** (stanzas   0.46   The music of the first stanza is repeated three additional times to
2–4)   new words. The opening instrumental ritornello separates one
   stanza from the next.

### 2. Orpheus' lament

| | |
|---|---|
| **1.** *Tu se' morta, mia vita, ed io respiro?* | **1.** You are dead, my life, and I still breathe? |
| *Tu se' da me partita per mai più non tornare, ed io rimango?* | You have left me, never to return, and I still remain? |
| *No, che se i versi alcuna cosa ponno,* | No! If my verses have any power, |
| *N'andrò sicuro a' più profondi abissi,* | I shall descend to hell's deepest abyss |
| *E, intenerito il cor del re de l'ombre,* | and, having softened the heart of the king of shadows, |
| *meco trarrotti a riveder le stelle.* | lead you back with me again to see the stars. |
| *O, se ciò negherammi empio destino,* | O, if I am thwarted by cruel destiny |
| *rimarrò teco in compagnia di morte.* | I will remain with you in the company of death. |
| *Addio terra, addio cielo e sole, addio.* | Farewell earth, farewell heaven and sun. |

**Recitative**   2.23   Monteverdi specifies that the accompaniment is to consist of
   organ and lute, lending it a properly hollow sound. Characteristics

**158**

of the recitative style are heard in the freedom of both melody and accompaniment from regular beat and rhythm; long-held chords by the instruments; a nontuneful, speechlike vocal line; and pungent dissonances on words such as *morta* ("death") and *intenerito* ("softened"). Awkward leaps by the voice also reflect Orpheus' heightened emotions. Vestiges of the expressive idiom of the madrigalists appear in phrases such as *profondi abissi* ("deepest abyss"), where the melodic line descends to the singer's lowest register. The end of Orpheus' lament reverts to a more melodious and rhythmically flowing style.

# Religious Music

Characteristics of the new baroque style—recitative, pronounced uses of dissonance, elimination of counterpoint, and smaller but more heterogeneous media—were slow to find their way into music for the church. Even innovators such as Monteverdi often reverted in their Masses and motets to densely contrapuntal textures in four or more vocal lines. Indeed, sacred music maintained a staunchly Renaissance style well into the eighteenth century, and audiences were at first inclined to accept the new baroque musical language as appropriate only to the opera theater or to the court, not to the service of worship.

## Monteverdi's Sacred Music

Monteverdi, to be sure, was not entirely opposed to innovation in religious music, with which he was increasingly involved after his appointment in 1613 as director of music in the Basilica of Saint Mark in Venice. This position was one of the most prestigious in all of Europe. For over a century, it had been held by a series of leading musicians who had forged a distinctive style of church music that proved widely influential. The Venetian style was marked by grandiose musical forces: Motets, for example, were written not for one but for several choirs of voices and often additional ensembles of instruments. These were positioned in the multiple galleries of the basilica in order to produce dramatic spatial effects. The Venetian composers also wrote works for brass and strings for the services of worship, and these rousing instrumental pieces also exploit "stereophonic" effects.

Monteverdi had decidedly eclectic tastes in his church music, which ranged from an old-fashioned Mass to monodylike motets for solo voice and

**Listening Guide**

### Claudio Monteverdi, "Domine ad adiuvandum"
Recording 5.2

*(Deus in adiutorium meum intende.*
*Domine ad adiuvandum me festina.*
*Gloria Patri et filio et Spiritui Sancto.*

O God, come to my aid.)
O Lord, make haste to help me.
Glory be to the Father, and to the
    Son, and to the Holy Ghost.

*Sicut erat in principio et nunc et semper*
   *et in secula seculorum Amen.*

As it was in the beginning, is now,
   and ever shall be, world without
   end. Amen.

*Alleluia.*

Hallelujah.

| | | |
|---|---|---|
| **Chant** | 0.00 | The motet is preceded by a phrase of Gregorian chant. |
| **A** | 0.13 | The first sentence of text, sung to repeated chords in the chorus, is joined to restless, energetic music in the instruments. Their main motive, in duple meter, begins |

| | | |
|---|---|---|
| **B** | 0.27 | A ritornello in the instruments changes to triple meter, a metric alternation typical of the Venetian style. It begins |

| | | |
|---|---|---|
| **A** | 0.36 | The next sentence repeats the first section of music with slight changes. |
| **B** | 0.52 | The ritornello is played again. |
| **A** | 1.02 | The final sentence of the text is sung to a third statement of the opening music, slightly varied. |
| **C** | 1.29 | Without pause, the music surges again into a triple meter on the word "Alleluia," leading to a rousing conclusion. |

basso continuo. He brilliantly adopted the Venetian style in the motet "Domine ad adiuvandum me festina" ("O Lord, Make Haste to Help Me," Recording 5.2), which was published in 1610 in a collection of church pieces. True to Venetian practices, Monteverdi calls in this motet for two large ensembles. The first is the chorus, consisting of six separate lines. The other is a band of brass, strings, and winds. There is also a basso continuo part, probably intended to be played by the organ.

Similar to much of the music of the Renaissance, "Domine ad adiuvandum" is not entirely original in its musical materials. The instruments play music that was earlier used for the prelude to *Orfeo,* as though alerting the listeners that now even church pieces will be charged with drama. The music for the chorus quotes a version of the very simple chant prescribed for use in a traditional Catholic service of worship. Monteverdi succeeds in bringing these contrasting resources together into a remarkably energetic whole, whose color and motion remind us of the baroque painting of Rubens. The equipoise of religious music of a composer such as Byrd is here totally displaced by a new, vitalized spirit, characteristic of a new era.

## *The Early Oratorio*

Even though some musicians of the seventeenth century questioned the appropriateness of the baroque style in church—linked, as it was, with the worldliness of the theater—they had no reservations about its use in religious music outside of the official services of worship. In Italy in the late 1500s, there arose many new Christian organizations that intended to make the work of the church more relevant to the people. The most important of these for the history of music was called the Congregation of the Oratory, founded in 1575 by a Roman priest named Philip Neri. This was originally a society of lay people who met in a separate room of Neri's church—an "oratory"—to hear preaching and to pray. Music was also a part of their gatherings, especially pieces that could bring alive the drama of Scripture.

Branches of Neri's organization spread rapidly throughout Italy, and musical presentations of biblical stories, called **oratorios** after the rooms where they were first given, emerged by about 1640 as a major new genre of religious music. Oratorios by this time used either Italian or Latin words drawn from a biblical story, most typically from the Old Testament. At first they were loose in their musical organization, but by the mid-seventeenth century they settled into a type of music resembling opera. Like opera, oratorios incorporated arias, recitatives, and choruses, although they were probably presented with few if any costumes and no scenery or staging. The genre reached its greatest heights in the late baroque period in the works of George Frideric Handel (see the discussion of *Messiah* in Chapter 6). Handel's inspiring oratorios would probably never have come into being were it not for the work of the first master of this genre, Giacomo Carissimi (1605–1674).

Carissimi lived virtually his entire life in Rome, where he was director of music in a Jesuit college that prepared Germans for the priesthood. His music includes Masses, motets, and oratorios. The specific circumstances for which he wrote his oratorios are not known, although they were probably performed at his own college and at the famous Oratory of the Most Holy Crucifix in Rome.

*Jephte,* Carissimi's most celebrated work, may well have been written for a performance at this oratory around the year 1650. The story, in Latin, deals with the ancient Israelite general Jephthah, as recounted in the Book of Judges 11:28–38. Before leading his troops against the Ammonites, Jephthah promises God that, if victorious, he will sacrifice the first creature that comes out of his house on his return. The enemy is crushed, but, returning home, Jephthah is greeted by his beloved daughter. Before the sacrifice is carried out, the daughter is allowed to roam the hills for two months, bewailing her fate. This story, which tells of absolute obedience to God's will, must have attracted Carissimi in part because it is charged with intense emotions that could be conveyed by the new musical language of the baroque period.

Carissimi's music calls for a large chorus, vocal soloists, and instrumental accompaniment. The text and music are divided into two large sections, of which the first is devoted primarily to narration (sung by a soloist, a chorus, or an ensemble of a few singers). The second and more dramatic part presents Jephthah's dialogue with his daughter, concluded by a chorus (Recording 5.3) lamenting the daughter's fate. Carissimi's music shows a keen awareness of Monteverdi's second practice and with other aspects of early opera. It differs from operatic music primarily in the emphasis that Carissimi gives to the chorus. Jephthah's lament "Heu, heu mihi!" ("Woe, woe is me!"), sung when he realizes that his daughter must be sacrificed, uses the same expressive resources of recitative that Monteverdi used in Orpheus' lament "Tu se' morta." Other solo passages have an arialike tunefulness.

The concluding section of the oratorio is a moving lament for chorus with instrumental accompaniment. Like most of Carissimi's choruses, this one is predominantly homophonic. It conveys its doleful message by the prominent use of dissonant sounds, much as occurs in Monteverdi's madrigals of the second practice, and by unusually rich harmonies. The melodic dimension itself attracts our attention less strongly, as it is subsumed in Carissimi's wonderfully expressive harmonic language.

**162**

**Listening Guide**

**Giacomo Carissimi, *Jephte*, concluding chorus, "Plorate filii Israel"**
Recording 5.3

| | |
|---|---|
| *Plorate filii Israel, plorate omnes virgines et filiam Jephte unigenitam, in carmine doloris lamentamini.* | Lament, children of Israel, lament ye virgins, for the one daughter of Jephthah, in mournful song lament. |

**A**   0.00   The performance on Recording 5.3 uses only one singer on each line in the chorus and an accompaniment consisting of lute, organ, and harp. Except for the delicate imitative texture on the words "in carmine doloris," the music is entirely homophonic, thus making the words all the more clearly understood.

**A′**   1.57   Both music and words are repeated, with a slightly varied ending.

## Instrumental Music

Only in the sixteenth century did instrumental music emerge as an important independent medium. Composers at that time began to write distinctive works for instruments, just as they had earlier for voices, and genres of instrumental music gained greater clarity and definition. Improvisation remained basic to the art of the instrumentalist, but no more so than to the art of the solo vocalist. Instrumental music of the early baroque period was much more tradition-bound than vocal music. Other than in isolated experiments, it did not at first adopt the innovations in style that we have observed in such vocal genres as recitative and monody.

The major instrumental genres early in the baroque differ in an important way from their modern counterparts: They are associated, in general, with no fixed medium. A canzona, for example, might have been a piece for keyboard alone or for an ensemble of winds and brass. The various types of dance music were played equally by any instrument or ensemble. This situation changed considerably by the late seventeenth century. At this time, as in works by Arcangelo Corelli, major instrumental genres became linked to definite types of ensembles.

# Music Today

## Ralph Kirkpatrick

The noble sound of the harpsichord playing Frescobaldi's canzone makes it surprising that from the end of the baroque period until the recent twentieth century, this instrument was infrequently played by the great virtuosi, who preferred the piano. Even when performing keyboard works specifically written for harpsichord, players opted for the piano or for harpsichords that had little in common with authentic baroque instruments.

The neglect of the harpsichord was repaired almost singlehandedly by the Polish-French virtuoso Wanda Landowska, who lived from 1879 to 1959. Her fascination with older music and historically correct performing practices led her to forgo the piano as a medium for baroque keyboard music in favor of the harpsichord. Even though the harpsichords that she had made for her tended to be more powerful and more colorful than their baroque ancestors, she proved that there is no true substitute for the original instruments.

Her pioneering work was brilliantly continued by her student Ralph Kirkpatrick. Born in Massachusetts in 1911, Kirkpatrick attended Harvard University prior to continuing his musical education in France and Germany. His studies with Landowska set him forth on the career of a virtuoso harpsichordist, whose per-

formances and recordings of Bach, Domenico Scarlatti, Couperin, Rameau, and other baroque masters established a level of competence and sensitivity that has inspired the present generation of early-music specialists. Kirkpatrick acquired his knowledge of historical performing practices by a firsthand reading of early documents, and this musicological work ultimately led to an authoritative study of the life and music of the baroque composer Domenico Scarlatti.

Kirkpatrick, like his mentor Landowska, was also vitally aware of the music of his own time. Just as Landowska played new pieces written for her by Manuel de Falla and Francis Poulenc, so too was Kirkpatrick the first interpreter of Elliott Carter's virtuosic Double Concerto.

At Kirkpatrick's death in 1984, Howard Schott emphasized the impact of his career on the modern generation of early music specialists: "In looking back on his career, . . . one sees him as a link between the generation of solitary pioneer figures . . . and the new wave of harpsichordists (many of them pupils or 'grand-pupils') that swept over the world after 1960."[*]

*Howard Schott, "Ralph Kirkpatrick (1911–1984)," *Early Music*, 12 (1984), 585.

In the discussion that follows, we shall survey several major instruments of the baroque period—the harpsichord, lute, and violin—and investigate typical works of music that they played.

## *Music for Keyboard*

The principal keyboard instruments of the baroque period were the harpsichord and the organ, both described in Chapter 2. In general, they played the same music interchangeably; that is, most keyboard pieces were just as well performed on one as the other. Baroque harpsichords were made in several sizes and shapes, and the terms **spinet** and **virginal** were sometimes also used to refer to harpsichords of this period. The organ, then as now, was encountered primarily in church.

Composers of baroque keyboard music showed their old-fashioned tastes nowhere more clearly than in their preference for polyphonic textures. Counterpoint, which was basic to all music of the Renaissance, had been largely cast aside in baroque vocal genres such as monody, aria, and recitative. But in keyboard pieces it lived on and reached new heights of intricacy and refinement. In the baroque period, works for keyboard in a contrapuntal texture carried genre titles such as *fugue, ricercar, fantasia,* and *canzona.* The canzona, for example, was typically a work in several sections. It was lively in tempo and polyphonic in texture.

Girolamo Frescobaldi (1583–1643) was one of the greatest masters of the keyboard during the early baroque period, especially in the composition of canzonas. Like Bach after him, Frescobaldi was renowned in his own day as a virtuoso organist. He worked primarily at Saint Peter's in Rome, and his influence was exerted equally by his teaching and by his musical compositions and brilliant playing. He composed keyboard works in virtually all of the genres existing in his day, plus ensemble pieces, madrigals and other Italian secular works, and music for the church.

The Canzona "La Vincenti" (Recording 5.4) was published two years after Frescobaldi's death. Its title continues the sixteenth-century tradition of attaching names to instrumental works (recall Josquin's "La Bernardina"), probably in reference to a patron or sponsor. Although no doubt intended primarily for organ or harpsichord, the piece could just as well be played by four instruments, since its texture consists of four equal and distinctly melodious lines. Like most of Frescobaldi's canzone, this work was probably intended for use in church.

In this canzona, Frescobaldi merges a fugal texture with variations form. The piece is clearly divided by cadences into five sections. In addition, it

**istening**
**Guide**

**Girolamo Frescobaldi, Canzona "La Vincenti"**
Recording 5.4

---

**A** (section 1)    0.00    A fugue in F major, in four imitative lines, makes up this section. The subject,

will be present in variations in all the remaining sections.

**A₁** (section 2)    0.40    In this small fugal passage, the subject is shortened and quicker in rhythm:

Clearly, however, it has the same contour as the subject of A, so we can conclude that it is a variation of the earlier melody. This section ends with a passage that produces a change of keynote, from F to A.

**A₂** (section 3)    1.04    Here the meter becomes triple and the key changes to B♭.

**Interlude**    1.20    This brief respite from the series of fugues serves to transport the key from B♭ to C.

**A₃** (section 4)    1.32    The character returns to that of the first section; so does the key (F major).

**A₄** (section 5)    2.15    The subject of the final fugue is distantly related to the opening melody:

**Coda**    2.50    The texture becomes freely polyphonic, leading to a brilliant conclusion.

---

has a brief interlude between sections 3 and 4, and it is ended by a rounding-off passage that is called a **coda** (Italian for "tail"). In each principal section, a fugue in four lines is constructed, and the subjects of each of these fugal passages are variations of the opening subject. The sections, furthermore, have very different characters, ranging from the stern opening to the dance-like third section to the lighthearted fifth section.

## Dance Music and the Dance Suite

Playing music to accompany dancing has always been an important activity for instrumentalists. In the Middle Ages, performers probably played dance tunes from memory, improvising at will, much like modern dance bands. By the baroque period, music that had become associated with various social dances began to separate from the dance itself and became a type of independent instrumental music, intended solely for listening. But the connection of such music to the original dances remained strong, as it influenced tempo, meter, character, and form. Dance music in the baroque period was played by virtually all instruments, including, in the late baroque period, orchestras and chamber ensembles.

The title of a dance piece is usually the same as the social dance that the music imitates. These names often refer to a characteristic dance step, as in the saltarello (from the Italian *saltare,* "to jump") or the courante (from the French *courir,* "to run"). Other names suggest geographic origins, such as allemande (French for "German") and pavane (from Pava, or Padua). The many Italian and French names rightly suggest that dance in the baroque period flourished especially in Italy and France.

Instrumental dance pieces throughout the baroque period are sometimes encountered as single, independent works but more characteristically as movements in larger cycles. The simplest such collections are dance pairs, such as a slow pavane followed by a lively gagliarda, linked together by a common keynote and, sometimes, by common themes. Gradually, larger successions of dances became the norm, creating the genre of the **suite** (French for "succession of things"). The exact content of suites varies greatly, although by the eighteenth century the sequence allemande, courante, sarabande, and gigue was very common. Many composers added a prelude before the allemande and additional light dances before the concluding gigue. The music of an entire suite normally remains in a single key.

The harpsichord and the lute were the two favored solo instruments for dance music. The quiet and refined lute was brought to Europe from the Arabic world during the Middle Ages, and by the fifteenth century it flourished as a solo medium and in the accompaniment of solo singing. Although Italy was the center of lute playing during the early baroque period, a distinguished school of performers and composers for the instrument arose in France as the seventeenth century progressed. The French lutenists had their own style: Their melodies were ornate, decorated by **graces,** quickly played groups of notes added to written melodies. The accompaniments tended to be very delicate, mixing polyphony of gossamer lightness with chords. So refined and, some say, artificial was the French style of lute music that it can be compared to French manners and language of the same time, which, in courtly circles, tended to be extravagant and precious.

The French dance style is heard in a Gigue in G Major for lute by Denis Gaultier (d. 1672). Gaultier was one of the founders of the French style of lute playing and composition, which is so enticing in its delicacy and esotericism. Little is known of his life, although he appears to have lived permanently in Paris, making his livelihood as a freelance performer and composer in aristocratic circles. His first important collection of lute music, from which the Gigue is drawn, appeared about 1650 under the title

**Denis Gaultier, Gigue in G Major from *Rhétorique des dieux***
Recording 5.5

| | | |
|---|---|---|
| **A** | 0.00 | The melody of this phrase begins in G major and cadences in D. It is highly elegant and refined in its rhythm and its use of graces. It begins |

| | | |
|---|---|---|
| **A** | 0.20 | The phrase is repeated. |
| **B** | 0.40 | The second phrase is longer than the first, with which it also contrasts in its imitative texture. This phrase reverses the plan of keynotes of the first section, as it moves from D back to G. |
| **B** | 1.05 | This phrase is also repeated. |

*Rhétorique des dieux* (*Rhetoric of the Gods*). It consists of lute dances, lavishly adorned by engravings and poetic commentaries.

Music of the gigue during Gaultier's lifetime was varied in style. In his hands it was usually quick in tempo, duple in meter, with highly intricate rhythms. Its form is usually binary. The Gigue in G Major (Recording 5.5) has two sections, each immediately repeated. The first is homophonic in texture, and the second begins with imitation of an ascending scalewise motive. The rhythm is especially sophisticated, exhibiting near the end of the piece swinging irregularities that may even remind us of jazz.

## The Baroque Sonata

Instrumental pieces called *sonatas* were composed by northern Italian musicians beginning in the late 1500s. The term itself (from the Italian *sonare*, "to play") indicates only that the piece was for instruments. The early examples were virtually synonymous with the type of music found in contemporary canzone. Like them, the early sonatas were used primarily in services of worship, to fill silences or to accompany a liturgical action. Such pieces were not linked to any specific medium, but ensembles of winds, brass, and strings were common.

As the seventeenth century progressed, the sonata emerged as an increasingly important genre with a more definite personality. It came to be associated especially with the violin, which in the latter half of the century was fast emerging as one of the most important instruments of the professional musician. Members of the violin family—which also includes the viola and the cello—had relatives in the Middle Ages and the Renaissance in instruments such as the viol and the rebec. Viols are stringed instruments that are visually similar to members of the violin family, but their sound is less penetrating, and they are less capable of virtuosic effects.

The essential features of the modern violin were perfected by craftsmen in the Italian cities of Cremona and Brescia in the seventeenth century. The work of Niccolò Amati (1596–1684) was especially important, not only in his innovations in violin construction but equally in his teaching. His apprentices included the most celebrated violin maker of all time, Antonio Stradivari (1644–1737). Stradivari (an instrument built by him is called a *Stradivarius*) found the ideal proportions and shape of the instrument, and his violins are still in use and greatly prized for their warmth of tone. The work of these craftsmen did much to stimulate interest in violin playing and, consequently, in the creation of musical genres, such as the sonata, that showed off the instrument's new capabilities.

*Mizzotint portrait of Arcangelo Corelli, by I. Smith Anglus after Hugh Howard.*

The sonatas of Arcangelo Corelli (1653–1713) not only helped to establish a distinctive and idiosyncratic style of violin writing but also firmly solidified the character of the genre. Corelli was born near Bologna, where he revealed a prodigious talent as a violinist. At the age of only 17, he was admitted to Bologna's prestigious Philharmonic Academy, an honor later extended to the 14-year-old Mozart. Around 1675 he moved permanently to Rome, where his playing soon gained him international esteem. Among his many influential Roman patrons was Cardinal Pietro Ottoboni, whose Monday evening concerts presented Italy's leading singers and instrumentalists.

Corelli's music consists primarily of sonatas. It is evidence of the remarkable rise in the importance of instrumental music that he apparently wrote no vocal music at all. His output was small, but very widely distributed in his own day and imitated by composers of many nationalities.

The sonata by Corelli's day was chamber music for one or two melody instruments plus accompaniment. Corelli's own favorite medium was two violins accompanied by harpsichord or organ. The keyboard's bass line was typically doubled by a cello or other instrument of bass range. A work of this type is called a **trio sonata** because there are three distinct lines of music, although a trio sonata is normally played by four instrumentalists. Corelli, like some of his predecessors, strictly distinguished between sonatas meant for use in the church and those intended for concert use, which he termed "chamber sonatas." These latter are dance suites, usually homophonic in texture, with each dance in binary form. Church sonatas typically have four movements that alternate slow and fast tempos. Their music is normally fugal in texture and not so overtly dancelike. Each movement is usually in binary form.

Corelli's Sonata in A Major (c. 1694; Recording 5.6) was the third sonata found in his fourth opus. Publishers in the seventeenth century began to label editions of instrumental music with opus numbers, which ostensibly give a continuous, chronological ordering of a composer's published works and help to identify the pieces that they contain. For some later composers, such as Mozart and Schubert, opus numbers (usually abbreviated *Op.,* followed by an arabic numeral) are incomplete and unreliable as aids to identification. But for Corelli, who wrote a modest amount of music, most of which was published during his lifetime, they are helpful. Publishers, by long-standing convention, issued works in groups of 3, 6, or 12, depending on the length of the pieces. In the first editions of Corelli's sonatas, 12 works make up a complete publication. So we can firmly identify this sonata by adding to its generic title and key the information "Op. 4, No. 3."

This is a typical example of a chamber trio sonata. Its melodic interest is carried by two violins, accompanied, in the performance on Recording 5.6, by harpsichord and cello. The piece consists of four movements, each in binary form and, after an initial prelude, each having the character of a dance. The prelude is slow in tempo and typically intense in its harmonic expressivity. The texture is homophonic, and the two violins toss a succession of short motives back and forth.

**Listening Guide**

**Arcangelo Corelli, Sonata in A Major, Op. 4, No. 3**
Recording 5.6

| | | |
|---|---|---|
| **Prelude** | 0.00 | This opening movement does not explicitly imitate a dance, although it has the binary dance form. Like most of Corelli's binary forms, the opening of the second section resembles the opening of the first section, as both share the same general rhythmic makeup. But the two sections are otherwise independent. When the sections are repeated, the performers on this recording improvise graces on the written melody. |
| **Corrente** | 2.36 | As in most of Corelli's binary forms, the first section moves from the home key (A) to a key five notes higher in an A-major scale (E). The second section reverses this motion, ending in the home key. |
| **Sarabande** | 4.02 | The slow sarabande invites improvised ornamentation, which the players on this recording add on the repeats of both sections. |
| **Gavotte** | 5.39 | The first section of this spirited dance uses a fleeting imitative texture in all three lines; the second section gives the melody primarily to the first violin. |

The second movement is an example of the Italian corrente. The melodic line, presented entirely in the first violin, is geared specifically to the violin. Unlike the music of Josquin's "La Bernardina," it would be hard to play on any other instrument, but its leaps and long-winded phrases are easily handled on the violin. The rhythm has a motoric steadiness created by a continuous flow of short values, which is a rhythmic style that became the norm in late baroque music in fast tempos.

The third movement is a sarabande, which among Italian baroque composers was normally a melodious piece in a slow tempo and in triple meter. The finale is in the spirit of the gavotte, a quick dance in duple meter.

## TOPICS FOR DISCUSSION AND WRITING

**1.** Compare and contrast Gaultier's Gigue in G Major (Recording 5.5) and the Prelude (movement 1) from Corelli's Sonata in A Major (Recording 5.6). Touch on the following points: tempo, overall form, melodic style, rhythm, and general spirit of the music. Which piece seems closer to true dance music?

**2.** The spirit of baroque painting resides in its greater degree of energy, motion, and drama in comparison to painting of the Renaissance. Compare the Venetian church style, as represented by Monteverdi's motet "Domine ad adiuvandum," to selected paintings by Rubens (such as *The Lion Hunt*), seeking the same "baroque" qualities in both. What musical features of Monteverdi's work suggest energy and motion?

**3.** Is Orpheus' lament "Tu se' morta" from Monteverdi's *Orfeo* an example of music of the "second practice"? Monteverdi stated that in music of this type, expression of the text was paramount, even if it necessitated harsh or unusual music. Carefully compare the text of the lament to the music in order to decide.

**4.** Explain the process of variation in Frescobaldi's Canzona "La Vincenti" (Recording 5.4). Describe the fugal subjects of the five major sections, and, as precisely as possible, tell how each differs from and is similar to the initial subject. Take into consideration rhythm, meter, contour, and length.

## ADDITIONAL LISTENING

### Caccini

Monodies from *Le nuove musiche*. The recordings of Alfred Deller (such as Harmonia Mundi France HM 228) are recommended.

### Carissimi

*Jephte* complete. The recording by the Gabrieli Consort and Players, Paul McCreesh, director, is recommended (Meridian CDE 84132). Church music by Carissimi's student Marc-Antoine Charpentier transplanted Carissimi's affective style to France. See especially Charpentier's *Messe de minuit pour Noël,* a charming work that quotes from French Christmas carols.

## Corelli

*Christmas Concerto,* Op. 6, No. 8. The genre of the concerto grosso will be discussed in Chapter 6.

## Frescobaldi

*Fiori musicali.* A monumental collection of organ music intended for use in the Mass. Genres include fugal ricercars and canzone.

## Monteverdi

*L'incoronazione di Poppea.* Monteverdi's last opera.

*Orfeo* complete.

*Vespers of the Blessed Virgin.* This is the 1610 publication in which the motet "Domine ad adiuvandum" is found.

## BIBLIOGRAPHY

Apel, Willi. *The History of Keyboard Music to 1700.* Translated and revised by Hans Tischler. Bloomington: Indiana University Press, 1972.

Arnold, Denis. *Monteverdi.* Master Musicians Series. Revised edition. London: Dent, 1975.

Bukofzer, Manfred. *Music in the Baroque Era: From Monteverdi to Bach.* New York: Norton, 1947.

Grout, Donald J. *A Short History of Opera.* Second edition. New York: Columbia University Press, 1965.

Hammond, Frederick. *Girolamo Frescobaldi.* Cambridge, Mass.: Harvard University Press, 1983.

Newman, William. *The Sonata in the Baroque Era.* Chapel Hill: University of North Carolina Press, 1959.

Palisca, Claude. *Baroque Music.* Third edition. Englewood Cliffs, N.J.: Prentice Hall, 1991.

Pincherle, Marc. *Corelli.* New York: Norton, 1956.

Schrade, Leo. *Monteverdi: Creator of Modern Music.* New York: Norton, 1950.

Smither, Howard. *A History of the Oratorio.* Volume 1: The Baroque Era. Chapel Hill: University of North Carolina Press, 1977.

Strunk, Oliver, ed. *Source Readings in Music History: The Baroque Era.* New York: Norton, 1965.

## NOTE

1. Oliver Strunk, ed. *Source Readings in Music History: The Baroque Era* (New York: Norton, 1965), p. 18.

# 6

## The Late Baroque Period, 1700–1750

## A Royal Concert

*The darkly lit room barely reveals a small but elegant gathering devoted to making and hearing music. The listeners are attentive and clearly charmed by what they hear. Their delight is no doubt increased because the flute soloist is none other than Frederick the Great, King of Prussia, and one of the most powerful rulers in the entire world. The audience has been carefully chosen from among friends of the king, connoisseurs, and illustrious visitors.*

Frederick's accompaniment is provided by a few strings and harpsichord. The latter is played by C. P. E. Bach, son of Johann Sebastian Bach and, in his own right, one of the great musicians of the eighteenth century. At the far left stands Carl Heinrich Graun, the king's director of music and a specialist in operatic composition. Standing at the far right is Johann Joachim Quantz, the king's flute teacher and his favorite composer of flute music. The work that Frederick is playing is almost certainly a concerto either by Quantz or by the king himself, who was equally skilled as an amateur flutist and as a composer.

This painting by Adolf Menzel, called "The Flute Concert" (1852), is a highly realistic depiction of one of the thrice weekly private concerts held in Frederick's palace, Sans Souci, located near Berlin. The lavish rococo decor of the king's music room reflects Frederick's taste for French language and culture. Formalities of manners at these concerts were evidently rigid. Only Quantz was allowed to comment on the king's playing or to express his approval for an especially good performance. Grumbling among the musicians was common. C. P. E. Bach was especially rankled by the lack of recognition of his talent. Although the king rewarded his favorite performers and composers with lavish salaries, Bach was never well paid, in part because he was not always indulgent of the king's limitations as a musician.

*Menzel's picture captures the intensely refined mood of the occasion, but also the decidedly elitist circumstances that surrounded music during the eighteenth century. Common men and women could hear little music outside of the opera theater or the church. Access to music at this time thus reflected the strict social hierarchy of the period. While the operas of George Frideric Handel were enjoyed by a large public audience in London, the magnificent works of a composer such as François Couperin were destined for the enlightenment of a very small circle of aristocrats at the French royal court. Only near the end of the century—the years of the great social upheaval of the French Revolution—did artistic music break out of the confines of palaces such as Sans Souci to become the property of people at large.*

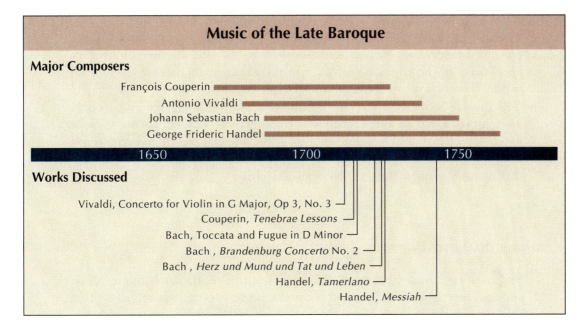

At the turn of the eighteenth century, Italian music reigned supreme every-where in Europe except for France. Its hegemony at this time was comparable to the dominance exerted by Franco-Flemish musicians in the fifteenth century or by German and Austrian composers at the turn of the twentieth century. If we could attend the performance of an opera in a city such as London, Berlin, Madrid, or Munich around the year 1700, it would likely be an opera sung in Italian by Italian singers. Only the French seemed able to resist the attraction of Italian music, and even they could not be entirely immune from its influence.

Curiously, this time of leadership for Italy in matters of music was one of weakness in politics and in the economy. Italy remained divided into numerous duchies, kingdoms, and city-states, most of which were controlled by foreigners. The Kingdoms of Naples and Sicily, which covered the entire southern half of the country, were ruled alternately by Spanish and Austrian kings, and the people of these regions suffered continual economic hardship. Most of the northern half of the country was controlled by Austria, leaving only a few independent city-states.

The determination of the French to have an independent type of music in the baroque period reflects the national consciousness and political might of France during the reign of Louis XIV. Music in France at this time closely

**179**

adhered to the king's own tastes, which ran to dance and theatrical works, chamber pieces, and harpsichord music. The growth in military might of the state of Brandenburg in northern Germany in the late seventeenth century foreshadowed the eventual rise of German-speaking composers in the musical world. The two great titans of late baroque music, George Frideric Handel and Johann Sebastian Bach, were both Germans, although in many works they imitated Italian and French contemporary composers. Their greatness foretells a change in musical geography in the late eighteenth and nineteenth centuries, when German composers would displace both the French and the Italians as the originators of new musical ideas.

## Vivaldi and Late Baroque Italian Music

Let us recall from Chapter 5 the main features of Italian baroque music around the year 1700. Opera had become supremely popular, so much so that its forms and styles were also used for concert works such as oratorios. Music in the church included motets with Latin words and instrumental pieces in a decidedly old-fashioned idiom that emphasized counterpoint and fugue. In concerts, dance music was most important. Composers wrote both suites and sonatas, which consisted similarly of a succession of dancelike movements for a variety of instrumental combinations.

Italian composers of the late baroque period favored opera most of all. This was the genre in which the greatest fame and fortune could be won. Ironically, some of the most successful composers of Italian opera in the late baroque were Germans, such as Handel and Johann Hasse. Italian composers also wrote music for the church, oratorios, and small unstaged operatic-type compositions called **cantatas.**

They also cultivated instrumental music. Around 1700 there emerged a new instrumental genre, the **concerto,** which was destined to endure to the present day. The term *concerto* (pronounced "con-CHAIR-tow") had been in use since the late 1500s. By 1700 it denoted a piece for orchestra, normally featuring one or more instruments as soloists. If there was more than one soloist, the work was termed a **concerto grosso** ("large concerto"). There was also a related type of music, now called the *orchestral concerto,* that had no soloists per se but in which motives were passed back and forth among various instruments of the orchestra. The overall form of the concerto quickly became standardized as three movements. The first was in a fast tempo, the second was slow (and sometimes very brief), and the finale was again fast.

The great master of the baroque concerto was Antonio Vivaldi (1678–1741). He was born in Venice, the son of a professional violinist who taught his son this instrument. He was ordained a priest in 1703, although his career was subsequently devoted almost solely to music. In that same year he became a teacher of violin at the Ospedale della Pietà, one of a number of remarkable institutions then existing in Venice. These orphanages for girls developed such reputations for their musical instruction that they became virtually conservatories. Vivaldi brought the level of musical performance at Pietà to a very high level, so much so that its concerts were internationally esteemed. He was made its musical director in 1735.

*This engraving of Antonio Vivaldi is based on a portrait by the Dutch engraver Morellon de La Cave, made about 1725.*

Although Vivaldi's early reputation was based on his publications of sonatas and concertos, he turned eventually to the career of an opera composer, at which he had only mixed success. In his later years, he traveled to promote his operas, and he died in Vienna, where, like Mozart after him, he was buried in an unmarked, common grave.

Vivaldi's music includes more than 20 operas, today little known, plus cantatas, church music, and trio sonatas. He is most famous for his concertos, of which he wrote over 500. These are mainly solo concertos, works that feature a single instrument with orchestral accompaniment. He also wrote concerti grossi and orchestral concertos (which he often called *sinfonie*). Since Vivaldi himself was a virtuoso on the violin, it is no surprise that most of his concertos feature this instrument, but he also wrote such works for cello, flute, oboe, bassoon, and other instruments.

Vivaldi's collection of 12 concertos, opus 3, first published in Amsterdam in 1711 under the title *L'estro armonico* (*Harmonic Inspiration*), vaulted him to fame as a composer of instrumental music. The wide influence of the works in this collection is shown by the attention given them by J. S. Bach, who, shortly after they appeared, rewrote no fewer than six of them for other media. The concertos of Vivaldi's opus 3 feature the violin, either alone or in groups of up to four. The orchestra that accompanied these soloists was probably flexible in size and makeup, though far smaller and more intimate than the modern symphony orchestra. An eighteenth-century performance of the concertos of opus 3 might have involved no more than nine performers: four violinists (from which the soloists were drawn), two violas, one cello, a harpsichord playing the basso continuo, and a string bass doubling the lowest line of the harpsichord part. The extent to which soloists were intended by Vivaldi to improvise on their written music is uncertain, but they most likely did, especially in the slow movements.

Not only did Vivaldi establish the three-movement form as the norm for concertos, but he also perfected a special plan for the first movements of these works, now called *ritornello form.* We encountered the term *ritornello* in Monteverdi's opera *Orfeo.* In that work it referred to a brief instrumental passage that periodically returned to bind together a scene mainly devoted to singing. Here its usage is similar since one or more melodies heard at the beginning of a movement periodically return amid contrasting melodic ideas. The ritornello form was widely imitated by all of the major composers of concertos in the late baroque period. It was used as well in operatic arias of the same time, and its vestiges remained even in the concertos of later eras.

The ritornello form, like all standard musical plans, was not used by composers in a doctrinaire manner, but freely, as suggested by the nature of melodic materials in a specific piece. A movement using this form begins with the entire orchestra playing an unbroken series of motives, all in the home key. There follows an alternation of passages for the solo instrument, playing either new melodies or ones already heard in the opening section, and passages for the full orchestra, playing a few of the initial motives. These quickly move into new keys, returning to the home key in the last one or two sections.

The first movement of Vivaldi's Concerto for Violin and Orchestra in G Major, Op. 3, No. 3 (Recording 6.1), exemplifies this composer's early application of the ritornello principle. The concerto itself has the typical three movements, in the sequence fast-slow-fast, with each movement about the same length. The first movement is subdivided into nine short sections. It begins with the full orchestra, then alternates between sections for orchestra and for the solo violin with a light accompaniment. The initial section of orchestral music consists of a chain of four short motives, some of which return in each successive orchestral section. Between these returning passages, the solo instrument plays its own melodies. Rhythms in this music, which is in a fast tempo, have the typical late-baroque motoric quality, driving ahead in even, short values. So great is the rhythmic continuity that it does not allow for any major cadences or other pauses in the motion, except at the very end of the movement.

**Listening Guide**

**Antonio Vivaldi, Concerto for Violin and Orchestra in G Major, Op. 3, No. 3**
Recording 6.1

| | | |
|---|---|---|
| **A** (orchestra) | 0.00 | Four motives are played in succession, all in the home key of G. Here is the first of these four: |

*[musical notation]*

| | | |
|---|---|---|
| **B** (solo violin) | 0.22 | The featured violin plays a new melody, accompanied lightly by strings: |

*[musical notation]*

| | | |
|---|---|---|
| **A'** (orchestra) | 0.29 | The full orchestra plays the first two motives from the opening passage; then new melodic material leads to the new key of D major. |
| **C** (solo violin) | 0.43 | The violin plays another new melody, in the key of D. |
| **A'** (orchestra) | 0.57 | Again the orchestra plays the first two motives of the opening passage, only now in D major. Then new melodies lead to the next key, B minor. |
| **B'** (solo violin) | 1.12 | The violinist now plays an extended version of the melody of the first solo passage. |
| **A'** (orchestra) | 1.27 | The orchestra plays the first orchestral motive three times in succession, first in B minor, then in D major, and finally in the home key of G major. |
| **B** (solo violin) | 1.39 | An exact repeat of the first solo section. |
| **A'** (orchestra) | 1.47 | The orchestra concludes with the fourth and first motives from the opening passage. |

# *François Couperin and the French Style*

French composers of the late baroque period also cultivated instrumental music, although they turned more often to the intimate, courtly genres of chamber music or solo harpsichord dances rather than to the concerto, which suggested a public forum. French taste also relished lavish ballets and a distinctive style of opera. A vigorous tradition of music for the church also flourished in France. The popularity of lute playing was gradually superseded during the baroque period by a brilliant school of harpsichord composition and performance centered at the French royal court. The harpsichordists adopted and extended the lutenists' art: They emphasized dances in a refined and ornamental style, and they cultivated a type of homophonic texture that had delicately fleeting moments of polyphony.

A genre of sacred music that was especially popular in France was the *Tenebrae lesson.* Tenebrae (Latin for "darkness") is a service in the Christian church celebrated on the three days before Easter. It takes its name from the ancient tradition of gradually extinguishing candles and leaving the church in darkness. In some of the Tenebrae services, verses from the Old Testament book of Lamentations, attributed to Jeremiah, are chanted or read (hence the term *lesson,* from the Latin *lectio,* "reading"). Composers since the early Renaissance had used these texts from Lamentations and their chants to create magnificent choral works. By the late baroque period, such pieces had become very popular in France, where audiences, starved for good singing by the closure of the opera theaters during Lent, flocked to church to hear their favorite singers perform during Tenebrae.

The greatest such composition—indeed, one of the greatest works in all of baroque music—is the set of *Tenebrae Lessons* by François Couperin (1668–1733). Couperin was born in Paris to a distinguished family of musicians. In 1693, he was appointed to the court of Louis XIV, whom he served as organist, harpsichordist, and composer until the

*François Couperin is depicted in his elegant courtly attire, confident and assured of his high position and accomplishment. The 1735 engraving is based on a portrait by André Boüys.*

**184**

king's death in 1715. His late years were devoted to composing, arranging to have his music published, and teaching harpsichord. Couperin's music consists primarily of harpsichord suites, church music, and ensemble sonatas, these last inspired by the trio sonatas of Corelli. His works combine both the distinctive features of the French baroque style and Italian elements. In the foreword to his dance suites *Les goûts réunis* (1724), he emphasized the compatibility of both types of music and urged an acceptance of the Italian style:

> The Italian taste and the French taste have long been separate in France in the domain of music. For my part, I have always valued things that are worthy of value, regardless of author or nationality, and the first Italian sonatas that appeared in Paris thirty years ago committed, to my mind, no errors.[1]

Couperin's *Tenebrae Lessons* (c. 1714) embody the union of the French and Italian tastes. From Italy come their intensity of expression, recitative and aria styles of singing, and medium of one or two solo voices accompanied by basso continuo. From the French style Couperin adopts a highly refined delicacy and heavily ornamented melodic line. Although Couperin stated that he had composed sets of lessons for all three days before Easter, only the first set survives. It consists of three separate sections, each having four or five verses from Lamentations.

On Recording 6.2 we hear the introduction and the first two verses of the first section. The music calls for one singer (a countertenor on this recording) and thorough bass, realized here by organ, bass viol, and lute. Couperin's melodic idiom is neither in the recitative nor in the aria styles as they existed in early baroque opera. Instead, it occupies a position midway between these two ways of singing, a compromise often called **arioso.** Like recitative, its rhythm is closely related to the rhythms of speech, and it also uses the expressive dissonances, leaps, and sequences that typified early Italian recitative. But its chords are not so sustained, and its melodic contour is more tuneful than recitative, although less so than in an aria such as "Vi ricorda" from *Orfeo.* Couperin's expressive arioso most resembles the melodic idiom of Caccini's monodies, works of which Couperin must surely have been aware.

In the opening sections, Couperin's melody is a paraphrase of the Gregorian chant that was traditionally used to sing the same words, to which he has added extra notes and melodic ornaments plus a regular rhythm and expressive harmonization. Beginning with the text "Quomodo sedet sola civitas," the melodic invention is freed from the chant.

**Listening Guide**

## François Couperin, *Leçons de ténèbres,* first lesson, opening verses
Recording 6.2

| | |
|---|---|
| *Incipit Lamentatio Jeremiae Prophetae.* | Here begins the lamentation of Jeremiah the Prophet. |
| ALEPH. *Quomodo sedet sola civitas plena populo: facta est quasi vidua domina Gentium: princeps provinciarum facta est sub tributo.* | ALEPH. How solitary lies the city, once so full of people! Once great among nations, now become a widow; once queen among provinces, now put to forced labor. |
| BETH. *Plorans ploravit in nocte, et lacrimae ejus in maxillis ejus: non est qui consoletur eam ex omnibus caris ejus. Omnes amici ejus spreverunt eam, et facti sunt ei inimici.* | BETH. Bitterly she weeps in the night, tears run down her cheeks; she has no one to bring her comfort among all that love her; all her friends turned traitor and became her enemies.[2] |

| | | |
|---|---|---|
| **Introduction** | 0.00 | The phrase "Incipit Lamentatio" is set to a melodic paraphrase of chant, coming to a full cadence in the home key of D major. |
| **Aleph** | 0.40 | The Hebrew letter *aleph* identifies the first poetic verse. Couperin sets the letter to music to form an independent musical section. Its melody is a paraphrase of chant, ornamented in the extreme. |
| **Verse 1** | 1.01 | This section of text, beginning "Quomodo sedet sola civitas," is arialike in its tunefulness and regular rhythm. Although the text is covered twice in succession, the music is different the second time. |
| **Beth** | 3.05 | *Beth* is the second letter of the Hebrew alphabet, used to identify the second verse of Lamentations. Its music is comparable in its florid style to that for *aleph.* |
| **Verse 2** | 4.12 | These words, beginning "Plorans ploravit," contain the heightened emotion desired by Italian composers of the second practice. And Couperin's treatment of them is worthy of Monteverdi or Caris- |

simi as he turns to the minor mode and explores the resources of dissonance, insistent textual repetition, and movement by ascending semitones to express their poignancy.

**Recitative**     6.31     On the words in the second verse "omnes amici," Couperin begins a new section, which he labels *recitative.* The melody, however, is virtually indistinguishable in style from the foregoing passages.

# Johann Sebastian Bach

In Johann Sebastian Bach (1685–1750) we encounter one of the greatest figures in Western music. As much as any composer in history, his work embodies a universal message that has overcome the passage of time and the vicissitudes of musical taste to inspire and delight generations of listeners.

Bach's music contains a summation of earlier baroque styles, and it also leads in new directions. He wrote in virtually all of the existing genres of his day, with the exception of opera, and, in addition to contributing to Lutheran church music, he also assimilated elements from French and Italian composition. In his last decades, Bach was keenly aware that the baroque style seemed to many of his contemporaries to be old-fashioned, even at times incomprehensible, especially when compared to the new and facile taste of the mid-eighteenth century. Perhaps for this reason, he left behind several encyclopedic collections of music that preserve in a monumental and enduring manner the compositional art of the Renaissance and the baroque.

## Bach's Life and Works

Bach's life and career were intimately connected with the music that he composed, since he usually concentrated on genres that were demanded by the terms of his employment. He was born in 1685 to a family of musicians in the village of Eisenach, in east-central Germany. In 1703 he became organist and choirmaster at the Lutheran church in Arnstadt, near his place of birth. Records of his four years in this position show that the young genius did not always conform to the usual expectations made of a church musician. Given a four-week leave to travel to the north to hear the great organist Dietrich Buxtehude, he stayed away for four months. And he appears to have taken delight in befuddling the Arnstadt churchgoers with his organ playing. A document by the church fathers notes:

> [Bach is reproved] for having hitherto made many curious variations in the hymn, and for mingling many strange tones in it, which has confused the congregation. In the future, if he wishes to introduce a wandering key, he must hold it out, and not turn too quickly to something else; or, as has hitherto been his habit, even play in a conflicting key.[3]

In 1707, Bach moved to Mühlhausen, where he continued his work as a church musician. Here he wrote his earliest surviving vocal pieces for the Lutheran service. His reputation as a virtuoso performer on the organ continued to grow, and in the following year, he was appointed organist to the court of a German state whose seat was in Weimar. He remained there until 1717, during which time he wrote some of his most famous works for the organ. He also continued to compose choral music for the church, and at this time he apparently made an intensive study of modern Italian works, especially those of Vivaldi.

The friction with his employers that marked his earlier years continued in Weimar. When he was invited to become the director of music at the court of Anhalt-Cöthen in 1717, he forcefully demanded his release, so forcefully, in fact, that he was made by his Weimar patron to serve a month in jail. But finally his release was granted and he moved to the small town of Cöthen to serve an appreciative and music-loving prince. His five years in Cöthen, where his duties were primarily confined to leading the small, virtuosic court orchestra, were among his happiest. For this ensemble Bach wrote some of his greatest instrumental music, including the six *Brandenburg Concertos.*

But after 1721 his patron's interest in music seems to have waned, and in 1723 he moved to the city of Leipzig to become director of music and "cantor" of the city's churches. His duties there were extensive. He was expected every week to provide choral and orchestral music for the city's two largest churches, whose performers he also had to rehearse and conduct. Furthermore, he taught music and Latin at the choir school attached to the Church of Saint Thomas. In Leipzig, Bach at first devoted himself to the composition of church choral music, demanded by the terms of his position, but he later stepped back from his grueling regimen to turn his interests to projects of a more monumental nature.

At the time of his death in Leipzig in 1750, Bach had achieved a reputation as an organist, a composer for keyboard, and a master of fugal composition. But the full extent and significance of his work were not widely known. Only in the mid-nineteenth century was his music revived and at last appreciated for its true greatness. A complete edition of his scores was not available until 1900. Since relatively little of his music was published during his own lifetime, opus numbers cannot be used to identify his works. Musicians instead use well-known titles or catalog numbers from Wolfgang Schmieder's *Bach-Werke-Verzeichnis* (*Catalog of Bach's Works*), abbreviated **BWV**.

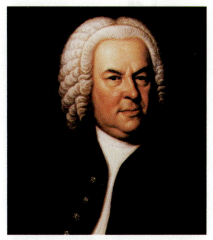

*This 1746 portrait of J. S. Bach by Elias Haussmann is considered the most authentic rendering of the composer. Bach is portrayed as the thoroughly accomplished artist.*

Although it is likely that many pieces of Bach are permanently lost, his surviving corpus of music is immense. It may be divided by medium into three categories: pieces for keyboard (primarily organ or harpsichord), other instrumental music, and works for voices (almost all of which are for the church). His keyboard pieces include many of the same genres found in the early baroque period, such as fugal compositions and dance suites. His organ music is often built around preexistent Lutheran hymns, and he also made keyboard arrangements of the music of other composers.

His chamber and orchestral works include concertos, suites of dances, and sonatas. Late in his life he wrote two monumental sets of fugues and canons, *The Musical Offering* (1747) and *Art of the Fugue* (1750, incomplete), for which he did not fully specify instrumentation. These are played nowadays by many different ensembles of instruments. Bach's vocal music consists primarily of pieces for chorus, solo voices, and orchestra intended to be sung in Lutheran services of worship.

### Bach's Church Cantatas

Martin Luther's reform of Catholicism had a far-reaching impact on church music in the German lands that embraced his ideas. With his rejection of the Latin Mass came the elimination of Gregorian chants. Luther recommended an alternative service of worship, but he made no demand that it be adopted by all congregations who followed his reforms. He urged that the services, whatever their form, be brought closer to the interests and understanding of the congregation. The Lutheran services were accordingly celebrated in the vernacular, and the congregation was encouraged to take part,

**189**

rather than simply look on. The Latin Mass continued to provide a model for the main Lutheran service, which, like the Mass, contained prayers, readings from the Bible, and a celebration of the Holy Communion. Unlike the Mass, however, it normally contained a lengthy sermon and congregational singing of hymns, called *chorales.*

By Bach's day it had become a tradition in most Lutheran parishes for the choir to sing an elaborate piece of music between the Gospel reading and the sermon. We now call such music a *cantata,* although this term was rarely used by Bach. The German church cantata uses religious texts, and its music calls for a chorus, often solo voices, and an accompaniment of organ or small orchestra. Some of Bach's cantatas consist of operalike successions of arias and recitatives, but in most ways they have little in common with Italian operatic music.

About 200 of Bach's church cantatas still exist. In general, these are written for chorus, solo voices, and a small orchestra. In overall form, they consist of several movements, which are devoted to solo singing, small groups of singers, and choruses, all with orchestral accompaniment. Bach himself probably assembled the words of many of the cantatas, drawing on biblical passages and hymn texts, although he sometimes chose religious poetry that was written and published expressly for the use of cantata composers.

Thanks to letters and other surviving documents, we are relatively well informed about Bach's own performing practices in these works. His choir consisted entirely of men and boys, usually three singers to a line. The soloists were drawn from the choir, and a small orchestra was put together from the town's string and wind players. Bach also composed cantatalike pieces called *oratorios* for the major holidays of Christmas and Easter and *passions* for Good Friday. He also wrote choral music to Latin words associated with the Catholic liturgy. His *Magnificat* was used in the Lutheran service on high feasts, and he also composed movements from the Latin Mass ordinary. His stirring B-minor Mass is a late composition, partly assembled from preexistent works. It appears to be a monumental reflection on the tradition of Mass composition rather than a work written for church use.

Although no one cantata can exemplify Bach's greatly varied choral music, the festive *Herz und Mund und Tat und Leben (Heart and Mouth and Deed and Life,* BWV 147) is reasonably typical. Movements of this cantata were composed during the Weimar period, and it was expanded in 1723 for use during Bach's first year in Leipzig. It is an unusually lengthy work, consisting of ten movements, of which the last four were probably performed after the sermon. Like almost all of Bach's cantatas, it was written for a specific occasion in the church year, in this case the Feast of the Visitation. This is the day

**Johann Sebastian Bach,** *Herz und Mund und Tat und Leben,*
**BWV 147, movement 6: "Wohl mir, daß ich Jesum habe"**
Recording 6.3

| | |
|---|---|
| *Wohl mir, daß ich Jesum habe,* | It is well that I have Jesus; |
| *o wie feste halt' ich ihn,* | O how firmly do I hold Him, |
| *daß er mir mein Herze labe,* | for He refreshes my heart, |
| *wenn ich krank und traurig bin.* | when I am ill and sad. |
| | |
| *Jesum hab' ich, der mich liebet* | I have Jesus, who loves me |
| *und sich mir zu eigen giebet,* | and gives Himself for me; |
| *ach drum lass' ich Jesum nicht,* | so I cannot leave Jesus, |
| *wenn mir gleich mein Herze bricht.* | even if my heart should break. |

**A**   0.00   The first two lines of text constitute the first unit of the hymn, which is preceded by an introductory phrase in the strings and oboes. Their melody is based on the first phrase of the hymn:

(Asterisks indicate the notes of the hymn appearing in the paraphrased melody.)

**A**   0.30   The music of the first two lines is repeated to the second two.

**B**   1.12   The remainder of the text is set to four short hymn phrases, around which the violins continue to intone their gentle soliloquy.

when the church celebrates the story told in the first chapter of the Gospel according to Luke of Mary's visit to her cousin Elizabeth.

The ten movements contain arias, recitatives, and choruses. The sixth movement (Recording 6.3) is especially ingenious, for here Bach borrows a stanza of the well-known hymn "Jesu, meiner Seelen Wonne" ("Jesu, Joy of Man's Desiring") and its tune to create music of inspiring originality. His treatment is at once deceptively simple and subtly elaborate. The choir sings the hymn in an unadorned manner, while the violins and oboes weave around and between its phrases a melody of great warmth and beauty in a gentle rocking rhythm. This melody is itself a paraphrase of the hymn tune, which Bach creates by adding notes to the preexistent melody and giving it a quicker rhythm and a different spirit. The result is a dialogue between the exquisite instrumental melody and the straightforward hymn, above which it wafts like a halo.

## Bach's Chamber and Orchestral Music

This division of Bach's oeuvre contains some of his most original musical ideas. He was evidently not interested in simple imitations of Italian genres, although he was intimately familiar with them. In his instrumental music, Bach tended, instead, to experiment with reinterpretations of the customary types of music that he had inherited from his predecessors. A concerto by Bach's day, for example, suggested the medium of orchestra plus featured instrument. But Bach wrote a so-called *Italian Concerto* for the medium of harpsichord alone. The form of the Vivaldian concerto is preserved, and its texture of soloist plus accompaniment is ingeniously imitated. Trio sonatas were works for three or more instruments, but Bach experimented with trio sonatas played by an organ alone. He also composed music for a single melody instrument in which he found ways to suggest a texture having both melody and accompaniment.

Bach composed the six *Brandenburg Concertos* during his years in Cöthen, during which he worked as conductor of a small court orchestra. Like most court ensembles in the baroque period, the orchestra in Cöthen was divided between soloists and group players. The soloists were presumably more accomplished on their instruments and better paid for their services. In the Cöthen orchestra these leading performers included a trumpeter, string players, and a few woodwind players. It is likely that Bach himself played the viola with the soloists or, as needed, the harpsichord.

In March 1721, a manuscript containing six concertos by Bach was forwarded to Christian Ludwig, the margrave of Brandenburg. Bach's music may have fulfilled a commission received earlier. The concertos, which were almost certainly written earlier for the Cöthen orchestra, fall into two types. Numbers 2, 4, and 5 are concerti grossi, since they have more than one featured soloist. The remaining three are examples of the orchestral concerto, mentioned earlier in reference to the works of Vivaldi. In these pieces, there is no soloist or solo group per se, although the overall form of the concerto is maintained. In these six concertos, Bach makes an exuberant use of the orchestra and of the expressive and virtuosic potential of his players. The fifth concerto is notable for its soloistic treatment of the harpsichord, certainly a showpiece for Bach himself. The sixth concerto is a study in unusual orchestral sonorities, since the ensemble consists of dark sounding violas, viols, and cellos.

*Brandenburg Concerto* No. 2 (c. 1721) is a classic example of the concerto grosso, and it also reveals Bach's tendency to push against the technical limits of the instruments. The soloists in this three-movement work consist of trumpet, recorder, oboe, and violin, and the orchestra adds strings and harpsichord. Of the four soloists, the trumpet is clearly the most prominent. Bach wrote music for this instrument in an exceedingly high register, demanding such agility and strength as to be a complex challenge to the player. The first movement (Recording 6.4) uses the Vivaldian ritornello form. But its elements are much more difficult to follow than in Vivaldi's G-major Concerto due to the similarity between solo and orchestral melodies. Bach often ac-

**Listening Guide**

**Johann Sebastian Bach,** *Brandenburg Concerto* **No. 2, BWV 1047, first movement**
Recording 6.4

**Orchestra**   0.00   The full orchestra (strings, harpsichord basso continuo, and solo group) plays a chain of short motives. Note that the rhythmic style has the typical late baroque motoric quality.

**Soloists**   0.20   Each of the four soloists plays a brief figure, illustrated here, separated by recurrences of the first of the orchestra's motives.

**Continuation**   0.57   Short orchestral ritornello passages alternate with solo passages, which either return to the motive shown above or to ritornello motives. The key moves away from the home key of F, returning to it near the end.

## Is There Music by Bach Waiting to Be Discovered?

*Bach's manuscript for his "Wir Christenleut" for organ, BWV 612.*

companies the four solo instruments with light orchestral music, making these passages very similar to those for full orchestra. But the basic formal plan is nevertheless the same as in Vivaldi's concerto: The full orchestra begins with a string of motives, leading to a passage for soloists, who play a new melody. The orchestral ritornello themes then alternate with solo passages, moving away from the home key and returning to it at the end.

### Music for Solo Organ and Harpsichord

In his own day, Bach was better known as a virtuoso organist than as a composer. His prowess as a performer was truly legendary. A contemporary named Constantin Bellermann recalled Bach's playing of the pedals of the instrument as the equal of others' use of the hands:

**194**

How much music did Bach actually write? Are there important works whose manuscripts are still to be discovered? These questions pique the curiosity of all lovers of his music. For a composer like Bach, most of whose music was not published until long after his death, it is indeed plausible that manuscripts may still exist that contain treasures of his music that are as yet totally unknown.

Shortly after his death in 1750, Bach's son C. P. E. Bach wrote a detailed obituary containing an enumeration of his father's compositions. He mentions "five full years of church pieces, for all the Sundays and holidays" and "five Passions." But what became of this music? At present only about half this number of church pieces are known to exist, and only two authentic Passions. Following his death, Bach's manuscripts were divided among his sons. Most went to Wilhelm Friedemann Bach, with disastrous consequences for the history of music. To pay his bills, he sold many of them, and their whereabouts have never been traced.

But Bach's music continues to resurface, although with tantalizing slowness and always under a cloud of controversy. The most startling recent "discovery" was made in 1984 by the Harvard Bach scholar Christoph Wolff, who found in the Yale Music Library a manuscript containing 33 organ works credited to Bach. After closely examining the music, Wolff declared, with considerable fanfare, that they were authentic. They are all pieces that contain Lutheran hymn tunes and appear to relate closely to Bach's early style as a composer.

But are they by Bach? Connoisseurs and specialists in his music are not uniformly certain. The manuscript was not copied by Bach himself but by someone probably after Bach's death. Whoever wrote out the music in this manuscript attributed it clearly enough to Bach, but could this be a fraud? Attributing music by minor composers to major ones has been done for centuries. The popular eighteenth-century composer Giovanni Pergolesi, for example, who died at the age of only 26, was said to have composed more music after he died than before on account of the number of pieces that were fraudulently ascribed to him.

It is likely that the new organ pieces will forever remain a source of controversy. Since they are now recorded, music lovers can form their own opinions.

He can by the use of his feet alone (while his fingers do either nothing or something else) achieve such an admirable, agitated, and rapid concord of sounds on the church organ that others would seem unable to imitate it even with their fingers. When he was called from Leipzig to Cassel to pronounce an organ properly restored, he ran over the pedals with this same facility, as if his feet had wings, making the organ resound with such fullness, and so penetrate the ears of those present like a thunderbolt, that Frederick, the legitimate hereditary Prince of Cassel, admired him with such astonishment that he drew a ring with a precious stone from his finger and gave it to Bach as soon as the sound had died away. If Bach earned such a gift for the agility of his feet, what, I ask, would the Prince have given him if he had called his hands into service as well?[4]

In Bach's day, the organ was a highly developed instrument found in most Lutheran churches. It was rich in different sonorities, with a characteristic **chiff,** a spitting sound at the onset of a note, and a low wind pressure that rendered a bright but relatively light sound. Organ music was frequently called for in the Lutheran service of worship: The organist played short pieces at various points, some of which incorporated hymn tunes and others of which were freely invented.

Bach composed both types, and his organ music stands today at the center of the repertory for the instrument. Over 160 pieces use preexistent hymn tunes, and among the others will be found many inspiring fugues. These works are often preceded by preludes in a homophonic texture. Bach also wrote variations and arrangements of music by other composers. His harpsichord music is similarly diverse. Most of the larger collections are devoted to dance music, including the *English Suites, French Suites,* "Partitas," and the *French Overture* (a suite despite its curious title), plus a massive set of variations called the *Goldberg Variations.*

The brilliance and drama of Bach's organ music are evident in his Toccata and Fugue in D Minor, BWV 565. The **toccata** (from the Italian *toccare,* "to touch") is a genre of instrumental piece, first appearing in the sixteenth century. It is characterized by a free, improvisatory spirit and by impetuous scales and chords. Bach often linked together toccatas and fugues in the same key which, as in BWV 565, share similar melodic materials. The date of this work is unknown, but it is thought to be an early composition.

The first section, the toccata, contains some of Bach's most powerful ideas. He creates the impression that the organist is improvising, since the music consists of a series of very different motives with little apparent connection among them. These are punctuated by silences in which the player seems to be contemplating the next phrase. The ideas are often spun out in sequences, in scalar lines, and in massive chords. The nature of this music, combined with the passionate key of D minor, creates a powerful sense of drama and of the unexpected.

At 2.28 the toccata draws to a close at a cadence, and the fugue begins straightaway. The term *fugue* has been used in this book so far to designate a texture of imitative polyphony (see Chapter 1). But in Bach's day it had also come to be a genre of music, begun in imitative polyphony, and also having an established overall form. A fugue normally begins with an **exposition.** This is a passage encountered at the beginning of the work in which each line of the piece successively imitates an initial basic melody, called a *subject.* For example, the fugue of BWV 565 has four distinct lines. The organist plays three of these with the hands and the fourth with the feet.

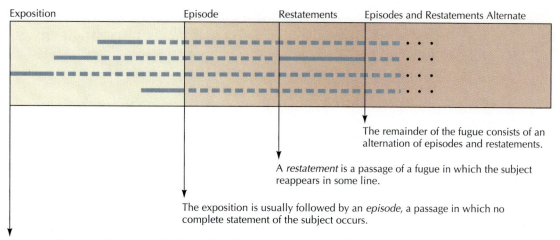

| Exposition | Episode | Restatements | Episodes and Restatements Alternate |

The remainder of the fugue consists of an alternation of episodes and restatements.

A *restatement* is a passage of a fugue in which the subject reappears in some line.

The exposition is usually followed by an *episode*, a passage in which no complete statement of the subject occurs.

The *exposition* is the first section of a fugue. Here the principal melody (called the *subject* and shown above by a solid line) is stated successively in each line. After its initial statement of the subject, each line continues with a polyphonic melody (shown by broken lines) that is not strictly imitative. Note that this diagram is not drawn to scale in terms of durations of the different sections.

**Figure 6.1**   *The basic elements of a Bach fugue in four lines.*

The exposition, which lasts from 2.29 to 3.30, begins monophonically with a concise subject shown in the Listening Guide. Just as this melody ends, it is imitated in a second line, which is distinguished from the first by a higher register. While the second line imitates the opening melody, the first line continues in free polyphony. These two lines continue until 2.53, when a third line, higher even than the second, enters with the subject; at 3.25, following more free polyphony in three strata, the fourth and final line appears. It is in the low register of the instrument, and it too begins with a statement of the subject.

The exposition ends when the last line of the work (in this case the fourth line) has completed its statement of the subject. In a Bach fugue, the next passage will normally be an **episode.** This is a passage of a fugue in which there is no complete appearance of the subject. The remainder of the work is an alternation of episodes and **restatements,** which are passages in which at least one line contains a complete reappearance of the subject. Figure 6.1 summarizes the form of a typical Bach fugue in four lines.

The final cadence of the D-minor Fugue is interrupted by a dramatic concluding passage that returns to the unpredictable, improvisatory spirit of the opening. Bach marks the beginning of this conclusion "recitativo"—enigmatically, since the melody is not particularly recitational. Yet the entire piece is so passionately rhetorical that Bach's reference to opera is nonetheless apposite.

## *L*istening *G*uide

**Johann Sebastian Bach, Toccata and Fugue in D Minor, BWV 565**
Recording 6.5

| | | |
|---|---|---|
| **Toccata** | 0.00 | The melodic ideas are made to seem unplanned and improvisatory, hence all the more dramatic. |
| **Fugue: Exposition** | 2.29 | The fugal subject is derived from the opening motive of the toccata, as shown here: |

(Asterisks identify notes in the subject from the opening motive.)
The fugue is in four lines, separated from one another by register.

| | | |
|---|---|---|
| **Episodes and Restatements** | 3.30 | These passages alternate, with an emphasis on episodes. |
| **"Recitativo"** | 6.38 | The concluding passage returns to the free and dramatic spirit of the opening, dispelling the intricate complexity of the fugue by a turn to dramatic rhetoric. |

# *G*eorge *F*rideric *H*andel

The lives and careers of Bach and Handel make a revealing comparison, since they exemplify the alternatives facing leading German musicians of the late baroque period. While Bach remained his entire life on German soil, devoting himself to the career of a church musician, Handel traveled across Europe, composing whatever types of music were most in demand and amassing an international reputation.

## Handel's Life and Works

The early years of Handel's life are remarkably similar to those of Bach. Handel was born in 1685 in Halle, scarcely more than 70 miles from Eisenach and in the same year as Bach. Both became string players and virtuoso organists. But soon their careers took entirely different directions. Handel received a university education, which Bach lacked, and in 1703 he moved to Italy to advance his education and his career. His success as a composer of Italian music—at this time including sonatas, cantatas, oratorios, and two operas—led to his appointment in 1710 to the court of Georg Ludwig, elector of Hanover. By then Handel was intent on making his reputation as a composer of Italian opera, which was in demand throughout Europe. He visited London to oversee productions of his operas, and in 1712 decided to remain there, not even petitioning his patron to be released from his former service.

*Thomas Hudson's portrait of George Frideric Handel, made three years before the composer's death in 1759, shows Handel in a solemn guise.*

As fate would have it, Georg Ludwig two years later ascended the English throne as King George I. But all was soon forgiven between Handel and the king. Handel lived on in London primarily as a free artist, working periodically for English nobility but primarily managing a commercial opera theater that mounted Italian works. By the late 1720s, popular taste for this repertory was fast waning, and in the 1730s he turned his attention to the composition of English-language oratorios. These proved immensely successful and have remained so ever since. Handel died in London in 1759 and is buried in Westminster Abbey.

His principal compositions are 40-odd operas, almost all written to Italian texts, and English oratorios. He also wrote Anglican church music, Italian cantatas, and, among the instrumental genres, keyboard music, sonatas, concertos, and suites. In this last category are found his ever-popular *Water Music* and *Royal Fireworks Music* for orchestra. Handel, much more than Bach, is representative of his secular and cosmopolitan age. Other than his late oratorios, his music is overwhelmingly secular and eclectic in its mixture of German, French, English, and Italian elements. His music is generally more accessible than Bach's and more attuned to the tastes of the eighteenth century, which admired Handel's clear melodiousness, his translucent textures, and his probing of the drama of human emotions.

## Handel and Late-Baroque Italian Opera

Italian opera by 1700 was a far cry from the experimental, courtly genre of Peri and Monteverdi. In the hands of composers such as Alessandro Scarlatti (1660–1725) and Handel, it had become an artificial, highly conventionalized, and decidedly commercial genre. It relied for its impact most of all on the expressive skills of great singers. Opera texts, called **libretti,** dealt typically with stories from history, embellished to project complicated tales of love, replete with exaggerated expressions of emotion. For musical reasons, all of the leading roles, both male and female, were usually sung by voices in the natural range of female singers. Men's roles were normally sung by castrati or sometimes by women dressed as men.

An opera libretto of this time normally had three acts and, in each, a long succession of scenes. Each scene usually consisted musically of a recitative passage, often introduced by orchestral music, and of an aria or a duet. After this musical high point, the singers left the stage—it was hoped, to applause.

The music that made up a late baroque opera resembled early opera in media but not in style. There were still instrumental passages, solo singing, ensembles such as duets, and an occasional chorus, but these were very different from their seventeenth-century counterparts. An opera in Handel's day normally began with an **overture** (called a *sinfonia* in Italian operas). This was played by the orchestra alone, which consisted by this time of a small group of strings, woodwinds, brass, and harpsichord. Recitatives had by and large lost the expressive, passionate quality found in Monteverdi. Instead, they were primarily opportunities for the characters to push the plot forward using a very speechlike declamation, accompanied solely by the harpsichord. Italian audiences of the day were famous for seeking other diversions during the recitatives! Choruses and vocal ensembles other than duets were uncommon.

The musical high points of opera were concentrated in the arias, which had become tuneful, often virtuosic, numbers for solo voice accompanied by orchestra. The drama during the arias was static, since the words, usually written as formal poetry in two stanzas, dwelt single-mindedly on an emotion that motivated the character at that point. Although the tempo and the spirit of arias were varied, reflecting the emotional situation of the character singing, their forms were almost invariably ternary. The first stanza of poetry was customarily sung to a section of music ended by a full cadence. The second stanza received contrasting music, also ending in a clear cadence. At this point, the composer simply entered the instruction *da capo* ("from the beginning") into the music, which instructed the performer to repeat the first section, usually with the addition of improvised vocal embellishments. The **da capo arias** of the late baroque often exhibited concertolike elements as well. In an aria of this type, the solo singer alternated with the orchestra to create a ritornello form.

Handel's opera *Tamerlano* was written in 1724 and enjoyed modest success in performances with Handel's own company at the King's Theatre in the Haymarket. The libretto (in Italian) was constructed by Nicola Haym, the official librettist of Handel's company, with whom Handel had many success-

## Nicola Haym and George Frideric Handel, *Tamerlano* (1724)

### Act 1.
Tamerlane has vanquished the Turks and taken their sultan, Bajazet, and his daughter, Asteria, prisoners. He soon falls in love with the daughter, despite his betrothal to Irene. He plans to soothe Irene's feelings by giving her to his friend Andronicus, a Greek prince. But secretly, Andronicus and Asteria have also fallen in love. This development causes conflicting emotions on all sides.

### Act 2.
Asteria seems willing to go along with Tamerlane's plan for their marriage, leading the others to suspect that she is blinded by ambition. But she secretly intends to murder him. At last, Asteria tells Tamerlane that she cannot marry him and that she intended all along to take his life. This news pushes him into a fury, and he declares that many will die!

### Act 3.
Tamerlane's rage is only increased when he learns that Asteria and Andronicus are in love. He commands that Bajazet be executed and Asteria married off to a slave. But Bajazet commits suicide, which softens Tamerlane's heart and leads him to give his blessings to Andronicus and Asteria. He vows to marry Irene, and a happy conclusion is reached.

ful collaborations. Libretto writing at this time was a near perfunctory exercise. It was entirely typical that Haym made no effort to be original; instead, he merely revised an existing Italian libretto used five years before in an opera by a lesser-known Italian composer.

The story is loosely based on the life of Tamerlane, a fourteenth-century Mongol warrior known for his military exploits and legendary ferocity. After defeating the Ottoman Turks, he took the Turkish sultan, Bajazet, prisoner. In Haym's libretto, as in countless earlier operas, there are two pairs of lovers whose natural alliances become crossed and confused. In the end, the rightful lovers reunite, and all ends happily. Other characters stand for exaggerated emotional states or ethical qualities. The prisoner Bajazet represents nobility of spirit: He prefers to die rather than to be subjugated by his enemy. Tamerlane represents power and ferocity. The female characters stand for various aspects of love and duty. Despite its formulaic quality, the story leaves the audience with a clear moral: A noble mind and a sense of duty can conquer all obstacles to happiness.

Asteria's aria "Se non mi vuol amar" ("If he loves me no more," Recording 6.6) occurs in Act 1, as she believes herself deserted by Andronicus and facing a loveless marriage to Tamerlane. The orchestral accompaniment consists of the subdued tones of strings, oboes, and basso continuo (played on the recording by harpsichord and lute), which reinforces the spirit of a lament, as does the use of minor mode, soothing rhythms, and an intensely lyrical melody.

**Listening Guide**

**George Frideric Handel, *Tamerlano*, Asteria's aria "Se non mi vuol amar" from Act 1**
Recording 6.6

| | |
|---|---|
| *Se non mi vuol amar,* | If he loves me no more, |
| *almeno il traditor,* | at least the traitor, |
| *perfido ingannator,* | the perfidious imposter, |
| *il cor mi renda.* | should return my heart. |
| | |
| *Se poi lo serba ancor,* | But if he wants to keep it, |
| *che non lo sprezzi almen,* | at least let him not despise it, |
| *o nel amarlo il sen,* | for, while loving it still, |
| *poi non l'offenda.* | he might wound it. |

**A**  0.00  The principal melody, shown here, is introduced by the orchestra, then repeated and developed by the singer. This section ends with a brief orchestral postlude, which reaches a cadence in the home key of E minor.

**B**  2.53  This section states the second poetic stanza, but more concisely than the opening section.

**A′**  4.03  The first section is repeated, with a few minor changes and with improvised ornaments by the singer.

The aria has the traditional ternary or da capo form, although it does not use ritornello devices or other concerto elements. The first section of the aria sets to music the first stanza of poetry, which is repeated several times, making this section the longer of the two. It begins with a brief orchestral introduction, whose main theme is taken up by the voice when it enters. The first of the three main sections is concluded by a brief orchestral postlude. The second section is more concise. It displays new melodic material and a change of keynote. Finally, there is a return to the opening section, during which the singer adds embellishments to the written melody.

### Handel's Oratorios and Messiah

Faced with the declining popularity of Italian opera among London audiences, Handel turned to the genre of the oratorio, with which he was intimately familiar from his earlier days in Rome. He did not, however, simply revive the type of music used by Carissimi; he transformed the genre to suit his own artistic purposes. Generalizations about Handel's oratorios are treacherous because of their great diversity. But by and large, these are works for chorus, solo voices, and orchestra using words in English that depict biblical dramas or ideas. They have the overall form of an opera in their succession of arias, recitatives, choruses, and ensembles, but they lack scenery, costumes, or staging, and, like the earlier oratorios, they place great emphasis on the chorus.

Most of Handel's oratorios are dramatic: They use libretti that tell a connected story drawn from the Old Testament, and they emphasize human experiences and emotions. They were usually performed by Handel's opera company in the Haymarket, alternating with opera performances. Handel tried to make them more appealing to the public by performing his own concertos for organ during intermissions.

*Messiah* is by far his best-known oratorio—perhaps the most beloved work of music in the entire English-speaking world—although it is far from typical. It is not a dramatic piece but rather a reflection on the biblical idea of the Messiah, who in Christian belief is identified as Jesus. Handel's librettist, Charles Jennens, mainly assembled passages from the Bible, and he divided and organized these into three large parts. The first concerns the advent and nativity of Jesus; the second, his Crucifixion and Resurrection; and the last, a reflection on the fate of humanity. In modern performances of *Messiah,* the first or second part is often presented independently.

Handel wrote the music in 1741 in the astoundingly short period of 21 days. He was planning a sojourn in Dublin, where the work was first presented in April 1742. The occasion was a charity benefit performance, whose considerable proceeds allowed for the release of 142 inmates from debtor's prison and assisted several hospitals. The next year it was performed in London, and thus began an unparalleled popularity that has continued to this day.

*Messiah* is a work of music (Beethoven's Fifth Symphony is another) that is capable of communicating profoundly to all persons, regardless of cultural or religious background or degree of experience with music. After the first performance in 1742, a Dublin reviewer summarized its impact after a single hearing:

> Words are wanting to express the exquisite delight it afforded to the admiring crowded audience. The sublime, the grand, and the tender, adapted to the most elevated, majestic and moving words, conspired to transport and charm the ravished heart and ear.[5]

These sentiments have been repeated by generations of listeners to this timeless masterpiece.

Handel revised the work several times, making minor changes in orchestration and composing a few new numbers; the orchestration was also redone later by Mozart, losing some of the splendor of the original. Musically, *Messiah* resembles an opera. It features an overture followed by a succession of recitatives, arias, and a few vocal ensembles. But unlike late-baroque opera, it also has many glorious choruses.

"Comfort Ye" (Recording 6.7) is a melodious tenor recitative occurring just after the overture. The words, from the biblical book of Isaiah, are ingeniously depicted. The major mode suggests the comfort mentioned in the text (all the more noticeable after the stern, minor-mode overture), as do the suave, stepwise melody and the stroking rhythms. The recitative is immediately followed by an aria for tenor, "Ev'ry Valley" (following on Recording 6.7), whose words, also from Isaiah, seem intended for musical interpretation. Handel does not lose an opportunity to paint the suggestive words with musical tones: The word *exalted* is given a soaring flourish. *Crooked* is made vivid by a jagged melodic contour, and the word *plain* is given to a single sustained note. But these expressive devices, repeatedly used by composers since the late Renaissance, are never allowed to become trivial or formulaic. They merge effortlessly into the melodious and invigorating expressiveness of the music.

*Listening Guide*

**George Frideric Handel, *Messiah*, tenor recitative and aria "Comfort Ye" and "Ev'ry Valley"**
Recording 6.7

| | | |
|---|---|---|
| **Recitative** | 0.00 | The melodic style of "Comfort Ye" is not the dry recitative so typical of opera but rather a melodious and expressive arioso accompanied by the orchestra. |
| **Aria** | 3.29 | In his oratorios, Handel generally avoided the full da capo aria forms that were standard in his operas. The aria "Ev'ry Valley" resembles in form solely the first section of a three-part da capo aria. This single section uses ritornello form, as the opening orchestral music returns twice in alternation with the vocal soloist. |

The chorus "Hallelujah" concludes the second part of the oratorio and forms the climax of the entire work, after which the remainder is but a dénouement. Audiences traditionally stand during the singing of this movement. Legend has it that King George II stood during an early performance, and others in the auditorium also stood in deference to the monarch, thus beginning the tradition. But this explanation seems scarcely sufficient to explain the practice. Handel's biographer Paul Henry Lang attributes it to our enduring awe, not of earthly rulers, but of the greatness of God: "And when the Hallelujah Chorus is thundered," he writes, "its wondrous strains exuding power and pomp, the audience gets to its feet to greet a mighty ruler in whose presence we do not kneel but stand at attention." There is indeed an excitement, an expressive force within the music itself, epitomized by the sharply etched rhythms of the opening of the "Hallelujah Chorus" (Recording 6.8), that by itself has long had the power to bring audiences to their feet.

The movement, whose words are drawn from passages of the Book of Revelation, uses chorus and a full orchestra of strings, woodwinds, trumpets, and timpani. It is free in form but carefully calculated to produce a steady buildup of excitement and to make the words crystal clear. Four subsections can be distinguished: The first consists of a succession of melodic motives in the chorus, each presented homophonically. At 1.37 there appears a short fugue on the words "And He shall reign for ever and ever," sentiments that are vividly conveyed by the strict and imperious rules of fugal composition. But the fugue soon dissolves, as the high voices pound out the stentorian phrase "King of Kings, and Lord of Lords," answered by the other voices, "forever and ever, Hallelujah." This passage marks the beginning of the climax of the movement, as the motive is repeated in an ever-higher spiral. A coda brings the chorus to a thunderous conclusion.

**Listening Guide**

**Handel,** *Messiah,* **"Hallelujah Chorus"**
Recording 6.8

| | | |
|---|---|---|
| **Preparation** | 0.00 | A succession of themes is presented by the chorus on the words "Hallelujah," "For the Lord God Omnipotent," and "The kingdom of this world." |
| **Fugue** | 1.37 | The fugue is based on the subject shown here, although it never becomes so dense as to obscure the words. |

and he shall reign for - e - ver and e - ver

| **Climax** | 2.40 | The antiphony between the higher and lower voices brings the music to a climax, followed by a mixing in of the fugue subject. |
|---|---|---|
| **Coda** | 3.13 | The rousing conclusion brings back several earlier motives. |

## TOPICS FOR DISCUSSION AND WRITING

**1.** Compare and contrast the recitative passage that ends the second verse of Couperin's first Tenebrae Lesson (Recording 6.2, from 6.31) to Monteverdi's recitative "Tu se' morta" from *Orfeo* (Recording 5.1, second part). Are the melodies equally speechlike? How do both composers find musical equivalents of the emotions expressed in the words? Also compare the harmonic and rhythmic styles of the accompanimental music.

**2.** Compare and contrast the uses of preexistent melodies in Josquin's Kyrie from the *Missa pange lingua* (Recording 4.3), the opening passages of Couperin's *Tenebrae Lessons* (Recording 6.2), and Bach's cantata *Herz und Mund und Tat und Leben*, BWV 147, movement 6 (Recording 6.3). Extend your comparison to include the ways in which the basic melodies are used, the likely purposes of such use, and the similarities or differences in the compositions that result.

**3.** Study the fugue in Bach's Toccata and Fugue in D Minor, BWV 565 (Recording 6.5), and try to distinguish the episodes from the restatements of the subject following the exposition. How would you characterize the episodes? Do they have anything in common with the subject?

**4.** Listen carefully to the words of the recitative "Comfort Ye" and the aria "Ev'ry Valley" from Handel's *Messiah* (Recording 6.7). Try to find all of the ways in which the composer portrays their meaning by musical devices. Review the history of such "word painting" in music that you have studied previously.

## ADDITIONAL LISTENING

### Bach

*Brandenburg Concerto* No. 5. The first movement features a stunning solo for the harpsichord.

Cantatas and cantata excerpts. The following are especially recommended:

> *Jauchzet Gott in allen Landen*, BWV 51. This is a virtuosic work for soprano and solo trumpet.
> *Ich habe genug*, BWV 82, especially the baritone aria "Schlummert ein."

*Jesu, der du meine Seele,* BWV 78, especially the duet "Wir eilen."

*Gottes Zeit ist die allerbeste Zeit,* BWV 106. An early cantata of remarkable beauty.

*Christmas Oratorio.* A compilation of cantatas originally performed on six days of the Christmas season in 1734–1735.

*Saint Matthew Passion.* Many connoisseurs consider this Bach's masterpiece. It is a lengthy cantatalike work first heard on Good Friday, 1727.

*Italian Concerto* for harpsichord. A vivacious work combining the Italianate concerto form with a solo harpsichord medium.

## Couperin

*Pièces de clavecin.* Couperin published 27 harpsichord suites, called "orders," in four volumes of *pièces.*

## Handel

*Concerti grossi,* Op. 6.

*Royal Fireworks Music.* Orchestral dances.

*Water Music.* Orchestral dances.

## Vivaldi

*The Four Seasons.* Four violin concertos, each descriptive of different seasons and prefaced by a sonnet describing that season.

## BIBLIOGRAPHY

(For general references to music of the baroque period, see the bibliography in Chapter 5.)

Dean, Winton. *Handel and the Opera Seria.* Berkeley: University of California Press, 1969.

————. *Handel's Dramatic Oratorios and Masques.* New York: Oxford University Press, 1959.

———— and John Knapp. *Handel's Operas, 1704–1726.* New York: Oxford University Press, 1986.

Geiringer, Karl. *Johann Sebastian Bach: The Culmination of an Era.* New York: Oxford University Press, 1966. An outstanding short study.

Lang, Paul Henry. *George Frideric Handel.* New York: Norton, 1966. Intended for the general reader.

Mellers, Wilfrid. *François Couperin and the French Classical Tradition.* New York: Dover, 1968. (Originally published in 1950.)

Pincherle, Marc. *Vivaldi.* Translated by Christopher Hatch. New York: Norton, 1957.

Schweitzer, Albert. *Johann Sebastian Bach.* Two volumes. Translated by Ernest Newman. New York: Dover, 1966. (Originally published in 1908.)

## NOTES

**1.** François Couperin, quoted in Wilfrid Mellers, *François Couperin and the French Classical Tradition* (London: Denis Dobson, 1950), p. 234. Translation by the author.

**2.** Translations of verses *aleph* and *beth* from *The New English Bible* (Oxford, Cambridge: Oxford University Press, Cambridge University Press, 1970), p. 992.

**3.** Hans T. David and Arthur Mendel, eds., *The Bach Reader* (New York: Norton, 1966), p. 52.

**4.** Ibid., p. 236.

**5.** *Dublin Journal,* April 17, 1742, quoted in Howard E. Smither, *A History of the Oratorio,* vol. 2 (Chapel Hill: University of North Carolina Press, 1977), p. 249.

# *Movement*
# III

# Music of
# Modern Times

The period from the middle of the eighteenth century to about 1900 has special importance for lovers of music. It was during this relatively brief span of time that most of the best-known composers wrote their works. In a period of scarcely 150 years, all of the masterpieces of Mozart, Haydn, Beethoven, Chopin, Schumann, Schubert, Brahms, Wagner, and Verdi were composed.

We shall see that these composers used several distinct styles, but they also had much in common. They all adhered to similar ways of expressing a keynote, and they all used major and minor scales, common rhythmic and metric patterns, and similar media, forms, and genres. So homogeneous was their music in technique and intent that it can be said that they followed a "common practice."

Although important composers of the common-practice period hailed from many different lands, those from Germany and Austria increasingly achieved preeminence. During the same 150 years, German political might and accomplishments in science and literature experienced comparable growth. But with the defeat of the German alliance in World War I, the common practice eroded and, with it, Germany's hitherto unquestioned leadership in music.

We can now see that the eighteenth and nineteenth centuries did not produce music that was necessarily superior to that of other times, although to people living then, committed in general to a progressivist outlook, this often seemed to be the case. All the same, it was a heyday for serious music, which flourished and increased everywhere in the world and captivated the attention of a large public with an intensity not duplicated before or since.

# 7

# Introduction
# to the Classical Style

———

## The Food of Love

The image of courtiers whiling away the hours amidst an idyllic natural setting reappears throughout eighteenth-century art. Following the death in 1715 of the militaristic French king Louis XIV, European society seemed to heave a collective sigh of relief. Social grace, elegant language and manners, and a worship of pleasure and sensuality quickly replaced the more civic-minded and duty-bound consciousness of the previous age. An especially characteristic pastime of the upper classes became the fête galante, a gathering of sumptuously dressed courtiers in a garden or other natural setting. Although conversation, relaxation, and entertainment were the main activities on such occasions, they were also especially well suited to the cultivation of love and passion.

For the French painter Jean-Antoine Watteau (1684–1721), the fête galante became a subject of enduring importance. His many paintings on this theme accurately record tastes in dress, manner, and entertainment among the French nobility of his day. They display with equal vividness Watteau's own fantasies on the emotional gratifications that such occasions provided. In his painting La Gamme d'amour (The Scale of Love), a lavishly dressed guitarist accompanies a lady in the singing of a song. Although others converse in the background, our attention is drawn to the musical encounter, which, in its understated intensity, implies sensual attraction between its two participants. Music was indeed central to the new social cult of the early eighteenth century, since it seemed uniquely capable of imparting a pleasure that was both refined and sensuously intense.

Watteau's paintings provide us with far more than a mere record of high society. Their greatness resides in the expressiveness of the painter's imagination, which, like his subjects, is infinitely refined and suggestive.

Music by the mid-eighteenth century came to share the spirit of the fête galante. Elegance, refinement, naturalness, and ease became the order of the day. Operas of this period clearly reflect the spirit of the age, with their emphasis on amorous encounters, sweetness, and good-natured fun. A new and popular musical style that was established by mid-century was, even then, termed "gallant," a word that suggested elegance, lightness of touch, and an attentiveness to the charms of women. But the gallant style was not destined to endure. As the century waned, it seemed more and more ephemeral, even downright frivolous. Together with the emotion-laden visions of Watteau, it was swept away by a renewed consciousness of the real world of political and social turmoil.

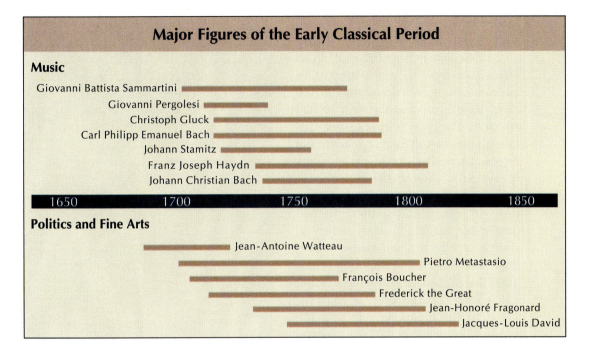

During the second quarter of the eighteenth century, a change of taste in music swept all of Europe. Provoked by a newly liberated attitude toward society and religion, it soon pushed the grandiose works of Bach and Handel into obscurity and ushered in a new musical style that we will call *classicism*. This term, which connotes the balance and serenity of Greek and Roman art, is appropriate to the new style because these qualities took on added importance. Classicism in music embraced the lifelike and the natural, it relished symmetry and simplicity, and it rejected anything that seemed contrived, overly complicated, or grandiloquent. Audiences by 1750 wished to be entertained or touched by music, not overawed or confused.

A forerunner of this new taste in the visual arts is the French painter Jean-Antoine Watteau. His works depart from the vigor and energy of baroque painting and seek instead the lyric, sensual, and idyllic moods of the *fête galante* or the gay frivolity of courtly life. *La Gamme d'amour (The Scale of Love,* see the opening of this chapter) depicts a relaxed and civilized scene of courtiers amid nature. The musician (a favorite subject of Watteau) accompanies the lady in a scene of sweet elegance laden with sensual and luxurious suggestion. Watteau's style was continued in later eighteenth-century France

**217**

by François Boucher (1703–1770) and Jean-Honoré Fragonard (1732–1806).

The playful lightness of Watteau's paintings has a counterpart in interior design and decoration in the early eighteenth-century style called **rococo.** The rococo interior is a fantasy of sensuously curved lines and organic shapes, in which gravity seems mysteriously absent. Although rococo interiors had their origin in France early in the century, they reached flamboyant heights by mid-century in church architecture in southern Germany and Austria. An imposing example is the pilgrimage church at Wies in the rolling countryside of Bavaria, shown at the right. The edifice is the work of the architect and stucco artist Dominikus Zimmermann and his brother, the fresco painter Johann Baptist Zimmermann. The interior captures a fantastic vision of lightness, color, and motion in which the straight lines of baroque architecture have totally surrendered to the curved shapes of nature. The nave is flooded with light, which brings a happy and vivacious spirit to the decorative interior and breathes life into the floating stucco work and its striking colors.

*The interior of the church in Wies, located in the shadow of the Bavarian Alps in the south of Germany, is a masterpiece of rococo church architecture. It was completed in 1749, the work of the brothers Johann and Dominikus Zimmermann.*

The music of Bach and Handel must have seemed daunting indeed to a public attuned to the gentle fantasies of Watteau and the brothers Zimmermann. In 1737 a music critic named Johann Adolph Scheibe assessed the music of Bach according to the new taste:

> This great man [Bach] would be the admiration of whole nations if he had more amenity, if he did not take away the natural element in his pieces by giving them a turgid and confused style, and if he did not darken their beauty by an excess of art. . . . Turgidity has led [him]

from the natural to the artificial, and from the lofty to the somber; and though one admires the onerous labor and uncommon effort, these, however, are vainly employed, since they conflict with Nature.[1]

For Scheibe, the rich ingenuity of Bach's music—its complicated fugal textures, motoric rhythms, and intense religiosity—was unnatural, too difficult, and hence unpleasing. Like most of his contemporaries at the approach of mid-century, Scheibe demanded a new and simpler order in music.

## Political, Intellectual, and Social Background

On its surface, the political situation in Europe in 1750 remained as it had been during the preceding century. European countries were ruled as monarchies, interlocked by treaties and by common interests, although bitter economic rivalries periodically erupted into warfare. Many of the powerful monarchs of Europe laid claim to lands far distant from their own. Thus the English and Spanish thrones administered colonies in the New World, and the Hapsburg monarchs in Austria ruled a vast region including parts of the modern-day Netherlands, Italy, Hungary, Czechoslovakia, and Poland. As before, the German states were allied in the Holy Roman Empire, by custom ruled by the Hapsburg monarch. As the century progressed, Prussia emerged as the most powerful German state and became a great rival of Austria.

The Hapsburg Empire, in which classical music rose to its greatest heights, was ruled from 1740 to 1780 by the remarkable Empress Maria Theresa. The 40 years of her reign saw reforms in taxation, improved living conditions for the peasantry, greater control of the church by governmental authorities, and increased opportunities for education. Maria Theresa was succeeded by her son Joseph II, who intensified the reforms begun by his mother and won a reputation as the most enlightened and benevolent monarch of his day.

*Empress Maria Theresa guided the Hapsburg Empire for much of the second half of the eighteenth century. During these years, Vienna, the Hapsburg capital, became preeminent in music.*

The rise of the classical style coincided with an extraordinary period of intellectual growth and innovation throughout Europe that is now termed the *Enlightenment*. The fountainhead of Enlightenment literature was Paris, home to a group of writers who called themselves *philosophes*. Denis Diderot, Voltaire, and the Baron de Montesquieu were leaders among their number. Their outlook echoed in the writings of authors throughout the world, including the Americans Thomas Jefferson and Benjamin Franklin.

Although their interests were varied, these authors were unified by a common view of religion and the church, an attachment to the scientific method of inquiry, and a liberal attitude toward human rights and the proper role of government. They were perhaps most insistent in wishing to limit the influence of the church and in rethinking the nature of God. They attacked authoritarian or superstitious elements of traditional religions, and many supported a natural or deistic religion in place of established dogma. In all intellectual matters, human reason was their true guide, and the belief was widespread that through the faculty of reason, humanity possessed a boundless capacity for knowledge, freedom, and progress.

Enlightenment philosophies had an important effect on eighteenth-century music and musical thought. They led to great advances in understanding the laws that govern this art, and they ultimately influenced musical style. A buoyant spirit and a preference for major mode, both distinctive features of the early classical style, mirror the heady confidence in the future that marks the writings of the French philosophes. Also, the aggressive secularism of the Enlightenment eventually led to a decline in the importance of sacred music, notable especially in the works of Beethoven.

Beethoven is the major classical composer most directly inspired by Enlightenment literature. His imagination was fired by his readings in Kant, Schiller, and Goethe, whose ideas of a brotherhood of humankind intent on virtuous actions and brotherly love were a lifelong inspiration to him. The most famous musical expression of these ideas of fraternity is in the Ninth Symphony. Beethoven's disdain for repressive government may have motivated his Third Symphony, and his attachment to the concept of the romantic hero is reflected in this work as in the opera *Fidelio* and the Overture to Goethe's *Egmont*.

Musical culture in the large cities of Europe in the eighteenth century was stimulated by a rising middle class. Ordinary citizens in unprecedented numbers were acquiring wealth, education, and artistic cultivation. They sought opportunities to hear and to be instructed in music, and they demanded printed music for use in the home. Before this period, people of modest means had little opportunity to hear music outside of the church or the opera theater. But in the classical period, concert series directed at a bourgeois public were initiated in several major cities. In London, orchestral music was heard beginning in 1765 at concerts organized by Johann Christian Bach and Carl Friedrich Abel, and later in the century, the orchestral concerts directed there by Johann Peter Salomon attracted international attention. In Paris in the eighteenth century, there were several competing series of public concerts. The *Concert spirituel,* for example, founded in 1725, presented sacred vocal music and instrumental pieces. Mozart composed works for their performances during a sojourn in Paris in 1778. The rival *Concert de la Loge olympique* succeeded in obtaining six new symphonies from Haydn to present to its subscribers during their concerts of 1785 and 1786.

The rise of an artistically inquisitive middle class produced a permanent change in the role of the professional musician in society. No longer was a composer's career limited to the service of an individual patron or to a church. Beginning in the later eighteenth century with Beethoven and Mozart, composers increasingly directed their works toward a large, anonymous audience of music lovers of any nationality or social standing. This audience was reached through the medium of music publishing, which underwent immense growth during the classic period, and by the public concert. Composers increasingly worked in genres that appealed to large audiences or were applicable to domestic music making. The new circumstances of composition also required that composers be able to tailor the style of their music to a particular audience. Some works were intended for a mass audience, and these had to be made direct in appeal and facile in comprehensibility. Other pieces were for the connoisseur, and they made no concessions to ease of understanding. Published music was often explicitly directed to the beginner or to the accomplished amateur.

## New Musical Genres of the Classical Period

The four most important genres of classical instrumental music are the symphony, string quartet, sonata, and concerto. Of these four, the **symphony** and the **string quartet** are new to the classical era. The concerto was carried over from the baroque period with appropriate changes in form and style, and the sonata, also in existence in the baroque period, underwent a complete redefinition by the late eighteenth century. Less important instrumental genres include the **serenade** (also called the *notturno, cassation,* or *divertimento*) and other chamber genres such as the **trio** or the **quintet.** The central type of music using voices is opera, which was introduced in the early baroque period. Secondary in importance are the oratorio and the Mass, both of which have a history extending well before the classical period. In the survey that follows, genres that are new to classical music—the symphony, string quartet, and keyboard sonata—will be defined and briefly described. The concerto, opera, oratorio, and Mass were introduced earlier in this book, and these will be touched on again later in this and the following chapter.

## The Symphony

The classical symphony is a work in three or, more typically, four movements for the medium of orchestra. Although new to the classical period, it was prefigured by the baroque orchestral concerto and the opera overture. Symphonies in the classical period were public pieces, works intended for a large audience, gathered at a private academy or a public concert. Accordingly, we can expect that they will express ideas of broad interest and do so in a direct manner.

The first movement of a symphony is the longest and weightiest of the four; it is moderately fast (sometimes introduced by a passage in a slow tempo), and it falls almost invariably into the sonata form (described shortly). The second movement establishes a new keynote; it is slow in tempo and lyric in expression. Its form may follow free sonata form, ternary form, or some other scheme.

The third movement of the four-movement symphony returns to the home key and imitates the **minuet,** a French baroque dance. This was a favorite aristocratic dance of the era of Louis XIV, named because of its minute steps. It has a slow and stately triple meter and binary form. For choreographic reasons, the baroque minuet was usually paired with a second minuet, after which the first minuet was repeated. Thus a large ternary form results: minuet 1, minuet 2, minuet 1. The second minuet usually contrasts with the first in character and by a reduced orchestration. In the baroque period, the second minuet might have been scored for only three instruments, whereupon it was called the *menuet en trio,* or "minuet for three." Although the central section of the third movement of the classical symphony is not so radically reduced in orchestration, it is still called the *trio.*

The classical minuet movement eventually lost the stately and refined character of the true French dance, taking on instead a quicker tempo and a more rollicking spirit. Composers such as Haydn and especially Beethoven sometimes avoided calling their third movements minuets, recognizing that the spirit of their music had nothing in common with the old aristocratic dance, even though the overall ternary form and triple meter were preserved.

They sometimes substituted the term **scherzo** (literally "joke") to characterize the spirit and mood of these movements.

The fourth movement of the eighteenth-century symphony, its finale, is quick in tempo and light or sparkling in style. It is also in the home key. It often uses rondo form (see Chapter 1), although other standard or hybrid forms are encountered as well.

The four movements of a classical symphony may be compared to an anthology of four short stories. The movements have a definite character and a definite relationship in their keynotes, but they do not usually share common themes. Beginning in the nineteenth century with Beethoven (and in a few earlier works by Haydn), the four movements of the symphony become more intimately linked by common melodic ideas and by an unbroken musical argument. At this time, we can begin to speak of the genre as a true cycle, comparable to a novel in four chapters, rather than as a mere anthology of unconnected stories.

The classical orchestra is made up of the same four subgroups as in the late baroque period—strings, woodwinds, brass, and percussion. But the classical orchestra was much changed in sonority because the brilliant trumpets of the baroque were relegated to a purely accompanimental role, the harpsichord was eliminated or became optional, and the strings were used to fill out harmonies more completely and with greater balance.

The string group is central, as it is entrusted with most of the melodic and harmonic materials. It consists of four lines of music: The highest is played in unison by several violins, the next lowest by "second" violins, the next lowest by violas, and the lowest of all, or "bass" line, by cellos and string basses playing in octaves. The exact number of strings that played these four lines varied according to the availability of performers and the size of the concert hall. Haydn's symphonies were performed by the court orchestra of the Esterházy family in the 1780s by a string section numbering about 17 players; in the Salomon concerts in London in the 1790s, Haydn's late symphonies were performed by a string complement of about 40. In either case, the string section of the classical orchestra was considerably smaller than its counterpart in the modern orchestra.

Next in importance to the strings in the classical orchestra is the woodwind section, which consists at its largest of pairs of flutes, oboes, clarinets, and bassoons. Clarinets became regular members of Viennese orchestras only around 1790. The brass section of the classical orchestra rarely played independent melodic material, and it was never used as an independent group. For the concert hall, it consisted maximally of pairs of French horns and trumpets, and trombones were often added in opera and music for the church. If trumpets were used, a pair of kettledrums was also called into service. In the woodwind and brass sections, only one player was normally used on a line of music since the doubling of parts was unnecessary to achieve a pleasing balance.

## The String Quartet

The string quartet is the most important of a category of genres called *chamber music,* or instrumental music for few solo players. In the classical period, chamber genres such as the trio (often for three stringed instruments or for piano, violin, and cello), quintet (usually for two violins, two violas, and cello), and other combinations involving piano were especially popular. Chamber works were generally in three or more movements, and they often resembled the serenade in their light character.

The overall form of the string quartet is indistinguishable from the four-movement symphony: fast sonata form, slow movement, minuet, and fast finale. Its medium consists of two violins, viola, and cello. But unlike the symphony or the serenade, the string quartet is normally music for the connoisseur: It has a rigor, a complicated texture, and often a sophisticated humor that make it ideal for the enjoyment of the experienced listener or for the pleasure of musicians themselves. When Haydn and Mozart met socially in Vienna in the 1780s, they often entertained themselves by playing quartets with other friends. This refined spirit of the quartet was perhaps best captured by Goethe when he remarked that listening to a string quartet was like overhearing a conversation among four intelligent people.

## The Sonata

In the late baroque period, sonatas were normally written for one or more melodic instruments and keyboard. Their form resembled a suite of dances, and they were used both as concert pieces and in church services. In the classical era, this character gradually changed, rendering the sonata a piece for piano or harpsichord alone or for piano accompanied by an instrument. By this time, sonatas had come to be written in only three movements—fast, slow, and fast—although other configurations are sometimes encountered.

Sonatas in the classical era also had a purpose different from that of their baroque forebears. At first, they were often written by a master teacher for his students, as in the case of the sonatas of Domenico Scarlatti (1685–1757), published as "exercises." The mature piano sonatas of Haydn, Mozart, and Beethoven are no longer works for amateurs, but professional pianists such as Beethoven rarely played their own sonatas in public concerts, preferring instead to improvise and to perform concertos.

## *The* Galant *Style*

In the second quarter of the eighteenth century, well before Haydn and Mozart established themselves as leading figures, the classical style began to emerge in works by a large number of composers scattered throughout Europe. There was no single dominant geographic center to this phenomenon. In Naples, a new type of comic opera that banished baroque exaggeration and artificiality appeared in works by Giovanni Battista Pergolesi (1710–1736), Leonardo Vinci (c. 1690–1730), and Leonardo Leo (1694–1744). In Milan, Giovanni Battista Sammartini (1701–1775) composed some of the earliest important symphonies in the classical manner. In Mannheim, an important center of symphonic composition arose at mid-century at the court of the elector Charles Theodore. A leader among the composer-performers in his service was the prolific symphonist Johann Stamitz (1717–1757). In London shortly after mid-century, Johann Christian Bach (1735–1782) composed symphonies, concertos, sonatas, and operas in the new taste. Bach was the youngest son of Johann Sebastian Bach, and his music was especially influential on Mozart.

Although it is impossible to interpret the music of these pioneers as establishing a unified style, their works all contain antibaroque tendencies that writers past and present have described by the French term *galant.* The **galant style** is lighthearted and elegant, simple and natural in texture and melodic expression, graceful in ornamentation, and straightforward in harmonic motion and phrase structure.

These features are clearly in evidence in the comic opera *La serva padrona (The Maid as Mistress,* 1733) by Pergolesi, one of the earliest celebrated works in the new manner. Originally, the two acts of *La serva padrona* were interpolated between the three acts of a serious opera, titled *Il prigionier superbo (The Proud Prisoner),* also by Pergolesi. This curious intertwining of the comic and the serious was commissioned and performed in Naples in 1733 as a tribute to the Austrian empress, Elisabeth Christine, since at this period in Italian history, the Kingdom of Naples was ruled by the Hapsburgs.

The libretto of *La serva padrona,* by the Neapolitan writer Gennarantonio Federico, is short, simple, and true to life. It uses only three characters: Uberto (bass) is the master of the house, Serpina (soprano) is his maid, and

Vespone (a mute role) is his valet. In the first act we learn that the maid in fact runs the household, pertly ordering everyone about, including Uberto. At wit's end, Uberto declares that he must marry in order to put Serpina in her place. To this Serpina rejoins that he should marry her, despite their differences in social station.

In the second act Serpina and Vespone hatch a plot to make Uberto agree to marry her. She tells Uberto that she is engaged to a soldier, since she will no longer be needed in his house after he is married. As Vespone is brought in disguised as the soldier, the scheme begins to work. Uberto longs to keep Serpina with him, and although the ruse is shortly unveiled, Uberto in the end resolves to marry his maid.

A comparison of the stories of *La serva padrona* and Handel's opera *Tamerlano,* discussed in Chapter 6, reveals such extensive differences between the baroque serious opera and the classical comic one that we must conclude that they represent entirely separate genres. All the same, their differences point up the change of taste that distinguishes the older baroque style from the newer classical manner, and it is all the more remarkable that the two operas were composed a scant nine years apart. Nicola Haym's libretto for *Tamerlano* is remote from everyday experience: It is a fictitious account of the clash between two early historical figures, and it dwells on exaggerated emotional states. Its overall point is didactic and moralizing. Federico's tale, on the contrary, is lifelike: It is set in the present day among people of the middle class, and it involves an unpretentious comic situation that everyone in the audience can understand. To facilitate and broaden its appeal, Federico used aspects of traditional Italian comedy: farcical scenes augmented by ludicrous disguise, stereotyped characters such as the soubrette maid and the stuffy master of the house, and, central to its comic impulse, an inversion of the accepted social order in which the maid gets the upper hand over her master.

The differences in musical language between the serious operas of Handel and the comic ones of Pergolesi are as striking as their differences in text. Uberto's aria "Sempre in contrasti" from Act 1 (Recording 7.1) exemplifies many of the features of the new *galant* style. Here Uberto commands an end to the bickering between Serpina and himself (see the translation in the Listening Guide).

The leading male part of Uberto is sung by a bass, a natural voice, rather than by the castrato voice that was preferred in serious opera. Uberto's part does not require great vocal agility or training, only good comic delivery. His lines are broken into many short phrases or motives that are expanded by repetition and sequence. Accordingly, there is much repetition in the words as well. As befits his character, Uberto occasionally breaks into a comic bluster, expressed by large leaps. At other times his singing creates a patter effect by the rapid delivery of quick, even rhythms where each note receives a syllable. All of these features later became the stock-in-trade of the comic bass in classical opera.

The music in general is exceedingly simple and straightforward. The aria maintains the familiar ternary or da capo form, the orchestra creates an unobtrusive accompaniment, and the mode is predominantly major. Only in the middle section does minor appear prominently, there to project a tone of mock pathos.

## *Listening Guide*

**Giovanni Battista Pergolesi, "Sempre in contrasti," from *La serva padrona***
Recording 7.1

| | |
|---|---|
| *Sempre in contrasti* | There are always arguments |
| *con te si sta,* | with you, |
| *e qua e là,* | here and there, |
| *e su e giù,* | up and down, |
| *e si e no;* | yes and no; |
| *or questo basti,* | that's enough, |
| *finir si può.* | let's stop! |
| *Ma che ti pare? Ah!* | [*To Vespone:*] So what do you think? |
| *Ho io a crepare?* | Do I have to die? |
| *Signor mio, no.* | No, my good sir! |
| *Però dovrai pur* | [*To Serpina:*] But you will |
| *sempre piangere* | forever bemoan |
| *la tua disgrazia,* | your disgrace, |
| *e allor dirai* | and then say |
| *che ben ti sta.* | it serves you right. |
| *Che dici tu?* | What do you say? |
| *Non è così?* | Is that not right? |
| *Ah! che! no! sì!* | Ah! What! Yes! No! |
| *Ma così è.* | But it is so. |

**Introduction**     0.00     Brief orchestral introduction containing the principal motive:

**A**          0.12          First part of the da capo aria, based on motives from the intro-
                               duction. Predominantly in major mode and based on a home key
                               (F) and other closely related tonalities.

**B**          1.49          Contrasting middle part, beginning with the words "Però dovrai
                               pur." Uberto's self-pity is expressed by the change to minor
                               mode and by the solemn unison passage at the beginning:

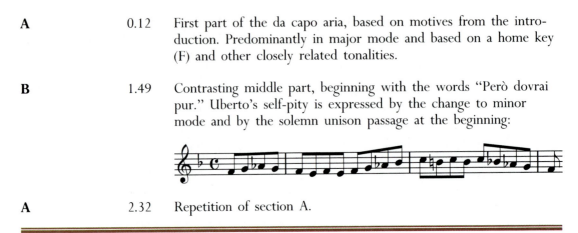

**A**          2.32          Repetition of section A.

The innovative *galant* style of Pergolesi's comic opera did not attract widespread attention in Europe until about the middle of the century. In 1752, it was performed on the stage of the Paris Opera, which at that time was still devoted primarily to French operas in the baroque manner. Despite the unassuming proportions of Pergolesi's work, it precipitated a spirited debate among musicians and writers (including Diderot, Rousseau, and the Baron von Grimm) on the attributes of French and Italian music. Beneath the argument, now called the *querelle des bouffons* ("quarrel of the buffoons"), was the issue of a change in taste in music at mid-century. While ostensibly debating national differences in music, the critics were primarily arguing about opposing directions in musical style: traditional baroque practices, as represented by French serious opera, versus the new classical taste, represented by comic Italian opera.

Elements of the *galant* style were preserved in music well into the second half of the eighteenth century. The mature phase of this reaction against baroque artifice is exemplified by the works of Johann Christian Bach. His life is typical of the cosmopolitan age in which he lived. After the death of his father in 1750, he studied in Berlin with his brother Carl Philipp Emanuel Bach. To further his education and to advance his reputation, he then went to Italy, where he pursued the career of a composer of opera. His success in this genre led him to resettle in 1762 in London, where he composed Italian operas for the King's Theatre in the Haymarket. He also entered into the employ of Queen Charlotte, wife of George III. In London, he collaborated with Carl Friedrich Abel on an important series of public orchestral concerts (1765–1781) for which he wrote approximately 90 pieces, mostly symphonies in the Italian manner.

The Symphony in D Major, Op. 18, No. 4, is typical of these pieces. The work is in three movements: the first, a lively opening; the second, a lyrical adagio; and the finale, a sprightly rondo. The three-movement form is characteristic of Italian symphonies of the classical period. In Italy, the genre was closely associated with late baroque Italian opera overtures (called *sinfonie,* hence the term *symphony*). In fact, Bach's symphony was published in 1781 as an "overture," and it may well have served the composer both as a concert piece and as an opera overture.

The music of the finale (Recording 7.2) illustrates the *galant* style. It is concise, bubbling in spirit, melodious, simple in structure, and predominantly homophonic in texture. The orchestra is somewhat larger than that used in most of Bach's other symphonies, as it calls for oboes, bassoons, horns, trumpets, and timpani in addition to the normal complement of strings. According to English custom in the

*J. C. Bach's great fame in London is attested by this portrait, executed by the renowned Thomas Gainsborough. The painter shows his subject true to life, with the refinement, vivacity, and apparent impatience for which the composer was known.*

eighteenth century, it is likely that a harpsichord or a piano was used in early performances to reinforce the harmonies and to allow the player to assist in conducting. The keyboard instrument, however, does not have independent music.

The brightness and simplicity associated with the *galant* style is further reinforced by the quick tempo, the use of major mode, and the even, sparkling rhythms. These avoid entirely the machinelike quality of baroque rhythms in fast tempos and move instead in differentiated patterns with many rests that allow the music to breathe. Our understanding of the work is also facilitated by the reigning homophonic texture. The melody is carried almost entirely by the violins, to which the winds and brass add only color and volume. In a few passages, the composer begins fugues, but these quickly dissolve into the more normal homophony.

Typical of many finales in classical instrumental music, this movement uses rondo form. According to this pattern, a melody presented at the beginning returns several times as a refrain. Bach makes the plan easy for us to follow since statements of the refrain melody contrast clearly with the intervening melodic materials (called *episodes*). All of the melodies are constructed in short phrases, and the many cadences help us to find our place within the form. Yet despite such rigid patterns, Bach never writes music that is studied or predictable. He invariably overcomes the restrictions of his formal plan and effortlessly conveys a sense of virtuosity and spontaneity.

**Johann Christian Bach, Symphony in D Major, Op. 18, No. 4, third movement (finale)**
Recording 7.2

**A (refrain)**     0.00     The melody is cast into a period form that is immediately repeated and that ends in a full cadence. It begins

**B (episode)**     0.25     Consists of a string of short melodic ideas, some set forth as brief
fugues. The music quickly changes to a new key (A major). The
episode begins with a rapid ascending scale:

**A (refrain)**     0.59     The opening melody and the home key of D return.

**C (episode)**     1.12     This passage begins in the minor mode in a lightly fugal texture.
In the middle, it returns to major, but on a new keynote (F), and
it finally repeats the material that opens the episode. The passage
is thus a small ternary form. It begins

**A (refrain)**     1.56     The opening melody returns again.

**Coda**     2.09     Based on a melody from the second episode (C), only returned to
the home key and brought to a definite conclusion.

# *Alternatives to the* Galant *Style*

The *galant* manner of Pergolesi and J. C. Bach was not the only new style in music of the early classical period. A group of composers associated with the court of Frederick the Great in Berlin around the middle of the eighteenth century took a different course that resulted in what is now called the *empfindsam* **("sensitive") style.** Its most important representative is Carl Philipp Emanuel Bach (1714–1788), another of the musically gifted sons of Johann Sebastian Bach. C. P. E. Bach served the Prussian court, primarily as a harpsichordist, from 1738 until 1768. His music for keyboard instruments is the most characteristic of his style, although he also composed concertos, symphonies, songs, and religious works.

Bach's music in the *empfindsam* style seeks to communicate intense emotions directly to the listener. To achieve this objective, his instrumental works often imitate the sound and delivery of emotional speech by their use of free and flexible rhythms, instrumental melodies that imitate impassioned operatic recitative, and unexpected and sudden changes of dynamics, key-notes, tempos, and mode.

Many of Bach's keyboard works capture the spontaneity and freshness of improvisations. Like most of the great composers for keyboard instruments, Bach was a master of the art of improvisation, especially on his favorite instrument, the clavichord. This instrument, a distant relative of the piano, produced a soft and delicate tone. The English historian Charles Burney heard Bach improvise on the clavichord in Hamburg in 1772, and his description of Bach's playing suggests the intense and refined emotionality that characterizes the *empfindsam* style:

> After dinner, which was elegantly served, and cheerfully eaten, I prevailed upon him to sit down again to a clavichord, and he played, with little intermission, till near eleven o'clock at night. During this time, he grew so animated and *possessed,* that he not only played, but looked like one inspired. His eyes were fixed, his under lip fell, and drops of effervescence distilled from his countenance. He said, if he were to be set to work frequently in this manner, he should grow young again.[2]

Although the *galant* and *empfindsam* styles conformed most closely to the new tastes of the early classical period, music in a baroque manner continued to exist. It was heard primarily in the genre of serious opera, which retained some of its popularity. The libretti of such works were, as in the

**231**

baroque period, fictionalized studies inspired by ancient history or myth. Their dramatic situations turned on heightened emotions in conflict with reason, duty, and noble behavior among the leading characters, and reason usually triumphed in the end. By far the most important writer of such libretti at mid-century was Pietro Metastasio (1698–1782), whose dramatic texts were set to music repeatedly by leading composers of the day. Their music by and large continued the conventions of late-baroque opera as it existed at the time of Handel.

Beginning in the 1760s, the genre of serious opera was refashioned to give it greater simplicity and naturalness. The chief figure in this operatic reform was Christoph Gluck (1714–1787). A German by birth, Gluck was trained in Italy and settled in Vienna in 1750. In his opera *Orfeo ed Euridice* (1762) and in later works, Gluck sought to reassert the importance of drama in opera. In his view, serious opera had become too dependent on virtuosic singing in its arias. He eliminated these in favor of an expressive, restrained arioso. His objectives, true to the spirit of the Age of Reason, were summarized in the dedication (1769) of his opera *Alceste*: "Simplicity, truth, and naturalness are the great principles of beauty in all artistic manifestations."

C. P. E. Bach's *empfindsam* style and Gluck's dramatic intensity are symptomatic of a broad reaction against the facility of *galant* or rococo art beginning in the 1760s. During this decade, the French painters Jean-Baptiste Greuze (1725–1805) and Jacques-Louis David (1748–1825) elicited great attention through paintings that glorified virtue, bravery, and heroism. The carefree and hedonistic tone of the rococo is remote to their values. David's *Oath of the Horatii* (page 233) is a celebrated example of this new direction in art. The painting depicts the three brothers Horatius, who swear to die in the defense of Rome, despite the distress of their sisters. The theme, drawn from ancient history, parallels the classical subjects that were used in contemporary serious opera.

German literature and theater of the 1770s were marked by a similar movement, called *Sturm und Drang* ("storm and stress"), in which unbridled emotion, rebellion, and heroism were exalted. Goethe's novel *Die Leiden des jungen Werthers* (*The Sorrows of Young Werther,* 1774) is a famous example. It deals with a young artist who ultimately commits suicide as a result of his unrequited passions and hopeless future.

Composers of the 1760s and 1770s such as Franz Joseph Haydn, to whom we now turn, also began to depart from the simplicity and monochromatic lightness of the *galant* style and to seek instead a new depth and passion in their music. Works in the minor mode gained a new currency, fugue and counterpoint returned to add weight, and melody and rhythm took on

*David's depiction in* **Oath of the Horatii** *of a scene from Roman history signals a new spirit in French painting. Rather than the frivolous sensuality of rococo art, David's painting speaks of duty, bravery, and heroism.*

greater expressivity. This music is, on the whole, eclectic in its mixing of styles, sometimes emphasizing the purely *galant* taste and at other times waxing intensely emotional.

## The Life and Early Music of Haydn

Franz Joseph Haydn (1732–1809) is the oldest of the dominating figures of the classical period. His career as an important composer began about 1760, during the early phase of the classical era. His works of this time touch on

**233**

## Music Today

### Back to Bach, or What's in a Name?

In 1965 the music world was rocked by the discovery of P. D. Q. Bach (1807–1742?), the last and least of Johann Sebastian Bach's 20 odd children. P. D. Q. Bach is the creation of composer and sometime musicologist Peter Schickele, whose "discovery" is actually a madcap conflation of the elder Bach and a number of his sons. Members of this illustrious musical family are, like P. D. Q., traditionally identified by their first initials, namely W. F. (Wilhelm Friedemann) and C. P. E. (Carl Philipp Emanuel), Bach's two oldest sons, and the youngest, J. C. (Johann Christian).

P. D. Q. was, according to Professor Schickele, the author of numerous strikingly original musical works, for example, the "Schleptet in E♭ Major," the "Toot Suite," and the "Pevertimento for Bicycle, Bagpipes, Balloons, and Orchestra." Schickele continues his crusade to bring these deathless masterpieces to a willing public through recordings and concerts, often enlisting the assistance of major symphony orchestras. The compositions are in reality highly sophisticated and extremely amusing parodies of the style of J. S. Bach, his sons, and other classical composers. The parody is revealed either by comic wrong notes, by highly peculiar musical events, or through outrageous texts credited to the ineptness or drinking problems of the unfortunate P. D. Q.

Schickele's attack on the sublime through the ridiculous builds on a tradition of comedy in music. In the 1940s and 1950s, the bandleader Spike Jones toured the country with his "Musical Depreciation Revue," featuring zany instruments and antics, musically gifted animals, and a "Latrinophone" made from a toilet seat provided with strings. Schickele hails Jones as the "granddaddy of us all," although Jones did not attempt to appeal to a highbrow audience that was genuinely committed to classical music, as Schickele does. In England in the 1950s, the illustrator and amateur musician Gerard Hoffnung organized festivals devoted to musical parodies of the masters, and Anna Russell exchanged a career as a singer for that of a hilariously irreverent lecturer on Wagnerian opera. In the United States, the zany skits of Danny Kaye and the pianistic travesties of Victor Borge have bridged the gap between audiences of vaudeville and the habitués of Carnegie Hall.

All of these comedians are skillful musicians in their own right and highly knowledgeable of the classics. Schickele is a very active and acclaimed composer of serious music. He and his forebears show us that in music, the serious and the comic are often surprisingly compatible.

several of the modern approaches to composition of his day, including the *galant* and *Sturm und Drang* manners. By his own admission, he was also profoundly influenced by the *empfindsam* style of C. P. E. Bach, whose music he carefully studied.

Haydn's long career spans the entire classical period, from its early phase through its maturity, finally prefiguring a new style that emerged in the early nineteenth century. Due to its comprehensive nature, we shall deal with his music in two segments. In this chapter we survey his life and investigate the compositions of his youth. In the next chapter we shall explore his mature works.

## Haydn's Life

Haydn was born in Rohrau, a small village on the Austro-Hungarian border, to the family of a wheelwright. Being an able boy soprano, he was accepted in 1740 into the choir school of the Cathedral of Saint Stephen in Vienna. Since women were not allowed to sing in the service of worship in Vienna at this time, boys were needed to supply high voices in church choirs. In return for these services, Haydn received room, board, and a rudimentary education.

In 1749, the young Haydn's voice changed, and he was summarily dismissed from his school. For the next 11 years he lived impecuniously in Vienna as a free-lance musician, playing street serenades, teaching, and continuing his musical education. He received lessons from the famous Italian composer and singing master Nicola Porpora.

*Joseph Haydn sat for his portrait, done by the artist Thomas Hardy, in 1791, during his first visit to London. He proved to be the toast of the city, entertained by nobility and acclaimed by music lovers from all walks of life.*

In 1761, Haydn was appointed assistant (later head) **Kapellmeister** ("musical director") of the court of Prince Paul Esterházy. In the eighteenth century, the duties of a Kapellmeister were partly administrative and partly musical. He organized and conducted performances at the request of his patron, he composed music, and he performed as his abilities permitted. The social status of a Kapellmeister, or of any musician, was comparable to that of a servant. At first Haydn was required to wear a uniform, and he could mingle only with other servants and musicians.

Fortunately for Haydn, the Esterházy family was unusually enlightened in artistic matters. They resided in palaces in Vienna, in nearby Eisenstadt, and, after 1766, at a new palatial residence called Esterháza. Most of Haydn's time was spent at Eisenstadt and Esterháza, where he was isolated from the new musical ideas afoot in Vienna.

*In 1683, princes of the Esterházy family built this magnificent palace in Eisenstadt, near Vienna. Haydn lived and worked in this palace for much of his lifetime of service to the Esterházys.*

But his music was too great to be kept long a secret within the prince's domains. His works were circulated in manuscripts, especially among Austria's musically active monasteries, and they soon became widely known. He was invited to write symphonies for concerts in Paris and London, and he was in demand among other music-loving princes throughout Europe.

On the death in 1790 of his patron Nicholas Esterházy, the private orchestra at Esterháza was disbanded. But by this time, Haydn's fame was so great that it was unthinkable that he would be dismissed. He received a stipend solely to be counted as an associate of the Esterházys, and he was at last given his freedom to travel and to work as he chose.

He made two triumphant visits to London, in 1791–1792 and 1794–1795, where he composed 12 symphonies for the concerts of the impresario Johann Peter Salomon. In London he was a regular visitor to Queen Charlotte, and the prince of Wales (later George IV) became a devoted advocate of his music. He received an honorary doctorate in 1791 from Oxford University. In 1795 he returned to Eisenstadt at the behest of a new Esterházy prince, Nicholas II, but his duties were then limited to composing one Mass each year. No longer was he a mere servant; he was an internationally renowned artist whose social status had risen to a high bourgeois level.

Haydn was an immensely prolific composer, in part due to the circumstances of his employment. During his years of active service for the Esterházys, he was required to write music to order. Most of his greatest works, however, were written after 1790, after he was freed from the day-to-day requirements for his patron. He composed in virtually all genres in existence in his day, among which his symphonies, string quartets, piano sonatas, Masses, and oratorios are best known.

## String Quartet in B♭ Major, Op. 1, No. 1

The genre of the string quartet occupies a special place in Haydn's oeuvre. He was central to its establishment as a major genre—a status that it has maintained to the present day—and he composed quartets from the beginning to the end of his lengthy career. He was probably attracted to the medium of two violins, viola, and cello because of its inherent musicality. The instruments blend together but are also capable of their own distinctive voices. They can play with both delicacy and power and with both flamboyant agility and lyrical sweetness.

Haydn's early biographer Georg Griesinger reports that Haydn began to write quartets during his visits in the 1750s to the country home of a patron named Karl Joseph von Fürnberg. If Griesinger's story is accurate, the String Quartet in B♭ may be one of the works that Haydn composed for Fürnberg. Its exact date of composition is unknown, although it was most likely written in the late 1750s. It was published in an early edition of Haydn's collected string quartets designated opus 1.

The quartet has five short movements, a number reminiscent of the baroque suite or of the serenade in the classical period. Shortly after composing the early quartets of his opera 1 and 2, however, Haydn settled on a four-movement sequence for his remaining quartets. The spirit of this work is entirely *galant* in its happy mood and accessibility. As in many of his early quartets and symphonies, the melodic material of the Quartet in B♭ is conferred primarily on the first violin.

In the first movement of this piece (Recording 7.3), we encounter an early example of sonata form. This pattern is somewhat complicated but important to understand since in the classical period it became the predictable plan of organization in the first movements of all major instrumental genres. In the words of Giorgio Pestelli, sonata form became "a way of musical thinking that was perhaps the fulcrum of the whole historical period."[3]

Although sonata form was essentially new to the early classical period, it grew from the binary form that was used by baroque composers in dance movements. Before studying Haydn's quartet movement, let us first discuss this baroque formal prototype. Dance pieces in the late baroque period (recall those in Corelli's Sonata in A Major from Chapter 5) were almost always in binary form. In general, such movements are short, consisting of two concise sections, each immediately repeated. In the first section, the melody begins in the home key. By the cadence at the end of this section, it will have changed to a new keynote. In the second section, this pattern is reversed, as the melody begins in the new key and returns at or near the end to the home key.

Baroque composers handled melodies in the second section in several ways. A typical approach was to begin the second section with a melody that was nearly identical (except for keynote) to the opening melody. After the first few seconds, this melody takes on its own identity. Then, roughly midway through the second section, the initial melody and the home key return, and the movement quickly comes to its conclusion. A summary of this pattern, called *rounded binary form,* is shown in Figure 7.1(a).

Turning now to the first movement of Haydn's Quartet in B♭, we will see many features that fit the description of rounded binary form but also others that suggest the existence of a new formal plan. Haydn's movement consists of two sections, each immediately repeated. The first begins with a melody in period form, ending in a cadence at 0.09. Let us call this part of the movement its *main theme.* It is followed by another melodic idea, during which the key changes from the home keynote of B♭ to F. Since this passage serves primarily to move from one key to another, we shall call it the **transition** (or **bridge**). It is followed by another new melodic idea, called the **subsidiary theme,** which is in the new key of F. This theme can be distinguished by its quicker rhythmic motion, leading to a definite cadence at 0.28, whereupon the entire first section is repeated. Since the first section contains the initial statements of all of the important themes of the entire movement, it is called the **exposition** of the sonata form. (Do not confuse this term with the exposition of a fugue, as described in Chapter 6.)

The second main section of the movement, from 0.57, begins by touching on motives from both the subsidiary theme and the main theme, which are presented in new shapes. It is thus called the **development** of the movement. Following a cadence at 1.17, the main theme returns in the

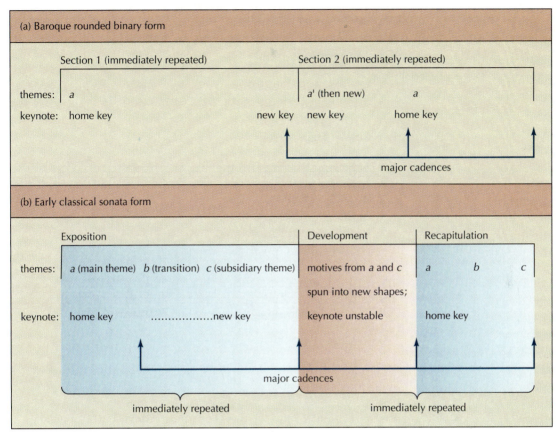

(a) Baroque rounded binary form

Section 1 (immediately repeated)             Section 2 (immediately repeated)

themes:    *a*                             *a'* (then new)          *a*

keynote:  home key             new key   new key         home key

major cadences

(b) Early classical sonata form

| Exposition | Development | Recapitulation |

themes:  *a* (main theme)  *b* (transition)  *c* (subsidiary theme)     motives from *a* and *c*     *a*     *b*     *c*

spun into new shapes;

keynote:  home key            .................new key     keynote unstable     home key

major cadences

immediately repeated                  immediately repeated

**Figure 7.1** *Baroque binary form and early classical sonata form.*

home key of B♭, followed by the remaining materials of the exposition (that is, the transition and the subsidiary theme). This passage is called the **recapitulation,** since it consists of a return of events of the exposition. It differs from the exposition in that its melodies do not change key. The entire second section is then repeated. These features of the early sonata form, as found in Haydn's quartet movement, are summarized in Figure 7.1(b).

    The mature classical sonata form differs from this incipient example in many important ways, although the main features of the form remain in place. We shall return to the sonata form in the next chapter, in the discussion of the first movement of Haydn's Symphony No. 102 in B♭ Major, in order to trace its expansion and solidification from these primitive beginnings to its mature shape.

**Franz Joseph Haydn, String Quartet in B♭ Major, Op. 1, No. 1, first movement**
Recording 7.3

A             0.00     Exposition: Main theme:

                  0.09        Transition to new key begins.

                  0.19        Subsidiary theme (in the new key):

A             0.28     Exposition is repeated.

B             0.57     Development: Motives from the main and subsidiary themes are spun into new shapes.

                  1.17        Recapitulation: Events of the exposition return, but all melodies remain in the home key, B♭.

B             1.44     Development and recapitulation are repeated.

## TOPICS FOR DISCUSSION AND WRITING

**1.** Assemble selected paintings by Watteau, Fragonard, and Boucher, and discuss the ways in which their themes, shapes, and colors conform to the *galant* style of music.

**2.** Compare the music of the aria ''Se non mi vuol amar'' from Handel's *Tamerlano* (Recording 6.6, discussed in Chapter 6) with that of ''Sempre in contrasti'' from Pergolesi's *La serva padrona* (Recording 7.1). Take into consideration overall form, orchestration, and the nature of the vocal line. How do the differences in style suggest the change of taste in music from the baroque to the early classical period?

**3.** Compare the music of the first movement of J. S. Bach's *Brandenburg Concerto* No. 2 (Recording 6.4) with the finale of J. C. Bach's *Symphony in D Major*, Op. 18,

No. 4 (Recording 7.2). Although these works are in two different genres, their styles will suggest general differences between baroque and classical music. Focus on the makeup of the two orchestras, the nature of rhythm and phrasing in the two pieces, the relative perceptibility of form, and the placement of cadences.

**4.** In what ways does Haydn's String Quartet in B♭ Major, Op. 1, No. 1, conform to the same *galant* style of the symphonic movement by J. C. Bach and the aria by Pergolesi also studied in this chapter? Take into consideration the mode of the three works, the prevailing texture, the general spirit conveyed by the pieces, the nature of the melodies, and the clarity of their rhythm and beat.

## ADDITIONAL LISTENING

The following pieces will be found enjoyable and informative and will provide a fuller understanding of the accomplishments of their composers. They are all readily available on long-playing records, compact disks, or tape.

### C. P. E. Bach

Sonata in F Major for harpsichord (*Prussian Sonata* No. 1, c. 1742). The slow movement of this work is a good introduction to Bach's *empfindsam* style, with its improvisatory, impassioned quality and evocation of operatic recitative.

Fantasia in C Major, Wotquenne 59, No. 6. This work appeared in a cycle of harpsichord sonatas, rondos, and fantasias collectively titled "Für Kenner und Liebhaber" ("For Connoisseurs and Amateurs"). Fantasias were one-movement pieces, usually for keyboard, that were improvisatory in character and free in form. They probably reflect Bach's own improvisatory practices at the clavichord, as mentioned by Burney.

### J. C. Bach

*Symphonie concertante* in A Major for violin, cello, and orchestra (c. 1770). The **symphonie concertante** was a favored genre of Bach. It was a concertolike piece for two or more solo instruments and orchestra. The overall form of this particular work is unusual in that it has only two movements.

### Gluck

*Orfeo ed Euridice* (1762; revised and translated into French, 1774). Listen especially for Orfeo's ravishing lament aria "Che farò senza Euridice?" in Act 3. Its melody is also heard in the laments that open Act 1.

### Haydn

(Also see Additional Listening in Chapter 8.)

Piano Sonata No. 20 in C Minor (1771). This work illustrates the *empfindsam* or storm-and-stress aspect of Haydn's music of the 1760s and 1770s.

String Quartet in C Major, Op. 20, No. 2. Like the Piano Sonata No. 20, this quartet is in the stormy idiom of the early 1770s. It is especially notable for its dense and complicated counterpoint, and its finale is cast in the form of a strict fugue.

Symphonies No. 6, 7, and 8 (*Le Matin, Le Midi, Le Soir,* 1761). As in the String Quartet in B♭ Major, Op. 1, No. 1, these symphonies feature the first violin. Their nicknames (*Morning, Afternoon, Evening*), given by the composer himself, probably refer to aspects of daily life at the Esterházy court that are suggested by the music.

### Pergolesi

*Stabat mater* (1736). This sacred composition, for solo voices and orchestra, mixes elements of the early classical style with an older church idiom.

*Pulcinella* by Igor Stravinsky (1920). This ballet score by the twentieth-century composer Stravinsky consists of arrangements of instrumental and vocal music attributed to Pergolesi. Its refreshing brightness depicts the *galant* style viewed through the eyes of an admiring modern interpreter.

## BIBLIOGRAPHY

### Early Classic Period in General

Blume, Friedrich. *Classic and Romantic Music.* Translated by M. D. Herter Norton. New York: Norton, 1970.

Burney, Charles. *The Present State of Music in Germany, the Netherlands and United Provinces.* Two volumes. Facsimile edition. Kassel, Germany: Bärenreiter, 1959. A delightful and informative diary of Dr. Burney's travels, originally published in 1773 and 1775.

Landon, H. C. Robbins. *Essays on the Viennese Classical Style.* New York: Macmillan, 1970. These articles are for the general reader. See especially Chapter 1 ("Rococo in Music") and Chapter 2 ("The Viennese Classical Period").

Lang, Paul Henry. *Music in Western Civilization.* New York: Norton, 1941. Chapters 12–15 deal with the classical style and its relation to contemporary intellectual and artistic history.

Pauly, Reinhard G. *Music in the Classic Period.* Second edition. Englewood Cliffs, N.J.: Prentice Hall, 1973.

Pestelli, Giorgio. *The Age of Mozart and Beethoven.* Translated by Eric Cross. Cambridge: Cambridge University Press, 1984.

Rosen, Charles. *The Classic Style: Haydn, Mozart, Beethoven.* New York: Viking Penguin, 1971.

Wangermann, Ernst. *The Austrian Achievement, 1700–1800.* Orlando, Fla.: Harcourt Brace Jovanovich, 1973. A short survey of political, intellectual, and artistic history.

**J. C. Bach**

Geiringer, Karl. *The Bach Family: Seven Generations of Creative Genius.* Second edition. New York: Oxford University Press, 1977.

Terry, Charles Sanford. *John Christian Bach.* Revised by H. C. Robbins Landon. London: Oxford University Press, 1967.

(For Haydn, see the bibliography to Chapter 8.)

## NOTES

1. Johann Adolph Scheibe, in *The Bach Reader,* ed. Hans T. David and Arthur Mendel (New York: Norton, 1966), p. 238.
2. Cedric Howard Glover (ed.), *Dr. Charles Burney's Continental Travels* (London: Blackie & Son, 1927), p. 239.
3. Giorgio Pestelli, *The Age of Mozart and Beethoven,* trans. Eric Cross (Cambridge: Cambridge University Press, 1984), p. 14.

# 8

*Viennese Classicism*

## The City of Music

Vienna is proudly known as "die Musikstadt," the City of Music. Its
reputation is justly deserved. Beginning in the eighteenth century, it
has been home to an incomparable number of leading musicians.
Haydn, Mozart, Beethoven, Schubert, Brahms, Bruckner, Mahler,
and Schoenberg have been only a few of its musically gifted residents.

There are many reasons that Vienna became preeminent in music.
First of all, it is situated at the crossroads between other areas where
music flourished, especially Italy, Bohemia, Germany, and Hungary,
and it attracted talented composers and performers from all of these
regions. But its main strength has been in the popularity of music

among its people. From the lowest of servants to the royalty of the Hapsburg family, nearly everyone in Vienna sang, played, and listened to music. The result was an extraordinary demand for professional music teachers, performers, publishers, and composers. "There's not a noble maid, not even a burger's daughter, who can't play the piano and sing as well," remarked the Viennese Joseph Richter in 1794.

Music in Vienna in the eighteenth century was especially focused in the palaces of the nobility, for whom elaborate music was both a passionate form of entertainment and a status symbol. The names of these patrons—Esterházy, Waldstätten, Lobkowitz, Lichnowsky, to cite but a few—loom large in the careers of the great Viennese classical composers. But music was also demanded by ordinary people, in the form of operas given at the Burgtheater or in suburban theaters, in church music performed in such magnificent sites as the Cathedral of Saint Stephen, and in summer concerts in parks.

The beauty and civility of Vienna in the mid-eighteenth century are captured in Bernardo Bellotto's "Vienna from the Upper Belvedere." Belvedere is a palace, built for the military hero Prince Eugene of Savoy and located in the suburbs of the city. The upper level—today used as an art gallery—provides an inspiring view of the city and the gentle hills lying to the northwest. The Venice-born Bellotto worked from 1759 until 1761 in the service of the Hapsburg

Empress, Maria Theresa. He specialized in panoramic "view paintings," such as the one shown here. The picture is almost photographic in its realism, although Bellotto is intent on showing the gardens and buildings in their most attractive light. The lake at the left belongs to the Schwarzenberg Palace, which stands opposite it. The formal gardens on the right are attached to the Belvedere, and here courtiers stroll and talk with an idealistic naturalness and refinement, just the way those of the nobility wished to view themselves. At the far end of the gardens is an orangery, a nursery where exotic trees and plants were grown and a common feature of palaces at the time. On the far left and right are the domes of suburban churches.

In the distance stands the city itself, dominated by the spire of Saint Stephen's Cathedral. We can see remnants of the medieval walls and battlements that still girded the city when the painting was completed in 1760. These were removed in the nineteenth century and replaced by the splendid circular avenue called the Ringstraße, which now gives the city so much of its charm.

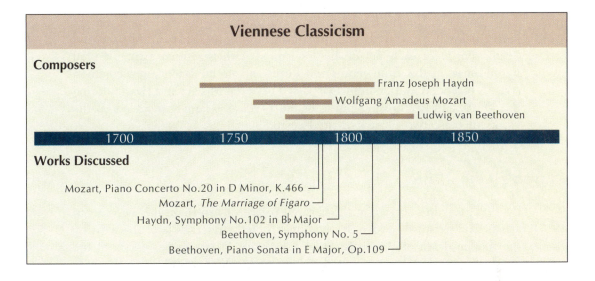

The history of the late classical period in music unfolds largely in the city of Vienna, for this was the center of activity for Franz Joseph Haydn, Wolfgang Amadeus Mozart, and Ludwig van Beethoven, the three preeminent masters of this age. Throughout the eighteenth century, musical culture in Vienna was vigorous in embracing different national tastes. Italian opera was in constant favor, although German opera was supported periodically by the Hapsburg court and heard regularly in suburban theaters. French opera enjoyed a period of popularity in the 1750s and 1760s, under the aegis of the Austrian chancellor Kaunitz. There was also a distinguished tradition of instrumental music in Vienna, including symphonic composition by figures such as Matthias Monn (1717–1750) and Georg Wagenseil (1715–1777) and chamber music by Karl Ditters von Dittersdorf (1739–1799) and Johann Baptist Vanhal (1739–1813).

Prior to the nineteenth century, music in Vienna was to a considerable degree confined to the private houses of aristocratic music lovers. Many wealthy individuals employed their own orchestras and chamber ensembles, and music heard publicly was limited in general to performances in church or in the theater. Public concerts, called academies, were usually isolated events, given either for charitable purposes or for the gain of a sponsoring musician. The importance of church music declined in Vienna toward the end of the century, partly due to the wane of the private chapel of the Austrian monarchy and partly due to the increasingly secular spirit of the age.

**249**

Never in the history of music have the leading composers of an era been so closely associated. The three crowning figures, Haydn, Mozart, and Beethoven, were each personally acquainted with the other two. They all wrote music in the same genres and forms and, to an extent, in a common style. A profound mutual influence passed between Mozart and Haydn during the 1780s, and Beethoven's music of the 1790s was largely modeled on the works of these two illustrious predecessors.

## Haydn's Late Music

By 1790, Haydn's service in the isolated palace of Esterháza had become an artistic and personal burden. He was unexpectedly released later that year by the sudden death of Prince Nicholas Esterházy. At last in possession of the freedom he craved, Haydn immediately moved to Vienna and began to weigh several attractive options. Despite his friend Mozart's pleas for him to remain in Vienna, Haydn accepted an offer, delivered in person, from the impresario Johann Peter Salomon to travel to London to write symphonies for Salomon's concerts. London at this time was well on the way to becoming a major industrial center, and it had a public eager for music. Haydn arrived there on January 1, 1791, and remained until the summer of 1792. In January 1794 he returned to London for a second sojourn, which lasted until 1795, at which time he returned permanently to Vienna.

Haydn received unparalleled attention and acclamation during his London trips, which was as gratifying to the aging master as it was unfamiliar to him after his years of isolation. His new artistic freedom and international recognition stimulated him to achieve new levels of productivity and greatness as a composer. From 1791 until he retired from composing in 1803, he produced 12 symphonies, 15 trios for piano, violin, and cello, 3 piano sonatas, 14 string quartets, 6 Masses, and 2 oratorios. All are among his greatest works. The symphonies are especially masterful, showing a depth of expression that reflects his great command of the orchestra as well as his contact with the profound expressiveness of Mozart's symphonies.

### Symphony No. 102 in B♭ Major

This is one of the six symphonies that Haydn composed during his second trip to London. It was written in 1794 and premiered in February of the following year at the Opera Concerts, a series that superseded Salomon's earlier subscription concerts at the King's Theatre. The orchestra was large (it

250

numbered about 60 players), and conforming to English tradition, Haydn assisted in the premiere performance by playing along at the piano. He calls in this work for a full classical orchestra, without clarinets, and he uses the standard four-movement plan in which the first movement dominates. The second movement will repay careful study, as it is one of the most inspiringly beautiful in any of Haydn's symphonies. The minuet movement has the earthy character of a peasant dance, and the finale is based on a cheerful folk melody.

In comparison with the symphony by J. C. Bach encountered in Chapter 7, Haydn's is distinguished by a grand sweep of ideas, an inexorable logic and forward motion, and a gripping interchange of themes. The *galant* spirit of the early classical period is almost entirely banished, as the music becomes a vast drama filled with color, motion, struggle, and conquest.

Predictably, Haydn uses sonata form in the first movement (Recording 8.1), here much expanded in comparison to the primitive example of this formal scheme encountered in his String Quartet in B♭, Op. 1, No. 1. The symphonic movement begins not with the main theme of the exposition but with a lengthy introductory passage in a slow tempo. The slow introduction to the first movement of a symphony was characteristic of Haydn's late works, and it was also used in a few symphonies by Mozart and in Beethoven's First, Second, Fourth, and Seventh Symphonies. First we hear the entire orchestra softly play a single note (B♭). The note grows ominously loud, and then dwindles away. Next, the violins state a four-note motive, which is passed around to various instruments during the remainder of the introduction. This motive and the long-held B♭ do not return per se after the introduction ends, but, characteristic of Haydn's striving for unity in his late music, they are subtly related to all of the subsequent melodic materials. The opening unison note is heard again in the first subsidiary theme, and the four-note motive underlies the main theme and transitional theme. Although these motivic connections among themes may be difficult to recognize at first, they make us hear this movement as a coherent musical argument, connected and unified from beginning to end.

At 2.32 the introduction ends and the music takes a bright turn as the tempo becomes faster and the rhythms quicker. The main theme is in period form, and it is heard twice in succession. Its cadence at 2.46 overlaps the beginning of the transition, which can be recognized for its loud volume and furious rhythmic energy. The transition leads to a new keynote (F), which is established by the full cadence at 3.25.

The first subsidiary theme is full of surprises. It begins with a loud note in unison, then an oddly placed silence, after which it continues. Other subsidiary themes ensue, leading to the cadence at 3.53 and the repeat of the

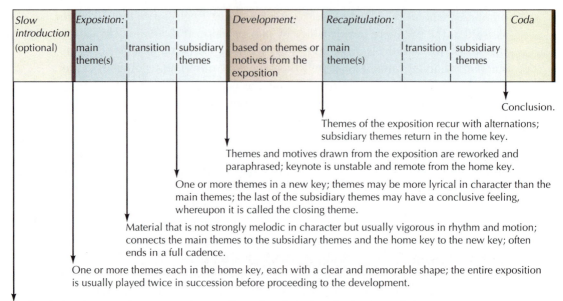

| Slow introduction (optional) | Exposition: | | | Development: | Recapitulation: | | | Coda |
|---|---|---|---|---|---|---|---|---|
| | main theme(s) | transition | subsidiary themes | based on themes or motives from the exposition | main theme(s) | transition | subsidiary themes | |

Conclusion.

Themes of the exposition recur with alternations; subsidiary themes return in the home key.

Themes and motives drawn from the exposition are reworked and paraphrased; keynote is unstable and remote from the home key.

One or more themes in a new key; themes may be more lyrical in character than the main themes; the last of the subsidiary themes may have a conclusive feeling, whereupon it is called the closing theme.

Material that is not strongly melodic in character but usually vigorous in rhythm and motion; connects the main themes to the subsidiary themes and the home key to the new key; often ends in a full cadence.

One or more themes each in the home key, each with a clear and memorable shape; the entire exposition is usually played twice in succession before proceeding to the development.

Optional; slow in tempo; themes or motives usually not heard after introduction has ended.

***Figure 8.1*** *Sonata form in the late eighteenth century: constituent parts.*

entire exposition. The development section spins out melodic ideas from both the main and subsidiary themes, turning them into ever-new shapes. At 6.01 a motive from the subsidiary themes is made into a brief fugue. The combatants in the fugue are finally separated (6.24), and a flute enters with the main theme. We are tempted to think that this is the recapitulation, but it cannot be since the home key (B♭) still has not been regained. The difference in orchestration in comparison with the beginning of the exposition also underscores that we have not yet reached the recapitulation. This passage, typical of Haydn's penchant for the unexpected, is an example of a *false recapitulation.*

At last, the key returns to B♭ and the true recapitulation begins. It brings back, with some changes, the melodic events of the exposition. In the recapitulation, the subsidiary themes remain in the home key (B♭), and in this movement, the main theme has one additional statement at 7.59.

Using this movement as a typical example, we can now summarize the features of sonata form as it is usually encountered in the first movements of late-classical instrumental pieces. It is misleading to see the details of this form in concrete or preestablished terms, since at most, sonata form is a general principle of organization susceptible to many varied realizations. A mature sonata-form movement (see Figure 8.1) is in two large parts, of which the first is immediately repeated. The second, the longer of the two, may or may not be repeated. The first part, called the *exposition,* contains the initial statement of the melodies or themes of the entire movement. It begins with one or more main themes, each in the home key and each having a definite and memorable shape. Next comes the *transition:* the passage in which the home key gradually gives way to the establishment of a new key. Transitions are usually not strongly melodious. They may develop motives already heard in the main themes or, sometimes, introduce new melodic ideas. But transitions are characterized more by their energetic rhythm than by their melodies. A transition ends on a new keynote, often coming to a full cadence.

The exposition is concluded by the statement of several subsidiary themes in the new key. Sometimes these melodies are more lyrical than the impetuous main themes. At times, the last of the subsidiary themes will have a conclusive character, whereupon it is called a *closing theme.* The exposition usually ends with a full cadence in the new key, and it is immediately repeated in toto.

The second large part of a movement in sonata form is divided into two primary subsections, the *development* and the *recapitulation.* In the development, themes or motives from the exposition are elaborated on, varied, or paraphrased, while the keynote is unsettled. The recapitulation returns to the home key and brings back the events of the exposition with certain changes. The home key remains in effect to the end of the movement.

A sonata-form movement may begin with an introduction in a slower tempo than the body of the movement itself. The melodies or motives of the introduction do not usually return after the introduction ends. The movement is usually closed by a short and conclusive *coda.*

**Franz Joseph Haydn, Symphony No. 102 in B♭ Major, first movement**
Recording 8.1

**Introduction**      0.00      Slow in tempo; based on two central motives that subtly underlie later themes:

| **Exposition** | 2.32 | Main theme: A melody in period form, immediately restated by different instruments. It begins |

| | 2.46 | Transition: A string of melodic ideas that are derived primarily from the main theme. Ends in a full cadence on the new keynote F. |

| | 3.26 | Subsidiary themes: A succession of themes all in the new key. The final one comes to a full cadence. The first subsidiary theme begins |

| **Exposition** | 3.54 | Repeated |

| **Development** | 5.15 | Part 1: Initial motives from the main theme and first subsidiary theme are reshaped while the keynote changes. |

| | 6.01 | Part 2: Brief fugue based on a motive from the transition, ending with a general pause and silence. |

| | 6.24 | Part 3: Begins with a restatement of the main theme in the flute (false recapitulation), followed by continued development of motives from the subsidiary themes. |

| **Recapitula-tion** | 7.02 | Main theme: More fully orchestrated and shorter than in the exposition. In the home key of B♭. |

| | 7.09 | Transition: Shortened in comparison to its appearance in the exposition. |

| | 7.33 | Subsidiary themes: All in the home key of B♭ and all modified in minor details in comparison to their appearance in the exposition. |

# *Wolfgang Amadeus Mozart (1756–1791)*

Mozart's career progressed very differently from that of his friend Haydn. Whereas Haydn made his real mark in instrumental composition, Mozart was constantly drawn to operatic music. Haydn lived under the patronage system in comfortable if isolated circumstances; Mozart traveled repeatedly to the major centers of European music in search of elusive, stable employment. Haydn's life spanned the entire classical period and early years of the nineteenth century, during which he acquired an international reputation; Mozart died at the age of 35, before the greatness of his music was widely recognized.

Mozart was born in Salzburg, then an independent city-state ruled by an archbishop and closely allied to the Hapsburg monarchy. His father, Leopold, was an accomplished violinist and composer who worked in the service of the ruling archbishop. The elder Mozart was a well-educated man who provided his son with all of his musical and general schooling.

It soon became clear that the child Mozart was an extraordinary musical prodigy. He quickly mastered the harpsichord and stringed instruments, he learned to improvise at the keyboard, he possessed an amazing memory for music, and he was able to compose in virtually any style he heard. His first compositions were made when he was a mere 6 years of age, and he wrote his first opera at 11. In an effort to advance the education of his prodigious son and to bring his gifts to wider recognition, Leopold Mozart and his wife took Wolfgang during the 1760s and 1770s on a series of travels to the major musical centers of Europe. At the age of 7 he performed for Maria Theresa in Vienna; the next year he played for Louis XV in Paris, continuing on to London in 1764, where he performed for King George III. During this trip to London he met Johann Christian Bach, who recognized the child's genius and with whom Mozart formed a touching friendship.

*The Parisian painter Louis Carrogis de Carmontelle recorded this image of a concert by the child Mozart (at the keyboard), his sister, and his father during the Mozart family visit to Paris in 1763–1764. Their elegant dress and the elder Mozart's casual stance suggest the gallant spirit that reigned in the arts in France during the 1760s.*

255

Mozart's tours were a valuable learning experience, leading him to compose in an eclectic fashion that produced very different results from the products of Haydn's isolation. Between his trips abroad, Mozart followed his father by entering into the musical service of the archbishop in Salzburg, Prince Hieronymus Colloredo, an employer whom he thoroughly disliked. From Munich, where Mozart had gone to oversee rehearsals of his opera *Idomeneo,* he expressed to his father, in typically salty language, his feelings for Colloredo:

> You know, my dear father, that it is only to please you that I am staying on there [in Salzburg], since, by heaven, if I had followed my inclination before leaving the other day, I would have wiped my arse with my last contract from him [Colloredo]. For I swear to you on my honor that it is not Salzburg itself but the Prince and his conceited nobility who become every day more intolerable to me.[1]

In 1781, Mozart left the service of the archbishop, determined to live in Vienna as a free artist. He was immediately a success, giving academies for his own benefit, publishing music, and teaching. He was happily married to Constanze Weber in 1782, and he became a fast friend of Haydn, who remarked to Mozart's father, "I tell you before God and as an honest man that your son is the greatest composer known to me, either personally or by reputation." In 1784, Mozart joined a Freemason's lodge in Vienna, where he relished the occult rituals and symbols, the spirit of fraternity, and the high-minded humanitarianism fostered by the Freemasons at this time.

But after about 1786, his fortunes began to decline, as he was less in demand as a teacher and a composer. He was especially frustrated in obtaining performances of his operas in Vienna, possibly due to opposition from the conductor of the court opera, Antonio Salieri, and from other rivals. Although finally in 1787 appointed to the musical staff of the Hapsburg court, he fell deeply into debt. He suddenly became ill from a condition that his physicians diagnosed as "severe military fever," and he died on December 5, 1791. As was the custom for people of lower social status, Mozart was buried in a common grave, near the outskirts of the city. Almost immediately after his death, rumors circulated that Mozart had been poisoned, possibly by his rival Salieri. There is no evidence for this suspicion, although it was later used as the basis for a play by Pushkin, *Mozart and Salieri,* and for the imaginative, though largely fictitious, play and film *Amadeus* by Peter Shaffer.

Mozart, like Haydn, composed in all of the major genres of his day, but he was most inclined toward operatic music. His talents as a virtuoso pianist also led him to the piano concerto. Like Haydn, Mozart composed music for specific performances, and this utilitarian approach led him to write an unusually large quantity of music. Most of his greatest compositions come from the last decade of his life.

Given the large number of works by Mozart (over 600) and the relative lack of contemporary publications bearing opus numbers, musicians today identify Mozart's music by so-called *Köchel* (abbreviated *K.*) *numbers.* These are the numbers assigned to Mozart's complete works in a catalog by the Austrian musicologist Ludwig von Köchel, published in Leipzig in 1862. In 1937, the Köchel catalog was revised, necessitating the change of many numbers. These revisions have not, however, replaced the older numbers in common usage.

Mozart composed approximately 50 symphonies, although the traditional numbering of his symphonies extends only to 41. The earliest are in the facile *galant* style of his mentor J. C. Bach, and the best known are the last six, composed from 1782 to 1788. These have a depth of expression that may well have inspired Haydn in his London symphonies.

The 23 piano concertos are among the glories of his work, indeed, of all of music. He also wrote concertos for orchestral instruments and several *symphonies concertantes.* Most of the piano concertos were composed during his final decade in Vienna, especially between the years 1783 and 1786, the period of his greatest fame as a performer. These are not simply showy or virtuosic pieces but instrumental music in which Mozart most consistently reveals his melodic and dramatic gifts.

Although Mozart's 26 string quartets include many masterpieces, the quartet was not one of his favorite genres. But his string quintets, written for the instruments of the string quartet plus an additional viola, are among his greatest chamber works. Mozart composed over 20 piano sonatas and more than twice that number for piano with instrumental accompaniment. These are generally *galant* in their simplicity and lightness of texture.

Mozart is unsurpassed in the history of music as a master of opera. Even as child, he was enraptured by great operatic singing, and he showed an uncanny ability to write music that could express different sentiments and characters. Mozart was a perceptive, if somewhat cynical, judge of people, and his operas abound in interesting characters that are brought to life by his music. The subjects of his operas are almost invariably filled with life and gaiety.

Mozart wrote operas of three types: Italian serious opera, Italian comic opera, and a category of German sentimental opera called **Singspiel.** *Idomeneo* (1781) and *La clemenza di Tito* (1791) are examples of the first type. These works rejuvenate styles from late-baroque opera, and their subjects are fanciful scenes from ancient history. Mozart collaborated with the librettist

Lorenzo da Ponte on his three mature Italian comic operas: *Le nozze di Figaro* (*The Marriage of Figaro,* 1786), *Don Giovanni* (1787), and *Così fan tutte* (*Thus Do They All,* 1790). Singspiel is a spoken German play interspersed with operatic music and usually based on a sentimental, romantic, or supernatural plot. Mozart's compositions *Die Entführung aus dem Serail* (*The Abduction from the Seraglio,* 1782) and *Die Zauberflöte* (*The Magic Flute,* 1791) are of this type.

Prior to his final decade in Vienna, Mozart wrote a large amount of music for the Catholic service of worship. Most is for the medium of chorus, solo voices, and orchestra. His Masses tend to be overtly operatic and popular in character, not surprisingly, since he was writing these pieces for the average worshiper and music lover. His final work of this type is a **Requiem Mass,** music for a special Mass for funerals. It was commissioned by a Viennese count, Franz Walsegg, to be performed as one of Walsegg's own compositions. At the time of Mozart's death in 1791, he had completed only the first movement, although most or all of the remaining movements were sketched. The incomplete passages were finished posthumously by Mozart's student Franz Süssmayr, who claimed that he, not Mozart, had composed the last three movements. The issue of authenticity in the Requiem has not been settled, although the work itself is esteemed as one of the master's most inspired creations.

### Piano Concerto No. 20 in D Minor, K. 466

In the late-baroque period, the concerto rose to a preeminent status among instrumental genres. It was equally important in the classical period. The overall form of the late-baroque concerto—three movements in the sequence fast, slow, fast—remained unchanged, as did the medium of solo instrument accompanied by orchestra. Although in the classical period many different instruments were used as soloists, the piano quickly became the most important.

Mozart's Piano Concerto No. 20 in D Minor, K. 466, was written in 1785, at the height of his popularity in Vienna as a pianist and a composer. Typically, it was written in a matter of only a few weeks and intended for use in a concert that Mozart organized for his own benefit. Despite somewhat strained relations with his son during this period, Leopold Mozart traveled to Vienna to hear the concert. After it, he wrote to his daughter, Maria Anna:

> We drove to his first subscription concert, at which a great many members of the aristocracy were present. Each person pays a souverain d'or or three ducats for these Lenten concerts. Your brother is giving them at the Mehlgrube and only pays half a

*Mozart wrote down his Piano Concerto No. 21 in C Major, K. 467, only days before its first performance in March 1785. This page from the slow movement (heard on Recording 1.1) shows the quickness with which Mozart worked, abbreviating the notation wherever possible. It also reveals remarkably few corrections or changes, suggesting that the concerto was entirely fixed in the composer's memory before he first set pen to paper.*

souverain d'or each time for the hall. The concert was magnificent and the orchestra played splendidly. In addition to the symphonies a female singer of the Italian theatre sang two arias. Then we had a new and very fine concerto by Wolfgang, which the copyist was still copying when we arrived, and the rondo of which your brother did not even have time to play through, as he had to supervise the copying.[2]

**259**

The overall form of the concerto is the familiar three-movement cycle: The first movement is fast and, given its length and pathos, carries the weight of the entire piece. The second movement, called a *romance* by the composer, is in rondo form, as is the impetuous finale. Like all of Mozart's late works in the minor mode, this piece is filled with a profound intensity and emotion that here seem to prefigure the tragic overtones of the Requiem, also in D minor.

In the first movements of concertos, classical composers never unanimously agreed on a standard form. Some aspects of ritornello form used by late-baroque composers in the fast movements of their concertos were preserved, and elements of the newer sonata form were present as well. Classical concertos also allowed for a display of the soloist's performing ability, something that was especially appealing to the public. The first movement of Piano Concerto No. 20 in D Minor (Recording 8.2) illustrates Mozart's amalgamation of both traditional and innovative formal elements, and it also contains some of his most passionate and lyrical music.

The movement opens with a section in which only the orchestra plays (Mozart as piano soloist may have played along with the orchestra in this opening passage, doubling the music of the orchestra). It contains a succession of themes, all but one in the home key of D minor, and it corresponds formally to the opening ritornello of a baroque concerto's first movement. Following a cadence at 2.25, a second major section begins, now featuring the soloist, who alternates with the orchestra. Some themes in this passage are new, and others have already been heard in the first section.

At 5.30 the orchestra reenters loudly with a theme from the opening ritornello, beginning a section in which themes heard earlier are developed and in which the pianist plays waves of notes designed to impress the audience. At 8.03 the orchestra again takes charge by restating the first theme in the home key of D minor. This resembles the beginning of the recapitulation of a sonata-form movement, an impression that is reinforced when other important themes from the first two major sections also return. The next point of demarcation occurs at 11.17, when the orchestra again enters loudly with a theme from the opening ritornello. This theme quickly leads to a full stop in the music. Now the pianist takes a turn at **improvisation,** playing extemporaneously without written music. At the end of the improvisation—called the **cadenza**—the orchestra concludes the movement with a final statement of themes from the opening ritornello.

The general order and nature of events in this somewhat complicated movement are summarized in the Listening Guide. Its form is reasonably typical of first movements in other mature classical concertos. Note especially

**Listening Guide**

**Wolfgang Amadeus Mozart, Piano Concerto No. 20 in D Minor, K. 466, first movement**
Recording 8.2

| | | |
|---|---|---|
| **Ritornello** | 0.00 | The orchestra plays a string of themes, mostly in the home key of D minor. The first of them begins |

| | | |
|---|---|---|
| **Solo episode** | 2.25 | The soloist is featured at first, introducing a new theme: |

Subsequently, the soloist alternates with the orchestra, mixing new themes with old and changing the key to F major.

| | | |
|---|---|---|
| **Ritornello and development** | 5.30 | The beginning of this section is marked by the loud entrance of the orchestra playing a theme from the opening passage. It is followed by the soloist and orchestra developing earlier themes, while the key proves unstable. |
| **Ritornello and recapitulation** | 8.03 | The orchestra returns with the first theme in the home key. The soloist and orchestra then alternate, bringing back several important earlier themes. |
| **Ritornello** | 11.17 | The orchestra loudly plays a theme from the very first section, quickly coming to a complete silence. |
| **Cadenza** | 11.39 | The soloist improvises. |
| **Ritornello (coda)** | 14.06 | The orchestra briefly plays themes from the opening ritornello to round off the movement. |

how baroque ritornello form and classical sonata form are intertwined. The alternation of playing by the soloist and by the full orchestra and the periodic recurrence of themes from the initial orchestral passage are holdovers from the baroque period. Sonata form is present in the change of key in the solo episode, the presence of a lengthy development section, and the recapitulation in the home key. The cadenza probably originated in operatic arias of the day, in which singers traditionally improvised near major cadences to show their virtuosity.

## *Le nozze di Figaro (The Marriage of Figaro)*

At about the time of the premiere of the D-minor Piano Concerto, Mozart began to compose a new opera based on a comic satire, *Le mariage de Figaro,* by the French writer Beaumarchais. Mozart's interest in Beaumarchais's comedies was stimulated when he saw an operatic version of this writer's earlier play *The Barber of Seville,* set to music by the Neapolitan composer Giovanni Paisiello. (A more famous opera based on *The Barber of Seville* was written later by Gioacchino Rossini.) Beaumarchais's *Marriage of Figaro* was a sequel to *The Barber of Seville,* and its brilliant wit, true-to-life characters, and overtones of social criticism captivated Mozart and convinced him of the play's suitability to the operatic stage.

At Mozart's suggestion, the poet and playwright Lorenzo da Ponte skillfully reshaped the play as an Italian libretto and tactfully eliminated much of its antiaristocratic content (with which Mozart was, all the same, no doubt sympathetic). The opera was first heard in Vienna on May 1, 1786, beginning a period of unprecedented popularity that has extended to the present day.

The story of *The Marriage of Figaro* contains high comedy and farce, without the stereotypes or simplifications found in Pergolesi's opera *La serva padrona.* Like this earlier opera, however, it relies on interactions of different social classes for its comic effects, for example, the servant Figaro getting the upper hand over his master, Count Almaviva. It also uses ludicrous disguises to produce farcical situations, such as the dressing of the page Cherubino as a woman. The characters of *The Marriage of Figaro*—a hypocritical nobleman, comic servants, a pompous doctor, a young swain, and a comic music teacher—are familiar to audiences of comedy. But unlike the characters of *La serva padrona,* those of *The Marriage of Figaro* come to life in truthful, multifaceted personalities who not only amuse us but also, in the manner of genuine drama, tell us about ourselves and about the eternal human condition. As in many comedies, the dramatic complications are finally resolved happily, and the story culminates in a wedding.

Mozart's opera is built of components familiar from earlier operas. The work begins with an overture in a free sonata form, and each act is divided into musical numbers consisting of arias, recitatives, ensembles, or choruses. The last three acts are concluded by lengthy sections called *finales*. These are multipart passages devoted primarily to ensemble singing and also, in passing, to recitative, chorus, and arialike interpolations. The words of the finales usually bring the plot to a point of climax, confusion, or resolution. Since they involve several major characters singing simultaneously or in succession, they allow Mozart an opportunity to distinguish and to define these characters in clear and dynamic ways.

The finales to Acts 2 and 4 are very long and involved character studies. The finale to Act 3 is short and relatively straightforward in organization, so we shall use this passage to illustrate the dramatic nature of Mozart's music (Recording 8.3). The finale begins as the count has caught Cherubino

---

**Listening Guide**

**Wolfgang Amadeus Mozart, *Le nozze di Figaro,* Act 3, finale**
Recording 8.3

| | | |
|---|---|---|
| **Introduction** | 0.00 | Wedding march. The key moves from G major to the central tonic, C major. |
| **A** | 1.47 | The tempo quickens, and a peasant duet and chorus begin: |

| | | |
|---|---|---|
| **B** | 2.58 | Fandango in A minor, slow tempo: |

| | | |
|---|---|---|
| **Transition** | 4.39 | Recitative accompanied by orchestra, during which the key changes from A minor to C major. |
| **A'** | 5.09 | Peasant chorus, C major, fast tempo. |

---

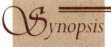

## Synopsis

**Le nozze di Figaro (The Marriage of Figaro), libretto by Lorenzo da Ponte, based on Beaumarchais's *Le mariage de Figaro* (1784)**

### Act 1.

Susanna and Figaro, servants to the Count and Countess Almaviva, are to be married, but Susanna fears that the philandering count will try to revive the *droit du seigneur*. According to this ancient practice, a nobleman could deflower a servant girl prior to giving her away in matrimony. Figaro is determined to use his wit to foil the count. His wedding is also threatened by the elderly Marcellina, who has a written contract from Figaro, promising to marry her as a pledge against an old unpaid debt.

The youthful page Cherubino is infatuated with all the ladies of the court, including the gardener's daughter Barbarina, Susanna, and, most of all, the countess. For this he has been banished by the jealous count and sent out for service in his regiment. Figaro makes fun of the "amorous butterfly," who will soon exchange the badinages of court life for the drudgery of the soldier.

### Act 2.

Figaro now hatches a plot to upset the plans of the count. He instructs Susanna to accept the count's proposal for a tryst that evening after dark in the garden, intending to send the disguised Cherubino in her place. After several comic escapades involving Cherubino, the musicians for the wedding arrive. The count is still determined to keep Susanna from marriage, and he declares that he will pass judgment on the legitimacy of Marcellina's claim.

once again among the ladies of the court. But before the count can punish the page, Figaro arrives to announce the beginning of the wedding procession. The count and countess sit to receive the couples to be married as the orchestra plays a wedding march.

The tempo then changes as peasant girls step forward, coached by Figaro, and praise the count for having abolished the hated custom of the *droit du seigneur*. A chorus of peasants extols his wisdom. Here and throughout the finale, Almaviva's hypocrisy is made increasingly blatant as a result of Figaro's meticulous plans made behind the scenes.

### Act 3.

Susanna meets the count and accepts his offer of a tryst, saying that she plans to use the money he has promised in dowry to pay off Marcellina. But he is still fearful of a double cross, so he passes judgment against Figaro: He must either pay his old debt or marry Marcellina. But in a sudden change of fortune, it is learned that Figaro is the long-lost son of Marcellina and Dr. Bartolo. Now there will be a double wedding as the older couple also decide to marry.

The countess dictates a romantic poem to the count, putatively from Susanna, to confirm their forthcoming assignation. The wedding procession enters the palace chambers. As Susanna kneels before the count to receive his blessing, she passes him the note. The couples then dance the traditional prenuptial fandango, and the count reads the letter elatedly.

### Act 4.

In the garden at dusk, all of the main characters intermingle in a tangle of mistaken identities. The count embraces "Susanna," actually the countess in disguise. Subsequently he stumbles on Figaro appearing to profess love to the countess. Temporarily outraged, the count finally penetrates the disguises and sees the foolishness of his own actions. He asks forgiveness of the countess, and all the characters return joyfully to the wedding banquet.

The tempo and meter now change to those of a stately courting dance called the fandango. Before she begins to dance, Susanna passes the count the note confirming their tryst, which he reads while the dance proceeds. While dancing, Figaro notices the count's pleasure in reading the letter, which he assumes to be from an unknown lady. This scene is filled with double meanings and erotic hints, suggested by the polyphony of the dance music and the traditional connotation of the fandango as a prelude to sexual pleasures. Mozart adds another level of meaning by quoting the fandango melody from Gluck's ballet *Don Juan,* a well-known work in Vienna at the time.

After a short accompanied recitative, in which the excited count invites everyone to the wedding banquet that evening, the music of the earlier chorus returns as the people again praise his goodness and wisdom.

The musical plan of this finale is symmetrical, and it is also unified by a single keynote. The opening wedding march functions as an introduction during which the main key of C is reached. The first duet and chorus, in C major, constitute the first main section, in which Figaro's plan to outwit and embarrass the count proceeds smoothly. The climactic middle section, the fandango in A minor, introduces an element of erotic intrigue and uncertainty. The dance on stage symbolizes the increasingly complex series of intrigues. The count is taken in by the fake note, the two couples anticipate their wedding, and Figaro is temporarily confused by seeing the count read a mysterious love letter. Finally, after a brief recitative transition, the music returns to that of the first section and to the opening key of C.

## Ludwig van Beethoven (1770–1827)

Beethoven's early years were similar in some respects to those of Mozart, although his career developed in a very different way. Like Mozart, he grew up in the family of a court musician and showed remarkable talent as a child performer and composer. He was born in the city of Bonn, which in 1770 was the seat of government of the electorate of Cologne. Like Salzburg, this was a small independent state ruled by an archbishop. Beethoven's father and grandfather were musicians in the service of this sovereign.

Unlike Mozart's father, however, Beethoven's did not carefully oversee his son's education and professional development. In fact, his father was an alcoholic who was often irresponsible as a parent. As a result, Beethoven did not receive a good general education, although he later developed a great interest in literature and modern ideas. But his musical development, which was guided primarily by the court organist, Christian Neefe, was prodigious. He was sent in 1787 to Vienna, probably

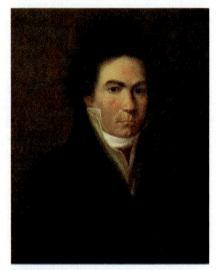

*Beethoven was 44 years old and at the height of his fame when this portrait was executed by Johann Christoph Heckel. The painter shows Beethoven in dark surroundings, serious as though lost in thought. Audiences in Beethoven's lifetime associated such brooding qualities with his fiery genius.*

to study with Mozart, but this sojourn was cut short by the illness of his mother.

In the summer of 1792, Haydn stopped in Bonn on his way back to Vienna after his first London sojourn. An arrangement was concluded whereby Beethoven would become his student. In November, Beethoven arrived in Vienna, where he remained for the rest of his life. His studies with Haydn were not entirely successful, probably due to Haydn's lack of interest in teaching and because of the difference in personality between the intense young artist and the established older one. Nevertheless, Beethoven imitated the music of Haydn in several early works, and he made great progress in attracting attention as a pianist. He was much in demand in the salons of Vienna's music-loving nobility, and his keyboard improvisations were found especially ingenious. His student Ferdinand Ries later recalled Beethoven's prodigious ability to improvise:

> Not a single artist of all that I have heard ever reached the plane in this respect which Beethoven occupied. The wealth of ideas which crowded in upon him, the moods to which he surrendered himself, the variety of treatment, the difficulties which offered themselves or were introduced by him, were inexhaustible.[3]

Around 1798, Beethoven became alarmed by problems with his hearing, which only increased as the years progressed. For this fiery young musician, the onset of deafness was catastrophic and depressive. In 1802, while spending the summer and fall in the Viennese suburb of Heiligenstadt, he wrote a last will and testament, addressed to his two brothers, which takes the form of a philosophical statement about his art and his physical disability.

> O you men who think or say that I am malevolent, stubborn, or misanthropic, how greatly do you wrong me. You do not know the secret cause which makes me seem that way to you. . . . Though born with a fiery, active temperament, even susceptible to the diversions of society, I was soon compelled to withdraw myself, to live life alone. If at times I tried to forget all this, oh, how harshly was I flung back by the doubly sad experience of my bad hearing. Yet it was impossible for me to say to people, "Speak louder, shout, for I am deaf." How could I possibly admit an infirmity in the *one sense* which ought to be more perfect in me than in others, a sense which I once possessed in the highest perfection, a perfection such as few in my profession enjoy or ever have enjoyed. . . .
>
> What a humiliation for me when someone standing next to me heard a flute in the distance and *I heard nothing,* or someone heard a

*shepherd singing* and again I heard nothing. Such incidents drove me almost to despair; a little more of that and I would have ended my life. It was only *my art* that held me back. . . .

It is my wish that you may have a better and freer life than I have had. Recommend *virtue* to your children; it alone, not money, can make them happy. I speak from experience: this was what upheld me in time of misery. Thanks to it and to my art, I did not end my life by suicide.[4]

In this remarkable document, which was discovered among the composers's papers only after his death, Beethoven states that he must live for his art and for virtue, not for his own comfort or enjoyment. His resolve to face his disability and to prevail over it coincided with a new period in his work. After 1802, his compositions strike out in new directions and less and less resemble the works of Haydn and Mozart, heretofore his models.

Beethoven was one of the first major composers who did not make his livelihood under the patronage system, by which a musician worked solely for another individual or institution. He lived instead as a free artist, who composed music for all humanity. He made money primarily by teaching, concertizing in both public and private, selling compositions to publishers, and composing on commission.

As a person he was described as moody, often intemperate, and shabby in his appearance and personal habits. But he succeeded in drawing attention to the greatness of his work in a way that always eluded Mozart.

His last decade was spent in near total deafness. People communicated with him by writing in conversation books, of which about 140 survive to the present day and give a vivid picture of his daily activities and thoughts. His music of this period has little in common with the earlier classical style; it takes on a grandiloquence and sometimes an exaggeration that is more akin to music in the nineteenth century. It can be intensely lyrical, at other times densely fugal. But regardless of which style he chose in his later works, Beethoven made his music serve the expression of an idea. In its heightened expressivity, it falls into the domain of the romantic era, to be discussed in Chapter 9.

Beethoven wrote many fewer pieces of music than either Mozart or Haydn, no doubt due to the different circumstances of his professional life and to his painstaking manner of sketching new works. He wrote 9 symphonies, 16 string quartets, 37 piano sonatas (5 of which are early pieces published without opus numbers), and 5 piano concertos. He composed only one opera, *Fidelio,* although this great work went through two substantial revisions. He wrote little for the church, in part because he was indifferent to organized religion, although his *Missa solemnis* is one of the masterpieces of his last years.

## Symphony No. 5 in C Minor

The Fifth Symphony, Op. 67, has been one of Beethoven's most popular works from his day to our own. This acclaim is not accidental. This is a work in which Beethoven wished to communicate to a large, general audience, not to a small circle of noble patrons or connoisseurs. The music is appropriately forceful and engaging, written in a language that can be immediately understood by many listeners, although it is nonetheless profound. The symphony was first heard at an academy for Beethoven's own benefit in 1808, where the Sixth Symphony (given the subtitle "Pastoral" by the composer) also received its premiere.

The Fifth Symphony has a conventional classical overall form of four movements. The first is fast and in sonata form, next comes a slow movement in a free variations form, the third movement is a ternary scherzo, and the finale is again in sonata form in a fast tempo. Several important features, however, deviate from the classical norm. The last two movements are played without pause between, and a theme from the scherzo is repeated in the finale. This last movement, rather than the first movement, carries the greatest weight. It is the longest of the four, the most grandiose, and the most forceful in orchestration. Beethoven expands the classical orchestra in the finale to include three trombones, piccolo (a small flute), and contrabassoon (a large bassoon), all intended to give the movement greater emphasis. The finale also shifts to major mode, a technique sometimes used by Mozart and Haydn in works beginning in minor. These innovations tend to give the symphony a dramatic connotation, in which the darkness and turbulence of the first movement are ultimately dispelled by the triumphant finale. So great is the unity of this symphony that we shall study it in its entirety.

The unusual features of the Fifth Symphony invite us to try to establish its meaning. Why does the mode turn to major in the finale? Why does Beethoven add trombones there? What is the meaning of the oboe solo in the recapitulation of the first movement? Why does the composer give this melody to the oboe rather than to some other instrument?

Some of the answers may derive from a remark putatively made by Beethoven about this piece to his assistant Anton Schindler. "One day in this author's presence," writes Schindler in *Beethoven as I Knew Him,* "he pointed

## Disability and the Arts

*The beginning of Beethoven's Heiligenstadt Testament.*

to the beginning of the first movement and expressed in these words the fundamental idea of this work: 'Thus fate knocks at the gate!'" Although the authenticity of Schindler's recollections has been questioned, a plausible interpretation of the Fifth Symphony can spring from this remark. Perhaps the work does, in fact, express Beethoven's struggle with his own fate, from the strife caused by deafness and depression to the ultimate triumph of the spirit.

Incredible as it may seem, Beethoven composed much of his greatest music, including the monumental Ninth Symphony and the *Missa solemnis,* after he became totally deaf. His superb accomplishment shows us that a physical handicap, even a serious one, does not necessarily limit human endeavor or achievement.

In 1988, the prestigious Sullivan Award for the nation's leading amateur athlete went to the baseball player Jim Abbott, who led America that year to a gold medal in the Olympics. In 1989, Abbott became a starting pitcher for the California Angels. Such outstanding accomplishments by any athlete deserve admiration, all the more so in Jim Abbott's case, since he was born without a right hand. Even in the sport of baseball, where manual dexterity is basic to success, Abbott rose to the top. Like Beethoven, his ability—determination, talent, and ambition—far outweighed his disability.

Handicapped people have always been among the greatest achievers in music. Even in the Middle Ages, the great composer and organist Francesco Landini, one of the major figures of his day, was blind. In the modern era, blindness has scarcely been a deterrent to the careers of many musicians. It is as though this deficiency in one sense makes the others more acute and more susceptible to development. The artistry of Stevie Wonder, Ray Charles, and George Shearing is known to all audiences who follow popular music and jazz. Yet many people are not aware that all three were blind from birth or from early childhood. The innate gifts of these artists and their determination to express themselves in music made their disability a spur rather than an obstacle to success.

The violinist Itzhak Perlman is known to popular as well as classical audiences. His musical virtuosity, jovial nature, and positive outlook make us forget that he is crippled. His disability, like that of Wonder, Charles, and Shearing, has been no hindrance to his career, which takes him repeatedly around the world.

A disability even in a sense that is basic to an art can be overcome by the human spirit. The French painter Claude Monet was a great interpreter of the forms of nature and a master of the use of color. Monet lost most of his sight in his later years, and yet this was precisely the time when he produced works of stunning originality in their approach to color and form, works that were an inspiration to abstract painters of the twentieth century. His achievements came from inner visions and a determination to create that could not be daunted. So too Beethoven. Although he lost, as he tells us in the Heiligenstadt testament, "that one sense which ought to be more perfect in me than in others," he did not lose more precious assets: a will to create and an inner ear that served as his unswerving guide.

## First Movement

In the first movement (Recording 8.4), conventional sonata form is expanded and made vividly dramatic. The work does not open with a main theme, as we might expect. Instead, we are presented with a four-note motivic fragment that is immediately repeated, both times coming to a pause. This motive is ambiguous in key and meter but crystal clear in its short-short-

**Ludwig van Beethoven, Symphony No. 5 in C Minor, first movement**
Recording 8.4

**Exposition**     0.00     Opening fragments and main theme. Note the open-endedness of the cadence of the theme, which rests on the note G rather than on the keynote C:

0.17     Transition. Based on the opening motive, the transition leads to a cadence preparing the key of E♭ major.

0.38     Subsidiary themes: A succession of three melodic ideas leads to a full cadence. The first subsidiary theme and its introductory fanfare begin

**Exposition**     1.18     The entire exposition is repeated.

**Development**     2.38     Part 1 is based on the opening of the main theme, unstable in key.

3.11     Part 2 is based on the horn introduction to the first subsidiary theme, leading climactically to the recapitulation.

| **Recapitula-tion** | 3.53 | Main theme, transition, and subsidiary themes return, the last unexpectedly in the major mode. |
| **Coda** | 5.21 | Further development of main and subsidiary themes and return to minor mode. |

short-long rhythm. The main theme is then introduced, itself based on several statements of the rhythm of the opening fragment. Indeed, this rhythmic idea is almost ever-present in the first movement, sometimes within melodies, at other times in the accompaniment. It also occurs prominently in other movements. The main theme soon comes to a cadence. But it does not suggest a full close since the melody does not reach its keynote. The music at this point has far too much energy to be brought to a full stop.

A short transition leads to another cadence, in the new key and mode of E♭ major. The entrance of the first subsidiary theme is heralded at 0.38 by the horns, which sound a variant of the opening fragments. Several subsidiary melodies are then strung together in the new tonality, leading to a full cadence and a repetition of the entire exposition.

The development deals at first with the main theme and subsequently with the horn fanfare preceding the first subsidiary theme. These motives dwindle almost to nothing, only to be revived in a mighty surge of rhythmic energy leading to the recapitulation. Several surprises are now in store. After the main theme is recapitulated, the orchestra suddenly falls silent and the oboe sounds a plaintive, recitativelike melody before the recapitulation continues. Perhaps the oboe represents the individual human voice, bemoaning the severe hand of fate. But its plaint is only momentary as the impetuous procession of ideas soon continues its journey. The subsidiary themes are brought back in the major mode, rather than in minor, as Mozart tended to do in his sonata-form movements in minor mode. In this way Beethoven prefigures the outright shift to major mode in the final movement.

The coda is no longer a simple rounding off of the movement but rather a lengthy passage in which the main and subsidiary themes are further developed and in which the music swirls back once again into the dark turbulence of the minor mode. In this movement, the basic sections of the sonata form—exposition, development, recapitulation, and coda—are almost exactly the same length.

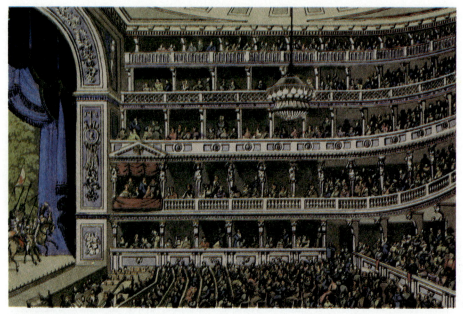

*The Theater an der Wien was opened in suburban Vienna in 1801. Under the management of Emanuel Schikaneder, the man who had earlier produced Mozart's* **Magic Flute**, *it came to be closely associated with performances of music by Beethoven. Beethoven's opera* **Fidelio** *had its first performance there in 1805, as did the premier performances of both the Fifth and Sixth Symphonies in 1808. This anonymous engraving dates from 1825.*

### Second Movement

The turbulence and impetuosity of the first movement are dispelled in the second (Recording 8.5), which settles squarely in the major mode and uses soothing melodies and graceful rhythms. The form of the movement is unusual, consisting of variations on two themes and elements of sonata form. The first theme is lilting in character. After several phrases it comes, almost reluctantly, to its cadence. The second follows immediately. After its initial appearance in A♭ major, this theme is restated majestically by the brass instruments in C major. This presentation looks both forward and backward in the symphony as a whole. It refers to the first movement by stating the short-short-short-long motive, and its profile and key suggest the main theme of the final movement.

The variations that follow are confined primarily to the first of the two melodies. They repeatedly paraphrase its rhythm and alter its form. The third variation turns to the spooky minor mode, suggesting that demons and goblins are never far from Beethoven's pastoral fantasies.

**274**

**Listening Guide**

**Ludwig van Beethoven, Symphony No. 5 in C Minor, second movement**
Recording 8.5

| | | |
|---|---|---|
| **A** | 0.00 | This is the primary theme for later variations and development. It begins |

| | | |
|---|---|---|
| **B** | 0.55 | The second theme begins |

It is immediately repeated in C major:

| | | |
|---|---|---|
| **Variation 1** | 2.04 | Themes A and B are paraphrased in turn. |
| **Variation 2** | 4.07 | Only theme A is heard, paraphrased by more rapid motion in the stringed instruments. |
| **Development** | 5.09 | Motives from theme A are developed as in a sonata-form movement. Theme B appears in a climactic presentation in the brass. |
| **Variation 3** | 6.54 | Theme A is again paraphrased, now in the woodwinds in A♭ minor. |
| **Variation 4 (recapitulation)** | 7.38 | Theme A returns in its original shape, in the home key of A♭ major. |
| **Coda** | 8.32 | Based on theme A. |

### Third and Fourth Movements

The third movement of the classical symphony is normally a minuet. But relatively few of Beethoven's works recapture the stately character of this baroque dance. They tend instead to be headlong in tempo and rollicking in spirit. Beethoven sometimes calls such movements *scherzos,* or "jokes," although he uses no such title in this symphony. The third movement (Recording 8.6) has the ternary form, fast tempo, and triple meter of the scherzo, but there is nothing joking about it. The goblins who peered briefly at us in the second movement now cavort openly and howl at the top of their lungs. The first section of the ternary form contains two themes in alternation. The first is a ghostly, rising figure in the basses in minor mode. The second theme (0.18) is a stentorian fanfare in the horns, which clearly contains the central rhythmic motive of the first movement.

**Ludwig van Beethoven, Symphony No. 5 in C Minor, third and fourth movements**
Recording 8.6

### Third Movement

**A**      0.00      Two themes alternate:

**B**      1.46      This trio turns to the major mode and begins with a free fugue.

**A/B**      3.10      On this recording, sections A and B are repeated.

**A′**      6.26      Shortened reprise of both themes from section A, now rescored and stated by plucked strings.

**Coda**      7.37      Distant references to the themes of section A are heard during an eerie stillness. A mighty increase in sound leads directly into the fourth movement.

## *Fourth Movement*

**Exposition**     0.00     Main theme: A long theme made up of a succession of distinctive motives. The key is C major, and the theme begins

Full orchestra

*ff*

               0.38     Transition: The key changes to G major while an important new theme is sounded triumphantly in the horns:

Horns

               1.07     Subsidiary themes: There are two important subsidiary themes, separated by a full cadence between them:

Strings

Woodwinds, strings

*sf*

**Exposition**     2.10     The exposition is repeated.

**Development**     4.20     Deals at first with the first subsidiary theme, but a new theme is later introduced:

Trombone, bassoon

*f*

                          The development ends in a full cadence.

**Episode**     6.02     A theme from the third movement is brought back.

**Recapitulation**     6.40     The major events of the exposition return, all in the home key of C major.

**Coda**     8.54     The two subsidiary themes are further developed, as is the transition theme (now transformed in a heroic manner). The tempo speeds up at the end, and the main theme makes a last triumphal appearance.

---

In the middle section, or trio, witches seem to gather for a diabolical dance, suggested by the impetuous fugue that Beethoven constructs. Wisps of the first-movement rhythmic motive are easily detected. The ternary form is completed by an abbreviated reprise of the first section. The music then settles quietly at 7.37 into a transitional coda, which leads without pause to the finale. In this linking passage, the timpani is at first the sole thematic instrument, restlessly muttering the rhythmic motive of the first movement. After this momentary respite, a great surge of energy carries us into the last movement.

The finale (also on Recording 8.6) is the longest of the four movements and the most forceful. Its main theme is fanfarelike and foursquare, with none of the ambiguities of the earlier themes. Its definitive turn to the major mode suggests a triumph over the turbulence of the first movement and the ghostly visions of the second and third. The movement has a typical sonata form except for the insertion of a passage from the scherzo between the development and the recapitulation (this passage is called an *episode* in the Listening Guide). The coda is greatly elongated and developmental as it reworks themes and motives from the exposition.

The unbroken logic and force of this great work were perceived as much by Beethoven's contemporaries as by modern listeners. In 1810, the German writer and musician E. T. A. Hoffmann found in this symphony, like listeners ever since, an incomparable union of genius and science:

> Can there be any work of Beethoven that confirms all this to a higher degree than his indescribably profound, magnificent Symphony in C minor? How this wonderful composition, in a climax that climbs on and on, leads the listener imperiously forward into the spirit world of the infinite![5]

### Piano Sonata in E Major, Op. 109

Beethoven's piano sonatas span his entire career as a composer, from his apprenticeship in Bonn well into his last decade. He often used the genre as a proving ground for new stylistic ideas. Many of the innovations seen in the Fifth Symphony of 1808, for example, such as the linking of movements and emphasis on the finale, were tried out first in piano sonatas composed five or six years earlier.

The last five sonatas, composed from 1816 to 1822, are often discussed as a group, despite their many differences in character. In them Beethoven continues the striking innovations in form and style that also characterized his piano sonatas of the preceding decade. In general, these works are irregular in overall form. Movements are often linked together, and the sequence of movements is unlike the earlier sonata cycles. In these works, we find large and imposing fugues, impetuous marches, immense theme and variations movements, idyllic lyrical passages in a free and improvisatory manner, and more conventional movements in sonata or ternary form.

The Sonata in E Major, Op. 109, was composed in 1820, at a time when Beethoven was devoting himself primarily to work on his great *Missa solemnis.* The sonata is dedicated to Maximiliane Brentano, daughter of Antonie Brentano. The latter is probably the "Immortal Beloved" to whom Beethoven addressed a passionate and frank expression of love in an unsent letter of 1812. At about this time, Beethoven was often a guest in the Brentano household. In a letter to Maximiliane of December 6, 1821, announcing the dedication of the work, Beethoven thinks back nostalgically to this crucial period in his emotional life and asserts that the dedication is made solely from personal feeling:

> This dedication is not misused, as happens in many cases. It is offered in the spirit which holds together nobler and better people on this earth and which can never be destroyed by time. This is what is now addressed to you and what recalls you to me as you were in your childhood years, so equally your beloved parents, your admirable and gifted mother, your father filled with truly good and noble qualities. . . . My memories of a noble family can never fade; may your memories of me be frequent and good.[6]

The intense nostalgia of these words echoes throughout this great work. And while dedicated explicitly to Maximiliane Brentano, we can suspect that the music also speaks from that place in Beethoven's heart occupied by her mother.

The first movement is relatively short, free in form, and intensely lyrical. The second movement is very fast and in ternary form, and the finale (Recording 8.7) is a theme and variations, to be played, so Beethoven writes in the music, "songfully, with the deepest feeling." The theme of the finale,

**Beethoven, Piano Sonata in E Major, Op. 109, third movement (finale)**
Recording 8.7

| | | |
|---|---|---|
| **Theme** | 0.00 | The theme is in two parts, each immediately repeated. The two parts begin |

| | | |
|---|---|---|
| **Variation 1** | 2.21 | The music has a slow and dancelike quality. |
| **Variation 2** | 4.22 | The character changes again, becoming light and detached in articulation. |
| **Variation 3** | 6.04 | The style is made to resemble baroque keyboard music, all the while obscuring the identity of the theme. |
| **Variation 4** | 6.30 | The theme becomes still more obscure, and the character of the music changes again, now somewhat slower in tempo. |
| **Variation 5** | 8.59 | Like variation 3, the music resembles baroque keyboard music in rhythm and percussiveness, only now much more imitative in texture. The form of the theme is not entirely preserved. |
| **Variation 6** | 9.54 | The theme is clearly audible at first, but it is soon submerged in the swirling rhythmic motion. |
| **Theme** | 12.07 | The theme is restated (more simply than at first) without the repeats of the two halves. |

typical of most in Beethoven's variations movements, is in binary form. Its two halves are placed in the middle and low registers of the instrument and played in a hushed tone. Its underlying harmonies are simple, and the melody itself is delicately ornamented and characterized by expressive leaps into higher and lower registers.

Six variations follow the theme. Each preserves at least part of the theme, but each also establishes its own character. The variations become progressively more remote to the theme, so much so that Beethoven does not label the last two by the term *variation*. In the first two variations, the theme is clearly present, since its harmonies, form, meter, and melodic outline are all preserved. Changes occur primarily in the rhythmic or textural aspects of its presentation.

The third variation imitates the sound of a baroque keyboard piece in its motoric rhythm, polyphonic texture, and percussive treatment of the piano. The meter changes to duple, but the overall form and harmonic implications of the theme are intact. The outline of the original melody is subtly embedded in otherwise new music. The outline is even more dimly heard in the fourth variation, sometimes disappearing entirely, although the harmonies and overall form of the original theme are maintained.

The fifth and sixth variations continue the processes of the earlier sections. The melody of the theme is made progressively more obscure, the character of the variations departs increasingly from that of the theme, and now the overall form of the theme is also lost by the insertion of new materials. At the conclusion of the movement, the theme is brought back in a starkly simplified version that, after the passionate, even ecstatic nature of the later variations, is overwhelmingly moving.

## TOPICS FOR DISCUSSION AND WRITING

**1.** Discuss the maturation of the classical style by comparing Haydn's Symphony No. 102, first movement (Recording 8.1), to the finale of J. C. Bach's Symphony in D Major (Recording 7.2). Consider the range of emotional expression, nature of themes and harmonies, makeup of the orchestra, and aspects of form in both works.

**2.** Debate the virtues and vices of attaching a poetic interpretation to Beethoven's Fifth Symphony. Isn't the work primarily an interplay of melodies, harmonies, and rhythms? Or do these necessarily represent some dramatic idea?

**3.** Compare the first movement of Haydn's Symphony No. 102 (Recording 8.1) with the first movement of Beethoven's Symphony No. 5 (Recording 8.4). Deal not only with technical features such as form, thematic usages, rhythms, and harmonies, but also the apparent dramatic content of both movements. As a former student of Haydn, what debt must Beethoven have owed his former teacher that is implicit in the Fifth Symphony?

**4.** Although the music of Mozart and of Vivaldi differ in style, Mozart still owed much to Vivaldi for devising a satisfying plan for the first movement of a concerto. Compare Vivaldi's Concerto for Violin in G Major, Op. 3, No. 3 (Recording 6.1) with Mozart's Concerto for Piano in D Minor (Recording 8.2) with an eye toward finding in the form of Mozart's work aspects of Vivaldi's ritornello pattern. What aspects of the Mozart have no analogy in Vivaldi?

## ADDITIONAL LISTENING

### Haydn

Andante and Variations in F Minor for Piano (Hoboken 17:6). An unusually somber and romantic work.

Concerto for Trumpet and Orchestra. This is one of Haydn's best-known concertos. It was written for a keyed bugle, a forerunner of the modern trumpet.

*The Creation,* especially the chorus "Die Himmel erzählen" (No. 13), the arioso "Und Gott schuf große Walfische" (No. 16), and the duet-chorus "Von deiner Gut" (No. 30).

Mass in C Major *(Missa in tempore belli)* and Mass in D Minor *(Nelson Mass).* These are two of the six late Masses written for Prince Nicholas II.

Piano Sonata No. 52 in E♭ Major. One of Haydn's last three piano sonatas, all written during his second sojourn in London.

String Quartet in C Major, Op. 76, No. 3 *(Emperor Quartet).* The slow movement consists of variations on the patriotic hymn that Haydn wrote in 1797 for the Hapsburg monarch, Francis II.

Symphony No. 94 in G Major *(Surprise);* Symphony No. 100 in G Major *(Military);* Symphony No. 104 in D Major *(London).* These are three of the symphonies written during Haydn's two trips to England.

### Mozart

Concertos: Concerto for Clarinet, K. 622; Piano Concerto in A, K. 488; *Symphonie concertante* for Violin, Viola, and Orchestra, K. 364.

Mass: *Coronation Mass,* K. 317

Operas: *Don Giovanni,* like *The Marriage of Figaro,* is set to a text by da Ponte, but it is a more serious work than *Figaro. The Magic Flute* is a German opera to a fantastic text that deals symbolically with ideas of Freemasonry.

Piano music: Fantasy in C Minor, K. 475.

Quintets: Quintet in G Minor for Strings, K. 516; Quintet in A for Clarinet and Strings, K. 581; Quintet in E♭ for Piano and Winds, K. 452.

*Requiem,* K. 626.

Serenades: Serenade in C Minor, K. 388; *Eine kleine Nachtmusik (A Little Night Music),* K. 525.

Symphonies: Symphony in G Minor, K. 550; Symphony in C Major *(Jupiter),* K. 551

### Beethoven

Concertos: Piano Concertos Nos. 4 and 5.

*Missa solemnis.* This grandiose Mass is intentionally archaic in style and not especially melodious but stunningly dramatic. Listen especially to the Credo and the Benedictus portion of the Sanctus.

Opera: *Fidelio,* Beethoven's sole opera, deals with heroism, fidelity, and the ultimate conquest of truth over evil.

Piano music:

> Piano Sonata in C Minor, Op. 13 *(Pathétique).* Listen especially to the slow movement, which shows Beethoven's melodiousness and sensitivity to the sonority of the piano.
>
> Piano Sonata in C♯ Minor, Op. 27, No. 2 *(Moonlight).* The first movement is based on a repetitive and placid accompanimental figure, which led to the nickname.
>
> Piano Sonata in A♭ Major, Op. 110.
>
> Quartets: String Quartet in F Major, Op. 18, No. 1; String Quartet in F Major, Op. 59, No. 1.
>
> Songs: "Adelaide"; *An die ferne Geliebte* (the second is a song cycle).
>
> Symphonies: Symphony No. 6 *(Pastoral);* Symphony No. 9. The latter work uses solo voices and chorus to words by Friedrich von Schiller.

## BIBLIOGRAPHY

### Haydn

Geiringer, Karl. *Haydn: A Creative Life in Music.* Third edition. Berkeley: University of California Press, 1982.

Hoboken, Anthony van. *Joseph Haydn: Thematisch-bibliographisches Werkverzeichnis.* Three volumes. Mainz: Schott, 1957–1978. The outstanding catalog of Haydn's complete works; in German, but useful to all students of Haydn's music.

Landon, H. C. Robbins. *The Collected Correspondence and London Notebooks of Joseph Haydn.* Fair Lawn, N.J.: Essential Books, 1959. See especially the correspondence of Haydn with Marianne Genzinger.

———. *Haydn: Chronicle and Works.* Five volumes. Bloomington: Indiana University Press, 1976–1980. Mammoth and comprehensive study.

———. *The Symphonies of Joseph Haydn.* London: Rockliff, 1955.

## Mozart

Anderson, Emily, ed. *The Letters of Mozart and His Family*. Second edition. New York: St. Martin's Press, 1966. The basic source of information about this composer.

Davies, Peter J. "Mozart's Illnesses and Death." *Musical Times* 125 (1984), 437–442, 554–561. A definitive study.

Dent, Edward. *Mozart's Operas: A Critical Study*. Second edition. London: Oxford University Press, 1947.

Einstein, Alfred. *Mozart: His Character, His Work*. Translated by Arthur Mendel and Nathan Broder. London: Oxford University Press, 1945. A general study that seeks to explain Mozart's personality.

Köchel, Ludwig von. *Chronologisch-thematisches Verzeichnis sämtlicher Tonwerke Wolfgang Amadé Mozart*. Revised by Alfred Einstein and others. Sixth edition. Wiesbaden: Breitkopf and Härtel, 1964. The source of the "K." numbers that identify Mozart's music.

Landon, H. C. Robbins. *1791: Mozart's Last Year*. New York: Schirmer Books, 1988. Written for the general reader.

_____, and Donald Mitchell. *The Mozart Companion*. New York: Norton, 1969. A collection of essays on Mozart's works, divided by genre.

Lang, Paul Henry, ed. *The Creative World of Mozart*. New York: Norton, 1963. A collection of essays on various topics.

Sadie, Stanley. *The New Grove Mozart*. New York: Norton, 1982. A short and factual general study.

## Beethoven

Anderson, Emily, ed. *The Letters of Beethoven*. Three volumes. London: Macmillan, 1961. Beethoven was not a great writer of letters, but this anthology is valuable all the same.

Arnold, Denis, and Nigel Fortune. *The Beethoven Reader*. New York: Norton, 1971. A collection of essays accessible to the general reader.

Kerman, Joseph, and Alan Tyson. *The New Grove Beethoven*. New York: Norton, 1983. A short and factual general study.

Kinsky, Georg, and Hans Halm. *Das Werk Beethovens*. Munich: Henle, 1955. Updated by several other publications; the standard catalog of the complete works of Beethoven.

Schindler, Anton. *Beethoven as I Knew Him*. Edited by Donald MacArdle. Translated by Constance Jolly. New York: Norton, 1966. Schindler served as Beethoven's assistant during his late period; these memoirs are valuable but often unreliable.

Solomon, Maynard. *Beethoven*. New York: Schirmer Books, 1977. An outstanding general study that emphasizes the composer's psychological makeup.

Thayer, Alexander. *Thayer's Life of Beethoven*. Edited and revised by Elliot Forbes. Revised edition. Princeton, N.J.: Princeton University Press, 1967. Thayer's massive incomplete biography is the basis for all later studies of Beethoven's life.

## NOTES

**1.** Wolfgang Amadeus Mozart, in *The Letters of Mozart and His Family,* 2nd ed., ed. Emily Anderson (New York: St. Martin's Press, 1966), vol. 2, p. 690.

**2.** Leopold Mozart, in ibid., pp. 885–886.

**3.** Ferdinand Ries, in *Beethoven Remembered: The Biographical Notes of Franz Wegeler and Ferdinand Ries,* trans. Frederick Noonan (Arlington, Va.: Great Ocean Publishers, 1987), pp. 87–88.

**4.** Ludwig van Beethoven, quoted in Maynard Solomon, *Beethoven* (New York: Schirmer Books, 1977), pp. 116–117.

**5.** E. T. A. Hoffmann, in *Source Readings in Music History: The Romantic Era,* ed. Oliver Strunk (New York: Norton, 1965), p. 38.

**6.** Ludwig van Beethoven, in Alexander Thayer, *Thayer's Life of Beethoven,* rev. and ed. Elliot Forbes (Princeton, N.J.: Princeton University Press, 1967), p. 781.

# 9

## The Age of Expression: Music in the Early Nineteenth Century

## Art as Emotion

*Sensual beauty, tears of hopeless love, and Christianity all mingle in this burial scene by Anne Louis Girodet-Trioson. Eschewing the classical subjects emphasized by his teacher, Jacques-Louis David, Girodet turned instead for this subject to the immensely popular contemporary novella* Atala *by François-René de Chateaubriand.* Atala *has all of the characteristics of writing that in the early nineteenth century were termed "romantic." The story, which has* parallels with Shakespeare's **Romeo and Juliet,** *is set in the wilds of the American Southeast. Its two central characters, Indians from rival tribes named Chactas and Atala, fall desperately in love. They flee into the wilderness of Kentucky, where they encounter the kindly Christian hermit, Father Aubry. Atala is a Christian, who cannot give herself to her beloved because of a vow of chastity made at her mother's urging. In a fit of passion, she poisons herself, after eliciting a vow from Chactas also to embrace Christianity. In the scene depicted by Girodet, Chactas and Father Aubry bury Atala in a woodland cave.*

*The lovers in* **Atala** *exist in a state of exaggerated feelings and emotions. In consonance with the ideas of the French writer Jean-Jacques Rousseau, their closeness to nature lends them a noble innocence, despite the sensuality of their setting and situation. Religion is not depicted by Chateaubriand, as it often was in Enlightenment literature, as restrictive of human development. Rather, it is shown as a source of beauty, sensitivity, and moderation of natural passions. At all times, Chateaubriand appeals to the heart rather than to faculties of reason.*

*Girodet's painting of this scene from the conclusion of the novella brings together all strands of the story. Erotic love is plainly evident, as Chactas clutches Atala's body, which has lost none of its beauty. Father Aubry represents Christianity and the reconciliation to fate that religion offers. The painting suggests none of the moralizing or* the appeal to civic duty that was so much a part of the paintings of David. Instead, its message, like that of most romantic artistry, is fully contained in its expression of emotions.

## The Early Nineteenth Century

**Major Composers**

Carl Maria von Weber

Gioachino Rossini

Franz Schubert

Hector Berlioz

Felix Mendelssohn

Robert Schumann

Frédéric Chopin

| 1750 | 1800 | 1850 | 1900 |

**Major Artists and Writers**

Johann Wolfgang von Goethe

Anne-Louis Girodet-Trioson

François-René de Chateaubriand

Jean-August-Dominique Ingres

Théodore Géricault

Eugène Delacroix

In a letter addressed in September 1781 to his father, Mozart spoke about the proper role of music: "Music, even when depicting the most terrible situations, must never offend the ear. It must instead please the listener, or, in other words, never cease to be music." His sentiments are true to the classical period, which emphasized simplicity and naturalness in art. The music of this age was regarded as a high form of entertainment, capable of expressing noble sentiments but nonetheless conceived as an elevated pastime.

Early in the nineteenth century, however, composers began to supplant this conception with new ideas. No longer was music always intended to please the listener. It became instead a medium by which complex ideas and profound emotions could be embodied and conveyed. Perhaps the most distinctive and persistent characteristic of music in the nineteenth century is direct and intense expression. Beethoven's Ninth Symphony, for example, avoids classical symmetry and balance in order better to express the power of joy and brotherly love. Near the turn of the twentieth century, Gustav Mahler chose the profoundly melancholy poetry of Friedrich Rückert, written after the death of two of Rückert's children, for songs titled *Kindertotenlieder (Songs*

**291**

*on the Death of Children).* Why would a composer dwell on such a painful topic in a musical composition? For Mahler, as for his nineteenth-century forebears, it was the depth of emotion that the words contained. Their intensity is heightened by Mahler's music, whose purpose is to express rather than to please.

The panorama of expression in nineteenth-century music brings into view not only composers' external worlds but, even more, their inner feelings. The personal voice of the composer is heard nowhere so clearly as in music of this period, and it often speaks from deep within a composer's private life. A tendency toward intense self-expression began strikingly with Beethoven, who, in many of his greatest compositions, brings us into his own innermost emotional world. The same propensity for self-exploration is found toward the end of the century, for example, in the music of Johannes Brahms. His *Alto Rhapsody* (1869) sets words by Goethe that speak of an isolated individual estranged from society and embittered by his fate. Surely Brahms identified with this protagonist, and the music that expresses these sentiments derives its moving beauty in part from the intensity of the composer's voice and the individuality of its message.

The nineteenth century was indeed the era of the individual. The French Revolution, which marked the end of the classical period, was carried forward by the idea of the rights of the individual, expressed in the motto "Liberty, equality, fraternity." This was the age when absolute monarchies were overturned throughout western Europe, feudalism was all but ended, and wealth and power passed once and for all from the aristocracy to the middle classes. It was a time when the hero was celebrated and the accomplishments of the individual, whether a military genius such as Napoléon or a virtuoso performer such as Niccolò Paganini or Franz Liszt, commanded the admiration of people from all walks of life.

The emphasis on individual expression in music led to numerous innovations in musical style. Melody and theme often avoided symmetrical period form in favor of longer, asymmetrical melodic shapes that better convey affective content. Harmony became more suggestive, especially through an increased use of dissonant chords. Composers were inclined to greater diversity in the choice of keynotes, indicating that certain keys were inherently more evocative of certain emotional states than other keys. Pieces in the minor mode became much more prevalent as composers delved ever more deeply into the realm of the subjective. In general, music of the nineteenth century wears its heart on its sleeve. It dispenses with classical restraint in favor of overt display, exaggeration, and impetuosity of feeling.

# Fine Arts and the Age of Romanticism

Musical innovations of the first half of the nineteenth century resonate in the other fine arts, where the same emotional individualism produced new modes of expression. So different is the art of the nineteenth century from that of the eighteenth that it creates a new period in the evolution of style, called **romanticism.** In the history of music, this new period extended from the early nineteenth century until about 1900. In some areas, romanticism persisted until World War I (1914–1918), and composers such as Richard Strauss (1864–1949) and Hans Pfitzner (1869–1949) continued to write in a romantic manner until the middle of the twentieth century.

The term *romantic* was first used in literary criticism near the turn of the nineteenth century, to describe writings of heightened imagination and emotion. Literature of this sort derived from several preexistent sources, especially German novels and plays in the *Sturm und Drang* manner (see Chapter 7) and essays and novels by the French writer Jean-Jacques Rousseau (1712–1778). From the Germans came the romantic emphasis on individualism, an exaltation of physical passion, and exaggerated states of emotion. In such writings by Rousseau as the *The New Héloïse* (1761) and *Discourse on the Origin and Bases of Inequality among Men* (1754), this author celebrates the individual who lives close to and in harmony with nature. All of these characteristics gained a sharper profile in nineteenth-century literature.

In painting, the expressive power inherent in romanticism reached a climax in the work of Eugène Delacroix (1798–1863). His approach to color, form, and the drama of human passions was inherited from his teacher, Théodore Géricault. In *Liberty Leading the People* (page 294), Delacroix creates an allegory of revolutionary emotion, inspired by the July Revolution of 1830. This very large painting depicts Parisians from all walks of life following the ideal of liberty, personified by the half-nude figure bearing a flag and a musket who strides over a tangle of bodies in the foreground. The great sense of motion, vivid color, and drama of this painting typify romantic exaggeration of emotion and unrestrained fantasy.

Delacroix's greatest rival was the painter Jean-August-Dominique Ingres (1780–1867), whose differences from Delacroix in technique and idea do not prevent their both contributing to a single romantic movement. *La grande odalisque* (page 295) suggests the flat surface of Greek vase painting, and the motionless repose and muted colors of the harem concubine differ sharply from the dramatic tumult of Delacroix's *Liberty*. Ingres's painting emphasizes the sensual and exotic in romantic art.

*The embodiment of romantic expressiveness: Eugène Delacroix's* **Liberty Leading the People** *(1830).*

Many of the qualities of romantic art and literature are evident in the musical works of the nineteenth century. The sentimentality of Rousseau reappears in the orchestral works of Pyotr Ilich Tchaikovsky, the unrestrained emotion and drama of Delacroix in the works of Hector Berlioz, and the pristine detachment of Ingres in the classical tones of Felix Mendelssohn.

## Orchestral Music

The orchestra became the medium through which composers of the nine-teenth century could best reach a growing middle-class audience. During this period, the once-only benefit concerts, academies, and private orchestral performances of the late eighteenth century were replaced by public orchestral concert series. Many famous orchestras were founded during the first half of the nineteenth century, including the "philharmonic" orchestras of Vienna, Berlin, London, and New York. In Paris, the *Société des concerts du conservatoire,* founded by François-Antoine Habeneck in 1828, was known for its brilliant performances of Beethoven's orchestral music.

The desire for ever-greater expressivity made the romantic orchestra different from its classical-era ancestor. Its size was increased, and new instruments, including harp, tuba, and **English horn** (a member of the oboe family), were added. The brass and woodwinds were regularly entrusted with melodic material, and all major subdivisions of the orchestra became capable of playing independently. The genres of orchestral music were multiplied in order to conform to the new expressivity. In addition to the concerto and the symphony of the classical period, there appeared several new types of orchestral music that overtly contained a literary or other nonmusical idea. This so-called **program music** is encountered in multimovement programmatic symphonies, one-movement **tone poems,** and symphonies using voices.

*Ingres's painting **La grande odalisque** (1814) merges neoclassical techniques and themes of the turn of the nineteenth century with a romantic warmth and sensuality.*

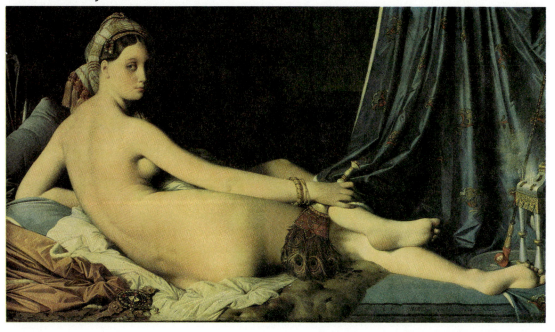

Beethoven's explorations of the orchestra as an expressive medium were continued in the early nineteenth century by Hector Berlioz (1803–1869). He was born near Grenoble and studied medicine in Paris, later turning to music. His artistic imagination was fired equally by the music of Beethoven and the literature of Shakespeare and Goethe. After a brief sojourn in Rome at the end of his apprenticeship, Berlioz settled in Paris, where he made his living mainly by writing musical criticism. His music, including orchestral pieces, songs, choral music, and opera, was supported by a small and devoted audience but never by the public at large, who found its originality confusing. In the 1840s and 1850s he undertook conducting tours, mainly in Germany, where he was assisted by such prominent musicians as Franz Liszt, Robert Schumann, and Felix Mendelssohn. His last major work was the monumental opera *Les troyens* (*The Trojans,* 1858).

*Symphonie fantastique* (*Fanciful Symphony,* 1830, revised 1832) was his first great accomplishment as a composer and shows his use of the orchestra and the symphonic genre to convey a vivid imagination, heightened emotionality, and autobiographical ideas. The work stemmed from the young composer's impetuous infatuation with the Irish actress Harriet Smithson, whom Berlioz saw acting the part of Ophelia in Shakespeare's *Hamlet* in Paris in 1827. "The impression made on my heart and mind by her extraordinary talent," he wrote in his *Memoirs,* "nay her dramatic genius, was equalled only by the havoc wrought in me by the poet she so nobly interpreted." *Symphonie fantastique,* at first titled *Episode from the Life of an Artist,* is a musical representation of Berlioz's own imagined love affair with Miss Smithson. Although he did not meet the actress prior to his completion of the symphony, they later married. It was an impetuous liaison that proved desperately unhappy for both.

Berlioz explained the poetic content of the symphony in a written program that was distributed at early performances. An artist falls passionately in love with an ideal woman. Her obsessive image in his mind is accompanied by a melody (Berlioz calls it the *idée fixe,* or "obsession"), which drives him through the gamut of emotions. It remains with him everywhere, at a ball, even in the countryside, where he has gone to seek tranquillity. He begins to have doubts about her fidelity (Berlioz had heard rumors that Miss Smithson was having an illicit affair with her theater manager), which plunges him into despair. In a state of depression he poisons himself with opium, only to fall into a fitful sleep. He dreams that he has murdered the beloved. He is led to the guillotine in a grim procession and executed for his crime. In the grotesque conclusion of the nightmare, his soul has descended to hell, where it is assailed by ghoulish witches in a perverse ritual or "sabbath." Among the hags is the beloved, who now taunts the artist in a tumultuous orgy.

Berlioz cautioned his early listeners that the music does not simply duplicate this fanciful tale but rather fills it in. The story, said Berlioz, connects the emotional content of the musical movements. But how can instrumental music fill in a story? Berlioz's main device was to make a melody symbolize a character in the story—the beloved—and to bring that melody back in every movement with changes that vividly suggest her own changes in personality. In the first movement the theme seems to embody her noble beauty in the eyes of the artist. In later movements it is transformed into a waltz melody and a pastoral folk tune, among other suggestive shapes. The composer also made ample use of obvious musical symbols. Church bells, for example, could aptly suggest a funeral, and a fugue could depict a grotesque gathering of witches.

Since his symphony was to fill in a story, Berlioz felt no need to adhere to the classical overall form of four movements. Instead, he uses five movements, although these five still remind us of the classical norm. The first movement is in a free sonata form with slow introduction; the second corresponds to a scherzo movement, the third to a slow movement. The fourth and fifth movements together correspond to the traditional finale.

The fifth movement (Recording 9.1) represents the riotous climax of the work, in which the artist suffers his ultimate debasement and punishment. The music bypasses all standard formal patterns and draws its logic instead from the narrative program. It begins with a slow introduction that suggests the frightful landscape of hell. No melodies are heard, no stable keynote appears, and rhythm, beat, and meter are fragmented and irregular. The music at 1.18 suddenly becomes fast, and from afar, the *idée fixe* tune is heard. Its prancing rhythm suggests the galloping approach of the former beloved. Her arrival is greeted joyously by the other witches, leading to a full restatement of her melody, now made taunting in rhythm and raucous in sound.

At 2.44 funeral bells are heard, leading at 3.08 to a quotation of the chant "Dies irae," from the funeral Mass of the Catholic church. The words of this familiar melody, although not used by Berlioz, speak of the tortures that await the sinful on the day of judgment. A gleeful round dance of the witches is depicted by an impetuous fugue, leading at 7.45 to a simultaneous statement of the "Dies irae" melody and the fugal subject. The work ends on a blazing major chord as the forces of hell triumph and annihilate the soul of the artist.

**Hector Berlioz,** *Symphonie fantastique,* **"Dream of a Witches' Sabbath" (movement 5)**
Recording 9.1

**Introduction**    0.00    Depiction of the eerie sounds of hell.

**A**    1.18    Arrival of the beloved, represented by the *idée fixe* melody:

**B**    2.44    Bells resound from the funeral of the artist; a fragment of the fugal subject in section D foretells the witches' grotesque dance.

**C**    3.08    Ophicleides (forerunners of the tuba) and contrabassoon stridently sound the opening of the melody of the chant "Dies irae" from the Catholic funeral mass:

It is echoed by prancing rhythms in the woodwinds, which represent the witches.

**D**    4.58    A fugue is constructed to depict a triumphant round dance of witches. Its subject is intricate, since it consists of two simultaneous lines. It begins

**E**    7.45    The fugal subject and "Dies irae" melody are stated simultaneously, thus mingling the sacred and the demonic.

**Coda**    9.00    A brief flourish in the full orchestra brings the movement and the work to a conclusion.

# Song

A *song* is a short piece in one concise movement for the medium of solo voice and piano. Late in the nineteenth century, the accompaniment was sometimes taken over by orchestra, and occasionally song composers called for one or more instruments in addition to piano. Songs were often compiled into **song cycles**—sets of several songs intended to be performed together. These are usually linked by a common poetic idea, a narrative, or recurring musical elements. Songs were written in the classical period, but the genre at that time was not as important as it became in the romantic era. Beethoven, for example, wrote songs as a diversion from his more important work in larger genres, although he composed memorable examples including "Adelaide" and the cycle *An die ferne Geliebte (To the Distant Beloved).*

Although composers of virtually all European and American nationalities wrote songs during the nineteenth century, the German development is clearly central. Perhaps the strength of interest in folk song in Germany and the general flourishing of musical culture there led to this preeminence. So dominating was the German contribution to songwriting that musicians often refer to the entire art of the song in the nineteenth century with the term **lied** (plural, **lieder**), which is the German word for "song." Later in the century, French composers such as Henri Duparc, Gabriel Fauré, and Claude Debussy rivaled their German contemporaries as songwriters. In Chapter 10, we shall examine songs by Fauré and by the American composer Stephen Foster; in this chapter we focus solely on the lied.

## Song Poetry

The art of the romantic song resides as much in poetry as in music. Indeed, the great accomplishment of the romantic masters of song was their uniting of these two in an intensely expressive whole. Almost always, composers of the nineteenth century chose preexistent poetry to be set to music. Depending on the degree of sophistication implicit in the poem, the musical treatment could be either simple, allowing the poetry to dominate, or elaborate, in which case the music interprets and reshapes poetic meaning.

Most of the poetry in romantic songs is *strophic;* that is, it is divided into several stanzas, each with the same number of lines, rhyme scheme, and scansion. Although the subjects that appear in song poetry are wonderfully varied, certain themes emerge repeatedly. Foremost among them is love, the eternal subject of songs of all types and all ages. Poetry in praise of the beauty of nature is also frequently encountered, and often the poet uses descriptions of nature to reveal aspects of inner emotional life. Many romantic composers were drawn also to poetry dealing with death, showing a persistent melancholy side of the romantic consciousness.

A composer who has chosen a strophic poem to set to music faces a basic choice. Will the song itself be strophic; that is, will music composed for the first stanza be repeated for all remaining stanzas? Or will the composer write new music for each stanza, thus producing a **through-composed** song? Most great songwriters have used both forms, allowing the nature of the poem to guide them. If the poem suggests simple, artless, or folklike ideas, the strophic form is usually chosen. If the poem is more complicated or if it demands enrichment by more elaborate music, through-composed form may result.

The most important poet in the early history of German song was Johann Wolfgang von Goethe (1749–1832), a figure who exerted an immense influence on romantic music of all types and nationalities. Goethe was born in Frankfurt and studied law before turning to the career of diplomat and writer. He also had training as a painter and a musician. He came to international attention in 1774 with his novel *The Sorrows of Young Werther,* a work in the *Sturm und Drang* style that was largely motivated by the author's personal experiences. He was appointed in 1775 to the court of Duke Charles Augustus in Weimar, which he served for the remainder of his life.

In addition to his writings, Goethe undertook scientific study, especially of plant biology, on which topic he wrote important treatises. Much of his poetry was written with the hope that it would be set to music, although Goethe rejected song settings in which the musical element was more than a backdrop to the words. His novels and plays also contain lyric poetry that was used by generations of song composers. Foremost among them are the related novels *Wilhelm Meisters Lehrjahre* (*Wilhelm Meister's Apprenticeship,* 1796) and *Wilhelm Meisters Wanderjahre* (*Wilhelm Meister's Travels,* 1829) and the epic philosophical drama *Faust* (two parts: 1808, 1832).

**The bright and lucid eyes of Johann Wolfgang von Goethe light up Franz Gerhard von Kügelgen's 1808 portrait of the great writer. Goethe's poetic writings stimulated an outburst of song composition by German composers of the early nineteenth century.**

*Franz Schubert and his friends often organized private song concerts, such as the one in 1826 depicted in this drawing by Moritz von Schwind. Schubert is playing the piano, accompanying the singer Johann Michael Vogl on his right.*

## Franz Schubert and "Erlkönig"

Franz Schubert (1797–1828) was the first great songwriter of the romantic period, the first major composer since the Renaissance to place the genre of song front and center in his oeuvre. He lived his short life in and around Vienna, where he was born to the family of a schoolmaster. After completing his education, for a while under Antonio Salieri, he resolved to live an impecunious, bohemian life, surrounded by other musicians, artists, and poets. His songs were often performed within this private circle, in gatherings that his friends called "Schubertiads." He died at the age of 31, never having received more than modest attention as a composer.

Schubert was a prodigious and remarkably productive figure. His symphonies, piano music, chamber works, and sacred choral compositions include masterpieces that are regularly performed in the present day. He wrote more than 600 songs, including two important cycles, *Die schöne Müllerin* (*The Beautiful Miller Girl,* 1823) and *Die Winterreise* (*The Winter Journey,* 1827). His favorite poet for songwriting was Goethe, from whose works he crafted every type of setting, from elaborate multisectional and through-composed pieces to others in simple or varied strophic patterns. The last of these types dominates, especially in his later years.

Regardless of the form, the accompaniment in Schubert's songs plays a vital role, setting the mood of the words, adding continuity, and often subtly commenting on the ideas in the poem. The voice parts tend to be expressive, usually with a touch of folklike straightforwardness. The songs are of great intimacy, in which depth of expression is concentrated in fleeting outward shapes.

"Erlkönig" ("Elf King," 1815) (Recording 9.2), written when the composer was only 18 years old, is an example of the great dramatic power that romantic songs could attain. The poem is a ballad by Goethe about an evil spirit of Scandinavian folklore. In eight stanzas, an eerie narrative is told. A father rides frantically through the forest, carrying his son. The child believes that he sees the dreaded Elf King, and despite his father's reassurances, when they arrive at their destination the child is dead. The poem itself is highly musical: It imitates the headlong rhythm of the hoofbeats with a relentless iambic meter and the recurrent hard, clipped *t*'s and *d*'s that end many syllables.

But Schubert was not content to let the emotion, drama, and musicality of the ballad be the only source of expression. He creates music that intensifies and reshapes the poetic ideas, making the music the equal of the words. Perhaps for this reason, Goethe did not so much as acknowledge receipt of this and other settings of his poetry when they were sent to him by Schubert.

Schubert uses his musical arsenal, first of all, to sharpen the drama of the poem. The setting is through-composed, in order to allow the music to follow the words in an intimate way. The characters in the diminutive drama take on vivid musical personalities: The child's lines are placed in the high register, and they ascend in dissonant shrillness and lose melodic shape as his terror increases. The father sings calmly in the low register as he tries to comfort the child. The Elf King sings in the middle register in a tuneful but cloying manner.

The piano accompaniment becomes an active expressive agent: Its rhythm at the opening suggests headlong flight through the forest, and when the Elf King speaks seductively to the child, the piano relents with a relaxed and lilting figure. Key and mode take on clearly dramatic functions. When the Elf King speaks, the foreboding minor mode changes suddenly to major, as the evil spirit tries to lure the child away. In these stanzas (especially in stanzas 3 and 5), the key is stable, whereas during the wrenching outcries of the child it loses focus.

In the final stanza the drama reaches its melancholy conclusion. The narrator relates that the father has at last arrived at home, whereupon the driving piano accompaniment falls silent. The last line, "In his arms, the child was dead," is delivered in recitative, a declamatory style that does not follow a strict beat and for which there is no continuous accompaniment. It is a memorably stark conclusion.

**Listening Guide**

## Franz Schubert, "Erlkönig"
Recording 9.2

1. *Wer reitet so spät durch Nacht und Wind?*
   *Es ist der Vater mit seinem Kind;*
   *er hat den Knaben wohl in dem Arm,*
   *er faßt ihn sicher, er hält ihn warm.*

2. *Mein Sohn, was birgst du so bang dein Gesicht?*
   *Siehst, Vater, du den Erlkönig nicht?*

   *den Erlenkönig, mit Kron' und Schweif?*
   *Mein Sohn, es ist ein Nebelstreif.*

3. *"Du liebes Kind, komm, geh mit mir!*
   *gar schöne Spiele spiel' ich mit dir;*
   *manch bunte Blumen sind an dem Strand,*
   *meine Mutter hat manch' gülden Gewand."*

1. Who rides so late through night and wind?
   It is the father with his child.
   He has the boy tight in his arm,
   he clasps him safely, he holds him warm.

2. My son, why do you hide your face so fearfully?
   Father, don't you see the Elf King?
   The Elf King with crown and train?
   My son, it is only a wisp of mist.

3. "You dear child, come with me!
   Pretty games I'll play with you;
   multicolored flowers are by the shore,
   my mother has many golden robes."

4. *Mein Vater, mein Vater, und hörest du nicht,*
   *was Erlenkönig mir leise verspricht?*

   *Sei ruhig, bleibe ruhig, mein Kind;*
   *in dürren Blättern säuselt der Wind.*

4. My father, my father, did you not hear
   what the Elf King softly promised me?

   Be quiet, be still, my child;
   'twas only the wind in the dry leaves.

5. *"Willst, feiner Knabe, du mit mir gehn?*
   *meine Töchter sollen dich warten schön;*
   *meine Töchter führen den nächtlichen Reihn;*
   *und wiegen und tanzen und singen dich ein."*

5. "Don't you want to go with me, fine boy?
   my daughters will wait upon you;
   my daughters lead the nightly revels;
   they'll swing, dance, and sing with you."

6. *Mein Vater, mein Vater, und siehst du nicht dort*
   *Erlkönigs Töchter am düstern Ort?*

   *Mein Sohn, mein Sohn, ich seh' es genau;*
   *es scheinen die alten Weiden so grau.*

6. My father, my father, don't you see there
   the Elf King's daughters in that dark place?

   My son, my son, I do indeed see it;
   it's just the old gray willows.

7. *"Ich liebe dich, mich reizt deine schöne Gestalt;*
   *und bist du nicht willig, so brauch' ich Gewalt."*
   *Mein Vater, mein Vater, jetzt faßt er mich an!*
   *Erlkönig hat mir ein Leids getan!*

7. "I love you, your beautiful shape charms me;
   and if you are not willing, I'll have to use force."
   My father, my father, he is grabbing me,
   Elf King has hurt me!

8. *Dem Vater grauset's, er reitet geschwind,*
   *er hält in Armen das ächzende Kind,*

   *erreicht den Hof mit Müh' und Not;*

   *in seinen Armen das Kind war tot.*

8. The father shudders, he rides swiftly,
   he holds in his arms the moaning child and
   arrives home with effort and distress.
   In his arms, the child was dead.

**Introduction**     0.00     The music of the piano pictures the urgent dash of the horse through the forest. Its mode is minor, centered on G:

**Stanza 1**     0.22     To the accompaniment of the introductory motives, a narrator describes the riders.

**Stanza 2**     0.56     The exchange of father and son is differentiated in register, and the introductory piano motive continues.

**Stanza 3**     1.30     The Elf King beckons the child with a singsong melody and a relaxed accompaniment. The mode becomes major and the key changes to a fresh tonic of B♭.

**Stanza 4**     1.54     The child's fearful response is set dissonantly, without a stable keynote. The driving introductory motive returns.

**Stanza 5**     2.17     The Elf King tries a new key (C major) and a new tune to seduce the child.

**Stanza 6**     2.36     The terrified child repeats his dissonant, unmelodious line heard in stanza 4, at a higher and more urgent level. The piano interlude after this stanza brings back the introductory motive.

**Stanza 7**     3.05     The impatient Elf King tries a final time to lure the boy off, now using the new key of E♭ major. On the final word, *Gewalt* ("force"), the music veers into the minor mode and the boy shrieks out a final time with his dissonant line, higher still.

**Stanza 8**     3.31     The music has returned to the home key of G minor, in which the narrator relates the arrival of the father. The impact of the final line is underscored by a melody that is close to speech.

# Music for Piano

In the late classical period, the piano emerged as the preeminent musical instrument, not only among professional players but also among amateurs from the aristocracy and the middle class. It was increasingly featured in concerts and so widely played that teaching piano and publishing piano music became basic to the careers of many professional musicians.

## Innovations in the Instrument and Its Music

The early nineteenth century witnessed ever-greater attention to the virtuosic skills of touring pianists such as Franz Liszt, Ignaz Moscheles, and Clara Wieck. Their immense popularity led by the 1830s to a new type of concert, the **recital,** in which one pianist was the sole performer. The works performed at these concerts increasingly included old music—sometimes going back to keyboard pieces by Bach—in addition to music written by the performer or other contemporary selections. Their atmosphere was more than a touch circuslike, as performers avoided the formality that attends modern recitals. A concert by Liszt in Saint Petersburg in 1842 is probably typical:

> Suddenly there was a commotion in the crowded Assembly Hall of the Nobility. We all turned around and saw Liszt, strolling arm in arm through the gallery behind the columns with the potbellied Count Mikhail Vielgorsky. . . . Most startling of all was his enormous mane of fair hair. In those days no one in Russia would have dared wear his hair that way. Just at that moment Liszt, noting the time, walked down from the gallery, elbowed his way through the crowd and moved quickly toward the stage. But instead of using the steps, he leaped onto the platform. He tore off his white kid gloves and tossed them on the floor, under the piano. . . . Without any preliminaries, Liszt began playing the opening cello phrase of the *William Tell* Overture. As soon as he finished, and while the hall was still rocking with applause, he moved swiftly to a second piano facing in the opposite direction.
>
> We had never in our lives heard anything like this; we had never been in the presence of such a brilliant, passionate, demonic temperament, at one moment rushing like a whirlwind, at another pouring forth cascades of tender beauty and grace. Liszt's playing was absolutely overwhelming.[1]

## *Music Today*

### "I Am Only Music"

With these few words, Dietrich Fischer-Dieskau deflected questions from an inquisitive reporter on his personal life. If Fischer-Dieskau is, in fact, only music, that is good enough for his thousands of fans around the world, who have acclaimed him for nearly a half-century as the world's greatest singer, perhaps the greatest of all times.

Dietrich Fischer-Dieskau was born near Berlin in 1925. His musical studies were interrupted by wartime military service, which resulted in his imprisonment by Allied forces in Italy. His artistry as a singer was recognized even then by his captors, who allowed him to sing German songs for prisoners of war in an attempt to boost their morale. Following the war, he quickly established a preeminent reputation as a singer equally adept at opera, oratorio, and song. It was in this last capacity that he made his greatest impact, especially in his renditions of the songs of Schubert and other German romantic lieder composers.

Dieskau's approach to singing is highly distinctive, so much so that a listener can very quickly recognize his voice in any context. He does not merely sing a song; he enters in every dimension into its spirit and meaning. He tends to underscore the sense of the words in a dramatic way, even if details of the music must be changed. No other modern lieder singer so penetratingly brings music to life.

His other unrivaled accomplishment is the breadth of musical literature that he has sung and recorded. Singers are generally limited to one type of singing—they are either opera singers, lieder singers, oratorio singers, specialists in modern music, specialists in early music, or some other. Dieskau is a master of all of these repertories, and he sings the songs of American, English, French, and Italian composers with the same insight that he brings to Schubert and Schumann. His number of operatic roles is equally vast, and he has appeared in all of the world's major opera houses.

Since the mid-1970s he has been active as an orchestral conductor. He also writes with great authority on musical topics, such as the songs of Schubert and the artistic relationship of Wagner and Nietzsche. He has won every major award for singing and has amassed the largest number of recordings ever for a singer. And he continues to sing, well into his sixties, giving concerts around the world and proving himself over and over again to be one of the most important ambassadors of the art of music.

---

The pyrotechnics for which Liszt was known were permitted, in considerable measure, by recent innovations in the construction of pianos. By the middle of the nineteenth century, the instrument had taken on a larger keyboard, allowing a greater total range and much greater resonance produced by heavier, felt-covered hammers and metal bracing that created greater string tension. Brilliant, fast-moving passages were facilitated by the introduction of a "double escapement" mechanism by which a note could be rapidly repeated.

The genres of solo piano music in the classical period were generally limited to large works such as sonatas and variations. Composers also wrote small pieces in a single movement, which were often presented as gifts to students. In the nineteenth century, these miniature pieces took on much more importance. Since they usually established some definite character, emotion, or mood, they can be called **character pieces.** Their titles are varied. Many imitate dances specified in their titles (the waltzes of Schubert are especially noteworthy). Others use terms that indicate a particular mood. The titles *musical moment, prelude, album leaf, rhapsody, song without words,* and *bagatelle* also appear, as do terms suggesting a tempo or form. Related to the romantic character piece is the **étude** (French for "study"), a work that drills some aspect of pianistic technique. In the hands of composers like Liszt, Debussy, Frédéric Chopin, and Alexander Scriabin, these study pieces attained great artistry and technical sophistication. Character pieces often had programmatic connotations, usually reflected in their titles, and they were often linked into cycles.

### Frédéric Chopin and the Nocturne in D♭ Major, Op. 27, No. 2

Of all the piano composers of the nineteenth century, Chopin (1810–1849) wrote music that most elicits the instrument's distinctive and poetic sonorities. His early years were spent in Warsaw, where he showed a precocious talent as a composer and a pianist. Beginning in 1829, he concertized in western Europe, settling in 1831 in Paris. Chopin quickly dispensed with the career of public recitalist, preferring instead private performances and teaching. His compositional muse was greatly inspired by his liaison with the writer Aurore Dudevant, known by her pen name, George Sand, with whom he lived for nine years. After their separation, his health and spirits declined rapidly.

Chopin was a specialist in composing for the piano. All of his music involves this instrument, and most is for solo piano, including three sonatas and a large number of character works. Among the latter are dances (especially waltzes and Polish dances called *mazurkas* and *polonaises*), études, impromptus, nocturnes, scherzos, and ballades. They contain great evocativeness and refinement, a wonderful exploitation of the sound of the instrument, and an imaginatively original treatment of harmony.

The Nocturne in Db Major, Op. 27, No. 2 (1835) (Recording 9.3) exhibits the inspired improvisatory element that runs through many of Chopin's best pieces (he was, in fact, a great master of improvisation). The descriptive title **nocturne,** suggesting a dreamy night piece, was first used for piano music in the character works of the Irish composer John Field, from whom Chopin adopted both the term and an intensely lyrical spirit. Chopin wrote 21 nocturnes and several other pieces with the nocturne character.

The form of the Nocturne in Db deviates from the ternary plan of most of Chopin's character works. Instead, an opening melody returns twice, each time following intervening melodic material. The form is closest to the rondo. The melodies heard between appearances of the main theme are improvisatory and highly ornamental. The texture is strictly homophonic as the pianist's right hand plays a broadly arched melody of operatic intensity. The accompaniment in the left hand consists of broken chords, often used by Chopin, giving the piece a delicate animation and lightness. Unexpected harmonic progressions add brilliance and color to this refined and elegant work.

*Frédéric Chopin was a close personal friend of the great artist Eugène Delacroix. The painter deeply admired Chopin's music and piano playing, as well as his strength of spirit. This latter quality is reflected in Delacroix's portrait of Chopin, painted in 1838.*

## Robert Schumann and "Grillen" from Fantasiestücke, Op. 12

Whereas Chopin's character pieces are evocative rather than overtly programmatic, those of Robert Schumann (1810–1856) are more concrete in their extramusical content. During his formative years, Schumann showed prodigious talent as a pianist, a composer, and also as a writer in the imaginative romantic manner. He was an outstanding improviser at the keyboard, and he was especially attracted to the piano works of Schubert and Beethoven. He attended law school but soon lost interest in favor of music.

His hopes of a career as a professional pianist were dashed by a malady affecting movement of one hand, and he then turned, like Berlioz, to work as a music critic. In 1840 he married the remarkable piano virtuoso Clara Wieck, the daughter of his piano teacher. Their courtship, beset by opposi-

**Listening Guide**

**Frédéric Chopin, Nocturne in D♭ Major, Op. 27, No. 2**
Recording 9.3

| | | |
|---|---|---|
| **A** | 0.00 | The strikingly beautiful main theme (illustrated below) is followed by several other melodic ideas. |

| | | |
|---|---|---|
| **A′** | 1.40 | The main theme returns, followed by variants of the additional melodies. |
| **A″** | 3.02 | The main theme reappears one final time. |
| **Coda** | 4.11 | A new melodic idea is introduced, subtly related to motives already heard: |

tion from Clara's father, stimulated a flood of songs composed in the year of the wedding. After that time, Schumann focused increasingly on orchestral and chamber works.

His piano music, overwhelmingly devoted to miniature forms, was composed primarily between 1830 and 1840. The diminutive pieces of these years are mostly collected into cycles with programmatic titles. In Schumann's music, still deeper meanings are hidden from view. He delighted in embedding in his music motives that had secret and deeply personal symbolism. In a letter to Clara in 1838 he explains the intimate connection between his music and the world around him:

> I am affected by everything that goes on in the world, and think it all over in my own way, politics, literature, and people, and then I long to express my feelings and find an outlet for them in music.

That is why my compositions are sometimes difficult to understand, because they are connected with distant interests.[2]

Schumann's *Fantasiestücke (Fantasy Pieces)* were composed in 1837. They consist of eight works, each with a suggestive title but no other programmatic associations. "Grillen" ("Whims") (Recording 9.4) is the fourth of the set and one of the most high-spirited. Here Schumann's humor shines through. The

*Listening Guide*

**Robert Schumann, "Grillen" from *Fantasiestücke*, Op. 12, No. 4**
Recording 9.4

**A** **a₁** 0.00 The humorous opening melody, which is immediately repeated, is a straightforward example of period form:

**a₂** 0.28 A new melodic element appears in the contrasting key of F minor:

**a₁** 0.54 The opening melody returns, in the home key.

**B** 1.08 The middle section of the ternary form consists of two alternating melodic ideas, of which the first is in the contrasting key of G♭ major:

**A'** 2.15 The material from section A returns, somewhat changed in its succession of keys.

music has the zest and gaiety of the dance, but it contains many unexpected turns. The opening melody contains a passage in which the metric emphasis temporarily leaps ahead one beat. The melody is also ambiguous in key, since the tonic is not clear until the melody reaches its last note.

# Chamber Music and Opera

The nineteenth century was not a great period for chamber music. After the flowering of string quartet writing in the works of Haydn, Beethoven, and Schubert, composers later in the nineteenth century were inclined to bypass this medium. The quartet and other chamber media suggested a certain strictness of form and homogeneity of sound that were out of keeping with romantic boldness and emotionality. The decline of the aristocracy dealt another blow to the development of chamber music. In Beethoven's day, several noblemen in Vienna employed their own private string quartets. It was in such private circumstances that Beethoven often tried out new works. In the nineteenth century there was no comparable institution to foster music of this type. The professional touring string quartet was still rare, and public concerts were dominated by virtuoso soloists or by orchestras.

It was primarily the composers of more conservative and traditional leanings who wrote chamber music in the early romantic period: Schumann, Felix Mendelssohn, and, later in the century, Johannes Brahms and Antonín Dvořák. Reflecting the hegemony of the piano in musical culture, there was much more emphasis in the nineteenth century than in the eighteenth on chamber genres including piano.

## Felix Mendelssohn and the Trio in D Minor, Op. 49

"Mendelssohn is the Mozart of the nineteenth century," wrote Robert Schumann about his friend. Indeed, in Mendelssohn's music, the classical spirit is almost always present, joined happily to a warmth and lyricism characteristic of the age of romanticism. Mendelssohn (1809–1847) grew up in Berlin in an affluent and artistically inclined family, and he received every possible encouragement in his musical and general development. He counted among his teachers Carl Friedrich Zelter, Goethe's musical adviser, through whom Mendelssohn met the great poet. Also through Zelter he became acquainted with the sacred vocal works of Bach. In 1829 he organized a performance in Berlin of Bach's *St. Matthew Passion,* an event that proved a milestone in the revival of Bach's music. Mendelssohn was later tireless in his organization of performances of the oratorios of Handel.

**Felix Mendelssohn, Trio in D Minor, Op. 49, first movement**
Recording 9.5

**Exposition**    0.00    *Main theme.* This melody is begun by the cello and continued in the violin. It has an expanded period shape and is in the key of D minor:

0.56    *Transition.* Begins with an allusion to the main theme but later introduces new motives. The key and mode are changed to A major.

1.43    *Subsidiary themes.* The principal subsidiary theme begins.

It is followed by several other melodic ideas. (The exposition is not repeated.)

**Development**    3.18    True to the classical model, this development passes quickly through several keys and touches on both the main theme and the principal subsidiary theme, transforming them and spinning them into new shapes.

**Recapitula-tion**    5.29    The main parts of the exposition are brought back, with minor changes in scoring and in the working out of themes. The key is now firmly in D (the principal subsidiary theme returns at 6.35 in the major mode; otherwise the mode is minor).

**Coda**    8.11    The main and subsidiary themes are heard one final time.

After a lengthy period of travel and composition, he settled in 1835 in Leipzig to conduct the Gewandhaus Orchestra. Not only did he raise the standards of this organization to a preeminent level, but his approach to conducting and programming, which combined masterpieces for orchestra from the time of Bach to his own day, created a model for orchestras still followed today. In the 1840s he added to his duties work as conductor and composer for the king of Prussia.

His mature music includes all of the major genres of his day except opera. His incidental music for Shakespeare's play *A Midsummer Night's Dream* is some of his most beloved, as are his five symphonies, his tone poems (which he termed "overtures"), and his intensely lyrical Violin Concerto in E Minor. He wrote eight volumes of *Lieder ohne Worte* ("songs without words") for piano, which are anthologies of character pieces. His chamber music included six string quartets, and he also composed songs and sacred choral music. His great oratorios *Elijah* and *St. Paul* evoke the memory of Handel.

His Trio in D Minor for violin, cello, and piano, Op. 49 (1839), exemplifies the wedding of classical form and romantic lyricism. It is a four-movement work in the classical manner, which elicited from Schumann comparisons with the chamber music of Beethoven and Schubert:

> This is the master-trio of the present, just as in their times were the trios of Beethoven in B♭ and D, and that of Schubert in E♭. It is a beautiful composition that years from now will delight our grandchildren and great-grandchildren.[3]

The first movement (Recording 9.5) is a straightforward example of sonata form. The themes are mostly based on period form, with clear points of departure and arrival. The tonal plan and harmonic language are the same as in the late classical period. In fact, the only aspect of this music to extend beyond the classical norm is the lyricism of its melodies, which have the warmth and emotionality of the romantic period.

### New Ideas in Opera

Opera in the early nineteenth century continued its hold over the public's attention, despite the rise of instrumental music. Although opera was a highly eclectic genre at this time, there emerged in Italy, Germany, and France reasonably distinct national types that diversified the hitherto Italian-dominated operatic world of the eighteenth century.

The subjects of Italian opera of this time could be either comic or serious, and its great appeal lay primarily in its reliance on virtuosic singing to convey heightened human emotions. These operas continued to be divided into subsections or "numbers," but the divisions became longer and more diverse in the musical styles that they contained.

The leading composer of Italian opera early in the nineteenth century was Gioacchino Rossini (1792–1868). After establishing his reputation in Italy in both the serious and comic veins, he moved permanently to Paris, then the operatic capital of Europe. There he produced both Italian and French works. The inexhaustible melodiousness of his vocal writing and his colorful overtures are exemplified in his most famous work, the comic opera *The Barber of Seville* (1815). His two most important successors prior to mid-century were Gaetano Donizetti (1797–1848) and Vincenzo Bellini (1801–1835).

Operas in the German language during the classical period form a genre that is now called *Singspiel.* These were spoken plays on sentimental, magical, or moralistic stories to which vocal and instrumental music were added. A new direction in a genuine German opera was initiated in 1821 by Carl Maria von Weber (1786–1826) with his masterpiece, *Der Freischütz (The Devil's Huntsman).* The story of this work derives from German folklore. It involves supernatural characters, is set amid common German folk, and includes main characters who represent ethical ideas and personality types. The action has a timeless quality in which forces of evil are ultimately defeated by the representatives of good. Weber called such works "romantic operas," referring to their supernatural elements, closeness to nature, and fantastic events.

Weber's music for *Der Freischütz* is distinctly German in spirit. He quotes folk songs, writes for rousing male choruses that were then popular in Germany, and integrates the orchestral music into the dramatic fabric in a way unknown in Italian or French opera. Romantic operas of this type were later a great inspiration to Richard Wagner.

Comic opera in France in the early nineteenth century continued to emphasize the simplicity and tunefulness of the late classical period. In the 1830s in France there appeared a new type of opera based on serious subjects, whose grandiosity—including spectacle, ballet, and massive choruses—led to its being labeled **grand opera.** It is symptomatic of the eclecticism of French grand opera that its leading composer, Giacomo Meyerbeer, was born and trained in Germany and rose to fame as an opera composer in Italy, where he had assimilated the style of Rossini. We will have a taste of the pageantry of grand opera in Verdi's *Aida,* which is discussed in Chapter 10.

## TOPICS FOR DISCUSSION AND WRITING

**1.** Compare Schubert's song "Erlkönig" with the setting of the same poem by Carl Loewe (written in 1818). Many striking similarities will be noted in the two settings, and the differences show Loewe's single-minded attention to the text. Loewe's "Erlkönig" may be found on numerous recordings, for example, EMI, IC 063-00 388 (performed by Dietrich Fischer-Dieskau).

**2.** Read Eduard Hanslick's short treatise *The Beautiful in Music* (translated by Gustav Cohen, Library of Liberal Arts, 1957), and test the validity of his critique of musical meaning against the finale of Berlioz's *Symphonie fantastique*. Hanslick was the leading Viennese music critic of the second half of the nineteenth century, and his treatise (which appeared in 1854) is an attack on the widespread notion that the role of music was to express poetic ideas or emotional states.

**3.** Compare Chopin's Nocturne in D♭ Major, Op. 27, No. 2, to the piece "Chopin" from Robert Schumann's *Carnaval*. In this work Schumann, an early admirer of Chopin, presents a good-natured imitation of Chopin's pianistic style. What aspects of Schumann's caricature ring true in comparison with Chopin's Nocturne?

**4.** The title of Schumann's piano piece "Grillen" poses a linguistic puzzle. The German word *Grillen* can mean either "crickets" or "silly ideas." After listening to the work several times, decide which meaning Schumann intended and explain why.

## ADDITIONAL LISTENING

### Berlioz

*Le carnaval romain (Roman Carnival Overture)*. This tone poem is made up of themes from Berlioz's early opera *Benvenuto Cellini*.

*L'enfance du Christ (The Childhood of Christ)*, Op. 45. This is an oratorio for chorus, orchestra, and solo voices based on texts appropriate to the Christmas season.

*Les nuits d'été*. A cycle of songs based on poetry by Théophile Gautier, *Summer Nights* was later orchestrated and is usually performed in this later version. The song "Absence" is especially ravishing.

### Chopin

Ballade No. 1 in G Minor.

Études, Op. 10.

Nocturne in E♭ Major, Op. 9, No. 2.

Polonaise in A♭ Major, Op. 53.

Preludes, Op. 28.

Sonata No. 2 for Piano in B♭ Minor. This contains a famous funeral march.

A recorded collection of Chopin's piano pieces by a major pianist. The recordings of Arthur Rubinstein are highly recommended.

## Mendelssohn

Concerto for Violin and Orchestra in E Minor, Op. 64.

*Hebrides Overture.*

*A Midsummer Night's Dream* (incidental music for orchestra, containing the famous wedding march).

Symphony No. 4 in A Major *(Italian Symphony).*

## Rossini

*The Barber of Seville.* This marvelously witty and spirited work is a setting of Beaumarchais's play of the same title. It is textually related to Mozart's *Marriage of Figaro.*

## Schubert

Quintet in A Major for Piano and Strings, D. 667 *(Trout Quintet).* This famous work contains variations on the melody of Schubert's earlier song "The Trout," hence its title. The "D." numbers identifying Schubert's music refer to a catalog of his complete music compiled by Otto Deutsch. They are comparable to the "K." numbers used for Mozart's music.

Sonata in B♭ for Piano, D. 960. Schubert's last piano sonata.

Song cycles *Die schöne Müllerin* and *Die Winterreise* and collections of songs sung by outstanding singers such as Dietrich Fischer-Dieskau, Gérard Souzay, and Elly Ameling.

Symphony No. 8 in B Minor *(Unfinished Symphony).* The numbering of the Schubert symphonies varies. This work was left in two movements, and it is unknown whether the composer considered it unfinished or complete as such.

Symphony No. 9 in C Major *(Great Symphony).*

## Schumann

Concerto for Piano and Orchestra in A Minor, Op. 54.

Piano music cycles *Carnaval,* Op. 9; *Kinderszenen,* Op. 15; *Papillons,* Op. 2.

Quintet for Piano and Strings in E♭ Major, Op. 44.

Song cycles *Dichterliebe* and *Liederkreis,* Op. 39 (to poetry by Eichendorff).

Symphony No. 3 in E♭ *(Rhenisch Symphony).* This work has the refreshing melodiousness of most of Schumann's symphonies. Its fourth movement is a stirring musical portrait of the cathedral in Cologne.

## Weber

*Der Freischütz.* A milestone in German operatic music.

## BIBLIOGRAPHY

General sources of information about romantic music, other fine arts, and history:

Abraham, Gerald. *A Hundred Years of Music*. Third edition. Hawthorne, N.Y.: Aldine, 1964. Coverage is from c. 1830–1930.

Blume, Friedrich. *Classic and Romantic Music: A Comprehensive Survey*. Translated by M. D. Herder Norton. New York: Norton, 1970. Blume theorizes that the classical and romantic periods should be viewed as a single stylistic continuum.

Einstein, Alfred. *Music in the Romantic Era*. New York: Norton, 1947. A pioneering study speculating about the interactions of musical style.

Griffiths, Paul. *The String Quartet: A History*. London: Thames & Hudson, 1983.

Grout, Donald J. *A Short History of Opera*. Second edition. New York: Columbia University Press, 1965.

Hobsbawm, E. J. *The Age of Revolution, 1789–1848*. New York: Mentor, 1962.

Jones, Howard M. *Revolution and Romanticism*. Cambridge, Mass.: Harvard University Press, 1974.

*Nineteenth-Century Music*. Journal published by the University of California Press three times annually since 1977.

Novotny, Fritz. *Painting and Sculpture in Europe, 1780–1880*. Second edition. New York: Viking Penguin, 1978.

Plantinga, Leon. *Romantic Music*. New York: Norton, 1984.

Stevens, Denis, ed. *A History of Song*. Revised edition. New York: Norton, 1960.

Welleck, René. "The Concept of Romanticism in Literary History." In *Concepts of Criticism*. New Haven, Conn.: Yale University Press, 1963, pp. 128–198.

Studies of composers mentioned in this chapter:

Barzun, Jacques. *Berlioz and the Romantic Century*. Third edition. New York: Columbia University Press, 1969.

Brown, Maurice J. E. *Schubert: A Critical Biography*. London: Macmillan, 1958. Updated by the same author in "Schubert: Discoveries of the Last Decade," *Musical Quarterly* 47 (1961) and 57 (1971).

Hedley, Arthur. *Chopin*. London: Dent, 1947.

Plantinga, Leon. *Schumann as Critic*. New Haven, Conn.: Yale University Press, 1967.

Warrack, John. *Carl Maria von Weber*. Second edition. Cambridge: Cambridge University Press, 1976.

Werner, Eric. *Mendelssohn*. Translated by Dika Newlin. New York: Da Capo, 1978.

## NOTES

1. Vladimir Vasilevich Stasov, *Selected Essays on Music,* trans. Florence Jonas (New York: Praeger, 1968), pp. 120–121
2. Robert Schumann, *Early Letters,* trans. May Herbert (London: Bell, 1888), p. 270.
3. Robert Schumann, in Leon Plantinga, *Schumann as Critic* (New Haven, Conn.: Yale University Press, 1967), p. 267.

# 10

---

# The Late Romantic Period,
## 1850–1900

---

### So That the Spirit Can Be Free

*In the lavish drawing room of his villa "Wahnfried," the great
composer Richard Wagner discusses his newest opera,* Parsifal.
*Joining him are his wife, Cosima, her father, the composer Franz
Liszt, and, at the far right, Wagner's editorial assistant, Hans von
Wolzogen. The picture, titled* Richard Wagner at His Home in
Bayreuth, *is by Wilhelm Beckmann. It is unlikely that it was
painted from life, since Wagner was far too busy before the premiere
of* Parsifal *to pose.*

But Beckmann's painting accurately captures the refined and intensely intellectual spirit that surrounded Wagner's daily activities in Bayreuth. The viewer is first struck by the great luxury of the appointments in the garden drawing room and the elegance of dress of all in attendance. The composer considered such amenities to be necessary for creative work. "For people like us," he wrote, "all extravagances have only one meaning, the achievement of peace and ease, so that the spirit can be free." Beckmann is also very accurate in reproducing details of the room. Above Cosima Wagner's head is a portrait of her painted by Franz von Lenbach. Behind her chair is a scene painting for **Parsifal**, executed by Paul von Joukowsky. Above Wagner's head is a depiction of the philosopher Schopenhauer, whose writings profoundly influenced the composer.

**Parsifal** (1882) was destined to be Wagner's last opera. The character Parsifal is encountered in Arthurian legend, although Wagner used as his direct model a romance by a medieval German poet, Wolfram von Eschenbach. The story is highly symbolic, tracing Parsifal's spiritual growth, his struggle with temptation, and his ultimate initiation into the mysteries of Christianity. Wagner held the opera in such high esteem that he wanted it to be performed only in his own theater in Bayreuth, a wish that was generally honored until 1913.

Wagner is joined in this picture by some of his closest and most trusted friends. Liszt was one of the greatest composers of the

*nineteenth century, who earlier had used his own prestige to further
the recognition of Wagner's music. Wolzogen was a well-known
writer and interpreter of Wagner's music. He was the editor of the
Bayreuther Blätter, a journal devoted to Wagner's theories and to
the greater understanding of his music. Wagner's wife, Cosima, the
daughter of Liszt and Marie d'Agoult, was herself a skillful pianist
and tireless supporter of her husband's ideas. But Wagner stands
above them all in Beckmann's depiction. Wagner's preeminence
proved to be a telling assessment. By the end of the romantic period,
his music and ideas had become signposts for new paths in virtually
all of the fine arts.*

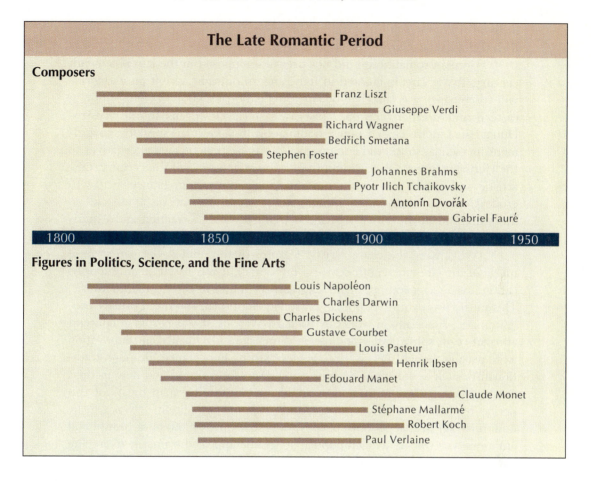

## The Late Romantic Period

**Composers**

Franz Liszt
Giuseppe Verdi
Richard Wagner
Bedřich Smetana
Stephen Foster
Johannes Brahms
Pyotr Ilich Tchaikovsky
Antonín Dvořák
Gabriel Fauré

| 1800 | 1850 | 1900 | 1950 |

**Figures in Politics, Science, and the Fine Arts**

Louis Napoléon
Charles Darwin
Charles Dickens
Gustave Courbet
Louis Pasteur
Henrik Ibsen
Edouard Manet
Claude Monet
Stéphane Mallarmé
Robert Koch
Paul Verlaine

The flowering of romanticism in Germany and Austria early in the nineteenth century laid the groundwork for a remarkable domination of the musical world during the second half of the century. Just as the political and economic power of the German states rose during this period, so too did the importance of German music, even to the point of exerting a true hegemony over musical culture around the world. Many of the leading late-nineteenth-century composers in the United States, including Horatio Parker, Edward MacDowell, and John Knowles Paine, received their training in Germany and, to a large extent, modeled their music on works by Germans. In France, despite bitter anti-German sentiment engendered by the Franco-Prussian War of 1870–1871, composers studied the music of Richard Wagner with

325

near-religious intensity. In Russia, prominent composers, including Pyotr Ilich Tchaikovsky, wrote music in a Germanic style.

German romanticism did not prevail unopposed in the late nineteenth century. It was largely ignored in Italy, and an outright assault on its world-wide dominance was launched by emerging national schools of composition in eastern and northern Europe. Just as eastern Europeans in the Austro-Hungarian Empire chafed under domination by a German-speaking government in Vienna, so too did composers from these regions seek alternatives to the Germanic approach to composition. Toward the end of the century, new artistic and intellectual forces, emanating especially from France, began to erode Germany's supremacy. Among them were antirealistic tendencies in literature and in the visual arts and a trend toward abstraction and experimentation in music.

What were the characteristic features of the unified German style of music of the late nineteenth century? First of all, it was based on an intensification, even exaggeration, of the expressivity found in early romantic music. This music was evocative, poetic, personal, emotional, and often overtly programmatic. Especially in works by Richard Wagner, it was heroic in content, affirmative in spirit, and grandiose in dimension. Originality and innovation were usually thought necessary to achieve lasting importance, although traditionalists such as Johannes Brahms mingled features of old and new in their music, shaping them into an inseparable composite. German music of this period tended to be serious, dense, and profound in content. It was usually nonutilitarian in that its only purpose was to express matters of beauty and emotion. As a rule, it avoided popular styles and appealed primarily to an elite and knowledgeable audience.

## Political, Social, and Artistic Developments

The upheavals experienced across Europe in 1848 did not succeed in changing the established political order, although these revolutions ushered in a new government in France, led by Louis Napoléon (1808–1873, later Napoléon III). In the German world, Prussia vied with Hapsburg Austria for leadership. Russia remained the most tradition-bound country of Europe, where feudalism endured until the 1860s and the tsars maintained absolute power. England was by far the industrial giant by mid-century and the leading imperial force in the entire world.

The second half of the century was a time of unprecedented advances in science, technology, and education. Improvements in farm technology greatly increased the food supply and allowed the population of Europe to double in this 50-year period. This was also a time of widespread migration, primarily of peasants from the country into large, industrialized cities and from various European lands to the New World. The Industrial Revolution was now felt throughout Europe, bringing with it improved communication, railroads, and mass-produced consumer goods, as well as the social evils of urban life. Many of the technologies that characterize modern society were invented or put in place during this half-century, including electricity, modern armaments, early automobiles, the telegraph, and the typewriter. For the first time, a true understanding of disease was established by such pioneers of microbiology as Louis Pasteur (1822–1895) and Robert Koch (1843–1910). The theory of evolution of species advanced by the naturalist Charles Darwin (1809–1882) revolutionized the biological and social sciences.

Nationalistic consciousness became ever more intense, especially among the bourgeoisie and the educated classes. Patriotic ideals, together with political and economic maneuvering, produced the unification of Italy and Germany and the establishment of independent governments in eastern Europe, including Hungary, Serbia, and Romania. The end of the century witnessed rampant imperialism, as the major European powers vied to establish either direct political or economic control over large portions of Africa and Asia.

Romantic literature of a sentimental type gave way by mid-century to writing, especially apparent in the novel, that was more realistic and dealt in a more objective way with human issues arising in an industrialized society. The novels of Charles Dickens (1812–1870) are examples of this trend toward social commentary. By the 1870s, realism (sometimes termed *naturalism*) also became the dominant trend in modern theater, led by the searching social studies of the Norwegian Henrik Ibsen (1828–1906). By the end of the century, the realist movement in play writing had penetrated the world of opera, especially in Italy, where it was termed **verismo.** Operas in this mode are usually set amid ordinary people, whose mundane problems are exacerbated by irremediable social forces, leading to acts of violence. Pietro Mascagni, Ruggiero Leoncavallo, and Giacomo Puccini wrote operas in this vein.

Toward the end of the nineteenth century, new trends in literature began to deflect attention away from social realism. A movement in French poetry of the 1880s termed **symbolism** was especially important in the dissolution of romantic realism, and it proved to be of great importance to French music at the turn of the twentieth century. Leaders of the symbolist movement, including Paul Verlaine (1844–1896) and Stéphane Mallarmé (1842–1898), wrote verse that avoided clear and logical narrative in favor of

*Gustave Courbet's depictions of the backbreaking labor of common people, as in* **The Stonebreakers** *(1849), pricked the social consciousness of many of his contemporaries. Not only does Courbet choose peasants and laborers as proper subjects for painting, but he shows their daily lives in a brutally objective manner.*

sensuous or imaginative symbols. The symbolists were much interested in music, which seemed to them able to move the emotions purely by immaterial, sonorous images, without recourse to mundane or realistic forms of discourse.

Painting at the middle of the nineteenth century followed a course similar to that of literature, whereby realism became entrenched as the dominant approach. Perhaps the most forceful spokesman for realism at this time was the French artist Gustave Courbet (1819–1877), whose canvases often depict people from lower social classes in mundane situations that elicit sympathy for their poverty. For Courbet, art could only rightly depict scenes from contemporary life. "I hold also," he wrote, "that painting is an essentially *concrete* art, and can consist only of the representation of things both *real* and *existing*."[1] His painting *The Stonebreakers* (see above) affirms the appropriateness of people in a mundane occupation as subjects for art.

In the 1860s in France, a powerful new school of painters in the realist vein emerged. These figures were followers of Edouard Manet (1832–1883) in depicting scenes from everyday life, but they did so with a new insight into the effects of light and color. Their movement was dubbed **impressionism,** a term at first used by critics as a pejorative. Their number included Claude Monet, Camille Pissarro, Auguste Renoir, and Edgar Degas, of whom Monet (1840–1926) most consistently presented their characteristic style.

The impressionists used as their subjects mundane and uncontrived scenes, especially landscapes, seascapes, and city scenes. These may include human figures, usually shown at a distance and almost always in comfortable or serene situations. Their basically realistic technique, especially in the works of Monet and Pissarro, is blurred by liquefied outlines and short, choppy brushstrokes. These suggest a dynamic play of light on the subject and a fleeting or spontaneous vision. Given certain conditions of light, the colors of an impressionist painting can be strong, emphasizing primary tones. These qualities are seen in Monet's *Roches Noires Hotel at Trouville* (page 330), in which the vivid blue of the sky and red of the flags, vibrating in the bright sunlight, convey not only the realistic power of color electrified by light but also the feelings of the painter. By studying this painting, we can almost feel the fresh sea air in Monet's face as he worked on the picture. The rough brushstrokes emphasize both these feelings and the realism of the windblown scene.

Realism in literature and painting did not produce direct analogies in music of the late romantic period, although new directions in painting by the impressionists and their successors and writers of the symbolist school stimulated musicians to seek new avenues of expression at the turn of the century. We shall analyze these musical developments in Chapter 11.

## Orchestral Music

Orchestral music of the late romantic period continued trends that were established earlier in the nineteenth century. The major genres remained the programmatic symphony, the tone poem, the symphony with voices, and the classical symphony. This last type is an example of **absolute music** because unlike the other three, it conveys no overt programmatic idea. Composers wrote for ever-larger and more diverse orchestras. The tuba and harp became regular members of the symphony orchestra, and some symphonists late in the period began using other unusual instruments such as the saxophone.

*A French impressionist painting,* Claude Monet's Hôtel des Roches Noires, Trouville *(1870).*

Despite the general allegiance of orchestral music after mid-century with early romantic models, several new avenues in symphonic writing were opened, including the use of nationalistic programs and a reassertion of traditional forms.

## A Return to Classicism

Clearly, the leading trend in nineteenth-century instrumental music was toward the expression of vivid and concrete ideas or intense emotions. This commitment to poetic expression carried with it the necessity of devising ever-newer musical means to convey programmatic content, including new forms, new modes of harmonic and melodic presentation, and ever-larger orchestras. In orchestral music at mid-century, programmatic content usually went hand in hand with an innovative style.

Around 1860 a group of musicians who were gathered about Franz Liszt in Weimar coined the term *New German School* to describe their highly innovative and expressive approach. They proudly thought of themselves as writing "music of the future." For other musicians of this time, however, their claim seemed excessive and an affront to the sublimity of music of the classical masters.

The most important traditionalist in the late romantic age was Johannes Brahms (1833–1897). Born in Hamburg to a family of musicians, he came to prominence in 1853 as a pianist and a composer. At that time he met Robert Schumann, who described him in these prophetic terms:

> I have held that someday there would and must suddenly appear one who would be called to give voice to the highest expression of the times, in an ideal manner, one who would bring us mastery, not as a gradual manifestation, but like Minerva, springing fully armored from the head of Cronus. And he has arrived, a young spirit, about whose cradle graces and heroes kept watch. His name is Johannes Brahms.[2]

In 1862, Brahms moved to Vienna, the home of the great classical composers of the previous century, to work as a conductor and a composer. Although he did not usually take part in polemics between the advocates of musical modernism and classicism, his music was sufficiently traditional in form and content to be held up by his supporters as an antidote to the avant-garde. Brahms himself signed a manifesto, published in the journal *Echo* in 1860, in which he expressed doubt about the validity of modernism as it was then practiced by Liszt's advocates: "The works of the leaders and pupils of the so-called 'New German School,' " he wrote, "are contrary to the innermost spirit of music, and are strongly to be deplored and condemned."

Brahms's music mixes classical and romantic elements in an intimate way. He avoided certain genres associated with the New German School, such as programmatic orchestral music, but his lieder and character piano pieces are squarely in the romantic manner. Even his works that have a classical outward shape are filled with an intense lyricism, often a dark romantic melancholy, and a subtly innovative reinterpretation of musical materials that defies distinctions between old and new.

His four symphonies and his chamber music are his most classical works. He approached the symphonic genre with the utmost respect, delaying the completion of his First Symphony until 1876. All of the symphonies are absolute works in the mold of Beethoven's symphonies. All use orchestras of modest proportions, and all apply traditional classical forms. Symphony No. 1 in C Minor exemplifies Brahms's merger of classical shape and romantic content. The work adheres to the traditional four-movement scheme, and the orchestra is approximately the same as for Beethoven's Fifth Symphony. Also like Beethoven's Fifth, the Brahms Symphony begins in C minor and ends triumphantly in C major.

The first movement (Recording 10.1) is cast in the classical sonata form, begun by a slow introduction. The introduction before the time of Beethoven did not share thematic material with the body of the movement. But in some of Beethoven's slow introductions, such as that of *Egmont* Overture, it contains fragmentary motives that later underlie major themes. This is the approach taken by Brahms in this movement. In the dense and brooding music of the introduction, we hear fleeting melodic ideas that will return subtly embedded within the themes of the movement to come. The result is a powerful unity lying just beneath a musical surface that is itself rich in invention and diversity.

After the slow introduction, the tempo becomes fast, and after a statement of a motive from the introduction, the main theme begins. It is highly irregular in shape. The main subsidiary theme occurs in the major mode, and its onset is clearly marked by a varied return of the motive that preceded the main theme. The exposition, which is repeated in the classical manner, ends in the stormy minor mode.

The development section spins the introductory motives and expositional themes into ever-new shapes, and the recapitulation brings back the thematic materials of the exposition in a fairly regular manner. A coda rounds the movement off in the major mode, which prepares us for the final movement, also in C major.

**Johannes Brahms, Symphony No. 1 in C Minor, first movement**
Recording 10.1

**Introduction**     0.00     A succession of motives is presented over a ponderously reiterated low C in the basses (a so-called *pedal point*). The dense texture and dark tone foreshadow the mood of the entire movement. The most important motive is illustrated below; its string of rising semitones (bracketed) are in evidence throughout the movement.

**Exposition**     2.49     The bracketed motive precedes the main theme, which is followed by a transition to the key of E♭ major and by several subsidiary themes. The entire exposition is repeated.

**Development**     9.16     Motives from the introduction are brought back in new shapes, and seemingly new themes emerge as transformations of preceding motives.

**Recapitulation**     12.27     The events of the exposition return, with many changes and with a new tonal plan whereby the home key of C is in effect throughout.

**Coda**     15.44     This closing passage has a slightly slower tempo; the opening introductory motive is much in evidence.

### Nationalism

Nationalistic and patriotic sentiments were a potent force in virtually all aspects of society in Europe and America in the nineteenth century. In the political sphere, they were stimulated by Napoléon's military subjugation of Europe at the turn of the century, and they later catalyzed the successful movements of unification among German and Italian states in the 1860s and

## Music Today

# The Pride of America's Music: Symphony Orchestras

Whereas European cities take pride in great traditions in music, outstanding opera theaters, and the legacies of the master composers, America's boast in the world of music is often its symphony orchestras. Throughout the twentieth century, the orchestras in Boston, New York, Philadelphia, Chicago, and elsewhere grew in importance, and by mid-century they had stunned the world with their virtuosity. No other country currently has so many orchestras of the first rank.

America's orchestras were firmly based on European models and trained by European specialists. In 1924, the Russian conductor Serge Koussevitzky arrived in America to conduct the Boston Symphony Orchestra. With the help of imported French players, he quickly elevated the orchestra to international esteem. In Cleveland, the Hungarian-born maestro George Szell created an orchestra that excelled all others in its precision and discipline. His countryman Fritz Reiner came to the Chicago Symphony in 1953 and produced what many people believe to be the outstanding orchestra of modern times, known for its incomparably powerful brass section. The strings have long been the pride of the Philadelphia Orchestra, whose lush sound was favored by its English conductor, Leopold Stokowski. The New York Philharmonic Orchestra has counted Gustav Mahler, Arturo Toscanini, and Leonard Bernstein among its composers.

In earlier times, not all instrumentalists aspired to careers as orchestral musicians, which often seemed full of drudgery. But this slighting attitude has now changed. Openings in the major orchestras are exceedingly rare, and often more than a hundred accomplished players audition for each position. The rewards are many. The minimum salaries of players in the top orchestras are more than $60,000 annually, an amount that can be doubled by recording, teaching, and additional free-lance playing. Most orchestras have a variety of performing opportunities—new music ensembles, chamber music, educational programs, and many more—that offer their members a rounded and challenging life in music.

And although the great early maestros of the podium such as Szell and Stokowski are now gone, the health of the American orchestra is sound. More orchestras in smaller cities are growing to major status, and the increasing number of regional orchestras and full-time chamber orchestras brings diversity to American musical culture. People living virtually anywhere in the United States are able to experience the thrill of hearing a first-rate orchestra live.

1870s. **Nationalism** was similarly prominent in the fine arts. In music, a national element is present when a composer adopts or imitates folk song or dance or uses tales from folk literature as the basis of dramatic or programmatic works.

National colorings were present in German music in both the classical and early romantic periods. Haydn and Beethoven sometimes quoted or imitated folk song in their symphonies, and many of the lieder of Schubert show a clear affinity for German folk music. But by the middle of the nineteenth century, as German musicians appeared to be establishing an international, unified musical language, folk coloring became less prominent in their works. At this time, composers outside of Germany, especially in eastern Europe, Scandinavia, Spain, and the United States, began to turn to folkloric elements as a way of asserting at least a limited degree of independence from the dominant German style.

Russian composers of this time were especially noteworthy in their use of their own musical folklore as a basis for musical innovations. In 1867, the critic Vladimir Stasov referred to a group of composers who sought to create a distinctively Russian approach to composition as the "mighty handful." Later, members of this group from Saint Petersburg were dubbed "the Five," and these figures were linked together by their insistence on an innovative harmonic language and by their use of folk song and folk texts. Most noteworthy among their number were their mentor, Mily Balakirev (1837–1910), and composers Modest Mussorgsky (1839–1881) and Nikolay Rimsky-Korsakov (1844–1908).

Other Russian composers of more Western orientation also made passing references to folk song. Chief among them is the remarkable Pyotr Ilich Tchaikovsky (1840–1893). His symphonies, tone poems, operas, and ballets rely primarily on the unified German style of the late romantic period. Although these pieces occasionally contain quotations of folk tunes, Tchaikovsky was not an aggressive nationalist in the manner of the Five. His music is overtly sentimental, often with a deep current of melancholy. Its profound lyricism is unsurpassed in the nineteenth century.

National movements also emerged in regions within the multicultural Hapsburg Empire, where German domination was both a political and an artistic reality. The career and work of Bedřich Smetana (1824–1884) are characteristic of a striving for recognition of the culture of eastern European lands. Smetana was born in Bohemia, a region of modern-day Czechoslovakia. Bohemia had enjoyed great political power and artistic distinction in the Middle Ages and the Renaissance, but in the sixteenth century it came under the rule of the Hapsburgs, where it remained a minor province until the twentieth century. German was the official language of state, although the people of Bohemia overwhelmingly spoke Czech. Czech patriotism was stimulated by uprisings in Prague in 1848, but still no satisfactory recognition of their independence or culture was made by the ruling Hapsburgs.

Like many educated Bohemians, Smetana spoke German rather than Czech, and his musical education and orientation were entirely Germanic. All the same, he was profoundly sympathetic to the patriotic yearnings of his fellow people. After a period in the 1850s and 1860s when he lived alternately in Bohemia and Sweden, he devoted himself to a musical career in Prague that would honor his homeland. He composed eight operas, most on patriotic subjects using the Czech language, and, among his works for orchestra, chamber ensembles, and piano, numerous programmatic compositions on nationalistic themes.

*Má vlast (My Homeland)* is a cycle of six tone poems written from 1874 to 1879. They depict the ancient castles of Bohemian royalty, Vysehrad and Tabor; scenes from the Bohemian landscape; and the legend of the female warrior Sarka. Their musical language conforms entirely to the dominant German style of the day, especially as found in the orchestral music of Richard Wagner and Franz Liszt (the latter was one of Smetana's most important patrons). Smetana's brand of nationalism, different from that of the Russian Five, contained no element of rebellion against German dominance, only a desire for the recognition of his homeland within a confederation of eastern European states.

*Vltava (The Moldau),* the second work of the cycle (Recording 10.2), depicts this river, which flows in a hook shape for nearly 300 miles, finally northward through Prague and into the Elbe River. The composer prefaced the published score with a verbal description of scenes that the music portrays:

> The Moldau. She rises from two springs, splashes gaily amid the rocks and glistens in the sun. As she grows wider, her banks echo with the sounds of hunting horns and peasant dancing.
> Moon light, round dances of nymphs.
> She reaches the St. John's Rapids, on whose rocks her waves break into a frothy spray. From there she flows broadly toward Prague, where she greets the venerable Vysehrad.

The music has immediate appeal in its great tunefulness and noble color. Smetana clearly wished the work to be enjoyed by all listeners, and the program is easily followed within the plainly descriptive music. The form, in one movement, consists of a succession of distinct sections, each depicting a

**The Moldau River (the Vltava in Czech) is the longest in Czechoslovakia, rising in the Bohemian Forest in the north, running through the capital city of Prague (shown here), and emptying finally into the Elbe River. It has inspired generations of Czech artists.**

leg of the river's journey. The main theme, representing in its broad and majestic continuity the river itself, comes back several times, thus acting as an element of continuity both in the music and in the program.

Smetana's celebration of his homeland was accomplished through an outright adoption of the dominant Germanic style of his era. The same approach characterizes the music of Antonín Dvořák (1841–1904), who continued Smetana's glorification of Bohemian legend and culture. Dvořák focused his work on operas in the Czech language (of which *Rusalka,* based on a fairy tale by Pushkin, is best known), symphonies, and chamber works. His music does not deviate from the style of Brahms and Wagner, although it often uses folk song quotations or imitations. From 1892 to 1895, Dvořák lived in the

**Listening Guide**

**Bedřich Smetana, *Vltava (The Moldau)* from *Má vlast (My Homeland)***
Recording 10.2

| | | |
|---|---|---|
| **Source of the Moldau** | 0.00 | Rapid scale passages in the woodwinds, accompanied by plucked strings, depict the bubbling of the springs. Their waters gradually converge into a noble river, represented by this melody: |

| | | |
|---|---|---|
| **Forest Hunt** | 2.50 | Hunting signals are heard in the horns and other brass instruments. |
| **Peasant Wedding** | 3.48 | A heavy-footed dance tune is unmistakable. Smetana here imitated a typical Czech folk melody, with its ponderous rhythm and limited tonal range: |

| | | |
|---|---|---|
| **Moonlight, Dance of Nymphs** | 5.27 | The fleeting figures in the woodwinds convey the dance of the imaginary nymphs, illumined by the moonlight of the strings. |
| **The Moldau** | 7.57 | After these episodes, the river continues its noble journey. The main theme returns. |
| **Saint John's Rapids** | 8.47 | Just as the river is broken up by the rapids, so too is the melody fragmented. |
| **The Moldau Flows Broadly Onward** | 10.01 | The main theme, representing the river, returns, now in the major mode. |

**Vysehrad**        10.27        As the river passes by the ruins of the ancient castle of Bohemian kings and princes, a noble melody is sounded by the brass and woodwinds:

United States, during which time he composed his celebrated Symphony No. 9 (*From the New World*). The rich melodies of this work imitate Negro spirituals, and Dvořák strongly urged American composers to incorporate their own native musical materials into artistic works rather than to continue to imitate European models.

## Song in the Late Nineteenth Century

German dominance of songwriting in the first half of the nineteenth century continued in the second, although it was then challenged by a related movement of song composition in France. Songs accompanied by orchestra rather than by piano were more common, and song cycles or collections centered on the works of a single poet were increasingly the norm. The art song of this half-century became even more intense, serious, and expressive than before. Simple strophic songs were less in evidence, as they were gradually replaced by through-composed or varied strophic plans.

The lieder of Johannes Brahms, Gustav Mahler, Richard Strauss, and Hugo Wolf continued the traditions of the romantic German song established by Schubert and Schumann. Those of Brahms and Mahler share an affinity with folk song, but their works in general have more sophistication than true folk music. Mahler was especially attracted to folk poetry from the anthology *Des Knaben Wunderhorn* as a source for texts in his early songs. Strauss generally eschewed the sophisticated verse of leading poets of his day, seeking instead more mundane poetry that would provide him with straightforward ideas and emotions. This quality of directness is also found in the music of many of his best-known songs. Hugo Wolf, on the contrary, dealt in general with poetry of high literary merit, including works by Goethe, Joseph von Eichendorff, and Eduard Mörike. The music of his songs makes a careful and often recondite expression of verbal ideas, and their melodies are usually more declamatory than tuneful.

### The French Mélodie

Late in the nineteenth century, there emerged a school of French song composers, led by Gabriel Fauré (1845–1924), Henri Duparc (1848–1933), and Claude Debussy (1862–1918), that could genuinely rival their German contemporaries in artistry and expressiveness. Their songs were called **mélodies,** a term suggesting an affinity in sophistication to the lied. Indeed, these composers imitated the approach to songwriting of the Germans, a model that was then enriched with distinctively French qualities. The serious tone and harmonic expressivity of the *mélodie* stemmed from the lied, but its rhythmic style was geared to the variable nature of accentuation of the French language. The ethos of French songs tends to be less philosophical or folklike than their German cousins, more understated, and with greater wit and playful sensuality.

Gabriel Fauré composed more than 100 songs. They exemplify both the similarities and the differences of the *mélodie* in comparison with the lied. "Dans la forêt de septembre" (1902) (Recording 10.3) is a setting of a poem

**Listening Guide**

**Gabriel Fauré, "Dans la forêt de septembre" ("In the Forest in September")**
Recording 10.3

*1. Ramure aux rumeurs amollies,*
*Troncs sonores que l'âge creuse,*

*L'antique forêt douloureuse*
*S'accorde à nos mélancolies.*

*2. Ô sapins agriffés au gouffre,*
*Nids déserts aux branches brisées,*
*Halliers brûlés, fleurs sans rosées,*

*Vous savez bien comme l'on souffre!*

1. Weakened murmuring branches,
   Sonorous tree trunks, hollowed
     by age,
   The ancient, aching forest
   Is in tune with our melancholy.

2. O fir trees clinging to the gorge,
   Dry nests in broken boughs,
   Burnt thickets, flowers without
     dew,
   You know of suffering!

3. *Et lorsque l'homme, passant blême,*
   *Pleure dans le bois solitaire,*
   *Des plaintes d'ombre et de mystère*
   *L'accueillent en pleurant de même.*

3. And when man, entering palely,
   Cries in your solitary woods,
   Shadowy and mysterious plaints
   Greet him with sympathetic
   tears.

4. *Bonne forêt! promesse ouverte*
   *De l'exil que la vie implore,*
   *Je viens d'un pas alerte encore*
   *Dans ta profondeur encore verte.*

4. Good forest! Open promise
   Of the exile that life implores,
   I come with footsteps still quick
   Into your depths still green.

5. *Mais d'un fin bouleau de la sente,*

   *Une feuille, un peu rousse, frôle*
   *Ma tête et tremble à mon épaule;*

   *C'est que la forêt vieillissante,*

5. But from a slender birch on the
   path,
   A russet leaf grazes
   My head and alights trembling
   on my shoulder.
   The aging forest—

6. *Sachant l'hiver où tout avorte,*

   *Déjà proche en moi comme en elle,*
   *Me fait l'aumône fraternelle*

   *De sa première feuille morte!*

6. Knowing that winter, when all
   comes to nought,
   Is now at hand in me as in it—
   Presents me with a fraternal
   tribute:
   Its first dead leaf!

**A** (stanza 1)    0.00    The music has a rich melodiousness that is soothing, refined, and restrained in emotion, thus creating the tone in which Fauré wishes the plaint of the narrator to be read. The music does not convey the specific meaning of words or phrases.

**B** (stanza 2)    0.37    A new melody is accompanied by a livelier rhythm on the piano.

**A** (stanza 3)    1.05    The melody of the first stanza returns.

**C** (stanzas 4–5)    1.39    A new contrasting melody is again accompanied by a more animated piano line. All of the fourth and the first three lines of the fifth stanza are run together.

**A** (stanzas 5–6)    2.25    The music of A returns with the last line of stanza 5, where a new thought is presented, and it continues throughout stanza 6.

by Catulle Mendès, one of the founders of the Parnassian school of French poets of the late nineteenth century. The Parnassians wrote in an elegant and restrained manner, and their poetry is highly musical in its sensitivity to the sounds and rhythms of words.

Mendès's poem, in six stanzas, tells of humanity's somber fate. A narrator describes a forest, weakened by age and suffering, with which the narrator identifies. When he enters the forest, the two seem to greet each other like brothers. Finally, the forest sends down a dead leaf as a fraternal token and symbol of their common fate. Fauré's music has the form of a rondo, in which the music of the first stanza returns in the third stanza and again at the end of the fifth. The music has an emotional restraint that mirrors the stoic passivity of the narration, and its gentle but constant lyricism acts as a foil to the melancholy of the words. The harmonic language is, by and large, rich and consonant, with only passing dissonant astringency.

## The American Household Song

The intensely artistic expression of the French *mélodie* and the German lied was by no means the only approach to songwriting in the nineteenth century. More popular, unsophisticated songs were intended for entertainment or for use among amateur musicians. These were composed in virtually all parts of the Western world, where they were sung and enjoyed by a larger audience than that of serious music.

In the United States, such songs were especially important to the largely vernacular musical culture of this period. The most important composer of such "household songs" was Stephen Foster (1826–1864). Of his roughly 200 songs, about 30 were written for use in minstrel shows, primarily for the Christy Minstrels, with whom Foster collaborated in the 1850s. The minstrel show was a popular form of theatrical entertainment in American cities at mid-century. It involved comic skits performed by actors in blackface, parodying the white audience's view of black culture. The shows also featured songs, often poking fun at classical music, dance tunes, and other songs in black dialect. Foster was a master of this last category of song, which includes such well-known examples as "Oh Susanna," "Camptown Races," and "Massa's in de Cold, Cold Ground."

Foster's work for minstrel shows was minor in comparison to his songs for use in the homes of America's middle classes. These pieces, many of which have become virtual folk songs by their continuous popularity in America, are usually for one voice and piano (sometimes guitar), strophic in structure, and simple enough to be played by amateur musicians. Their words are sentimental and nostalgic, sometimes affecting a cultivated or genteel tone. "Ah! May the Red Rose Live Alway" (1850) is typical of this type. The words were probably written by Foster himself, and they speak in an artificial and sentimental way about the beauty of nature. The music (Recording 10.4), with its simplicity and copious repetition, perfectly captures the naïveté of these words. The setting is strophic, with the first line of text and music in each stanza repeated as the last line. A short piano prelude returns in the middle and again at the end. The harmonic language is simplified but occasionally imitates high art.

## Music for Piano

The character piece for piano saw its brightest moments during the first half of the nineteenth century in the works of Schubert, Schumann, Chopin, and Mendelssohn. Among the major composers of the second half of the century, it was kept alive as an important genre primarily by Brahms and Liszt. Brahms's early piano music is devoted mainly to the classically oriented sonata and large variation cycles. Late in his career, from about 1878 to 1893, his lyric muse once again awakened to the composition of short and intensely expressive music for piano. The descriptives that he chose for these works—capriccio, intermezzo, rhapsody, fantasy, ballade, and romance—betray no programmatic content, but their diversity of mood, from the ebullient to the dark and melancholy, places them squarely in the romantic tradition of Schumann.

In its enormous size and diversity, the piano music of Franz Liszt (1811–1886) runs the gamut of nineteenth-century styles and genres. Liszt was born in Hungary but never learned to speak the language of his homeland. From childhood until the early 1840s, he toured all of Europe as a virtuoso pianist. The works that he performed, primarily variations, character pieces, and transcriptions of music by other composers, were typical of the repertory of the nineteenth-century virtuoso.

In the 1840s he retired as a traveling performer and settled in Weimar, where he conducted the orchestra of the court of Duke Carl Alexander. At this time he focused on orchestral composition, and he used his great prestige to support the work of other composers (including Berlioz and Wagner). In the 1860s he lived primarily in Rome, where he took minor orders of the Catholic church and composed a large number of sacred choral pieces. His late years, from 1869, were spent alternately in Weimar, Budapest, and Rome.

Liszt's vast number of compositions includes works in all of the major genres of the nineteenth century, with greatest emphasis on piano music, songs, tone poems, and chorus. He wrote relatively little chamber music, no classical symphonies, and only one early opera. His piano music is dominated

**Liszt at the Piano** *(1840) by Joseph Danhauser depicts an imaginary soirée at the home of Franz Liszt. Liszt plays at the piano, looking up at his bust of Beethoven for inspiration. His consort, Countess Marie d'Agoult, sits reclining against the piano, while the leading Parisian musicians and writers listen intently. From left to right are Alexandre Dumas Sr., Victor Hugo, George Sand, Niccolò Paganini, and Gioacchino Rossini.*

by character pieces and transcriptions and also includes a strikingly original Sonata in B Minor and two piano concertos.

Pianistic reflections on his years of travel appear in three collections of character works, all sharing the title *Années de pèlerinage (Years of Pilgrimage)*. The first volume (published in 1855) contains portraits from his journeys in Switzerland. The second collection, subtitled *Italy,* contains musical interpretations of artworks and literature from this country. The third collection comes from Liszt's late years and projects religious sentiments and reflections on Italian scenes.

**344**

**Franz Liszt, "Au bord d'une source" ("At the Edge of a Spring") from *Années de pèlerinage,* volume 1: *Switzerland***
Recording 10.5

| | | |
|---|---|---|
| **Theme** | 0.00 | The theme captures the effervescent quality of the spring and ends with a bubbling flourish in the high register: |

| | | |
|---|---|---|
| **Variation 1** | 0.38 | The theme returns, although its sequence of keynotes is changed. |
| **Variation 2** | 1.31 | The theme returns in a disjointed version. |
| **Variation 3** | 2.14 | The theme is now entirely stated in the home key of A♭ major. |
| **Coda** | 2.44 | The coda begins with the theme and ends with a simple and quiet postlude. |

"Au bord d'une source" ("At the Edge of a Spring") (Recording 10.5) is from the first or Swiss volume of the *Années.* It was composed during the composer's travels in Switzerland in 1835 and 1836, first published in 1842, and revised in 1855 for use in the *Années.* Like most of the pieces in this collection, it depicts with great clarity a scene from the Swiss landscape, in this case a bubbling spring. The animated accompaniment, a swinging rhythm, and a sensitive use of the bright sound of the upper register of the piano all capture Liszt's vivid and no doubt happy memories of the scene.

The form of the piece consists of free variations on the opening melody. This principal theme begins like a melody in period form, except that the consequent phrase is greatly extended and changes key. Its cadence is not marked by a return to the keynote but instead by a flourish in the high register suggesting the effervescence of the spring's water. Three variations of this melody follow, and the end is marked by a quiet and simple reflection on the beauty of what has been depicted. Although the music is in need of no additional description, Liszt added to the published score a line from Schiller: "In murmuring coolness, the play of young nature begins."

## Music for Chorus

Prior to the nineteenth century, choruses were found primarily in opera, in churches, and in occasional concert performances of cantatas or oratorios. In the romantic period, they became much more a part of amateur music making and were increasingly heard outside of church. In England during this century, clubs of amateur male singers met to perform a type of unaccompanied choral music of lively character called **glee.** A comparable movement arose in Germany near the turn of the nineteenth century, in which male singing groups met regularly to socialize and to make music. These organizations sang patriotic pieces, folk songs, or artistic works. Schumann, Weber, and Brahms wrote music for such amateur male choruses, and their rousing style of singing was also used by German opera composers.

The revival of choral singing outside of the church went hand in hand with a revival of interest throughout Europe in the choral music of Bach and Handel. Handel's oratorios had been performed continuously in England since the early eighteenth century, and in the nineteenth, massive performances of works such as *Messiah* were a regular part of English concert life. Musicians in Germany were increasingly interested in reviving works by Bach and Handel. Mendelssohn was especially important in this revival, as was Schumann. In 1850 a group of German connoisseurs founded the Bach-Gesellschaft (Bach Society), whose primary mission was to foster the publication of the complete works of Bach. Their goal was reached in 1900, and the Bach-Gesellschaft edition is to this day a model for reliable editorial practices.

Connected with the heightened historical awareness of early music that fueled the Bach and Handel revivals was a renewal of interest in the Masses and motets of Palestrina and other sixteenth-century masters. This repertory, which was scarcely known to musicians or audiences in 1800, came under increasing scrutiny, both for its inherent beauty and as a model for contemporary composers of church music. Beethoven in his last years undertook a careful study of the Palestrinian style, which he imitated in passages in his *Missa solemnis* (1824). Church music, especially in Catholic parts of Germany, began to imitate the solemn, unaccompanied textures of Palestrina and also to revive authentic versions of Gregorian chant.

## *Brahms's* **Ein deutsches Requiem**

Brahms typifies the romantic composer's renewal of interest in choral music outside of the church. His secular works for chorus include the *Alto Rhapsody* (for alto voice, male chorus, and orchestra), *Schicksalslied (Song of Destiny),* and *Nänie (Elegy).* Although indifferent to organized religion, Brahms composed numerous choral works of a philosophical and religious nature. The greatest of these is no doubt *Ein deutsches Requiem* (1857–1868). Music for this work was sketched in the 1850s but completed only after the death of his mother in 1865.

Brahms's Requiem is very different from the traditional musical Requiems composed by Mozart, Berlioz, and others. Those works are settings of the Latin text for the Catholic funeral Mass. Brahms makes no reference to the liturgical Requiem, piecing together instead his own text from the Bible. The words deal with the Christian idea of death and salvation and the comfort that religion offers the faithful.

The work is in seven movements and calls for mixed chorus, solo voices, and orchestra. The sixth movement, "Denn wir haben hie keine bleibende Statt" (Recording 10.6; see the translation in the Listening Guide), is the dramatic climax. Here Brahms uses words primarily from 1 Corinthians 15, in which the Apostle Paul predicts a future "mystery" by which the faithful will be instantly transformed and made immortal.

The movement is divided into several sections, which follow the meaning of the text in their construction and style. The first part speaks of the search by humankind for a permanent home. It is set to music for chorus and orchestra such that the steadily walking bass line in the orchestra suggests the process of search. The tonality of this passage is G rather than C, the overall tonic of the movement. The transition from G to the more permanent C later in the movement captures precisely the sentiments expressed in the text.

In the second section there is an exchange between a baritone soloist, who issues Saint Paul's vision of the last judgment, and the chorus, representing humankind. At the apostle's stirring words, "We shall all be changed in a flash, in the twinkling of an eye, at the last trumpet-call," the key finally settles on C and the tempo becomes very fast. The chorus builds to a grandiose climax on the words, "O Death, where is your sting?" and the music soars into the triumphant major mode. The movement is concluded by a massive fugue, reminiscent of those from the Handel oratorios, as the voices of humanity praise God.

**Johannes Brahms,** *Ein deutsches Requiem (A German Requiem),*
**sixth movement ("Denn wir haben hie keine bleibende Statt")**
Recording 10.6

*Denn wir haben hie keine bleibende Statt, sondern die zukünftige suchen wir.*
*Siehe, ich sage euch ein Geheimnis: Wir werden nicht alle entschlafen,*
*wir werden aber alle verwandelt werden; und dasselbige plötzlich in einem*
*Augenblick, zu der Zeit der letzten Posaune. Denn es wird die Posaune schallen,*
*und die Toten werden auferstehen unverweslich; und wir werden verwandelt*
*werden. Dann wird erfüllet werden das Wort, das geschrieben steht: Der Tod ist*
*verschlungen in den Sieg. Tod, wo ist dein Stachel! Hölle, wo ist dein Sieg!*
*Herr, Du bist würdig zu nehmen Preis und Ehre und Kraft, denn Du*
*hast alle Dinge erschaffen, und durch Deinen Willen haben sie das Wesen und*
*sind geschaffen.*

### Translation

For here we have no permanent home, but we are seekers after the
city which is to come. [Hebrews 13:14]
Listen! I will unfold a mystery: we shall not all die, but we
shall all be changed in a flash, in the twinkling of an eye, at the last
trumpet-call. For the trumpet will sound, and the dead will rise
immortal, and we shall be changed. Then the saying of Scripture will
come true: "Death is swallowed up; victory is won!" "O Death,
where is your victory, O Death, where is your sting?" [1 Corinthians
15:51–52, 54–55]
Thou art worthy, O Lord our God, to receive glory and
honour and power, because thou didst create all things; by thy will
they were created, and have their being! [Revelation 4:11][3]

**Part 1**

Chorus and orchestra. The choral music alternates between homophonic and imitative textures.

**Part 2**

A baritone soloist issues Saint Paul's description of the last judgment, alternating with chorus. At his words, "zu der Zeit der
letzten Posaune" ("at the sound of the last trumpet") our recorded excerpt begins (0.00).

348

**Part 3**     0.26     Fast tempo. The chorus sings two subsections (both begun by the melody shown here), separated by a phrase for baritone solo. The second choral section leads to a climax and a shift to major mode.

**Part 4**     3.21     Fugue on this subject:

Herr, Du bist  wür-dig zu  neh-men Preis und  Eh  -  re und Kraft.

## Opera in the Late Nineteenth Century

Operatic developments in Italy and Germany in the second half of the nineteenth century were dominated by two great masters: Giuseppe Verdi and Richard Wagner. Verdi was true to the conception of opera established earlier by Rossini, although he used the Rossinian model in an original and ingenious manner. Wagner likewise wrote his early operas in the style of the earlier romantic operas of Carl Maria von Weber, but unlike Verdi, he transformed this model in an unprecedented direction.

### Giuseppe Verdi

The operas of all earlier Italian masters—including Rossini, Donizetti, and Bellini—were pushed from center stage by mid-century by the works of Giuseppe Verdi (1813–1901). His operas summarized a century of development in Italian opera and brought the genre to its greatest heights. Verdi was born in northern Italy and scored his first major success at Milan's La Scala Theater in 1842 with *Nabucco.* From then until his final opera, *Falstaff* (1893), he specialized in operatic composition. He lived in Paris in the 1850s, for whose theaters he wrote several works. Following the completion of *Aida* in 1871, he retired from the stage, only to be lured back by the prospect of setting to music the Shakespeare-inspired librettos to *Otello* and *Falstaff.*

349

Verdi's operas are decidedly weighted toward serious subjects, especially those inspired by plays of Shakespeare and Schiller. Although not literally nationalistic, they contain many rousing scenes that Verdi's audiences interpreted as patriotic. Indeed, Verdi sympathized with the Italian Risorgimento movement, which aimed toward political unification of Italy and the freeing of northern Italian states from Austrian domination. His operas became so symbolic of the patriotic strivings of his day that a common rallying cry was "Viva Verdi," in which Verdi's name became the acronym for *Vittorio Emanuele, Re d'Italia* (Victor Emmanuel, King of Italy). Victor Emmanuel II, the king of Sardinia, was a central figure in Risorgimento politics.

The story of *Aida* (1871) is based on a sketch by the French-born Egyptologist Auguste Mariette. His ideas were expanded by Camille du Locle and Verdi himself and then placed into Italian verse by Antonio Ghislanzoni. The work was commissioned by the viceroy of Egypt shortly after the opening of the Suez Canal, and it received its premier performance in Cairo in 1871.

The story is set in Memphis and Thebes, in ancient times. Egypt is under attack by Ethiopia, and the king must choose a commander for his armies. He selects the brave Radamès, who at this moment is in emotional turmoil. The king's daughter Amneris loves him, but he is in love with her Ethiopian slave, Aida. Aida's allegiances are torn between her love for Radamès and her attachment to her homeland, where she is the daughter of King Amonasro. In the finale of Act 2, Radamès's armies return to Thebes victorious. Contrary to the vindictive wishes of the priests, Radamès asks that his captives—among whom is Amonasro—be freed.

Egypt is soon again under attack from Ethiopia, and Amonasro commands his daughter to obtain secret military information from Radamès. When he unwittingly gives the information, Radamès is overheard by the jealous Amneris, who accuses him of treason. Offering no defense and deaf to Amneris's pleas for clemency, Radamès is condemned to death by entombment. In the final scene, presented on a stage divided into two levels, Aida steals into Radamès's cell and dies with him while Amneris, above, prays for his soul.

The finale to Act 2 (Recording 10.7) is the dramatic core of the entire work and one of the grandest theatrical and musical displays in all of opera. Its structural plan is essentially ternary. The first part does not advance the story but is purely a treat for the eyes and the ears. The people and officials of Thebes gather to greet the victorious armies of Radamès. There is dancing, stirring marches accompanied by onstage bands, and general rejoicing. The middle section is, on the contrary, dramatic. Radamès asks that his prisoners be released, thus siding with the people but opposing the priests and fool-heartedly ignoring the realistic advice of the chief priest, Ramfis. Amonasro is revealed to be the father of Aida, but he conceals his identity as Ethiopia's king and immediately begins to plot his revenge on the Egyptians. The music of this middle passage consists of a succession of subsections alternating recitative, aria, chorus, and ensemble. The large ensembles are especially ingenious, as the opinions of different characters and groups are stated simultaneously. Finally, the opening music returns.

**Giuseppe Verdi,** *Aida,* **finale to Act 2 (excerpt)**
Recording 10.7

**A**      0.00      (On Recording 10.7, the opening passages of the finale are omitted, beginning instead with the conclusive "Vieni, o guerriero vindice.") Here the victorious troops enter, with Radamès appearing last. A succession of melodies is sung by the chorus of people and priests, all closely centered on the key of E♭. The first melody praises the glory of Egypt:

**B**      2.19      A succession of sections in recitative, aria, ensemble, and choral styles develops the essential dramatic conflicts. Keynotes and mode change rapidly.

**A′**      13.00      The opening hymn of praise returns, but its continuation is varied. At 14.32 Verdi combines three previous melodies, giving a vivid musical portrait of the tumultuous mixing of emotions and objectives that have emerged. In a brief codetta, onstage trumpets sound the music that earlier led the troops into Thebes.

## Richard Wagner and the Music Drama

As Verdi reigned over Italian operatic composition in the late nineteenth century, Richard Wagner (1813–1883) prevailed in Germany. Wagner grew up in Leipzig and Dresden, where he developed a passion for theater and music. He traveled from city to city as a theatrical music director, settling in Dresden in the 1840s. Involvement in the uprisings there in 1849 led to his banishment from German lands and his exile to Switzerland. There he theorized about the future of opera and began to forge an innovative compositional approach that emerged in *Tristan und Isolde* (1859) and later works.

After receiving a partial amnesty from the state of Saxony, he was invited in 1864 to Munich, where he received lavish patronage from the Bavarian king, Ludwig II, who financed the premiere of *Tristan* in 1865 and paid Wagner's immense accumulation of debt. In 1872, Wagner moved permanently to the Bavarian town of Bayreuth, where he raised funds to build a festival theater for his own music. His four-day cycle of operas, *Der Ring des Nibelungen (The Ring of the Nibelung),* was first performed there in 1876.

Like Verdi, Wagner wrote few significant compositions outside of the genre of opera. Most of his early works, including *The Flying Dutchman* (1841), *Tannhäuser* (1844), and *Lohengrin* (1847), are in the genre of romantic opera as established by Carl Maria von Weber. His later ones—the *Ring* cycle, *Tristan und Isolde, Die Meistersinger von Nürnberg (The Master Singers of Nuremberg,* 1867), and *Parsifal* (1882)—are of a new but related type that Wagner called **music drama.**

Wagner wrote all of his own librettos, which are generally based on myth or German legend. He pares his stories of extraneous aspects of plot, leaving only a central, symbolic action. Such texts, he theorized, were universal in meaning and eternal in importance. His later operas are not clearly divided into musical numbers but consist instead of lengthy sections of a homogeneous melodic style falling roughly between aria and recitative. The term *endless melody* or *infinite melody* is often used to designate this seamless continuity, although Wagner used these terms more to suggest that his music was infinitely or continuously expressive.

The orchestral part of his operas is very different from that of Verdi's, which tends to be either a simple accompaniment to singing or occasionally an excuse for colorful pageantry. Wagner's orchestra is as expressive as the singing, and often more so. It is rich in texture, as he expanded the customary opera orchestra to a much larger size and entrusted it with a web of motives that symbolize dramatic ideas. Such a musical figure is normally called a **leitmotif,** although this term was not used by Wagner himself. A leitmotif is a short melodic and harmonic fragment stated by the orchestra that designates or recollects a dramatic character, thing, or idea. Listing such motives and their associative content is a useful undertaking for newcomers to Wagner's operas, although more experienced listeners may find such lists to be overly simplified and even misleading. The motives appear especially clearly in the *Ring* operas, where they are constantly in flux as the drama unfolds. The technique of the leitmotif had antecedents in the programmatic symphony, where recurrent themes (such as Berioz's *idée fixe* in the *Symphonie fantastique*) often symbolized dramatic ideas.

Wagner also strove to achieve what he termed a *Gesamtkunstwerk,* or "total artwork." He theorized that the fine arts after the ancient Greeks had fallen into decline, the leading symptom of which was their separation into music, dance, poetry, and visual arts. Traditional opera, he believed, did not improve on this separateness because music was clearly dominant. In his own works he intended the sister arts to merge or synthesize into a supremely expressive dramatic medium. His operas and music dramas take on immense lengths, befitting the titanic issues they treat; they are extreme examples of the tendency of late romantic music toward heroic affirmation of the human spirit.

The texts of Wagner's massive tetralogy of operas, *Der Ring des Nibelungen,* were written between 1848 and 1852 and published separately in 1853. They still have considerable interest as purely literary works. In them Wagner melds aspects of Teutonic myth, medieval chivalric legend, Shakespearean themes, and his own personal theories concerning property and human relationships. The story is set in the world of Germanic myth, a realm ruled by the god Wotan. The central point of his universe is an ash tree whose roots reach throughout the cosmos. From beneath the ash tree flows a spring of wisdom, where Wotan drank, leaving an eye in return.

Wotan and the other gods are not immortal; they live only by eating golden apples tended by the goddess Freia. They are aware that, apples or no, they will eventually be destroyed in a great cataclysm in which all living things, all good and evil, will be destroyed. After this disaster, life will be regenerated on a higher level. Awaiting this fate, Wotan resides in his palace, Valhalla, surrounded by earthly heroes killed in battle and transported to the palace by his fierce, winged daughters, the Valkyries.

In Wagner's treatment of the myth, Wotan strives to establish a lawful and orderly existence in the cosmos. But at every step he is frustrated in this aim by the ramifications of a primal sin, symbolized by his wrongful use of a horde of gold taken from the Rhine River to pay for the construction of Valhalla. Only a mortal man, of his own free will, can right this wrong by returning the gold to the earth, its rightful owner. Wotan wishes humans to achieve this independence from the gods, even though it will lead to their destruction.

The basic message of the *Ring,* told in highly symbolic terms, is that the universe contains two great forces inevitably in conflict: the power of wealth and the power of love. Of these, the power of love is the greater. The first

*The influence of the operas of Richard Wagner extended well beyond music, having an impact as well on the visual and literary arts of the late nineteenth century. The American painter Albert Pinkham Ryder (1847–1917) several times chose themes from Wagner's operas as subjects of his work. In* Siegfried and the Rhine Maidens *(1888–1891), he depicts a scene from* Götterdämmerung. *Siegfried is on a nocturnal hunt near the Rhine River, where he encounters three Rhine maidens who foretell of his fate.*

*At Wagner's own festival theater in Bayreuth, the visual effects in his operas were intended to produce a sense of realistic illusion. The Rhine maidens from* **Götterdämmerung,** *depicted by Albert Ryder on p. 354, were allowed their realistic swimming motions as shown in this drawing.*

opera of the cycle—*Das Rheingold*—tells of Wotan's building of Valhalla, paid for by the Rhine gold, which is fashioned into a ring. The ring symbolizes the power of wealth, but its bearer must also suffer the curse of foreswearing love. In the opera *Siegfried,* the fearless hero Siegfried is born from an illicit union between Wotan's children Siegmund and Sieglinde. Siegfried gains possession of the ring and, by his bravery, cannot be deterred, even by Wotan. This is the hero who will supersede the gods and cleanse the earth of its evil. On his knightly journeys, he comes on an armed woman, asleep on a mountain ringed by fire. She is Brünnhilde, a former Valkyrie made mortal as punishment for disobedience, and when she is awakened by Siegfried, they fall in love.

In the final opera of the cycle, *Götterdämmerung (Twilight of the Gods),* the Norns, sister goddesses of fate, spin the rope of fate while recounting the narration to that point. Wotan, they say, has cut the world ash into firewood, which is stacked ominously around Valhalla. When they reach the question of the theft of the Rhine gold, the rope of fate breaks. No longer is humanity's fate in the hands of the gods. Humans can now freely control their own destiny. The conclusion of the lengthy Prelude (Recording 10.8) is a love duet between Siegfried and his new bride, Brünnhilde, during which the knight errant takes leave of his beloved. She has used her magic to protect him against harm, except for his back, since she knows that he will turn his back

**Richard Wagner, *Götterdämmerung (Twilight of the Gods)*, duet of Siegfried and Brünnhilde from the Prelude**
Recording 10.8

| | | |
|---|---|---|
| **Orchestral Introduction** | 0.00 | Dawn breaks on the mountain where Siegfried has met Brünnhilde. The orchestral music is dominated by their motives: |

Siegfried:

*ff*

Brünnhilde:

| | | |
|---|---|---|
| **Brünnhilde's Confession** | 3.12 | Brünnhilde has given Siegfried wisdom and lore but has lost her strength to him as well. Her motive abounds in the orchestral music. |
| **Siegfried's Response** | 5.21 | Siegfried admits that he lacks the power fully to understand her gift. Both of their motives are prominent. |
| **Summary** | 6.14 | Brünnhilde recounts the circumstances of their meeting and marriage. Both of their motives remain in force. |
| **Exchange of Pledges** | 8.08 | Siegfried gives Brünnhilde the ring in troth; she gives him her horse Grane to carry him hence in search of glory. In addition to their motives, we also hear these: |

Ring:

Valkyrie (on mention of Grane's earlier mission at the scenes of battle):

| | | |
|---|---|---|
| **Peroration** | 10.29 | Siegfried and Brünnhilde sing each other's praises, whereupon Siegfried departs. |

to no enemy. He gives her the ring as a pledge of his fidelity, and she presents him with her steed, named Grane.

The body of *Götterdämmerung* is a complex tale of love potions, magical changes of identity, and treachery by which the evil Hagen tries to gain possession of the ring. On a nocturnal hunt, Hagen stabs Siegfried in the back, and Siegfried dies. At this emotional climax, the voices typically fall silent and the orchestra wells up in a funeral interlude in which, by motivic associations alone, the history of Siegfried is eloquently recounted. Brünnhilde commands that a funeral pyre be built and lit for Siegfried, into which she also rides. The Rhine swells up out of its banks and destroys everything remaining, thus returning the ring to the earth. Above, Valhalla is in flames.

The duet that concludes the Prelude to *Götterdämmerung* illustrates the stylistic features of Wagnerian music drama. The music is seamlessly continuous, and the voices, though highly expressive, do not dominate as in an Italian operatic aria. The orchestral music is largely made up of recurrent associative motives, some of the most important of which are illustrated in the Listening Guide. The section is unified by the keynote E♭, which returns periodically; by the recurrent motives; and by the continuity of the text.

## TOPICS FOR DISCUSSION AND WRITING

**1.** Both Liszt's "Au bord d'une source" and the opening of Smetana's *Moldau* depict a spring. Compare the musical devices that the two composers use to paint this picture from nature, and discuss how vividly the sights and sounds of a spring are re-created. Which composer is more successful in his depiction? Which composer better conveys the feelings of the observer in the midst of a natural setting?

**2.** Compare the first movement of Brahms's Symphony No. 1 with the first movement of Haydn's Symphony No. 102 in B♭ Major (Recording 8.1). Using Haydn's music as an example of the mature classical style, try to find similar classical elements in Brahms's work. In what ways does Brahms's symphony deviate from the classical norm? Take into consideration the nature of the orchestra, the form of the work, the quality of the melodies, and the expressive nature of harmony.

**3.** Compare the music of Fauré's song "Dans la forêt de septembre" and Schubert's "Erlkönig" (Recording 9.2) in order to summarize differences between the French and German styles of songwriting. How do these differences exert opposing forces on melodic styles?

**4.** Focusing strictly on musical style, compare the finale of Act 2 from Verdi's *Aida* with Wagner's *Götterdämmerung* duet from the Prelude. Deal primarily with melodic style, the nature of harmony, and the role of the orchestra.

## ADDITIONAL LISTENING

### Brahms

Symphonies No. 2, 3, and 4. Each of the four Brahms symphonies is a masterpiece, notable for great lyricism.

### Dvořák

Symphony No. 9 (*From the New World*). Certain melodies of this work skillfully imitate Negro spirituals.

### Fauré

Requiem, Op. 48.

### Liszt

Concerto No. 1 for Piano and Orchestra. This brilliant work exhibits an unusual form, in which movements are played without pause.

*Les préludes.* This is a tone poem based freely on poetry by Lamartine.

### Mussorgsky

*Pictures at an Exhibition.* Originally a cycle of programmatic character pieces for piano, the work is better known in a brilliant orchestration by Maurice Ravel.

### Richard Strauss

*Don Juan.* An exciting tone poem based on the dramatic poem by Lenau.

*Four Last Songs.* These romantic songs for voice and orchestra were written by the composer shortly before his death in 1949.

### Tchaikovsky

*Romeo and Juliet.* Tchaikovsky's great melodic gift is much in evidence in this tone poem based on Shakespeare.

Symphony No. 6 (*Pathétique*). This melancholy and immensely lyrical symphony has a freedom of form that is typically romantic.

### Verdi

Requiem. This sacred work, composed on the death of the Italian novelist and patriot Alessandro Manzoni, is wholly operatic in style.

*Rigoletto.* One of Verdi's greatest operas from his middle period, based on a play by Victor Hugo.

**Wagner**

Orchestral music from *Der Ring des Nibelungen*. Especially popular is "Ride of the Valkyries."

*Tannhäuser*. This early romantic opera is filled with stirring choruses and inspired melodies, much more in the Italian style than the *Ring* operas.

*Tristan und Isolde,* Prelude and "Liebestod." These excerpts, drawn from the beginning and end of the opera, are its best-known music.

## BIBLIOGRAPHY

See the Bibliography for Chapter 9 for general works on nineteenth-century music. The following sources deal with the life and music of composers mentioned in this chapter.

Brahms, Johannes. *Letters of Clara Schumann and Johannes Brahms, 1853–1896*. Edited by Berthold Litzmann. New York: Longman, 1927.

Brown, David. *Tchaikovsky*. 4 volumes. New York: Norton, 1978–1992.

Budden, Julian. *The Operas of Verdi*. 3 volumes. New York: Oxford University Press, 1981.

Fay, Amy. *Music-Study in Germany in the Nineteenth Century*. New York: Dover, 1965. Fascinating memoirs by an American piano student of Liszt, originally published in 1880.

Geiringer, Karl. *Brahms: His Life and Work*. Second edition. London: Allen & Unwin, 1948.

Newman, Ernest. *The Wagner Operas*. New York: Knopf, 1972.

Orledge, Robert. *Gabriel Fauré*. London: Eulenberg, 1979.

Searle, Humphrey. *The Music of Liszt*. Second edition. New York: Dover, 1966.

Wagner, Richard. *The Ring of the Nibelung*. Translated by Stewart Robb. New York: Dutton, 1960. A translation of the entire four-opera text.

Walker, Alan. *Franz Liszt*. 2 volumes to date. New York: Knopf, 1983–1989.

Westernhagen, Curt von. *Wagner: A Biography*. Translated by Mary Whittall. Cambridge: Cambridge University Press, 1978.

## NOTES

1. Gustave Courbet, quoted in *Artists on Art,* ed. Robert Goldwater, Marco Treves, 3rd ed. (New York: Pantheon, 1958), p. 296.
2. Robert Schumann, "Neue Bahnen," *Neue Zeitschrift für Musik,* October 28, 1853, p. 185. Translation by the author.
3. *The New English Bible* (1961).

# 11

## The Rebellion Against Romanticism, 1900–1945

## Impressions in Color and Sound

On New Year's Day 1911, the Russian-born artist Vasili Kandinsky, together with several other young painters, attended a concert of new music in Munich. On the program were two works by the Viennese composer Arnold Schoenberg, one a string quartet, the other a collection of piano pieces. Kandinsky and his friends probably knew of Schoenberg's reputation as an experimenter with sounds, a composer using only dissonant chords who avoided the appearance of a keynote. Kandinsky was himself highly musical. Not only did he play piano and cello, but he was also convinced that colors themselves had musical properties.

But it is unlikely that Kandinsky and the others in his party anticipated the impact of the music they heard on that day in 1911. Clearly, it was baffling to them. It seemed different from all traditional music, but nevertheless it was profoundly engaging. How could such music have meaning? Was it related to their own experiments in color and form? Kandinsky and his friends immediately began to speculate on these questions. Franz Marc, who also attended the concert, thought Schoenberg intended to erase all of the laws of music and to approach this art on a purely instinctive basis, like a primitive artist. Marianne Werefkin opined that Schoenberg must have intended to juxtapose unrelated or unmixed sounds, without regard for any broader harmonizing.

Kandinsky's own response to the concert took the form not of a theory, but of this painting. The term "impression" was used by the artist for paintings that stemmed directly from some external stimulus, in this case, a concert. Although largely abstract, the painting still has vestiges of the shapes that Kandinsky recalled from the concert. The large black form suggests a piano, and the heads of the audience and performers are plainly in evidence. But these recognizable objects are only subsidiary to the impact of the painting, which relies instead on the pure and direct expressivity of color. Our attention is first drawn to the brilliant yellow field at the right, which seems to engulf the black shape and to encroach on the busier forms at the left.

In his treatise "Concerning the Spiritual in Art" (1911), Kandinsky wrote that yellow had the power to move toward an observer and to produce a disquieting effect that was the equivalent of a shrill and piercing trumpet. Black, on the contrary, suggested a deathly void, an eternal silence, and an utter absence of tone.

Shortly after completing the painting, Kandinsky wrote to Schoenberg to inquire further about the composer's ideas, which seemed to reinforce Kandinsky's own. They both agreed that modern art and music must reject logical or traditional forms and rely instead on the expressive instincts of the individual artist. "When one is actually at work," wrote Kandinsky, "there should be no thought, but the 'inner voice' alone should speak and control."

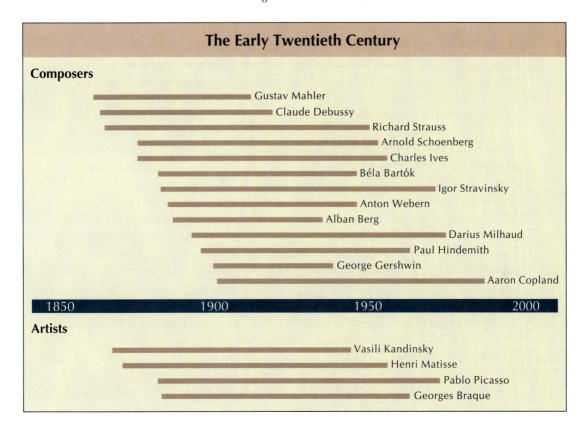

## The Early Twentieth Century

**Composers**

Gustav Mahler
Claude Debussy
Richard Strauss
Arnold Schoenberg
Charles Ives
Béla Bartók
Igor Stravinsky
Anton Webern
Alban Berg
Darius Milhaud
Paul Hindemith
George Gershwin
Aaron Copland

1850          1900          1950          2000

**Artists**

Vasili Kandinsky
Henri Matisse
Pablo Picasso
Georges Braque

Musical style during the first half of the twentieth century underwent an unprecedented change. In a space of less than 50 years, major composers throughout the Western world removed elements of music that for centuries had been basic to its understanding and enjoyment. Keynote, consonant harmony, major and minor scales, regular beat and meter, and tuneful melodies were bypassed in favor of new and untried materials. Composers rushed to create a new musical language, confident that it would communicate fresh ideas and concerns.

What led musicians to such a drastic path? Their motives often involved nonmusical sentiments, especially political feelings and philosophical ideas. But perhaps the most important consideration is found in the very nature of the late-romantic style, which contained elements that seemed to ensure its ultimate downfall. Romanticism emphasized originality and progress in its musical materials. "Art means new art," wrote the composer

**365**

Arnold Schoenberg. "This is the code of honor of all the great in art."[1] As the romantic style matured, it approached practical limitations to further innovation. Music could hardly become more grandiose than Wagner, more evocative than Chopin, or more intensely melodious than Brahms. For musicians such as Schoenberg, committed to the romantic outlook, the only course of development was, ironically, a renunciation of its essential language.

But whatever motives underlay their bold reshaping of the world of music, composers after the turn of the century produced pervasive and far-reaching innovations that document a rebellion against music as it was known to that time. The background against which this rebellion took place was the unified German romantic style, which, at the turn of the twentieth century, still dominated European and American music. Music lovers throughout Europe flocked to Bayreuth to hear Wagner's music dramas, in performances that acquired cultic importance. Listeners of more traditional inclination admiringly pondered the symphonies of Brahms. American serious musical life was strongly oriented toward Germany. The Boston composer Charles Ruggles, for example, changed his first name to Carl, hoping that its German sound would bring him professional opportunities. This German domination continued until the time of World War I (1914–1918), and it ended in part because of a worldwide reaction against Germany's militaristic politics.

Increasingly during the first two decades of the century, important new musical voices were heard from outside of Germany, among them Claude Debussy and Maurice Ravel in France, Alexander Scriabin and Igor Stravinsky in Russia, Béla Bartók in Hungary, and Charles Ives in America. Together with modernists living in Germany and Austria, these pioneers began to transform the language of German romanticism in ways that would lead to its downfall after World War I.

## Modernism in Letters and the Visual Arts

Modernism in the arts and letters at the turn of the twentieth century was informed by a general rejection of realism. Rather than continuing to investigate the external human condition, artists and writers were increasingly inclined to explore the inner psyche and the irrational sources of behavior. These motives underlay such developments in the visual arts as cubism in France and expressionism in Germany and Austria. Cubism was formulated by Georges Braque (1882–1963) and Pablo Picasso (1881–1973) in the years immediately preceding World War I. In their paintings in this style, objects are distorted into angular, geometric, or planar shapes in which several per-

***Pablo Picasso's* Houses on the Hill, Horta de Ebro *(1909), is a milestone in the development of cubist art. The artist depicts the houses of a Spanish village by assembling geometric, planar shapes.***

spectives are manifest simultaneously. In Picasso's *Houses on the Hill, Horta de Ebro* (see above), the space created by houses and hills is transformed into a fantasy of geometric shapes. As the realistic portrayal of objects became more remote to the cubist aesthetic, painters relied increasingly on instinct as their guide. "When I came to the conclusion that I had to be free to work without a model," wrote Braque,

> I did not find it at all easy. But I struggled on, following my intuitions, and gradually found that I had become more and more detached from motifs. At such time, one has to follow dictates which are almost unconscious.[2]

The unconscious mind was also an object of interest to German painters of the **expressionist** movement. Artists in this loosely defined development were inspired by the themes and techniques of earlier modernists,
including Vincent Van Gogh (1853–1890) and Henri Matisse (1869–1954), in
which a forceful, often distorted expression of the painter's feelings is paramount. Van Gogh's famous statement, "Instead of trying to reproduce exactly
what I have before my eyes, I use color more arbitrarily in order to express
myself forcibly,"[3] applies equally well to the early German expressionists.

A leader of the expressionist manifestation in Munich was the Russian-
born Vasili Kandinsky (1866–1944). His early paintings are strongly influenced by Matisse in their impressionistic subjects, often drawn from nature
and depicted in intense though unrealistic colors that communicate the painter's inner feelings. Kandinsky and his colleagues emphasized the role of the
spirit in art, which led them away from realistic visions toward the expression

*Vasili Kandinsky's series of "compositions," executed about 1911, are some of the
earliest important nonrepresentational paintings. This is* **Composition IV.**

of inner ones. *Composition IV* (see p. 368) is one of a cycle of pictures in which Kandinsky removed virtually all references to naturalistic forms. In his booklet *Concerning the Spiritual in Art,* he describes these works. A "composition," he writes, is

> an expression of a slowly formed inner feeling, which comes to utterance only after long maturing. . . . In this, reason, consciousness, purpose play an overwhelming part. But of the calculation nothing appears, only the feeling.[4]

Kandinsky's doctrine of intuitive art has remarkable parallels in the contemporary trend toward atonal music, which will be discussed shortly.

The expressionist movement in German and Austrian art was related to a development in German writing (especially for theater and cinema) that is also described as expressionist. It originated in the late plays of August Strindberg and incorporated decadent images from the French symbolists. An expressionist play, as by August Stramm, Walter Hasenclever, or Ernst Toller, is typically in one brief act. Its characters, usually few in number, embody larger-than-life principles and often lack proper names. The action, which usually centers on perverse or violent behavior, symbolizes a universal condition that often takes a nightmarish form. As in music of the same time, the language of expressionist writing abandoned traditional modes, adopting in their place a symbolic and often cryptic idiom, laced through by fragmentary thoughts and elliptical silences. Plays of this sort were regularly made into opera librettos by composers early in the century, one of which, Alban Berg's *Wozzeck,* will be studied shortly.

## Music Before World War I

The brief period from 1900 until the outbreak of World War I in 1914 was an astonishing time in the development of European music. It mingled traditional musical values with experiment, the latter often guided by an increased sensitivity to new directions in the sciences, philosophy, and the sister arts. Although a full-fledged reaction against romanticism was not felt until the 1920s, the groundwork for that rebellion was laid by the new musical ideas of composers both outside of Germany—including Claude Debussy, Igor Stravinsky, and Béla Bartók—as well as by modernists such as Arnold Schoenberg living in Germany or Austria.

## Gustav Mahler, Arnold Schoenberg, and the Twilight of Romanticism

The German romantic musical language was extended into the twentieth century by a group of brilliantly original composers that included Gustav Mahler (1860–1911), Richard Strauss (1864–1949), Max Reger (1873–1916), and Arnold Schoenberg (1874–1951). Mahler, like Strauss, divided his career between conducting and composing. His music falls almost entirely into the genres of the symphony and song. Typical of German and Austrian composers of a modernistic outlook, his early symphonies are intensely programmatic and often autobiographical in content. The later ones become increasingly nonreferential, reflecting a general trend toward abstraction in music after the turn of the century.

Mahler was born in Bohemia and educated in Vienna. He established an international reputation as an operatic conductor, holding major positions in Kassel, Prague, Leipzig, Budapest, Vienna, and New York. His composing was usually confined to summer vacations, which he spent in the Austrian Alps. He composed ten symphonies (the last one incomplete), a "song-symphony" titled *Das Lied von der Erde* (*The Song of the Earth*), and numerous songs, mostly with orchestral accompaniment.

The orchestral song "Ich bin der Welt abhanden gekommen" ("I Have Lost Track of the World," 1901) (Recording 11.1) illustrates Mahler's intensely romantic outlook as it explores the individual's retreat from the outer to the inner world. It was written at a crucial time. Mahler's early songs had relied primarily on folk poetry from the anthology *Des Knaben Wunderhorn* (*The Youth's Magic Horn*), but at the turn of the century he turned his attention to the writings of Friedrich Rückert (1788–1866). Their intensely personal tone, oriental flavor, and intellectuality resonated in Mahler's own imagination.

### Gustav Mahler, "Ich bin der Welt abhanden gekommen"
Recording 11.1

*1. Ich bin der Welt abhanden gekommen,*
   *Mit der ich sonst viele Zeit verdorben;*
   *Sie hat so lange nichts von mir*
      *vernommen,*
   *Sie mag wohl glauben, ich sei*
      *gestorben!*

*1.* I have lost track of the world,
   on which I earlier lost much time;
   for long it has not heard from
      me;
   it probably thinks that I am
      dead!

| | |
|---|---|
| **2.** *Es ist mir auch gar nichts daran gelegen,*<br>*Ob sie mich für gestorben hält.*<br>*Ich kann auch gar nichts sagen dagegen,*<br>*Denn wirklich bin ich gestorben,*<br>*gestorben der Welt.* | **2.** It's all the same to me<br><br>if it thinks me dead.<br>I certainly can't deny it,<br><br>for I am truly dead, dead to the world. |
| **3.** *Ich bin gestorben dem Weltgetümmel*<br><br>*Und ruh' in einem stillen Gebiet.*<br>*Ich leb' allein in meinem Himmel,*<br>*In meinem Lieben, in meinem Lied.* | **3.** I am dead to the world's turmoil,<br>and I rest in a quiet place.<br>I live alone in my heaven,<br>in my love, in my song. |

**Introduction**   0.00   The principal motive (below) is presented in a leisurely, hesitating fashion, without a strong sense of conclusion. The harmonies are not built on the keynote.

By rearranging the notes of the motive into a scale, its pentatonic content can be seen:

**Stanza 1**   1.00   The voice begins with the introductory motive but then continues freely. The keynote appears after much delay.

**Stanza 2**   2.34   New melodies are heard, and on the narrator's admission that he is indeed dead to the world, the music moves to a fresh keynote (D) in the major mode.

**Stanza 3**   3.56   A new melody distantly suggests the introductory motive. The orchestral postlude returns to the tonic note F and to earlier motives.

Rückert's poem "Ich bin der Welt abhanden gekommen" is in three stanzas. A narrator describes his symbolic death, through which he alienates himself from the external world and attains a blissful, isolated serenity. The poem suggests the attainment of a state akin to nirvana in Buddhism, and it reflects Rückert's authoritative studies in Eastern literature and philosophy. Mahler, like Wagner and many other German composers of the late nineteenth century, shared Rückert's fascination with oriental philosophy, an interest that emerges most prominently in Mahler's *Das Lied von der Erde* (a setting of ancient Chinese poetry).

In its slow pacing and long phrases, Mahler's setting perfectly mirrors the lost-to-the-world sentiments of Rückert's poem. The music is through-composed, although the initial motive heard in the orchestral introduction returns several times. The Eastern flavor of the poem is captured by the scale that underlies this principal motive. It resembles the major scale on F, the tonic of the work, but two notes are consistently omitted, making it a five-note or **pentatonic scale.** The music of many Eastern cultures (see Chapter 14) is based on scales of this type.

The melodic phrases are highly irregular in structure, and the harmonies have a dissonant piquancy created by the sinuous winding of melodies around underlying chords. The texture of the song is decidedly rich, as the primary melody, in the voice, is shadowed constantly by related melodic ideas in the orchestra.

The late romantic style of composers such as Mahler was strongly progressive. It emphasized innovation and originality of musical means, tending toward an ever more intense expressivity. It was found by many listeners to be difficult to understand, given its increased use of dissonant chords, melodies in which all 12 notes of the octave vied for equality, and textures and rhythms of complicated density and turgidity. These features were pushed to new extremes in the music of the Viennese composer Arnold Schoenberg. Schoenberg's early works consist primarily of songs and programmatic instrumental pieces, all in the late-nineteenth-century manner. About 1908, he carried this idiom in a new direction. Dissonant chords entirely replaced triads and other familiar harmonies, and any sense of keynote was meticulously avoided. In his music after this time, major and minor scales no longer had priority, as they were replaced by the **chromatic scale,** consisting of all 12 notes of the octave. Such music is called *atonal*. It maintains many aspects of the late romantic style, but it is heard by most listeners as something quite new. In addition to its radically innovative harmonic language, it is also more abstract in its avoidance of programmatic meaning, in its conciseness, and in the terseness of its melodies.

As Schoenberg eliminated the formal constraints of earlier music, he was left with only his intuition as a compositional guide. In his early atonal works, he relished the lack of external rules and asserted his intuition as a superior source of coherence. To Vasili Kandinsky he wrote on January 24,

**372**

1911, that he wished the "elimination of the conscious will in art." "Art belongs to the unconscious," he continued, echoing Kandinsky's own thoughts as applied to painting.

> One must express *oneself!* Express oneself *directly*. Not acquired characteristics like taste, training, intelligence, knowledge, but that which is *inborn* or *instinctive*. Whoever is capable of listening to himself, recognizing his own instincts, engrossing himself reflectively in every problem will not need the crutch of established forms.[5]

The music that Schoenberg wrote from 1908 until about 1912 stems from this radical theory of composition, so akin to the intuitive formulations of Kandinsky of the same period. But Schoenberg later came to question intuition or the unconscious mind as the sole source of art, and he sought some new method that would replace the former laws of music. By 1921 he had developed a new compositional approach, which he called the "method of composing with twelve tones, related only one to another." We shall see it at work in his *Survivor from Warsaw,* discussed in Chapter 12, and in Webern's String Quartet, discussed later in this chapter.

## Debussy and Musical Impressionism

While progressive figures in German music at the turn of the century began to transform the romantic musical language from within—by pushing its own distinctive features to unprecedented extremes—composers outside of Germany initiated a more direct assault in the formulation of a new language that was both anti-German and antiromantic. This phase in the rebellion against romanticism was felt especially strongly in France, both before and after World War I. It was spurred onward by nationalistic sentiments and by an assimilation into music of new directions in the other fine arts, especially the impressionist movement in painting.

Impressionism (discussed in Chapter 10) is a tendency in French painting of the late nineteenth century that explores the relationship of light and color in depicting uncontrived scenes from nature. The term *impressionism* was also applied by French critics, usually pejoratively, to new music, especially to that of Claude Debussy (1862–1918). Although Debussy himself strongly rejected this analogy with painting, his music suggests parallels with the visual arts that help us to assess its powerful originality. Like the impressionist painters, Debussy repeatedly evokes scenes from nature with an unaffected spontaneity. He seeks to capture, in his words, "the invisible sentiments of nature" without directly copying natural sounds. "Music is allied to the

## *Music Today*

## Bayreuth

Since late in the nineteenth century, this small and idyllic town in northern Bavaria has been synonymous with the art of Richard Wagner. It was here in 1872 that Wagner decided to settle and to construct a theater devoted exclusively to the performance of his own works. He acquired land for a villa from his greatest patron, Ludwig II, king of Bavaria, and then set about raising money for the construction of a theater that would incorporate his visionary theories of opera, scenography, and drama. In the summer of 1876, the building was completed, and Wagner oversaw the first festival of his works, devoted to complete performances of his tetralogy *(Der Ring des Nibelungen)*. The second festival took place in 1882, this time with performances of *Parsifal*, Wagner's last work. The composer intended this opera to be performed only at Bayreuth.

After Wagner's death in 1883, the continuation of the festivals in Bayreuth became subject to the iron will of his widow, Cosima Liszt Wagner. She expanded the repertory to include earlier Wagner operas and demanded a near-religious adherence to her husband's ideas. In 1906 she turned control of the festivals over to her son, Siegfried. Following a temporary cessation of festivals from 1914 until 1924, Siegfried Wagner began to allow changes in his father's realistic conception of staging, scenery, and costume, admitting abstractions and symbolic treatments.

World War II was a dark period in Bayreuth's illustrious history. Hitler himself was a frequent and welcomed guest, and the organizers of the festivals, of necessity, hewed to his ideas in staging and repertory. But after the war, under the leadership of Wagner's grand-

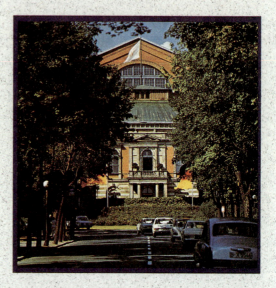

son Wieland Wagner, the theater reopened and reestablished its preeminence in Germany's cultural life. In 1973 leadership of the Bayreuth Festival passed from Wagner's heirs to a foundation.

The theater itself is utilitarian. It is unprepossessing from the outside; emphasis is directed most toward the interior functions. It is acoustically superb. The seats are notorious for being uncomfortable, given the length of Wagner's works, but such inconveniences are of little significance to the faithful. The orchestra plays in a deeply sunken and recessed pit, making it invisible to the audience. In recent years, stagings, even at Bayreuth, have reflected an international trend in operatic productions in which the composer's ideas on costume and scenography are entirely set aside and treated in a symbolic or reinterpretive manner. For many of Wagner's devoted audiences, these productions border on heresy, but they continue the tradition of Bayreuth in the vanguard of new operatic ideas.

movement of the waters," he wrote, "to the play of curves described by the changing breezes. Nothing is more musical than a sunset!"[6] His avoidance of strict beat suggests the liquefied outlines of a Pissarro landscape, and his reliance on pure instrumental colors may remind us of the vibrating tones of Monet's *Roches Noires Hotel* (page 330). Like impressionist painting, Debussy's music is richly evocative of images, impressions, and recollections.

Debussy grew up in Paris and attended the Paris Conservatory from 1873 until 1884. Like many young artists living in Paris at this time, he developed a taste for exotic art, including Japanese prints and the music of Russia and the Orient. He was strongly attracted to the music dramas of Wagner, but he professed a desire in his own music to allow the melodic line, rather than the orchestra, to be the main bearer of expression. He was increasingly impatient with the adulation of Wagner typical of French musical amateurs, and he sought a distinctively French musical idiom that did not entirely reject Wagnerian influence.

His first major success was his operatic setting (1902) of the symbolist play *Pelléas et Mélisande* by Maurice Maeterlinck. The play has strong connections with Wagnerian texts, although its heightened symbolism, suggestion rather than narrative, and lightness of tone differ clearly from the Wagnerian model. Debussy's music is similarly understated and subtle, using silence or ellipsis to suggest emotional states and a delicacy of musical utterance much at odds with Wagnerian rhetoric. Debussy's other music falls into the typical genres of the romantic period, emphasizing song, character works for piano, and orchestral tone poems.

The latent impressionism of Debussy's music is clearly evident in his character work "Reflets dans l'eau" ("Reflections in the Water," Recording 11.2), from a cycle titled *Images* (1905). Like landscape paintings of Monet, this work for piano produces its effect by refined suggestion and subtle evocativeness. A rigid sense of beat or regular meter is nowhere in evidence, as Debussy imitates the irregular movements of water. The brilliant manipulation of color that characterizes impressionist painting is approximated by Debussy's great sensitivity to the coloristic potential of harmony and of the piano. Like Liszt's water piece for piano, "Au bord d'une source," Debussy's "Reflets" brilliantly captures the mysterious essence of a shimmering pond. Full-blown melodies are not heard. The melodic element consists instead of a succession of brief, fragmentary motives, which suggest the shapes made by ripples in the water. But our attention is drawn in this work not so much to melodies as to textures, pure sounds of chords, surging arabesques of notes, and other evocations of sunlight glistening in water.

Debussy's use of the piano to create images and illusions of reality places this work in the company of character pieces by Chopin and Schumann, as Debussy himself suggested in a letter to Jacques Durand on September 11, 1905: "Without false vanity, I think these three pieces work well and will take their place in piano literature . . . to the left of Schumann or to the right of Chopin."[7]

The form of "Reflets" is exceedingly free. It consists of a number of sections that flow together without a sense of cadence. The three-note melodic fragment of the opening returns at 1.54 and at 3.41, contributing to a fleeting sense of conventional form. But form in this work derives from no preestablished plan. It imitates, instead, our encounter with the object that it evokes. We view the watery reflections, marveling at their ever-changing color and motion; we linger over their beauty; then we depart.

Debussy helps to free his listeners from traditional notions of form by removing strict beat, familiar harmonic progressions, and even a strong sense of keynote. Most of the melodic fragments are not based on familiar major and minor scales but on a scale consisting of rising or falling successions of whole steps. Scales of this sort have no inherent tonic note, and their ambiguity all the more accommodates Debussy's new sense of form.

## Modernism in Russia

In the late nineteenth century, several outstanding Russian composers used nationalistic ideas to assert their independence from Western musical styles. Their innovative spirit was inherited in the early twentieth century by modernists including Alexander Scriabin, Sergei Prokofiev, and Igor Stravinsky. Scriabin's early music imitated the romantic idiom of Chopin and Wagner, but about 1908 he began to write atonal music in a style very different from Schoenberg's contemporary atonal experiments. Prokofiev, the youngest of the group, came to attention in the West as a radical modernist, although he later returned to composition of music of romantic melodiousness. Igor Stravinsky (1882–1971) had the greatest impact of all, as he presciently sensed emerging directions in European music and shaped them to fit his own distinctive musical outlook.

Stravinsky decided on music as a career only after legal studies in his native Saint Petersburg. He studied composition with Nikolay Rimsky-Korsakov, in whose brilliant style Stravinsky wrote his early works. Stravinsky's music was brought before European audiences by the impresario Sergey Diaghilev (1872–1929), whose Ballets Russes exported virtuosic Russian dancers and composers to eager Western audiences. Between 1910 and 1923, Stravinsky wrote the music for five ballets commissioned by Diaghilev. Most are modernistic works, nationalistic in their stories and use of folk tunes. Like all of the ballets created by Diaghilev, they are fairly short, consisting of continuous music that meticulously expresses a pantomimed scenario.

Stravinsky's music after about 1920 underwent a major change of direction. After this time it was more international than regional, less overtly experimental, and closer in spirit to works of the baroque and classical periods. This reorientation was part of a general "neoclassical" movement in Europe and America during the interwar period. Its onset coincided with Stravinsky's emigration from Russia to France, and it continued even after he moved permanently to the United States in 1939. After the completion of his opera *The Rake's Progress* (1951), a work in a Mozartean vein, Stravinsky underwent yet another change

*In 1939 Igor Stravinsky visited Hollywood, where music from his ballet* The Rite of Spring *had recently been used in Walt Disney's film* Fantasia. *A Disney artist at that time drew this cartoon of the composer.*

of style, as he put aside the neoclassical language and embraced a dissonant and abstract manner that was de rigueur among younger composers following World War II.

*Le sacre du printemps* (*The Rite of Spring,* 1913) was Stravinsky's third ballet for Diaghilev and the high-water mark of his exploration of new musical resources. Its scenario, conceived by Stravinsky in collaboration with the Russian primitivist painter Nicholas Roerich, presents scenes from prehistoric Russia as tribes gather to celebrate the arrival of spring. There is group dancing, interrupted by the appearance of an elder, whose ritual kiss of the earth sends the tribes into pandemonium. At the conclusion, a virgin is chosen to perform a "sacrificial dance," in which she dances herself to death to gain the favor of the gods. This scenario, with its clearly elemental, barbaric tone, conforms to the primitive themes that had become common in French painting from the time of Paul Gauguin and resurfaced in pictures by Matisse and Picasso.

In its evocativeness and huge orchestral requirements, *The Rite of Spring* reminds us of romantic orchestral music. But the music otherwise has few, if any, models. The melodic element is clearly in the background, consisting of short motives that are repeated in hypnotic fashion. Many of these are fragments of eastern European folk song. The music has no stable keynote, and blatantly dissonant chords outweigh familiar harmonies.

The "Danse sacrale" ("Sacrificial Dance," Recording 11.3) that ends the ballet is the primary opportunity for solo dancing. Here a virgin is seized by an elemental frenzy that pushes her into a tumultuous and fatal dance. The music—cast into a refrain form—is clearly geared to depict her wild dis-

## Igor Stravinsky, "Danse sacrale" ("Sacrificial Dance") from *Le sacre du printemps (The Rite of Spring)*
Recording 11.3

| | | |
|---|---|---|
| **A** (refrain) | 0.00 | The refrain is characterized by its constantly shifting beat, irregular meter, and dissonant harmonies. No full-blown melodies appear. |
| **B** (episode) | 0.29 | A quiet though forbidding accompaniment builds tension, which is cut through by shrieklike motives in the brass. |
| **A′** | 2.02 | The refrain music returns a half-step lower than in its earlier appearance. |
| **C** (episode) | 2.30 | The orchestra creates the illusion of frantic flight, punctuated by a hypnotically repeated motive: |
| **A′** | 3.09 | The refrain music briefly returns. |
| **C′** | 3.15 | The second episode continues, building to a gigantic and raucous climax. |
| **A′** | 3.39 | The refrain returns a final time. |
| **Coda** | 4.35 | A brief conclusion. |

order. The immense orchestra blares out cacophonous dissonances, and a regular beat is heard only briefly. The orchestra percussively delineates a constantly shifting pulse that is gathered into irregular, unstable metric units.

It is quite probably this unorthodox rhythmic element, wed to a pagan and barbaric tale, that led to a near riot in Paris at the first performance of the work in 1913. The American writer Carl Van Vechten was present at the memorable event:

> A certain part of the audience was thrilled by what it considered to be a blasphemous attempt to destroy music as an art, and, swept away with wrath, began, very soon after the rise of the curtain, to make cat-calls and to offer audible suggestions as to how the performance should proceed. The orchestra played unheard, except occasionally when a slight lull occurred. The young man seated behind me in the box stood up during the course of the ballet to enable himself to see more clearly. The intense excitement under which he was labouring betrayed itself presently when he began to beat rhythmically on the top of my head with his fists. My emotion was so great that I did not feel the blows for some time.[8]

## Bartók and Nationalism

The nationalistic schools of composition that flourished in eastern Europe and Scandinavia in the late nineteenth century intensified in the first two decades of the twentieth and expanded to include composers in Spain and the New World. We have just seen Stravinsky's affinity for folk song and Russian folklore in his early ballets. The American composer Charles Ives wove popular American tunes into his music, and the Spaniard Manuel de Falla evoked the folk music of his native Andalusia. The most original nationalist composer in eastern Europe was the Hungarian Béla Bartók (1881–1945), who used the peasant music of his homeland as a guide in the creation of works of great power.

Bartók was born in a Hungarian town that is now part of Romania. He lived from the age of 12 in Pozsony (modern Bratislava, Czechoslovakia), called Preßburg by its influential German population. He proudly returned to the Hungarian capital of Budapest to attend conservatory, and he was rankled that his composition teacher, Hans Koessler, would speak only German to him and use only German music as a model for correct composition. Spurred on by national pride, he began in 1904 a systematic study of folk songs preserved by Magyar peasants, an undertaking that he later found "as necessary to me as fresh air is to other people." In these folk songs he discovered an antidote to romantic grandiloquence, which he increasingly disdained. "Folk music," he wrote in 1921, "expresses an idea musically in the most concise form, with the greatest simplicity of means, with freshness and life, briefly yet completely and properly proportioned."[9]

Bartók taught piano at the Budapest Academy of Music from 1907 until 1934, at which time he devoted himself primarily to ethnomusicological research. In 1941 he immigrated to the United States, where he lived in New York until his death in 1945.

Bartók's music consists primarily of piano character pieces, chamber works (of which his six string quartets are masterpieces), opera and ballet, and orchestral music. It is highly eclectic in its mixture of folk elements, traditional Western idioms, and new elements derived from Debussy, Stravinsky, and the German modernists, but his music is decidedly antiromantic.

Bartók's "Allegro barbaro" ("Barbaric Allegro," Recording 11.4) is a piano character piece that exemplifies this mixture of diverse musical impulses. It was written in 1911, early in Bartók's career, and it makes no overt use of folk tunes. But it is infused, all the same, with the spirit of eastern European folk music. The piece consists of a succession of short melodies, each based on a small segment of a scale. These motives are repeated with simple variations, but not developed. Like all folk music, a keynote is evident, here F♯, which is reiterated at the beginning and end and in passing throughout the piece. The driving rhythm, always preserving a clear sense of pulse, has its origin in similar rhythms in Hungarian dance tunes. These folk melodies were probably performed with much rubato, which Bartók imitates as he repeatedly places the tempo in flux.

## Music Between the World Wars

The end of World War I in 1918 marked the onset of a major new style in the history of music, in which romanticism, led by German and Austrian composers, was forcefully rejected. This change of taste had been prefigured earlier in the music of Stravinsky, Debussy, and Bartók, but the cataclysm of war made the rebellion against romanticism complete. Germany and Austria were viewed by much of the rest of the world as the perpetrators of the war. After its conclusion, these countries suffered economic turmoil, marked by runaway inflation and desperate shortages of food and basic necessities. It was in such circumstances that leadership in the world of music slipped away.

The musical situation in the United States after 1918 dramatically reflected the rejection of German domination. The Boston Symphony, for example, from its founding in 1881 had been conducted by Germans and largely staffed by imported German instrumentalists. But in 1924 the orchestra looked to France for a new conductor, bringing the Franco-Russian émigré Serge Koussevitzky to the United States. Koussevitzky had a solidly Gallic orientation that remained in force with this orchestra until the 1960s. No longer did the outstanding young American composers travel to Germany to seek higher musical education, as they uniformly did in the late nineteenth century. A generation of young American musicians, including Aaron Copland, Virgil Thomson, and Roy Harris, now went to France to begin their careers in music.

After 1918, virtually all of the major features of the late romantic style were overturned. The constant striving for originality was replaced by an acceptance of older musical models, especially those from the baroque period. The ultraserious, dense, and difficult aura of romantic music was dispelled in works of simplicity, clarity, and lightness. Music was no longer elitist or strictly nonutilitarian. It aimed for a broader audience, and it could legitimately afford light entertainment in addition to a loftier message.

Expressivity—the keystone of romantic musical style—was no longer a central issue. Igor Stravinsky spoke for the new generation when he wrote in 1936 in his autobiography:

> I consider that music is, by its very nature, essentially powerless to *express* anything at all, whether a feeling, an attitude of mind, a psychological mood, a phenomenon of nature, etc. *Expression* has never been an inherent property of music. That is by no means the purpose of its existence. If, as is nearly always the case, music appears to express something, this is only an illusion and not a reality.[10]

## Neoclassicism

The rebellion against romanticism was at its strongest in France in the years between the world wars. Stravinsky resettled there in 1920 and turned away from the primitivism and forceful atonality of *Le sacre du printemps,* finding in its place a style that embraced older values in a nonetheless original manner. The French composer Erik Satie (1866–1925) wrote simple, tuneful music of lighthearted wit, intentionally approaching triviality, as a way of rejecting both German romanticism and French impressionism. The writer

Jean Cocteau proved to be an articulate spokesman for Satie's aesthetic, as he praised a new spirit in French music that

> no longer grimaces, or wears a mask, or hides, or shirks, and is not afraid to admire or to stand up for what it admires. It hates paradox and eclecticism. It despises their smile and faded elegance. It also shuns the colossal. That is what I call *escaping from Germany*.[11]

Stravinsky, Satie, and Cocteau all represented in the 1920s a musical style that is now termed **neoclassicism.** Its main musical features were simplicity and clarity. Melodious, homophonic textures were the order of the day, and familiar, triadic harmonies were revived. The motoric rhythms of the baroque were often imitated, and, in general, there was less emphasis on evocativeness or programmatic meaning. The vitality of popular music was regularly imitated.

Satie and Cocteau were mentors to young French composers who in the 1920s extended the neoclassical idiom. "They represented new attitudes in music and the spirit of the period," wrote Aaron Copland, who shared their milieu in Paris in the early 1920s.

> They signified the absolute end of the Germanic Brahmsian and Wagnerian approach—the one that seemed to say you had to listen to music in a very solemn and sacrosanct manner with your eyes closed and your head in your hands. They were not long-haired romantic genius types.[12]

Darius Milhaud (1892–1974) was one such composer whom Copland met and praised. Like a genuine French neoclassicist, he had little patience for Wagner and shared in the high spirits of Cocteau's circle. After completing his studies at the Paris Conservatory, he was hired by the poet and diplomat Paul Claudel as secretary to the French embassy in Rio de Janeiro. His exposure to Latin American dance music was subsequently reflected in his piano character works *Saudades do Brasil (Longing for Brazil,* 1921). In 1922 he visited New York, where he heard New Orleans–style jazz:

> The music I heard was absolutely different from anything I had ever heard before and was a revelation to me. Against the beat of the drums the melodic lines criss-crossed in a breathless pattern of broken and twisted rhythms.[13]

These impressions were used in the writing of a ballet, *La création du monde (The Creation of the World,* 1923), that exemplifies aspects of the neoclassical idiom. Milhaud was commissioned by Rolf de Maré, whose Swedish

Ballet was a rival of Diaghilev's Russian troupe. The scenario, by Blaise Cendrars, is set among prehistoric African tribes who act out African legends about the world's creation. At the conclusion, a newly created man and woman engage in a frenzied "Dance of Desire." Clearly, Cendrars's story is spun off from Stravinsky's *Rite of Spring*, although Milhaud's music is of a very different sort. Rather than the huge orchestra of the Stravinsky, Milhaud chooses a small ensemble with piano, saxophone, and expanded percussion. These instruments suggest the diverse sonorities of a jazz band, and jazz idioms are imitated throughout. After a brief musical introduction, the first scene or "tableau" (Recording 11.5) depicts chaos before the creation, as

**Darius Milhaud, *La création du monde (The Creation of the World)*, tableau 1**
Recording 11.5

| | | |
|---|---|---|
| **Fugal exposi-tion** | 0.00 | The fugal subject contains several "blue notes," characteristic of jazz (see Chapter 13). These notes, marked by an asterisk in the notation below, are lowered a half-step from their normal placement in the major scale. |

| | | |
|---|---|---|
| **Episode** | 0.33 | A new melody appears in the cello and oboe, based on motives from the subject: |

| | | |
|---|---|---|
| **Restatements** | 0.40 | A succession of restatements of the fugal subject is heard. |
| **Episode** | 1.04 | The original episodic figure returns, leading to its simultaneous combination at 1.11 with the fugal subject. The first tableau is connected to the second by a brief interlude. |

shapeless masses of bodies fill the stage. In this scene Milhaud uses the form of a strict fugue, which evokes both baroque instrumental music and the polyphonic textures of an improvising New Orleans jazz band. The fugal subject is first stated in the string bass, accompanied by jazzy figures in the percussion and piano. The subject is imitated in turn by trombone, saxophone, and trumpet. The remainder of the fugue is made up of ever more frenzied restatements of the subject, alternating with other melodic ideas.

The idea of using jazz idioms in an otherwise "serious" composition was a recurrent element in neoclassical music as composers sought to break down the distinction between high and popular art. Milhaud's music has a spirited directness, a clarity of rhythm and pulse, and a familiarity of form in the use of fugue that distinguish it from romanticism and bring it into line with the mood of the 1920s. But Milhaud is by no means a traditionalist. In fact, throughout his long career, he showed a constant interest in innovative musical ideas. In his early years, when *Création* was written, he experimented repeatedly with the harmonic and tonal implications of **polytonality,** having two or more distinct keys in effect simultaneously in different strata of a composition. Polytonality is essayed in *Création,* for example, in the first episode of the first scene. In this passage, half of the instruments play in C major and the others in D major. The result is a pungent dissonance reminiscent of jazz.

### Music in America

Musical culture in the United States in the nineteenth century was characterized by an unusually vigorous popular and folk element. Religious songs of many different types, patriotic tunes, band music, and minstrel and household songs were enjoyed by people from all walks of life, and they left an indelible mark on the imagination of American musicians. Serious or concert music in the nineteenth century tended to be unoriginal in style, despite the notable accomplishments of composers such as Edward MacDowell (1860–1908), George Chadwick (1854–1931), John Knowles Paine (1839–1906), and Horatio Parker (1863–1919). All of these figures received their musical education in Germany, and their music hewed, by and large, to European models.

Beginning in the early twentieth century, there appeared in America composers of serious music who were not attached to European examples. They were imbued with an experimental spirit and a desire to reflect their American homeland in their music. The remarkable Yankee composer Charles Ives (1874–1954) is best known among this group of American modernists.

Ives was born in rural Connecticut and grew up in the family of a free-thinking municipal band director. He learned to play organ as a child and had a good knowledge of European music. But he was closer in spirit to the popular tunes that he heard at camp meetings, parades and other patriotic gatherings, and the band concerts conducted by his father.

He attended Yale University, where he studied composition with Horatio Parker, although he never came to share Parker's strictly European outlook. After graduating, he made his career as an insurance executive, soon proving immensely successful and helping to found the modern American insurance industry. He composed in his free time and only rarely had his music performed publicly. Due to uncertain health and, perhaps, a loss of inspiration, he stopped composing around 1920, after which he cautiously attempted to make his music known to a larger public. In the 1930s and 1940s his works were championed by the conductor Nicolas Slonimsky and the pianist John Kirkpatrick, and their striking originality was acknowledged.

Ives's philosophy of music was very different from the accepted notions of the nineteenth century. He held that all art stemmed from a spiritual side of humanity. It did not necessarily require a special gift or training, and it was in no way elitist. Art could be found everywhere: in mundane activities, in people, in nature. Its message was not abstract or refined but spiritual, moral, and civilizing. This is the conception of music that he attributes to Henry David Thoreau: "Thoreau was a great musician," Ives wrote, "not because he played the flute, but because he did not have to go to Boston to hear 'the Symphony.' "[14]

All great music, in Ives's view, had "substance," which was marked by its genuineness, spirit, and high character. Conventional beauty and coherence had nothing to do with substance, and Ives was very suspicious of these qualities. They imbued a composition only with "manner," something of little value. The works of the late romantic period—especially those of Wagner, Debussy, and Tchaikovsky—were dismissed by Ives as consisting solely of this shallowness. Manner was revealed in art in many ways:

> The sculptors' overinsistence on the "mold"; the outer rather than
> the inner subject or content of his statue—overenthusiasm for local
> color—overinterest in the multiplicity of techniques, in the idiomatic,
> in the effect as shown by the appreciation of an audience rather than
> in the effect on the ideals of the inner conscience of the artist or the
> composer.[15]

For Ives to give his own music substance, he had to make it speak of his own interests and background. This he accomplished by quoting the popular tunes that he recalled from his youth or by imitating the way that common people made music. A good antidote for manner was a healthy dose of dissonance. In general, his music, which includes symphonies and tone poems, chamber works, piano character pieces, songs, and choral music, is both nationalistic and eclectic. It combines many different styles, ranging from the simplicity of a Sunday school hymn to a raucous frenzy. His music celebrates everyday American values as he came to understand them.

The song "Charlie Rutlage" (c. 1920) (Recording 11.6) illustrates this eclecticism and the great dramatic power that Ives discovered in everyday American scenes. It is a setting of a ballad, cast as a succession of couplets, that narrates the death of the "good cowpuncher" Charlie Rutlage. Despite its artlessness, the poem speaks movingly of a common man's encounter with fate. Ives's music dramatizes these sentiments with the same forcefulness as Schubert's "Erlkönig," although their musical materials are very different. The song is in ternary form, in which the outer sections imitate folk music. The melody is based mainly on a pentatonic scale, and it has the easy gait of a cowboy tune. This style contrasts greatly with the middle part. Here the voice declaims the words in a spoken recitation and the pianist plays ever more frantically and dissonantly, finally pounding out chords with the fists to portray Charlie's death beneath his falling horse.

*Listening Guide*

**Charlie Ives, "Charlie Rutlage"**
Recording 11.6

| | | |
|---|---|---|
| **A** | 0.00 | The main theme (below) at first uses a folklike pentatonic scale; it then changes keynote quickly and unexpectedly. |

(Voice:)

| | | |
|---|---|---|
| **B** | 0.56 | The voice recites the dramatic climax of the narrative while the piano plays ever faster and more frantically. |
| **A′** | 2.03 | The main theme returns, ending with a hymnlike cadence. |

*Grant Wood's* **Spring Turning *(1936) typifies regionalism in American art.***

Ives's experimental spirit was maintained in American music between the world wars by his fellow Yankee Carl Ruggles, the New Yorkers Leo Ornstein and Edgard Varèse, and a group of West Coast composers including Henry Cowell, Harry Partch, John Cage, and Lou Harrison. But their avant-gardism was not central to the spirit of the times, which in America had come to emphasize traditional values, simplicity and directness, and a forthright regionalism. These qualities are apparent in the paintings of the 1930s of Grant Wood (1892–1942) and Thomas Hart Benton (1889–1975). Wood's *Spring Turning* (see above) pictures the rolling lands of the Midwest, whose fertility and abundance are suggested by a matronly shape. The painting rejects the subjectivity and complication of modern European painting in favor of a charmingly direct and clearly regional language.

The leading American composers between the world wars projected similar qualities. Aaron Copland, Virgil Thomson, Roy Harris, and Walter Piston were populists who embraced traditional musical values. They were strongly oriented toward French neoclassical music, although their works speak with a distinctively American accent. "We wanted to find a music that would speak of universal things in a vernacular of American speech rhythms," wrote Copland. "We wanted to write music with a largeness of utterance wholly representative of the country that Whitman had envisaged."[16]

The vernacular of American speech, which Copland wanted in American music, many composers found in jazz, which they used to give vigor and spontaneity to their own serious works. George Gershwin (1898–1937), although known primarily for his popular music, composed many serious pieces flavored by jazz. Gershwin, like Copland, was born to a family of Russian immigrants in New York. Even as a teenager, he attracted nationwide attention for his popular songs, and he later wrote classics for the musical theater and for film. But throughout his short life, he also composed such works as the Piano Concerto, the tone poem *An American in Paris,* and the folk opera *Porgy and Bess.*

His three Piano Preludes (1926) mix several jazz styles with experimental devices and formal procedures drawn from the world of art music. The first of these pieces (Recording 11.7) has a classical ternary form, touches of bitonality worthy of Milhaud, and an expressive and free use of dissonance. But the spirit of the work is drawn from jazz. The opening melodic gesture contains blue notes suggestive of a jazz singer's expressive bending of scale tones downward. The rhythm of the opening has the irregular pulse of Latin dance music, and the accompaniment is drawn from the "stride" piano style of ragtime. In this idiom, the pianist's left hand regularly alternates notes in a low register and chords in a middle register.

**George Gershwin, Piano Prelude No. 1**
Recording 11.7

A        0.00    After a brief introduction that presages the main theme and establishes the Latin rhythm of the accompaniment, the principal theme is stated:

B        0.28    A new melody is heard in the middle section, which is accompanied bitonally by a left-hand figure in a conflicting key.

A′       1.19    The main theme returns.

Aaron Copland (1900–1990) was the most outstanding of the American populist composers of the interwar decades. After graduating from high school, he traveled to France to complete his musical education, studying there with the remarkable teacher Nadia Boulanger (1887–1979). Boulanger was subsequently the mentor to several generations of leading American musicians. Although she was not doctrinaire about the style in which her students composed, she insisted that all music exhibit what she called a *grande ligne* ("long line"). "It is difficult adequately to explain the meaning of that phrase to the layman," Copland later commented.

> To be properly understood in relation to a piece of music, it must be felt. In mere words, it simply means that every good piece of music must give us a sense of flow—a sense of continuity from first note to last. . . . A great symphony is a man-made Mississippi down which we irresistibly flow from the instant of our leave-taking to a long foreseen destination.[17]

After returning to the United States, Copland quickly made his mark as a composer of jazz-inspired pieces. By 1930, he put jazz aside and cultivated a more abstract, percussive, and astringent manner, although he also continued to write works of broader appeal. These latter, highly regional in content, include the ballet scores for *Rodeo, Billy the Kid,* and *Appalachian Spring* and patriotic wartime pieces including *Lincoln Portrait* and *Fanfare for the Common Man*.

Despite its diminutive size and unassuming character, the *Fanfare* (Recording 11.8) has proved to be one of Copland's most enduring and most imitated works. It illustrates the continuity or "long line" that runs through all of his music. It was commissioned in 1943 by the Cincinnati Symphony as a patriotic gesture, and it calls for brass and percussion. Following a stentorian introduction in the drums and cymbals, the trumpets state a theme resembling a bugle call, made up of large intervals. Its cadences are punctuated by the return of the drums. The theme is then twice varied, each time with more brass instruments added, and a coda brings the work to a blazing conclusion.

## Music in Germany and Austria

The neoclassical movement in France and America in the 1920s was felt in Germany and Austria as well, even though these areas had been the hotbeds of modernism before World War I. The horrors of the war and its aftermath sparked a rebellion against experimentation in music, as well as in

*George Grosz's 1918 depiction of a German army medical examination is typical of the cynical tone of art after World War I. Here the army doctor declares the skeleton "fit for active service," as officers tell jokes in the foreground. Social criticism was pronounced in all of the fine arts in Germany of the postwar period. (The Museum of Modern Art, N.Y. A Conger Goodyear Fund.)*

literature and painting. Rather than presenting the distorted and symbolic images of expressionism, many German artists and writers after the war were inclined to return to realism, but then with a trenchant critique of the society that had seemingly produced the war. Bertolt Brecht wrote plays in the 1920s, such as *Die Dreigroschenoper* (*The Three-Penny Opera,* 1928), satirizing Germany's bourgeois society. Kurt Weill added popular songs to this play, which is intended to sensitize the audience to social issues. A related movement in the visual arts in Germany in the mid-1920s was termed the "New Objectivity," in which painters such as George Grosz and Otto Dix depicted the horrors of war and made grotesque caricatures of the German establishment.

Paul Hindemith (1895–1963) emerged as the leading German neoclassicist of the interwar period. Before about 1923, Hindemith was an experimenter. He set shocking expressionist plays as one-act operas, delved into American jazz idioms, and imitated the atonal style of the Viennese modernists. But later he settled on a more traditional type of music that suggested the baroque period in its rhythmic mechanism and contrapuntal textures and revived tonality, albeit in a transformed manner. Hindemith became a vitriolic opponent of the direction of music represented by Schoenberg and his circle, which he found arbitrary and snobbish. He wanted, instead, music that would communicate an ethical message to its hearers and would embrace traditional values and materials. His music of the 1920s is often compared to paintings of the New Objectivity, although the attitude of social criticism and satire associated with this artistic movement had increasingly little in common with Hindemith's lofty ideal of music as ethical discourse.

There remained in German-speaking lands in the years between the world wars a residue of modernism, including techniques of liberated dissonance and atonality, that were inherited from the prewar period. The main force behind music of this type was the Viennese modernist school led by Arnold Schoenberg. But even Schoenberg, who had nothing but disdain for neoclassicism, responded to the more conservative spirit of the time by writing music in a more direct manner.

In his atonal pieces composed before World War I, he sometimes wrote in a stream of consciousness, listening to his inner musical ear for guidance, avoiding familiar chords and banishing any sense of keynote, and pursuing a spontaneous sense of form. In the years during and immediately following the war, he sensed the need for a more concrete method to guide him. By 1923 he had developed what he termed the "method of composing with twelve-tones, related only one to another." The details of the method are not of primary importance for the listener. In fact, Schoenberg considered them solely as a composer's guide and not at all pertinent outside of his own workshop. His method was intended to ensure the constant recirculation of all 12 notes and to unify the melodic and harmonic dimensions of a work by making them share the same constellations of intervals. Twelve-tone music does not suggest any uniform style, although the music that it produces is nor-

*In addition to being one of the leading modernist composers of the twentieth century, Arnold Schoenberg was also a skillful amateur painter. His portrait of his student Alban Berg was made about 1910, roughly at the end of Berg's period of study.*

mally atonal, chromatic, and highly dissonant. We will examine one of Schoenberg's 12-tone pieces, *A Survivor from Warsaw,* in Chapter 12.

Schoenberg's two leading students, Alban Berg (1885–1935) and Anton Webern (1883–1945), followed their mentor along the road from late romantic composition to atonality and, finally, to 12-tone composition. Berg was a lifelong resident of Vienna, and he began his compositional studies with Schoenberg in 1904. He came to prominence as a composer only in 1925, with the premiere in Berlin of his opera *Wozzeck.* Before his untimely death in 1935, he wrote a relatively small amount of music, including *Wozzeck* and its companion piece *Lulu,* orchestral essays, songs, and chamber works.

Berg adapted the text of *Wozzeck* from a fragmentary spoken play by Georg Büchner (1813–1837). The play was based on the life of a soldier named Johann Woyzeck, who in 1824 murdered his mistress, a crime for which he was executed. Büchner expands on the historical circumstances by making Wozzeck and his mistress helpless victims of fate and of social injustice. His play anticipates by almost a century aspects of German expressionist theater in its use of violence as a symbol of social and psychic disintegration and its symbolic treatment of characters. Wozzeck, for example, is preyed on by a doctor, representing science gone mad; a captain, symbolizing the hypocrisy of a militaristic society; and a drum major, who symbolizes its brutish elements.

Wozzeck is an impoverished soldier who lives with his common-law wife, Marie, and their child. To earn a few pennies, he allows the doctor to perform experiments on him, which are driving him to insanity. Marie is seduced by the dashing drum major, as she sees no reason to resist. But Wozzeck discovers earrings that the man has given her and, in a demented rage, murders her and then drowns himself.

To make up the text for his opera, Berg selected 15 scenes from Büchner's play, which he then distributed over three acts. The music of each scene is modeled on a genre or form of classical instrumental music. As though to compensate for the lack of traditional harmonies and key, Berg emphasized recurrent leitmotifs and other devices to make the music express the words. Depending on the text, the voices sometimes sing in a traditional fashion or they use a type of singing called **speech melody.** Devised earlier by Schoenberg, this combined strict musical rhythms with a speechlike use of pitches.

The second scene of Act 3 (Recording 11.9) is the climax of the opera. Wozzeck takes Marie to a deserted lake, where he has resolved to murder her for her infidelity with the drum major. As the moon rises blood-red, he stabs her to death in a frenzy. At this point, all of Marie's leitmotifs rush past in the orchestral music, just as it is said that a person's whole life flashes in review at the moment of death. According to Berg's formal plan, this scene is an "invention upon a note," by which he means that a single note (B) is ever-present. The note represents the obsessive idea of murder, which does not leave Wozzeck until after his crime is committed.

**Alban Berg, *Wozzeck*, Act 3, Scene 2**
Recording 11.9

A forest path by a lake. It is dark. Marie and Wozzeck enter from the right.

| | |
|---|---|
| *Dort links geht's in die Stadt. 's ist noch weit. Komm schneller.* | MARIE: The way to the left goes toward town. It's still far, hurry! |
| *Du sollst dableiben, Marie. Komm, setz' Dich, komm.* | WOZZECK: You should rest here, Marie. Come, sit down, come. |
| *Aber ich muß fort.* | MARIE: But I must go! |
| *Bist weit gegangen, Marie. Sollst Dir die Füße nicht mehr wund laufen. 's ist still hier! Und so dunkel. Weißt noch, Marie, wie lang es jetzt ist, daß wir uns kennen?* | WOZZECK: You've gone far, Marie. You shouldn't run further with sore feet. It's quiet here! And so dark. Do you still remember, Marie, how long it has been that we've known each other? |
| *Zu Pfingsten drei Jahre.* | MARIE: On Whitsunday, three years. |
| *Und was meinst, wie lang es noch dauern wird?* | WOZZECK: And how long do you think it will continue? |
| *Ich muß fort.* | MARIE: I must go! |
| *Fürchst Dich, Marie? Und bist doch fromm? Und gut! Und treu! Was Du für süße Lippen hast, Marie! Den Himmel gäb' ich drum und die Seligkeit, wenn ich Dich noch oft so küssen dürft. Aber ich darf nicht! Was zitterst?* | WOZZECK: Are you afraid, Marie? Aren't you virtuous, and good, and true? What sweet lips you have, Marie. I would give all heaven and salvation if I might still kiss you. But I cannot! Why are you trembling? |
| *Der Nachttau fällt.* | MARIE: The night's dew is falling. |
| *Wer kalt ist, den friert nicht mehr! Dich wird beim Morgentau nicht frieren.* | WOZZECK: Whoever is cold will freeze no more! You won't be frozen by the morning dew. |
| *Was sagst Du da?* | MARIE: What are you saying? |
| *Nix.* | WOZZECK: Nothing. |
| *Wie der Mond roth aufgeht!* | MARIE: How red is the rising moon! |
| *Wie ein blutig Eisen!* | WOZZECK: Like a bloody knife! |
| *Was zitterst? Was willst?* | MARIE: Why do you tremble? What are you going to do? |

| | |
|---|---|
| *Ich nicht, Marie! und kein Andrer auch nicht!* | WOZZECK: If not me, Marie, then no one else! |
| *Hülfe!* | MARIE: Help! [*He stabs her in the throat with the knife.*] |
| *Todt!* | WOZZECK: Dead! [*He stands up timidly and dashes silently off.*] |

**Part 1**      0.00      Few of the important leitmotifs of the opera appear in this section, as Wozzeck and Marie rest by the lake. When Wozzeck praises Marie's sweet lips, the harmonies become sweetly triadic.

**Part 2**      3.12      Wozzeck tells Marie that he means nothing by his proverb about the morning dew, but the note B, on which he sings "Nix," tells us that he means murder. This ominous moment is underscored by a long silence, after which part 2 begins. The moon rises blood-red, which is depicted by a rising figure in the orchestra over a growling low B. At Wozzeck's comparison of the moon to a bloody knife, the leitmotif that throughout the opera represents the knife is sounded by the muted horns:

After Marie is stabbed, several of her motives rush by. The curtain falls as the orchestra plays a dramatic crescendo solely on the note B, leading to a rhythmic motive that will be central to the next scene.

---

Anton Webern also became a student of Schoenberg's in 1904, while he was completing doctoral studies in musicology at the University of Vienna. His music was of such originality that it never attracted much attention during his own lifetime. He made his living primarily by teaching, conducting, and consulting for the publisher Universal Edition, and his career is an inspiring study in total devotion to the art of music. Toward the end of World War II, he moved from Vienna to Mittersill (near Innsbruck), in order to live with his daughter and son-in-law. In a tragic accident, he was shot to death there in 1945 by an American occupation soldier.

**Anton Webern, String Quartet, Op. 28, first movement**
Recording 11.10

**Theme**         0.00     The theme was intended by Webern to be heard as a period form
divided into two halves at 0.11. Its rhythmic values are relatively
simple, although its contour and its sense of continuity are unorthodox. The end of the theme is marked off by a slowing of
the tempo. The "antecedent" phrase of the theme is

**Variation 1**   0.30     This variation is relatively close to the theme in its dispositions of
the basic two-note motive, division into two parts (corresponding
to antecedent and consequent phrases of a period form), and alternation of bowed and plucked passages.

**Variation 2**   1.02     Here the tempo becomes faster and there is a greater sense of
motivic continuity in the various lines.

**Variation 3**   1.32     This variation corresponds to the middle (contrasting) part of a
ternary form, in that it has a denser and darker texture.

**Variation 4**   2.10     Listen for the imitations of the opening soloistic gesture in the
violin, which recurs in the other instruments in a free fugue. The
rhythmic activity in this variation is clearly increased.

**Variation 5**   2.43     This variation corresponds to the reprise of an A B A (ternary)
form. Its tempo is the same as the beginning, and it repeats the
bold angularity of the opening.

**Variation 6**   3.13     This codalike passage contains a more chordal presentation of the
basic motive, dwindling finally to a hushed echo.

Webern's earliest pieces were written in the late romantic style, but most of his works are atonal. He adopted the 12-tone method in the 1920s and used it with great strictness. Most of his music is characterized by extreme brevity and concentration (a style called **aphoristic**). It is exceedingly understated and refined, to the point where minute gestures assume major importance. The texture of his works is remarkable for its spareness and disjunction of line. The melodic element is highly abbreviated and elliptical, and it often passes quickly among several different instruments and is further fragmented by the interpolation of silences and large, angular leaps.

All of these qualities are present in his String Quartet, Op. 28 (1937). Its three movements last a total of about eight minutes (long by Webern's standards). The first movement (Recording 11.10), we know by Webern's own description, is to be construed in a theme and variations form, also having a freely ternary shape. We are struck at first by the seeming lack of a melodic line. Melody appears to be replaced by small groups of notes continuously passed among the instruments. Repeated listenings cause us to hear more connections between these groups, but Webern's notion of melody and theme is still very different from the conventional one and demands that we bring to it new strategies for listening.

A basic compositional premise in this piece is the fitting together of constant recurrences of an opening two-note motive. The notes of this figure are usually separated by a wide and dissonant interval. The ever-changing ways in which statements of the motive fit together create the effect of a kaleidoscope. Sometimes the motive appears with rhythmic values that are long, other times very short; sometimes the notes are played with the bow, sometimes by plucked strings. Sometimes the presentations overlap or appear simultaneously, other times they emerge side by side. The major structural junctures in the movement are all marked off by a temporary slowing of the tempo and, sometimes, by the interjection of a momentary silence. It is absolutely crucial in Webern's music that attention be paid to minutiae, for his is an art of the utmost concentration and refinement.

## TOPICS FOR DISCUSSION AND WRITING

**1.** Was Debussy an "impressionist" composer? Compare his "Reflets dans l'eau" with Claude Monet's paintings *Bathing at La Grenouillère* and *Sailboat at Petit-Gennevilliers* or to other impressionist art that depicts water. Why might Debussy so vociferously have rejected the epithet *impressionistic* for his music?

**2.** Compare Milhaud's *La Création du monde* with Louis Armstrong's "West End Blues" (Recording 13.5), and isolate the elements of New Orleans jazz present in the Armstrong recording that appear in Milhaud's imitation.

**396**

**3.** Read Georg Büchner's play *Woyzeck* and compare it with the atonal musical style of Berg's opera *Wozzeck*. Does atonality correspond necessarily to the psychotic world of Wozzeck? Would a more conventional musical style express Wozzeck's plight equally well? Can atonal music express other types of emotions?

**4.** Analyze the first movement of Webern's String Quartet, seeking conventional musical elements. Make as strong a case as possible that the music is related to conventional music and should be heard in the same way as music of earlier times.

## ADDITIONAL LISTENING

### Bartók

Concerto for Orchestra. This late piece is one of Bartók's most accessible. Its brilliant and virtuosic treatment of the orchestra is concertolike in that many instruments are featured as soloists.

*Duke Bluebeard's Castle.* Bartók's only opera. The text is a version of the Bluebeard legend, treated in a dreamlike, symbolic manner.

### Berg

Concerto for Violin. Berg's last complete work. Elegiac in tone, the concerto contains quotations of a Lutheran hymn (in a harmonization by Bach) and an Austrian folk song.

*Lyric Suite* for String Quartet. This passionate work is secretly descriptive of Berg's love for Hanna Fuchs.

### Debussy

*Pelléas et Mélisande.* Debussy's only completed opera. Its delicate and refined texture perfectly captures the spirit of the symbolist play by Maurice Maeterlinck on which it is based.

Prelude to *L'après-midi d'un faune (Afternoon of a Faun).* A tone poem that interprets a symbolist poem by Stéphane Mallarmé.

*La mer (The Sea).* A tone poem showing Debussy's great love for nature and ability to evoke its magical essence.

### Mahler

Symphony No. 4 in G Major. This is Mahler's most classical symphony. In its finale, a soprano sings folk poetry on the joys of heavenly life.

Symphony No. 6 in A Minor. Mahler's most personal work. The symphony outlines the composer's titanic, although futile, struggle with his own fate.

### Milhaud

*Saudades do Brasil.* Twelve character pieces for piano, each of which imitates a Latin American dance, also using Milhaud's pungent bitonal harmonies.

## Schoenberg

*Gurrelieder*. An immense cantata for large orchestra and voices, firmly in the Wagnerian vein.

*Pierrot lunaire (Moonstruck Peter)*. This atonal and partly expressionistic work is for speaker and a chamber orchestra.

## Stravinsky

*L'oiseau de feu (The Firebird)*. Stravinsky's first ballet score and the work that brought him international attention. Its style resembles that of his teacher, Rimsky-Korsakov.

*Mass*. This 1948 work is in the composer's neoclassical style.

*Octet*. An early neoclassical work.

## Webern

Arrangement of Bach's Ricercar in six voices from *The Musical Offering*. The arrangement is for chamber orchestra and shows Webern's colorful and fragmented style of orchestration.

## BIBLIOGRAPHY

### General Works on Twentieth-Century Music

Austin, William. *Music in the 20th Century*. New York: Norton, 1966.

Machlis, Joseph. *Introduction to Contemporary Music*. New York: Norton, 1961. Despite the title, Machlis covers primarily composers of the first half of the century.

Mitchell, Donald. *The Language of Modern Music*. New York: St. Martin's Press, 1970. Emphasis on Schoenberg and on the interdisciplinary connections of modern music.

Salzman, Eric. *Twentieth-Century Music: An Introduction*. Third edition. Englewood Cliffs, N.J.: Prentice Hall, 1988.

Simms, Bryan R. *Music of the Twentieth Century: Style and Structure*. New York: Schirmer Books, 1986.

### Studies of Composers Discussed in This Chapter

Debussy, Claude. *Debussy on Music*. Translated and edited by Richard Langham Smith. Collected by François Lesure. Ithaca, N.Y.: Cornell University Press, 1971.

La Grange, Henry-Louis de. *Mahler*. Garden City, N.Y.: Doubleday, 1973. One volume to date in English, following the composer's life in great detail to 1902. Other volumes are available currently in French only.

Lockspeiser, Edward. *Debussy: His Life and Mind*. Two volumes. Cambridge: Cambridge University Press 1978. Lockspeiser pursues a strongly interdisciplinary approach to Debussy's work.

Moldenhauer, Hans and Rosaleen Moldenhauer. *Anton von Webern: A Chronicle of His Life and Work*. New York: Knopf, 1979. An exhaustive musical and biographical study.

Perle, George. *The Operas of Alban Berg*. Volume 1 *(Wozzeck)*. Berkeley: University of California Press, 1980.

Redlich, Hans. *Alban Berg*. London: Calder, 1954. See especially Berg's lecture on *Wozzeck*, included as an appendix.

Schoenberg, Arnold. *Style and Idea*. Edited by Leonard Stein. Translated by Leo Black. Berkeley: University of California Press, 1984. A collection of Schoenberg's writings. Basic for an understanding of his music.

Stevens, Halsey. *The Life and Music of Béla Bartók*. Revised edition. New York: Oxford University Press, 1964.

Stuckenschmidt, H. H. *Schoenberg: His Life, World and Work*. Translated by Humphrey Searle. New York: Schirmer Books, 1977. The most detailed biography.

White, Eric Walter. *Stravinsky: The Composer and His Works*. Second edition. Berkeley: University of California Press, 1979.

## NOTES

1. Arnold Schoenberg, *Style and Idea*, ed. Leonard Stein, trans. Leo Black (Berkeley: University of California Press, 1984), p. 114.
2. Georges Braque, quoted in Sam Hunter and John Jacobus, *Modern Art*, 2nd ed. (Englewood Cliffs, N.J.: Prentice Hall, 1985), p. 138.
3. Vincent Van Gogh, *The Complete Letters*, eds. J. Van Gogh-Bonger, W. V. Van Gogh (Greenwich, Conn.: New York Graphic Society, 1958), vol. 3, p. 6.
4. Wassily Kandinsky, *Concerning the Spiritual in Art*, trans. M. T. H. Sadler (New York: Dover, 1977), p. 57.
5. *Arnold Schoenberg, Wassily Kandinsky: Letters, Pictures and Documents*, ed. Jelena Hahl-Koch, trans. John C. Crawford (London, Boston: Faber and Faber, 1984), p. 23.
6. Claude Debussy, *Debussy on Music*, trans. and ed. Richard Langham Smith, coll. François Lesure (Ithaca, N.Y.: Cornell University Press, 1971), p. 199.
7. Claude Debussy, *Debussy Letters*, trans. Roger Nichols (Cambridge, Mass.: Harvard University Press, 1987), p. 158.
8. Carl Van Vechten, in Eric Walter White, *Stravinsky* (Berkeley: University of California Press, 1969), p. 176.
9. Béla Bartók, "The Relation of Folk Song to the Development of the Art Music of Our Time," in *Béla Bartók Essays*, ed. Benjamin Suchoff (London: Faber and Faber, 1976), p. 322.
10. Igor Stravinsky, *An Autobiography* (New York: Norton, 1962), p. 53.
11. Jean Cocteau, *A Call to Order*, trans. Rollo H. Myers (New York: Haskell House, 1974), p. 3.
12. Aaron Copland, *Copland, 1900–1942* (New York: St. Martin's Press, 1984), p. 71.

13. Darius Milhaud, *Notes Without Music* (New York: Knopf, 1953), p. 136.
14. Charles Ives, *Essays Before a Sonata*, ed. Howard Boatwright (New York: Norton, 1970), p. 51.
15. Ibid., pp. 77–78.
16. Aaron Copland, *Music and Imagination* (New York: Mentor, 1959), p. 111.
17. Aaron Copland, *What to Listen For in Music*, rev. ed. (New York: McGraw-Hill, 1957), p. 30.

# 12

## Music in the Age of Anxiety,
### 1945 to the Present

## Autumn Rhythm

*Jackson Pollock's painting Autumn Rhythm (1950) invites several
conflicting interpretations. At first sight, its immense size (more than
17 feet wide and 8 feet tall) and its confusing density of fractured
lines imply an overwhelming angst bordering on obsession and
violence. Further examination may lead us to question how the
painting was made, as though the painter's obvious engagement and
intensity in his work constitute its subject. Still further study may
suggest a whirling rhythm reminiscent of a complicated jazz
improvisation and even a subtle lyricism of colors rising from the
neutral background of the canvas. But whatever the interpretation,
the viewer will find it virtually impossible to be passive when
confronted with the painting's aggressive presence.*

Pollock studied painting with Thomas Hart Benton, a realist artist of muscular images of everyday American life. Pollock essayed a few pictures in Benton's manner, but he was quickly diverted by the more modernist directions of cubism and surrealism as well as by the works of Mexican mural painters, especially José Orozco and David Siqueiros. Pollock's pictures of the 1930s are linked by a tendency toward grotesque, tortured images of humankind, depicted in impenetrably dense, dark shapes or by savagely brilliant colors. In the 1940s, living in New York City, he made his paintings increasingly abstract, though no less aggressive and intense. He was identified with a group of New York painters called "abstract expressionists," although his highly idiosyncratic style is not easily referable to any larger movement.

In the late 1940s Pollock developed a distinctive way of making paintings. A canvas was placed on the floor and paint was flung, spattered, and dripped on it, such that chance and spontaneous actions acquired a hitherto unprecedented importance in the artist's technique. These "drip" paintings, of which **Autumn Rhythm** is an example, have several striking analogies with developments in music during the postwar decade. Their spontaneity reminds us not only of jazz improvisation, a type of music beloved by Pollock, but also of experimental compositions in which performers had to make crucial on-the-spot choices. Composers of the early 1950s, such as John Cage, also wrote pieces in which selections of pitch, rhythm, and *texture were governed by chance. In the early 1960s, European composers such as György Ligeti and Krzysztof Penderecki experimented with "textural" compositions that are directly analogous to Pollock's homogeneous, holistic conceptions. In textural music, elements such as lines, chords, and rhythms are subsumed into masses of sound, which themselves become the indivisible building blocks of a composition.*

## The Age of Anxiety (1945 to the Present)

**Composers**

| | 1900 | 1925 | 1950 | 1975 | 2000 |
|---|---|---|---|---|---|

Elliott Carter
John Cage
Conlon Nancarrow
Milton Babbitt
Gunther Schuller
Pierre Boulez
Morton Feldman
Karlheinz Stockhausen
Krzysztof Penderecki
Peter Maxwell Davies
Terry Riley
Steve Reich
Phillip Glass
Ellen Taaffe Zwilich
Charles Dodge
John Adams

**Artists**

Mark Rothko
Willem de Kooning
Arshile Gorky
Jackson Pollock

"To write poetry after Auschwitz is barbaric." These words of the philosopher and musician Theodor Adorno echoed throughout the artistic world after World War II. The unspeakable horrors of the war made conventional forms of artistic expression seem hollow, even fraudulent. And the aftermath of war, the threat of nuclear holocaust and a dehumanizing technological society cast a forbidding shadow over the traditional values of enjoyment and ennoblement that art had always promised. For the musician, the cheerful, simple, and tuneful music of prewar neoclassicism appeared a false reflection of life in the atomic age. A continuation of neoclassicism after 1945, especially for young composers in Europe and America, became unthinkable.

For three decades after the war, serious music underwent a remarkable transformation that pushed neoclassicism and traditionalism—hitherto the

**405**

dominant trends both in Europe and America—far from the center of attention. In their place arose an aggressive experimentalism that seemed determined to wipe the historical slate clean and to build an entirely new conception of music.

This penchant for experiment is mirrored in painting, sculpture, and architecture of the postwar decades. In New York in the mid-1940s there emerged a loosely defined school of painting whose intensely emotional and nonrepresentational style was termed *abstract expressionism*. As was the case in American avant-garde music of the same time, abstract expressionism was led by a group of European refugees, among them Arshile Gorky (1905–1948), Willem de Kooning (b. 1904), and Hans Hofmann (1880–1966), and American-born artists such as Jackson Pollock (1912–1956).

Pollock's pictures are among the most original of the entire movement. Works such as *Autumn Rhythm* (1950; page 402) use a "drip" technique in which paint is flung and spattered on a canvas. The viewer is first drawn into the sense of how the painting is made, toward the process more than toward a premeditated structure or form. Its boldness, extravagance, and larger-than-life size suggest an intensely emotional involvement on the part of the painter in the creation of his works.

The paintings of Mark Rothko (1903–1970), like those of Pollock, banish any suggestion of naturalistic subjects, but their greater contemplativeness does not deny an intense emotional expression. Rothko's *Four Darks on Red* (1958; page 407) is one of a series of large paintings often described as "color fields." In them, blocks of intense, expressive colors and rectangular shapes create an emotional language attuned to the postwar spirit.

## Revival of the Avant-Garde, 1945–1975

The Second World War was as shattering an experience for European and American musical culture as was the First. World War I brought an end to late romantic experiment in music and helped to install neoclassicism in its place. World War II had the opposite effect, as it marked a temporary end of traditionalism in music and the beginning of a period of innovation and experiment. The American musician Elliott Carter, himself a populist composer in the late 1930s, spoke about the effects of the war on his own artistic development:

> Before the end of the Second World War, it became clear to me,
> partly as a result of rereading Freud and others and thinking about

*A typical abstract expressionist painting of the 1950s: Mark Rothko's* **Four Darks on Red** *(1958).*

psychoanalysis, that we were living in a world where this physical and intellectual violence would always be a problem and that the whole conception of human nature underlying the neoclassic esthetic amounted to a sweeping under the rug of things that, it seemed to me, we had to deal with in a less oblique and resigned way.[1]

The three decades following the end of the war witnessed both remarkable innovations in music and a revival and extension of the modernistic tendencies of the early years of the century, especially atonality and 12-tone music associated with Schoenberg and his school. Music of this time also embraced newly developed electronic devices capable of sound production and manipulation and explored ways in which music could merge with theater.

One of the most important innovations of the postwar decade came from America. John Cage (1912–1992) wrote pieces in which his choice of musical elements was guided by chance, rather than by musical laws, taste, or intuition. **Chance** or **aleatoric music** was informed by Cage's contacts in New York with modern painting and with his study of Zen Buddhism. It was his way of bringing music closer to nature and of allowing sound per se to be the listener's sole point of focus. To accomplish these objectives, Cage felt compelled to suppress his own distinctive musical preferences.

Music in which compositional decisions were made by following chance procedures was said by Cage to be "indeterminate of composition." Later he expanded the element of chance by presenting the performer with geometric diagrams on which to improvise in any fitting way. The materials of such pieces consisted of the performers' playing, silences, or background noises. These musical works became solely occasions for an audience's contemplation of sounds, which contained or conveyed none of the composer's artistic ideas or intentions.

Other composers after World War II explored the possibility of new textures in music, alternatives, that is, to traditional interactions of lines and chords. The Hungarian György Ligeti and the Pole Krzysztof Penderecki found imaginative ways to deploy masses of sound, in which the basic audible element was not the individual interval, line, chord, or pulse but a conglomerate of such particles, which could then be shaped into an artistic form. The music of the French composer Pierre Boulez (b. 1925) contains virtuosic explosions of sound that banish conventional textures, although their high-speed delivery keeps them from merging into sound masses. Boulez, known equally for his work as an orchestral conductor, was highly critical of the conventional textures used in the atonal and 12-tone music of Schoenberg. He embraced the rational element of Schoenberg's 12-tone method but transformed it so that it would not lead him to music with traditional lines, chords, or rhythms.

## The Revival of Atonality and Serialism

During the war, atonal and 12-tone music were almost entirely banished from the European musical scene by the Nazis, who considered it the

**408**

height of "cultural Bolshevism" and artistic degeneracy. The leading representative of music of this type, Arnold Schoenberg, had fled to America in 1934, where he was accorded respect but where his music seemed out of keeping with the reigning populist spirit. Following the war, composers in both Europe and America began a restudy of his music and that of his student Webern, and extensions or imitations of their styles were common.

The 12-tone method contains a principle of order, called **serialism,** that guides a composer's choice of pitches as they are laid out in time through a piece. Composers after the war, including the American Milton Babbitt and Europeans Boulez and Karlheinz Stockhausen, extended serialism to rhythm, dynamics, and other elements. Most of the crucial choices in such works were guided by an elaborate rational apparatus. This ultrarationalism was an artistic response to the sense of chaos that the war had produced.

In terms of style, the recondite structural scaffolding supported music that was dense, abstract, and depersonalized. The familiar elements of traditional music had no further role, and in their place arose a maximal diversity of musical components. All 12 notes were used evenly, banishing any sense of keynote or traditional scale. All different registers, from very high to very low, came into play, dispelling the normal sense of melodic line. Regular beat, rhythm, and meter were eliminated by the vastly increased number of durational values, among which there existed no simple relationship.

The 12-tone music that Schoenberg himself composed after the war, to be sure, seemed almost conservative compared to the totally serialized pieces of his younger contemporaries, although nonetheless masterful in its construction and immediate in impact. *A Survivor from Warsaw* (1947) (Recording 12.1) is one of the most powerful works of his later years, showing that the complex innovations of atonality and 12-tone pitch selection could not just coexist with music of powerful emotionality but even enhance it. The work, in one movement, calls for narrator, orchestra, and male chorus. Schoenberg himself wrote the words, based on reports of the heroic uprising in the Jewish ghetto of Warsaw in February 1943 and its brutal aftermath in which survivors were systematically murdered. The narrator impersonates a survivor of the uprising who is first beaten unconscious, only later to witness the selection of fellow prisoners to be sent to the gas chambers. As a final, defiant gesture, the prisoners sing the traditional Hebrew hymn, "Shema Yisroel."

Schoenberg's music is in one continuous section, and it closely follows and expresses ideas contained in the words. It has no keynote, and all 12 notes of the octave are used freely. Schoenberg follows a form of 12-tone composition, although it is not strictly serial and not always intended to recirculate all 12 pitches.

**Arnold Schoenberg, *A Survivor from Warsaw***
Recording 12.1

**Introduction**    0.00    The trumpets begin with a reveille motive that recurs later to suggest the awakening of the prisoners. The music has a busy, nervous rhythm and texture that suggest the frightful events to come.

**Narration**    0.42    The anxiety of the music is enhanced by imitations of the shrill German of the Nazi sergeant. The reveille motive is much in evidence.

**Hymn**    5.26    The Hebrew text of the traditional "Shema" is quoted:

*Shema Yisroel, Adonoy elohenoo, Adonoy ehod. Veohavto es Adonoy eloheho, behol levoveho oovehol nafsheho, oovehol meodeho. Vehoyoo haddevoreem hoelleh, asher onohee metsavveho hayyom, al levoveho. Veshinnantom levoneho, vedibbarto bom, beshivteho beveteho, oovelehteho baddereh, ooveshohbeho oovekoomeho.*

Hear, O Israel, the Lord our God, The Lord is one. And you shall love the Lord your God with all your heart and soul and mind. And these words that I command you this day shall be upon your heart. And you will teach them to your children. And you shall speak of them when you sit down in your house and when you walk on your way and when you lie down and rise up.

Although Schoenberg uses this traditional Hebrew text, he writes a new, 12-tone melody for it, which is sung in unison by the male chorus. It begins

She-ma Yis-ro-el,    A-do-noy _ el-o-he-noo,    A-do-noy  e-hod.

## Electronic Music and Mixed Media

Composers during the postwar decade began to construct music whose sounds were generated, modified, or reproduced by electronic devices. Such works of **electronic music** stemmed directly from the postwar boom in technology and the readiness of avant-garde artists to plumb its communicative potential. Like all major innovations in the history of music, it had forerunners in earlier times. In the years around World War I, a group of modernistic Italian painters created a movement called *futurism*. Their main contribution was in the visual arts, but at least one of their members, the painter Luigi Russolo, also tried his hand at a type of music made from noises. Early-twentieth-century composers also experimented with electronic musical instruments. French musicians including Arthur Honegger and Olivier Messiaen wrote for an electronic keyboard instrument called the *ondes musicales* ("musical waves"), invented in 1928 by the Parisian musician Maurice Martenot. Other electronic sound makers such as the Trautonium and the Theremin were used experimentally by major European composers of the 1930s.

These tentative uses of electronic technology became much more important in the adventuresome atmosphere of the late 1940s and the 1950s. Beginning in 1948, a French radio technician, Pierre Schaeffer, experimented with recorded musical works made up of a collage of prerecorded sound effects. Since Schaeffer did not work "abstractly" with musical notation, he termed his studies **musique concrète.** He later achieved impressive results in collaboration with the composer Pierre Henry, and a studio in Paris for musique concrète was visited by major composers including Boulez, Stockhausen, and Edgard Varèse.

In 1951 at the German Radio in Cologne, a studio for electronic music was founded by a group of composers, technicians, and communications theorists. Their intentions differed from those of their French counterparts in that they began with sounds that were produced electronically, rather than with sounds recorded in a natural setting, as in musique concrète. Their efforts gained attention when they were joined by the young composer Karlheinz Stockhausen (b. 1928). His *Gesang der Jünglinge* (*Song of the Adolescents,* 1956), which combines the concrète sound of the human voice with electronic sounds, is one of the earliest masterpieces of the new medium.

In the 1960s and 1970s, electronic music was furthered by a series of technical innovations that made the work of the composer quicker and simpler. The most important of these new devices was the **synthesizer,** a term that refers to equipment, highly diverse in type, that speeds and integrates the production, manipulation, and reconstitution of electronic musical sounds.

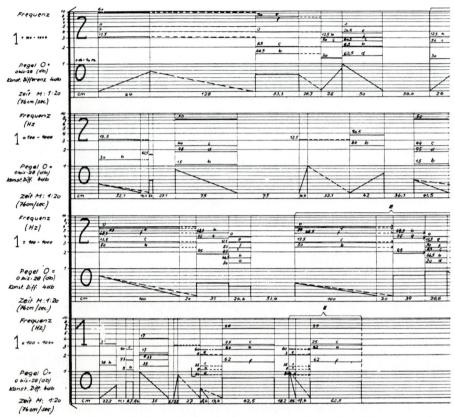

*Although a composer of electronic music does not usually work with a score, the German Karlheinz Stockhausen used this diagram to construct his early electronic composition **Elektronische Studie I** (1953). The first five seconds of the piece are represented.*

During this same period, electronic compositions produced solely on tape declined in importance, as composers sought ways in which live performances could be joined with the new realms of sound and expression provided by electronic devices. Live performance coordinated with tape was used by composers including Mario Davidovsky and Jacob Druckman. Other musicians experimented with live performances in which the sounds of the performers were transformed electronically on the spot. Innovations of this sort had a great impact on rock music, which continues to exploit the electronic experiments of serious composers of the 1950s and 1960s.

Since the mid-1970s, electronic music has battled for its identity against two powerful opposing forces: a general trend away from experimentation in serious music and the relentless assimilation of electronic musical technology by popular music. A distinctive style of serious electronic music of this more recent period has been produced by the use of computer programs capable of speech synthesis. Charles Dodge's *Speech Songs* (1973) is an example of the computerized reassembly of speech in songlike form. The first song, "When I Am With You" (Recording 12.2), manipulates its poem in a witty manner, interlacing it with subtle gestures from serious music, notably a musical motive constructed from the letters of the name Bach, which in German is equivalent to the notes B♭, A, C, and B:

Bb    A    C    B (=H)

The humor underlying Dodge's *Speech Songs* became common in music of the postwar period, arising almost spontaneously as a leavening ingredient in an otherwise hyperserious musical culture. Experiment in some musical circles became so intense that it dissolved by itself into a mad, absurd theater of mixed media, having little if anything to do with serious music of even the recent past. The influence of John Cage was basic to this development. Increasingly in his aleatoric works of the 1950s and 1960s, incongruous visual or absurdly theatrical images accompany his meditations on sound.

In the early 1960s, a group of artists and musicians sponsored such "happenings" in New York under the aegis of a group called Fluxus. A sample Fluxus work is La Monte Young's "Piano Piece for Terry Riley, No. 1," which is contained in these instructions:

> Push the piano up to a wall and put the flat side flush against it. Then continue pushing into the wall. Push as hard as you can. If the piano goes through the wall, keep pushing in the same direction regardless of new obstacles and continue to push as hard as you can whether the piano is stopped against an obstacle or moving. The piece is over when you are too exhausted to push any longer.[2]

"Danger music" was another specialty of Fluxus. In works of this type, some action is carried out that puts the performers or the audience in peril. La Monte Young's "Composition 1960, No. 2" is exemplary:

> Build a fire in front of the audience. Preferably, use wood, although other combustibles may be used as necessary for starting the fire or controlling the kind of smoke. The fire may be of any size, but it should not be the kind which is associated with another object, such as a candle or a cigarette lighter. The lights may be turned out. . . . [3]

The spirit of Fluxus is present in mixed-media compositions of Peter Maxwell Davies (b. 1934), although without the element of absurdity associated with Cage and with Fluxus. Born and educated in Manchester, England, Davies continued his musical studies in Italy and America. In 1967, he organized a group called the Pierrot Players, devoted to the performance of modern music. His own music, which touches on all major vocal and instrumental genres, is eclectic, using preexistent music in various ways and assimilating many different styles.

His most celebrated work is *Eight Songs for a Mad King* (1969), which was composed for his ensemble. Here Davies sets to music texts written by Randolph Stow that portray the insanity of King George III (1738–1820), in part drawn from the king's own recorded statements. These words are sung and declaimed by an actor impersonating the monarch, accompanied by an orchestra of woodwinds, strings, percussion, and piano. Some of these players sit in bird cages, acting out the part of birds who were given to the deranged king, which he tried to teach to sing.

---

*Listening Guide*

**Peter Maxwell Davies, *Eight Songs for a Mad King*, No. 7, "Country Dance (Scotch Bonnett)"**
Recording 12.3

| | | |
|---|---|---|
| **Part 1** | 0.00 | The king, a great advocate of the music of Handel, begins by singing a madcap version of "Comfort Ye, My People," from *Messiah,* transformed into a cheap cocktail song. |
| **Part 2** | 1.09 | To the music of a fox-trot, the king exhorts the people of Windsor to merrymaking. |
| **Part 3** | 1.40 | His high spirits suddenly turn dark as he begins to rail on the sinfulness of the world. The music becomes grotesque. He takes the violin from one of the orchestra members and hysterically breaks it to pieces, symbolic of his self-destruction. |
| **Part 4** | 3.26 | In a ludicrous recitative, the king admits to his own contemplation of evil but vows to rule "with a rod of iron." A reference to Handel leads to a distorted postlude. |

---

The seventh song, "Country Dance (Scotch Bonnett)" (Recording 12.3), shows the mixture of styles that characterizes the entire work. Popular music mixes with quotations from Handel's *Messiah* and with raucous atonality, all projecting the tortuous changes in mood of the unfortunate king.

## Music in America

Following World War II, American composers became, in general, much more prominent in international circles of modern music and more inclined to be leaders in the presentation of new styles than they had been at any earlier time. American musical culture was greatly stimulated by the arrival during the war of émigré musicians from Europe, including Arnold Schoenberg, Igor Stravinsky, and Paul Hindemith. Some of the émigrés, among them Ernst Toch, Dimitri Tiomkin, and Ingolf Dahl, found a challenging new outlet for their work in the American film industry. Others, such as Hindemith and Schoenberg, became university teachers and through this forum exerted an influence on the next generation of native-born composers. Hindemith's teaching at Yale University was especially important, as he counted among his students Mel Powell, Yehudi Wyner, and Lukas Foss. Schoenberg, who taught primarily at the University of California in Los Angeles, had among his American students Leonard Stein, Dika Newlin, and Gerald Strang. Stravinsky also lived in southern California, although he had little personal contact with Schoenberg. Stravinsky did not teach, but the brightness and originality of his music drew to him an informal circle of younger composers including Irving Fine and Ingolf Dahl.

As was the case in Europe, the postwar decade in America witnessed the end of dominance of neoclassical or traditional composition and its replacement at center stage by an intense and often experimental modernism. So great was the movement toward atonality, serialism, and other modernistic idioms that even the leaders of prewar neoclassicism now began to write chromatic, dissonant, and keyless music. The most startling convert was Stravinsky. After his Mozartean opera *The Rake's Progress* (1951), Stravinsky began to imitate the works of Webern in their spare, disjunct textures, abstract content, and chromatic, dissonant harmonies. Even Paul Hindemith, who had dismissed the work of Schoenberg and the postwar serialists as music by "imps and snobs," began to write angular, chromatic, and bitingly dissonant music, as in his *Mass* (1963). Aaron Copland, America's greatest composer in the populist vein of the prewar decades, turned to a form of 12-tone composition in his Piano Fantasy, Piano Quartet, and tone poem *Connotations*.

**415**

Experiment of a more radical sort was carried out by John Cage, in his application of chance and improvisation to music. Cage's works were immensely influential on European composers. Boulez, Stockhausen, and the Polish composer Witold Lutosławski used aspects of chance (which they were inclined to called "aleatory") to give their music a lively unpredictability. In America, Cage's experiments with indeterminacy were extended by Earle Brown, Christian Wolff, and Morton Feldman. Feldman (1926–1987) developed Cage's interests in pure sound in a more conventional direction. His works tend to be quiet, extremely extended in length, and intuitively constructed, aiming at a blended and slowly evolving wash of sound.

*The composer John Cage.*

The experimental and distinctively non-European spirit of music in the United States following World War II is seen especially clearly in works by Elliott Carter (b. 1908), Milton Babbitt (b. 1916), and George Crumb (b. 1929). Carter's early career was typical of the American populist composer of the interwar period. He pursued his musical education in Paris under Nadia Boulanger, and his early music, such as *Three Poems by Robert Frost* (1942), is in a traditional, almost folklike manner. In the 1950s, his style changed radically in a series of chamber and orchestral works, including the first of four string quartets and Variations for Orchestra. In these pieces, the listener is confronted by an immense complication of materials, especially in the rhythmic dimension. The music is divided into several layers, each with its own ever-changing beat. His works do not contain normal melodic statements and developments, and they express dramatic ideas in a highly recondite fashion.

Milton Babbitt, long a professor at Princeton University, exerted his influence as a music theoretician and analyst as well as a composer. He used mathematical set theory to explore the potential of the 12-tone method of composition devised by Schoenberg, and he then applied mathematical ideas to govern rigorously all or most elements of a composition. His music, like Carter's, suggests a profound complication and abstraction that makes it accessible to relatively few listeners. In his article "Who Cares if You Listen?" (a title that he subsequently disclaimed), Babbitt compares the comprehension of his brand of modern music to the comprehension of modern science:

**416**

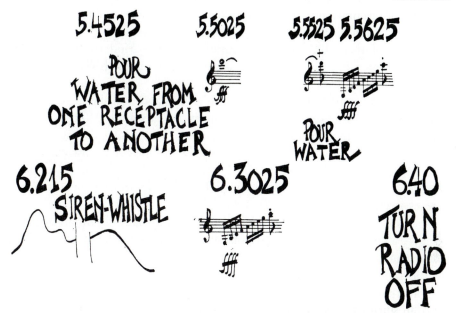

*Cage: Water Music*

**John Cage pioneered the use of "graphic" scores, which were guides for performers that did not employ normal musical notation. An example is this excerpt from his Water Music (1952). In this largely improvised piece, a performer not only plays on the piano but also whistles, pours water, and manipulates a radio.**

> The time has passed when the normally well-educated man without special preparation could understand the most advanced work in, for example, mathematics, philosophy, and physics. Advanced music, to the extent that it reflects the knowledge and originality of the informed composer, scarcely can be expected to appear more intelligible than these arts and sciences.[4]

George Crumb, since 1965 a professor at the University of Pennsylvania, has continued the exploration of pure sound that underlies so much of the modernist movement in American music. Most of his pieces are for heterogeneous ensembles, sometimes using live electronic enhancement. Many are theatrical in their application of dance and costume, and they often convey a sense of ritual. Crumb's innovative treatment of the voice is especially noteworthy, and his music often takes on elaborate levels of meaning by its use of quotations of earlier music and its evocation of exotic cultures.

The power of jazz and other modes of popular music were continuously felt by American composers, even by those of an experimental and modernistic orientation. Gunther Schuller (b. 1925) expanded his work as a composer of 12-tone music by linking such serious idioms with the emerging "cool" jazz of the 1950s. In collaboration with the Modern Jazz Quartet, Schuller composed pieces that he called *third stream*, in which serialized music alternates with jazz.

The music of Conlon Nancarrow (b. 1912) accomplishes a remarkable conjunction of jazz and experimental applications of sound. After his participation with the Abraham Lincoln Brigade in the Spanish Civil War, Nancarrow emigrated to Mexico. Out of necessity, he composed almost exclusively in the medium of player piano, tediously transferring his music to paper piano rolls. Most of these "studies" use jazz rhythms, but some are provocative and abstract portraits in sound.

His "Study 3a" (Recording 12.4) uses the jazz idiom of **boogie-woogie**, a style of piano music popular in America in the late 1930s and the 1940s. The tempo of such pieces is fast, with a driving, repetitive bass line, and they consist formally of continuous variations on a 12-measure "blues" harmonic pattern (see Chapter 13 for a further discussion of blues). Nancarrow reproduces the basic elements of boogie-woogie but compounds them into a fantasy of different metric and temporal layers and projects them at a much higher speed than could be played by any pianist. His music welds the spirit of jazz to the richness and inventiveness of experimental music in its great complication and intricacy.

## Return to the Known: Music from 1975 to the Present

The sorting out of emerging trends in any contemporary art is perilous and uncertain. Before music has stood the test of time, many different and conflicting directions appear to compete with one another. But it is now tentatively clear that during the 1970s a major change in musical taste was felt. In the 30 years following the end of World War II, modernism had become a doctrinaire movement that ruled the international musical scene. Its musical by-products were abstract, difficult, innovative, rationalistic, and sometimes absurd. But in the 1970s these qualities began to weaken in favor of music of wider appeal and greater familiarity of means. Critics increasingly interpreted the modernism of the postwar years as producing "academic" music, a pejorative epithet suggesting excessive complexity and dryness and appeal only in a scholarly setting.

As was the case in music of the late romantic period, the era of postwar modernism contained the seeds of its own destruction. Its continual striving for innovation and novelty after three decades reached a practical limit. To many observers, everything new had been tried, and the pendulum began, almost by itself, to swing back in the direction of traditional values. Furthermore, the anxieties that fueled postwar music had by the mid-1970s in part abated, suggesting to both composers and audiences that doctrinaire modernism was no longer so compellingly needed.

What were the features of the new taste of the 1970s and 1980s? It valued music that was less complicated and abstract, more traditional in materials, and more customary in the demands that it made on the listener. It insisted on the presence of the known: jazz or popular idioms, assimilations of foregoing styles such as romanticism, quotations of familiar music, or the copying of the style of some particular earlier composer.

The change of style of the mid-1970s can rightly be compared to that of the decade following World War I. At both times, a complex and elitist art was set aside in favor of music made in a traditional manner that would appeal to a larger audience. Both changes of direction were rebellions against an immediate artistic past and a reaching back to earlier and more appealing types of music.

## Minimalism

The American minimalist movement shows clearly how experiment of the 1960s was transformed into populism in the 1970s. **Minimalism** emerged as a distinct movement in the 1960s, based on music composed by four Americans: Terry Riley, Philip Glass, La Monte Young, and Steve Reich. At first it was a highly experimental idiom, somewhat akin to music heard in the Fluxus happenings, in which several of the minimalists were active. A minimalist work is one in which an entire piece (often of great length) is generated by repetition of brief musical figures (a musical device called **ostinato**). These recurrent motives often contain a clear and regular pulse and are themselves constructed on familiar scales or harmonic progressions. Slight and gradual changes normally occur, producing a sense of evolution amid an otherwise static and repetitive continuum.

Terry Riley's *In C* (1964) was one of the earliest important minimalist works. It is based on 53 short melodic motives, played by any group of instruments. All players begin with the first motive, which they repeat over and over in a strict tempo established by a pianist, who strikes the note C repeatedly to create a beat. Gradually, all players move on to the second motive, and so forth, bringing the piece to an end after all 53 figures have been covered. An element of Cage-like chance and improvisation is present in the choice of medium and in the lack of strict coordination as the players move from motive to motive. The great duration of the work and its calculated monotony reinforce the sense of an experimental, modernistic idiom.

Steve Reich's earliest minimalist pieces were constructed in the medium of musique concrète. Working in an electronic music studio in San Francisco in the mid-1960s, Reich recorded interesting speakers and experimented with reconstituting their words in musical form by placing a phrase of speech on a tape loop. His *Come Out* (1965) uses only a single phrase spoken by a youth in Harlem, "Come out to show them," which is repeated over and over in the two channels of a stereo tape recorder. Gradually, the two channels come out of phase, as one moves very slowly ahead of the other. The texture is later enhanced by overdubbing, and the listener slowly loses track of the words and perceives instead a gradually changing rhythmic pattern created by the interaction of the channels. Like much early minimalist music, Reich's early works are "process" pieces: The entire composition is created by a plan and a process that the composer determines in advance and then sets in motion. It is strikingly modernistic, in that it is made up of speech sounds rather than strictly musical ones, and it lacks any semblance of orthodox melody or form.

At about the same time as Reich composed *Come Out,* Philip Glass (b. 1937) began writing repetitive, minimalistic works. Glass had a traditional musical education, and like most young composers of the 1950s and 1960s, he wrote 12-tone works. He continued his education with Nadia Boulanger in Paris, where he developed a distaste for the doctrinaire quality of his own idiom. After encountering music of the Indian virtuoso Ravi Shankar, he began to write works of an entirely original sort. These were based on brief motivic patterns and spun out by continuous repetition with gradual change.

Living in New York after his return from France, Glass organized his own performing ensemble, consisting of amplified electric keyboards and woodwinds. His group toured abroad and in America, and he quickly developed an enthusiastic following outside of the musical establishment.

*Einstein on the Beach* is a work of musical theater that in 1976 brought Glass to the attention of traditional musical audiences. It was written in collaboration with the dramatist Robert Wilson. Wilson specialized in extremely lengthy theatrical portraits of famous people (including Stalin, Queen Victoria, and Frederick the Great). These are presented without narrative but instead by a succession of loosely related images, speeches, and dances. *Einstein* consists of recurrent images of a train, a trial, and a field. These are placed into nine scenes in four acts, which are framed and connected by interludes called "knee plays." Although a violinist impersonating Albert Ein-

*Early American minimalist composers had much in common with avant-garde artists of the same period. Bridget Riley's* Disturbance (1964) *is strikingly similar to a process piece by Steve Reich. In both, initial decisions give rise to automated processes that generate the form of an entire artwork.*

stein stands to the side of the stage, the scenery, dialogue, and music express no specific story about the great physicist or about any other subject. Their meaning must be supplied instead by the listener.

The music, which Glass considers postminimalist, is formed primarily by repetition and gradual change. Its scalar and harmonic bases are drawn from traditional music, and it has a clear pulse. The instrumental music of *Einstein* is provided by Glass's ensemble of loudly amplified keyboards and woodwinds, to which a chorus is occasionally added.

The second scene of Act 1 is typical of the strict organization that prevails throughout the music. Visually, this scene depicts a trial. Two judges read incongruous texts while other actors impersonate figures in a court-room. The violinist impersonating Einstein sits between the orchestra and the actors. The music of the scene is divided into two subsections, the first following a brief introduction, the second followed by a brief postlude. The second of the two subsections (Recording 12.5) introduces a musical theme that recurs in the later trial scenes (Act 3, Scene 1, and Act 4, Scene 2):

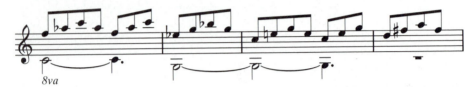

The short figure is repeated constantly by the electric organ, but rarely are the repetitions exact. The phrase is instead expanded and contracted by the addition or subtraction of one or a few notes. A clear and regular pulse is always present, although the metric organization changes as notes are added and removed. The notes themselves form familiar chords. Above this music a judge reads a text dealing with the ladies of Paris. It is charmingly witty, but in no way does it deal with the content of the music or with Einstein, who remains only one of many images in the work.

Strict minimalism did not endure beyond the mid-1970s, when it was replaced by a more conventional style that maintained, sometimes in passing, aspects of minimalistic repetitiveness, clear pulse, and simple motives and harmonies. The element of experiment that fueled the early minimalist move-ment was banished, and its vestiges were reworked in music of broad appeal, which in some instances became overtly popular. Glass's album of popular songs, *Songs for Liquid Days,* is an example of this transition from an experi-mental style to a popular one. Terry Riley's music of the 1970s, such as his "Rainbow in Curved Air," comes to resemble jazz improvisations, enhanced by electronic manipulations and by minimalistic ostinatos.

The idiom of the minimalists of the 1960s had an immense interna-tional impact, both on avant-garde rock and on serious music. The American composer John Adams (b. 1947) was one of many early followers. In the 1970s he wrote minimalistic pieces for piano or chamber ensembles. In the 1980s, appointed adviser on new music by the San Francisco Symphony, he turned to large works for orchestra, sometimes with chorus, as in his *Harmo-nium.* Minimalist repetition is still present in these works, but in other ways they imitate the romantic orchestral idiom. The style of the Finnish romantic composer Jean Sibelius is especially prominent. In 1987, Adams completed the opera *Nixon in China,* dealing with Richard Nixon's historic visit to Peking in 1972. The style of Glass from *Einstein* is clearly in the background of this skillful and witty work, but the experimentalism that informed the original minimalist movement is almost entirely absent.

## Neoromanticism

The neoclassical movement of the 1920s in general avoided stylistic references to the romantic period. It was, after all, largely motivated by a rejection of romantic taste. But in the 1970s and 1980s, romantic music—especially late romantic music—proved to be a fertile source of ideas that could be adapted to new modes of composition. Beginning in the 1960s with Leonard Bernstein's performances of the Mahler symphonies with the New York Philharmonic Orchestra, interest revived in Mahler and other less-known composers, such as Alexander Zemlinsky (1871–1942). Their idiom was resuscitated in a movement that can be called **neoromanticism.**

One of the first major composers to embrace romanticism was the American George Rochberg (b. 1918). Rochberg's early music conformed to the modernistic spirit of the postwar period, but by the 1970s he found such music limited in expressive means. "There can be no justification for music," he wrote, "if it does not convey eloquently and elegantly the passions of the human heart." These were the qualities that he found missing in the modernism of his day. To recapture them, he proposed a return to the same values and materials used by the great masters of the past, especially those of the romantic period:

> The renewal of music depends on the renewal of the art of composition itself. If we value Wagner and Brahms for the power of their harmony, why, then, have we given up harmony? If we value Mozart and Chopin for the elegance of their melodies, why, then, have we given up the melodic line?[5]

Rochberg's solution was to write music that overtly imitated several different models from the past and thus to enrich the expressive quality that he sought in music in general. He had a particular affinity for romantic composers, such as Brahms, Wagner, and Mahler.

A single-minded revival of romantic styles was made by the American composer David Del Tredici (b. 1937). Predictably, his early music consisted of abstract 12-tone studies. But from 1968 his imagination was fired by the writings of Lewis Carroll, and he devoted himself to a series of works, increasingly in the late romantic style, that dealt with Carroll's children's tales. He adopts a technique of thematic recurrence reminiscent of the music of Liszt, and his compositions contain autobiographical allusions in the manner of Schumann. The ecstatic quality of his music, such as in the Pulitzer Prize winner *In Memory of a Summer Day* (1980), reflects similar qualities in the Mahler symphonies.

Music of the Polish composer Krzysztof Penderecki (b. 1933) underwent a similar transformation to that of Rochberg and Del Tredici. Penderecki was part of a remarkable flowering of musical modernism in Poland in the early 1960s. He immigrated to the West in 1966 and has subsequently taught in both Europe and America.

Penderecki's early music was never in the doctrinaire language of Webernesque serialism. Around 1960 he essayed a style using complex textures or masses of sound as the basic compositional elements. These were deployed in works for large orchestral or vocal media, which, like his *Threnody for Victims of Hiroshima* (1960), address monumental themes. In 1965, with his *St. Luke Passion,* his music became highly eclectic, touching on a number of styles including atonality and romanticism.

By the 1980s he had adopted a unified style based on romantic models. His *Lacrimosa* (1980) is an example. This work was commissioned by Lech Walensa and the Solidarity labor movement of Poland as a memorial for workers killed during a factory strike. It was later incorporated into Penderecki's *Polish Requiem.* Its words, from the Roman Catholic funeral Mass, lament the dead, promise retribution, and pray for eternal peace. Works such as the *Lacrimosa* will no doubt be viewed in the future as artistic precursors of the movement of political liberation in eastern Europe, much as Verdi's operas prefigure the unification of Italy in the nineteenth century.

The *Lacrimosa* (Recording 12.6) is for soprano, chorus, and orchestra; it is in one concise movement in a freely through-composed form. It is romantic in its slow and even ponderous sense of motion (a quality that most of Penderecki's music shares), its darkness of orchestration and harmony, and its rich and sometimes contrapuntal texture. The large orchestra is synonymous with that of the late nineteenth century, and, most romantic of all, the music is intensely expressive of the sentiments contained in the words.

A central melodic motive recurs throughout, in the manner of a Wagnerian leitmotif, signifying the "weeping" suggested by the word *lacrimosa*. In a romantic manner, this motive contains an expressive leap to a tone (D♭) just above the note contained in the underlying harmony (C). After holding out this neighbor tone, it falls back to the chordal tone. The work is not based on a traditional use of key, although keynotes are heard in local contexts.

## Krzysztof Penderecki, *Lacrimosa*, from the *Polish Requiem*
Recording 12.6

| | |
|---|---|
| *Lacrimosa dies illa, qua resurget ex favilla judicandus homo reus.* | That day is one of weeping, on which the guilty one will rise again from the ashes, to be judged. |
| *Huic ergo parce Deus, pie Jesu Domine, dona eis requiem.* | Therefore spare him, O God, merciful Lord Jesus, give them rest. |

**Introduction**  0.00  The orchestra begins with slow, ponderous rhythms, minor mode based on the keynote F, and statements of the central motive:

**Verse 1**  0.37  The soprano solo and chorus reiterate variants of the basic motive as the keynote progressively changes.

**Verse 2**  2.05  The music moves to a climax in a brief orchestral interlude, settling in the key of F♯ major at the conclusion.

## *A New Orthodoxy in Modern Music*

The serious music that was most often performed in America in the 1980s traveled in the middle of the road. It partook of some elements of the modernist revolution of the early twentieth century and its recrudescence in the decades following World War II. These include a liberated treatment of dissonance, a freeing of tonality, and an increased reliance on the expressive capacity of sound. But in most ways it was traditional: It sought to be expressive, it had conventional lengths and pacing, it used familiar textures made from lines and chords, it featured melody above other elements, and it avoided disturbing subjects or unexpected effects. It assiduously avoided any qualities that might be dubbed "academic" or any extravagantly experimental

## *Music Today*

### The Kronos Quartet

The genre of the string quartet has figured strongly in twentieth-century composition. After losing favor among the romantic composers, the quartet returned to center stage in the modern period, resuming the importance it had enjoyed in the classical era. The leanness of sound, clarity of line, and a suggestion of seriousness and rigor all made the string quartet an appealing medium for the modern musician.

But who will play the daunting, complex quartets of the twentieth century? The technical and physical demands of this music regularly exceed the patience and taste of many professional ensembles attuned more to the classical symmetry of Haydn and Mozart. Schoenberg's 4 quartets, Bartók's 6, and Carter's 4 are some of the most difficult ensemble music ever written, not to mention Dmitri Shostakovich's 15 quartets, Milhaud's 18, and Hindemith's 6!

ideas such as chance, theater, or ultrarationalism. It was very often eclectic, reminding us of one or more earlier styles or even specific earlier works or composers. It was music that, at its best, shows the keen musical ear and masterful training of its composer. It was what one might term "politely modern" music.

Compositions by the Americans John Adams, John Harbison, Joseph Schwantner, and Ellen Taaffe Zwilich (b. 1939) represent this style at its best. Zwilich began her musical career as a professional violinist, and her practical experience as an orchestral player is evident in her skillful use of the orchestra. She studied composition with Elliott Carter and Roger Sessions, and she holds a doctorate from the Juilliard School.

The gulf that separated the patent greatness and importance of this modern literature and the inclinations and technical limitations of many quartets gave rise early in the century to a new phenomenon: the professional string quartet that specialized in contemporary music. One of the earliest such ensembles was founded by four young Hungarian musicians in 1909, led by Imre Waldbauer, expressly to devote themselves to the noble complication of Bartók's early quartets. This ensemble remained together until the end of World War II.

In 1922 the composer Paul Hindemith, also a virtuoso player of viola, founded the Amar Quartet, which was devoted to modern chamber music and first performed many of Hindemith's own works. In the same year, the young Viennese violinist Rudolf Kolisch founded a quartet that also specialized in modern music, giving first performances of the quartets of Arnold Schoenberg (Kolisch's teacher and later his brother-in-law). Following World War II, several important quartets specializing in modern music appeared, including the Concord Quartet, known for its recordings of the music of George Rochberg, and the Composers Quartet, which first unraveled the complexities of quartets by Carter.

In 1973 there appeared an ensemble destined to be the most important modern music quartet of the day: the Kronos Quartet. Its members, David Harrington, John Sherba, Hank Dutt, and Joan Jeanrenaud, all lived in San Francisco. All were classically trained and shared an intense interest in contemporary music and a belief in the importance of the quartet medium to new music of any type. Their public image is nothing like the quartet heretofore. They wear unconventional dress and project an appearance with more than a passing resemblance to punk rockers.

Their music is as unorthodox as their dress. Their concerts almost invariably include a significant work from early in the century, and then they move on to what they do best—playing new music, much of which they have commissioned, in a panoply of different styles. They are equally partial to jazz, multimedia effects, and electronic enhancement, as well as to music with more traditional values. Their bravura conviction in their work, their utter lack of elitism, and their rejection of the doctrinaire in modern music have made the Kronos Quartet one of the most exciting forces in contemporary music.

The excellence of her music was recognized in 1983, when she was awarded the Pulitzer Prize, given for her First Symphony (1982). She was the first female composer to receive this prestigious award. Her music is composed for conventional media and in familiar genres such as the symphony, song, and string quartet. Her tone poem *Celebration* (1984; Recording 12.7) was commissioned by the Indianapolis Symphony to inaugurate a new concert hall. It is a work of about eight minutes in length, in one movement. It has great exuberance and color, and it makes the orchestra sound especially attractive. Its materials are conventional. It has a strict rhythmic pulse, basically homophonic texture, clearly reiterated motives, and predominantly consonant harmonies. The form of the work is arch-shaped. The initial motives are developed in the introspective middle parts and recapitulated briefly near the end. The principal motive is heard at the beginning in the trumpets and is then never long absent from the piece.

## TOPICS FOR DISCUSSION AND WRITING

**1.** In 1952, only months after the death of Schoenberg, Pierre Boulez wrote a polemic titled "Schoenberg Is Dead." He was critical of a traditional element that he found in Schoenberg's 12-tone music. Based on your study of Schoenberg's *Survivor from Warsaw,* discuss the pros and cons of Boulez's position. What aspects of Schoenberg's work are, in fact, traditional to music of the nineteenth century and before? What elements are decidedly new?

**2.** Regarding the narrative content of his theater piece *Einstein on the Beach,* the composer Philip Glass has written:

> Fundamental to our approach was the assumption that the audience itself completed the work. In the case of *Einstein on the Beach,* the "story" was supplied by the imaginations of the audience, and there was no way for us to predict, even if we had wanted to, what the "story" might be for any particular person.[6]

Discuss the relation of Act 1, Scene 2, of Glass's *Einstein on the Beach* to some logical narrative, whether about the career of Einstein or some other focal idea. Has Glass succeeded in provoking you to complete the story? How so or why not?

**3.** Draw a diagram or picture that shows the progressive adding of layers of distinct metric structure in Nancarrow's "Study 3a." How are the layers distinguished from one another?

**4.** Argue both sides of this assertion: Penderecki's *Lacrimosa* is more a romantic piece than a modern one. Observe and explain the features of this work that suggest nineteenth-century music and those that suggest the twentieth century.

## ADDITIONAL LISTENING

### Boulez

*Le marteau sans maître (The Hammer Without Master).* For voice and chamber ensemble. The music has the freedom and virtuosic brilliance that are characteristic of Boulez.

### Cage

*Sonatas and Interludes for Prepared Piano.* A piano is "prepared" when mutes are inserted into its strings, giving it the quality of a percussion ensemble.

## Crumb

*Ancient Voices of Children*. A virtuosic study for soprano and chamber ensemble, setting surrealistic poetry by Federico García Lorca.

## Del Tredici

*In Memory of a Summer Day*. Freely based on Lewis Carroll's *Alice* tales and clearly in the romantic manner.

## Glass

*Glassworks*. An album of Glass's music performed by his own ensemble.

## Reich

*Come Out*. A phase process piece of musique concrète.

*Tehillim*. A setting of Hebrew psalms for voices and orchestra, postminimalist in its mixture of styles.

## Riley

*In C*. A seminal work in the history of minimalism.

*Salome Dances for Peace*. For string quartet.

## Schoenberg

*Ode to Napoleon Buonaparte*. A companion piece to *A Survivor from Warsaw,* for narrator, string quartet, and piano. The poem is by Lord Byron.

## Stockhausen

*Gesang der Jünglinge*. An early electronic work for boy soprano and electronic sounds.

## BIBLIOGRAPHY

### General Works on Music Since 1945

Brindle, Reginald Smith. *The New Music: The Avant-Garde Since 1945*. Second edition. New York: Oxford University Press, 1987.

Griffiths, Paul. *A Guide to Electronic Music*. New York: Thames & Hudson, 1979.

———. *Modern Music: The Avant Garde Since 1945*. New York: Braziller, 1981.

Nyman, Michael. *Experimental Music: Cage and Beyond*. New York: Schirmer Books, 1974.

Poggioli, Renato. *The Theory of the Avant-Garde*. Translated by Gerald Fitzgerald. Cambridge, Mass.: Harvard University Press, 1968.

Rockwell, John. *All-American Music: Composition in the Late Twentieth Century*. New York: Vintage Books, 1983.

Schwartz, Elliott. *Electronic Music: A Listener's Guide*. New York: Praeger, 1973.

**Studies of Composers Mentioned in This Chapter**

Cage, John. *Silence*. Middletown, Conn.: Wesleyan University Press, 1961. A collection of essays.

Carter, Elliott. *The Writings of Elliott Carter*. Edited by Else Stone and Kurt Stone. Bloomington: Indiana University Press, 1977.

Edwards, Allen. *Flawed Words and Stubborn Sounds: A Conversation with Elliott Carter*. New York: Norton, 1971.

Glass, Philip. *Music by Philip Glass*. New York: HarperCollins, 1987.

Griffiths, Paul. *Boulez*. Oxford Studies of Composers, volume 16. London: Oxford University Press, 1978.

———. *Cage*. Oxford Studies of Composers, volume 18. London: Oxford University Press, 1981.

———. *Peter Maxwell Davies*. London: Robson Books, 1981.

Maconie, Robin. *The Works of Karlheinz Stockhausen*. London: Oxford University Press, 1976.

Peyser, Joan. *Boulez: Composer, Conductor, Enigma*. New York: Schirmer Books, 1976.

Reich, Steve. *Writings About Music*. New York: New York University Press, 1974.

Rochberg, George. *The Aesthetics of Survival: A Composer's View of Twentieth-Century Music*. Ann Arbor: University of Michigan Press, 1984.

Schiff, David. *The Music of Elliott Carter*. New York: Da Capo Press, 1983. A technical and analytical discussion.

Schoenberg, Arnold. See the bibliography for Chapter 11.

# NOTES

**1.** Elliott Carter, in Allen Edwards, *Flawed Words and Stubborn Sounds* (New York: Norton, 1971), p. 61.

**2.** La Monte Young, in Michael Nyman, *Experimental Music: Cage and Beyond* (New York: Schirmer Books, 1974), p. 70.

**3.** Ibid.

**4.** Milton Babbitt, "Who Cares if You Listen?" *High Fidelity,* 8 (Feb. 1958), p. 40.

**5.** George Rochberg, "Reflections on the Renewal of Music," in *The Aesthetics of Survival* (Ann Arbor: University of Michigan Press, 1984), p. 237.

**6.** Philip Glass, *Music by Philip Glass* (New York: HarperCollins, 1987), p. 35.

# Movement IV

# Jazz and Non-Western Music

In the final two chapters, we turn our attention from artistic music in the European tradition to explore American jazz and selected non-Western musical cultures. Jazz has proved to be the most important type of popular music throughout the world in the twentieth century. It also possesses the decidedly "classical" features of stylistic growth, sophistication, and longevity. Jazz and classical music throughout this century have mutually influenced each other. Following World War I, as European and American composers first became generally aware of jazz, they often adopted its melodic spontaneity and rhythmic energy into new serious works, and following World War II, avant-garde jazz performers began to explore the extravagant innovations that were then dominating the world of classical music.

A knowledge of music in major non-Western cultures has in the twentieth century become increasingly indispensable to musicians and to lovers of music. Great treasures of music are to be found in virtually all regions of the world. Classical works that rest on ancient practices and elaborate aesthetic ideas are as much a part of Eastern culture as they are Western. Folk music and vigorous types of popular music exist everywhere, and they will give us new insights into the lives of people throughout the world.

As we look forward to the beginning of the twenty-first century, we can see that all of the musical currents encountered in this book are merging into a multifaceted cultural stream. Early music is no longer ignored or viewed as an academic speciality. It is recognized instead for its relevance to our modern musical enjoyment. Jazz cannot now be confined solely to the cultural milieu of African-Americans; it has become an important feature of the mainstream of music. And as the world draws closer together, the musical traditions of the entire world seem poised to enter decisively into our musical life.

# 13

---

## Jazz

---

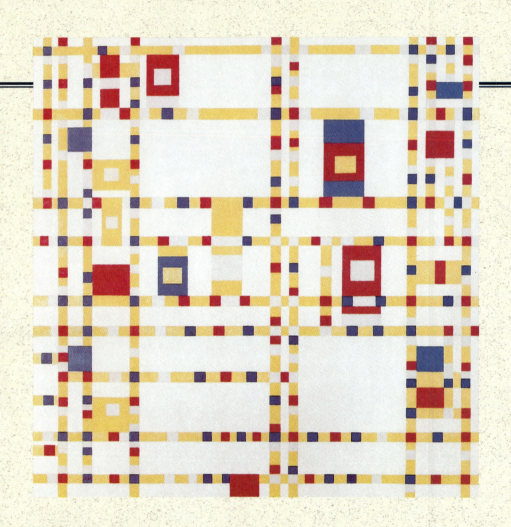

### Boogie-Woogie

*The pianist's left hand begins a driving phrase that moves
methodically over a few simple harmonies. The phrase is played over
and over in a mesmerizing, breathless ostinato. The listener is riveted
by its impulsive and relentless energy. Its endless rhythm is then
punctuated by electric flashes in the trumpets and trombones. At last,
the saxophones wail out a melody in counterpoint to the piano's*

incessant rhythms. The result is a type of jazz called "boogie-woogie."

When the painter Piet Mondrian arrived in New York City in 1940, he immersed himself in jazz. He found this type of music to be a quintessential expression of the American spirit, which impressed him as refreshingly informal and open to new ideas. The skyscrapers of New York possessed the pure geometry that fired his artistic imagination, and the jazz clubs on Broadway exuded a dynamic restlessness that quickly found expression in his paintings.

Broadway Boogie-Woogie (1942–1943) was one of Mondrian's first reflections on his new homeland. Its rectilinear organization duplicates the strict rhythms of this form of jazz, and its cubes of bright color suggest the brassy staccato chords that punctuate its driving bass lines.

Mondrian's paintings were not always so clearly expressive of an external or realistic content. Living in Paris after World War I, he perfected an artistic style that he termed "neoplasticism." A work of this type, he said, "must be produced or constructed. One must create as objectively as possible a representation of forms and relations. Such work can never be empty, because the opposition of its constructive elements and its execution will arouse emotion." His painting thus became imposing organizations of straight black lines meeting at right angles on a white background. Some of the squares and rectangles, especially at the margins of the canvas, were filled with bright, pure colors that exerted a feeling of pressure on the otherwise neutral construction. Such paintings were, in the artist's words, "expressions of the essence of art through a rhythm of lines, colors, and relationships."

Mondrian believed that his neoplastic works achieved a universal artistic statement that conformed to external natural laws. He rejected the reliance on purely instinctive expression, such as Kandinsky had postulated in his prewar writings. A genuine emotional response to a painting, Mondrian countered, could only result if the artist had struck a balance between subjective and objective states. Mondrian's appeal for rational construction resounded throughout the world of art in the period following World War I. In music it helped to produce Schoenberg's 12-tone method of composition and the return to traditional modes of expression associated with neoclassicism. The clear-eyed objectivity in Mondrian's own paintings seemed to him perfectly attuned to the bright and brassy sounds of American jazz.

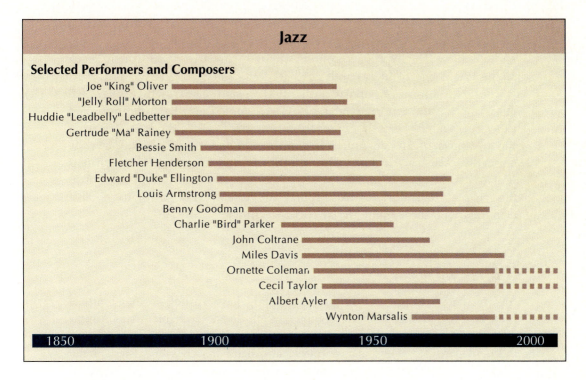

## Jazz

**Selected Performers and Composers**

Joe "King" Oliver
"Jelly Roll" Morton
Huddie "Leadbelly" Ledbetter
Gertrude "Ma" Rainey
Bessie Smith
Fletcher Henderson
Edward "Duke" Ellington
Louis Armstrong
Benny Goodman
Charlie "Bird" Parker
John Coltrane
Miles Davis
Ornette Coleman
Cecil Taylor
Albert Ayler
Wynton Marsalis

1850    1900    1950    2000

America's contribution to musical culture in the twentieth century has stemmed not only from the nation's serious composers but, perhaps even more important, from its unusually vigorous and diverse popular music. The development of a sophisticated musical vernacular in the United States came from the melting pot of peoples who immigrated to America from all corners of the world. The artistic traditions that they brought with them were quickly transformed and intermingled, and their music flourished among a large and affluent middle class that sought entertainment.

By the early years of the twentieth century, a broad and multifaceted category of popular music called **jazz** had emerged. In its originality and vitality, jazz was destined to capture the attention of all elements of American society and be adopted as well by people outside of the United States. It quickly left its mark on popular music of many nationalities as well as on the serious music of both European and American composers. Its impact continues undiminished in the present day.

What is jazz? Even so basic a question cannot receive a simple answer, since the term *jazz* has always been used loosely and broadly to designate

**437**

many types of popular music. Jazz can refer equally to a musical form such as the blues, a style with swinging rhythms, or a performance idiom involving improvisation. The expressive content of jazz is similarly broad: It may speak of the tragic side of life as well as of its joys.

Jazz is a form of popular music. It is created primarily by professional musicians for the entertainment of a large audience, whose interests and experiences it addresses. It derives from earlier popular music as well as from the folk music of African-Americans. In some of its forms, it also displays the decidedly "classical" features of sophistication and longevity. Although it is probably futile to seek an all-purpose definition of jazz, we shall attempt in this chapter to survey its background and touch on some of its notable manifestations throughout the twentieth century.

# The Origins of Jazz

An art that is so diverse as jazz could only have sprung from a musical background that was similarly complex. Such diversity characterizes American popular music of the nineteenth century. Spirituals and gospel hymns, folk and patriotic songs, dance music, and band marches coexisted in the United States in a mélange that mirrored American society and its interests.

It is probable that the folk music from West Africa, brought to America by slaves, also informed aspects of jazz. But exactly how is virtually impossible to specify, given the scarcity of documentation, the many different approaches to music on the continent of Africa itself, and the quickness of acculturation of the slaves in the New World. It is well documented that slaves who were brought to America and to the West Indies had a great love of dancing, drumming, and singing. Their main musical instruments were drums of various sizes and the *banza* (later called the "banjo"). Several descriptions of slaves' music mention continuous alternations of phrases sung by a soloist and answered by a group. Their music often had a utilitarian quality, functioning especially in rituals, social gatherings, and work situations. In general, however, the scanty information that exists about the music that the slaves brought from Africa does not conclusively identify it as a direct antecedent of jazz.

## The African-American Musical Heritage

Background sources of jazz are more readily identifiable in African-American folk and popular music of the nineteenth century. On the planta-

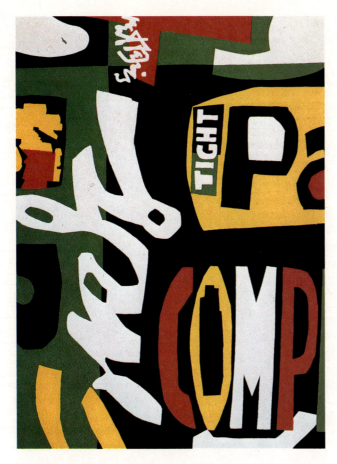

*The paintings of Stuart Davis, such as **Blips and Ifs** (1964), merge the flat geometry of cubism with the bright colors of American life. The rhythms and impulsiveness of jazz are among his recurrent themes. His paintings represent a confluence of images drawn from both high and popular art.*

tions, slaves made their labor easier by singing largely improvised work songs and **field hollers.** The work songs were sung by gangs of men. In later recorded examples, the African form of call and response is often preserved. A leader calls out a line of words, using a musical form of speech, that is then answered by the rest of the group. A field holler is similar, except sung by a single worker.

An especially important body of African-American folk songs was developed for use among black religious congregations. These **spirituals** made use of the simple harmonic language of European hymns, but they retained the syncopated rhythmic figures, swinging rhythms, and deviations from prevailing scales that are later found in jazz. The gospel hymn was the urban counterpart to the spiritual of the American Southeast. These strophic hymns, in which each stanza was usually concluded by a recurrent refrain or **chorus,** were delivered in a powerful manner of singing that reappears among the early blues singers. They are often accompanied by hand clapping and performed with a revivalistic fervor.

The minstrel shows of the middle of the nineteenth century—already touched on in Chapter 10—brought the music of black Americans to a larger urban audience. The minstrel show was a theatrical presentation in which black actors or whites in blackface parodied the white audience's stereotyped views of black culture. Comic skits alternated with music and dance. Songs using black dialect were heard, as were dance pieces played by a band that regularly included African instruments such as the banjo. The most typical dance was the jig, often played by the banjo at headlong speed and with intricate rhythms. The vitality and driving rhythms of these dances were revived in ragtime piano music at the turn of the twentieth century.

*As interest in ragtime in America began to wane after World War I, it had just begun to ignite enthusiasm among musicians in Europe. Its syncopated rhythms were imitated by Stravinsky in his* **Ragtime** *of 1918. Stravinsky's friend Pablo Picasso drew this cover for the first edition of 1919.*

## Ragtime

**Ragtime** is an immediate predecessor of jazz—so close, in fact, that some commentators early in the century equated the two. The term *ragtime* was used around the turn of the twentieth century in both a broad and a specific sense. Broadly speaking, it designates any popular music—songs, dances, or marches—using a syncopated rhythm in its melodic line. More precisely, the term designates a genre of piano music, closely resembling the march, that uses syncopation. The term itself no doubt stems from the "ragged" quality of syncopated rhythms.

**Syncopation** is a rhythmic phenomenon in which notes begin slightly before and end slightly after a beat. The transformation of a regular, unsyncopated rhythm into a syncopated one can be observed in Figure 13.1. The

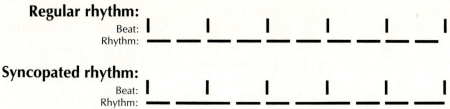

**Figure 13.1**  *Syncopated rhythm*

rhythm illustrated at the top simply subdivides the time between beats into two equal parts. Below, some of the successive notes are joined together in duration, making them begin and end between the beats. The result is a syncopated rhythm.

Rhythms of this sort may have African origins. They began to emerge prominently in banjo jigs and minstrel songs of the nineteenth century, and they were especially prominent in a plantation dance called the **cakewalk.** In this dance, slave couples dressed in finery imitated the manners of their white masters in a ballroom promenade. They were accompanied by a march with syncopated rhythms, and the couple with the most attractive gait and gesture was rewarded by "taking the cake" as a prize.

By the 1890s, the ragged, carefree rhythms of the cakewalk had spread to virtually all of the popular music associated with American blacks. Even renditions of musical classics were often "ragged," that is, given a syncopated treatment. At this time there emerged a new genre of popular piano music incorporating the infectiously bouncy syncopations: It was called the **rag.** The piano rag had a strong connection to the cakewalk and to other marches, which at this time were commonly used as dance as well as military music. Like the march, the rag was in duple meter and usually moderate in tempo. Rags were composed ordinarily by trained musicians, usually written down, and published in prodigious numbers. The pianist performed a rag in a percussive manner, often keeping the pulse by stamping one foot. The performer's right hand carried the syncopated melody, and the left hand played chords in a simpler rhythm, often striding regularly from bass notes in a low register to chords in the middle of the keyboard.

The forms of piano rags were similar to those of band marches. In general, one concise movement was divided into several short sections, each having a new tune. A typical rag began with a brief introduction and then launched into the first melodic section or *strain.* This initial phrase was then immediately repeated. A second strain, containing a new tune, followed, and it was also repeated. Next came one or two strains in a new key, collectively called the *trio.* The rag could end in this new key, or it might adopt a large ternary form by returning to the initial strains in the home key. Although later jazz styles did not always embrace the distinctive rhythms of ragtime, they often kept this general formal outline.

The best-known composer of piano rags was Scott Joplin (1868–1917). Born in Arkansas, Joplin received a good musical education before moving to Saint Louis, where he earned his living as a pianist. He played for a still larger audience at the World's Fair in Chicago in 1893. By the end of the century, his popular compositions, primarily rags for piano, had become best-sellers. In 1907 he moved to New York, where he was active as a teacher as well as a pianist and composer. He was not satisfied with a career solely as a writer of simple rags but aspired instead to merge their idiom with classical forms. He wrote two ragtime operas, one of which, *Treemonisha* (1911), has been revived and recorded.

His most popular composition was "Maple Leaf Rag" (1899), named after a dance hall in Sedalia, Missouri. Like most successful rags, it was published and enjoyed by both blacks and whites and among all social classes. Joplin himself recorded the work on player piano rolls. His performance of 1916 (Recording 13.1) shows authentic elements of the ragtime style. Although this piano roll does not preserve nuances of Joplin's touch, the percussive style of ragtime is nevertheless reproduced.

"Maple Leaf Rag" has the typical rag or march form. It is made up of several strains, most immediately repeated, and it moves at the middle to a trio in a new key. The right hand carries the syncopated melody, accompanied simply by the rhythmically regular left hand. The meter, predictably, is duple.

The ragtime craze in America largely came to an end in 1918 following World War I, although it remained a powerful influence on early jazz for decades following. In postwar Europe, however, ragtime was just being discovered and eagerly imitated by serious as well as by popular composers. Its directness, lack of artifice, and bright spirits seemed just the right antidote for the melancholy of war and the economic turmoil that followed. In the works of composers including Stravinsky, Satie, and Milhaud, the ragtime idiom is repeatedly encountered and is closely associated with the neoclassical style.

## Blues

The **blues** is a genre of folk song, largely improvised, that originally grew out of the cultural milieu of American blacks. Like ragtime, it was a predecessor of jazz whose styles and forms were quickly taken over by jazz

**Listening Guide**

**Scott Joplin, "Maple Leaf Rag"**
Recording 13.1

**Part 1**

A      0.00      This strain is immediately repeated. Its melody, typical of much ragtime, is not in itself memorable, but the jollity of the rhythm holds our attention. The key is A♭ major.

B      0.43      This second strain is also in A♭ and also immediately repeated.

A      1.25      A return to the first strain (not repeated) rounds out the first part of the rag.

**Part 2 (Trio)**

C      1.46      The trio is marked by a shift to a new key, D♭ major. This strain is immediately repeated.

D      2.28      The final strain (repeated) returns to the home key of A♭.

musicians. Unlike ragtime, however, blues continued to develop parallel to jazz, and the two idioms became so closely intertwined as to be inseparable. The history of blues prior to the earliest recordings, made about 1920, is largely conjectural, since it grew from an improvised folk music for which there is virtually no documentation.

It is likely that blues originated in various types of vocal folk music sung by blacks in the American Southeast. Ballads that glorified black heroes, older work songs, and field hollers were, in all likelihood, forerunners. At some point in the late nineteenth or early twentieth century, presumably at first in rural areas, these antecedents merged into a type of folk song having the formal and stylistic traits that are characteristic of blues: strophic variations on a simple harmonic pattern, texts that deal with the melancholy or dark side of life among blacks, and an expressive vocal style in which the singer slides between pitches, sometimes imitating speech more than song.

The "rural" blues of the early twentieth century was usually sung by men who accompanied themselves on guitar. Their music and words were entirely improvised, although based on standard patterns and themes. Recordings by "songsters" such as Papa Charlie Jackson, Blind Lemon Jefferson, and Robert Johnson appeared, though sparingly, in the 1920s and later. Perhaps best known of their number in the present day is "Leadbelly," the pseudonym of Huddie Ledbetter (1885–1949). Born in Louisiana, he made a reputation as a blues singer in the country manner, accompanying himself on the guitar. He sang all kinds of black folk music, including re-creations of slave hollers, work songs that he learned from convicts during his lengthy prison sentences, blues, and pop music. He recorded many of his songs in the 1930s for the archives of the Library of Congress, and in the 1940s he worked as an entertainer in a more popular idiom.

Leadbelly's "Outskirts of Town" (1947) (Recording 13.2) exemplifies the country blues, although it contains, in typically eclectic fashion, styles of singing that are also characteristic of professional entertainers of the 1940s. The song is accompanied by guitar and harmonica, played on the recording by Woody Guthrie and Cisco Houston. The words, quite possibly improvised by the singer, deal with a man's resolve to move with his lady out of town. Like many country blues, its words are coarse, as at the end, where the man warns his partner, "If we have any children, all of them better look just like me."

The first stanza of text has the standard blues form:

I'm gonna move way on the outskirts of town,
I'm gonna move way on the outskirts of town.
You know I don't want nobody always hangin' 'round.

It consists of three lines, of which the first two are identical and in which the rhyming third line explains the sentiments contained in the first two. Later stanzas, however, are not in the conventional blues pattern. Their first lines contain new thoughts, but then they return to the second and third lines of the first stanza. The sixth and final stanza returns to the conventional form:

It may seem funny, baby, funny as it can be,
It may seem funny, baby, funny as it can be.
If we have any children, all of them better look just like me.

The music consists of variations, each called a *chorus* and each corresponding to one stanza of the text. The key and succession of harmonies in each chorus are the same. The succession of harmonies is especially characteristic of blues. Normally, it begins with a major triad built on the keynote (G) in the bass, which is sustained continuously for the duration of the first line of

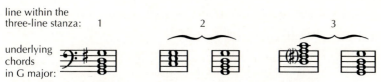

**Figure 13.2** *Standard succession of harmonies in a blues chorus*

text. The second line of words begins with a harmony made of a major triad on the fourth note of the G major scale (C), then returning to the chord on G. The third and final line begins harmonically with a chord built on the fifth note of the scale (D), returning again to the initial or tonic chord on G. These underlying chords are illustrated in Figure 13.2. They are extremely simple, and they may have been derived by the early blues singers from the uncomplicated harmonies of hymns and spirituals.

Leadbelly's singing is very speechlike, almost a melodious form of narration. As such, it does not strictly adhere to the pitches of a G major scale but instead slides between notes and freely uses the rhythm of speech. Consistently, however, the third note of the scale, B, is lowered to B♭, giving the melody a twangy pungency. Such lowered notes within the major scale, including, in other works, the seventh and sometimes the fifth scale degrees, are termed **blue notes.**

The melody of the first stanza is preserved, with simple variations, throughout, and the basic harmonic progression is unchanging. In the fourth and fifth choruses, the voice falls silent and the melody is taken by the harmonica, which imitates the pungent, narrative quality of Leadbelly's voice. Woody Guthrie's guitar accompaniment is unobtrusive except in the introduction and in stanzas 4 and 5, where it becomes driving in rhythm and melodic in its outlining of chords. Such a bass line, typical in blues performances of the 1930s and 1940s, creates a style called *boogie-woogie*. The rhythms of the singer and accompanists "swing," suggesting that they are constantly propelled forward, slightly anticipating the beat. The subdivision of the space between beats in a swinging style is normally in thirds, expressed by rhythms in which a long value, equaling two-thirds of this space, is followed by a short value of one-third. This rhythmic style, characteristic of most jazz but very different from ragtime, is illustrated in Figure 13.3.

**Figure 13.3** *Swinging rhythms (The longer notes are twice as long as the shorter ones.)*

445

**Listening Guide**

**Leadbelly, "Outskirts of Town"**
Recording 13.2

| | | |
|---|---|---|
| **Introduction** | 0.00 | The instruments state the basic 12-bar harmonic progression, realized by the guitar in a boogie-woogie style. |
| **Chorus 1** | 0.20 | The voice sings the first stanza of text, improvising a basic melody that fits the standard underlying harmonies: |

| | | |
|---|---|---|
| **Chorus 2** | 0.41 | The melody is generally preserved, although some new words are added. |
| **Chorus 3** | 1.01 | Still new words are added to music that is essentially the same as in the second chorus. |
| **Chorus 4** | 1.21 | The harmonica now enunciates an expressive variation of the basic melody while the guitar plays the basic chords in a more animated boogie-woogie fashion. The singer urges the instrumentalists onward. |
| **Chorus 5** | 1.41 | The harmonica and guitar state another variation of the basic materials. |
| **Choruses 6–7** | 1.59 | The song is concluded by the reentry of the voice to sing the final two stanzas of words. |

A somewhat different interpretation of the blues was made by professional singers in minstrel shows during the 1910s and 1920s, leading to a phenomenon called the "classic" or "urban" blues. These singers were normally women, and they were accompanied typically by jazz bands or piano rather than accompanying themselves on guitar. Their songs dealt with themes of life among blacks, but from a female perspective that often became

**446**

melancholy. They tended to adhere more closely to a standardized blues form than did their male counterparts in the rural tradition, and their singing is often more polished in technique.

The first great classic blues singer was Gertrude "Ma" Rainey (1886–1939). From about 1900 she toured as a singer with the Rabbit Foot Minstrels, and she quickly developed a devoted following among black Americans. In 1923 she began a recording career in which she worked with outstanding instrumentalists such as the trumpeter Louis Armstrong. Some of her most characteristic recordings are of "Jelly Bean Blues," "See See Rider," and "Bo-Weavil Blues."

In 1912, Rainey's minstrel act was joined by another young singer, Bessie Smith (1894–1937), who rose in the 1920s to a position of preeminence in blues singing and whose many recordings established a level of excellence in urban blues that has never been surpassed. Smith was born in Chattanooga, Tennessee, and after touring on the vaudeville circuit, she began making immensely successful recordings in New York. Her artistry is marked especially by an intense expressivity, clear enunciation of words, and high musical standards.

Bessie Smith composed and recorded "Lost Your Head Blues" (Recording 13.3) in New York in 1926. She is accompanied by several leading jazz instrumentalists, including the pianist Fletcher Henderson and the cornetist Joe Smith. Her words, spread over six stanzas, are the narrative plaint of a good woman who has been ungratefully abandoned by her man after he came into money. The poetic form in each stanza hews unvaryingly to the standard blues pattern of two identical lines followed by a rhyming third line.

The music is also highly regular, although nonetheless expressive. Following a short introduction, each of the five stanzas is based on the unchanging 12-measure blues progression of harmonies shown in Figure 13.2 (here in the key of E♭ major). These chords are played unobtrusively by the pianist. In the first stanza, Smith weaves a melody, probably improvised on the spot, above these chords. This tune will itself be subject to variation in each of the ensuing stanzas.

Another typical and highly expressive

*Bessie Smith was the greatest blues singer of the 1920s. She brought an unparalleled artistry and refinement to her singing, which helped to establish jazz as a major art form.*

feature of the urban blues is found in this example in the music of the cornet. After each line of text, it adds a chattering, improvised response, as though making a commentary on the sentiments of the line just concluded. Joe Smith's playing is almost an echo of the voice: He slides between notes like the singer and skillfully imitates her brassy tone, speechlike rhythms, and tight vibrato. By playing some of the notes with the valves of his trumpet pushed only halfway down, he varies the color of his responses, capturing the melancholy of the words. This relation of voice and instrument may well be a distant reminder of the call-and-response singing of slave work crews of bygone years.

**Bessie Smith, "Lost Your Head Blues"**
Recording 13.3

| | | |
|---|---|---|
| **Introduction** | 0.00 | The cornet plays a melodic fragment that anticipates part of the melody sung in the first stanza. |
| **Chorus 1** | 0.11 | The voice states the basic melody above the standard blues harmonies. The melody begins |

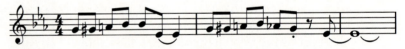

| | | |
|---|---|---|
| **Choruses 2–5** | 0.43 | The accompaniment remains virtually unchanged as the voice spins out a series of variations on the underlying harmonies and on the melody of stanza 1. The variations are primarily rhythmic, since the singer must accommodate lines of greatly varying length to the basic melodic and harmonic pattern. |

# Jazz in the 1920s, 1930s, and 1940s

Ragtime and blues set the stage for the emergence of jazz. Ragtime lent its syncopated rhythms and multithematic forms to jazz. From the blues, jazz derived its seriousness of tone, swinging rhythms, improvisatory techniques, and monothematic forms. The birthplace of jazz was New Orleans, a city with a unique social and cultural background, and it quickly spread to other cities and diversified its already eclectic musical personality.

### The New Orleans Style

By 1900, the city of New Orleans had acquired a vast appetite for popular music and an explosive mixture of musical forces. Here was a melting pot of nationalities and races that prided itself on its tolerance of differences and on a zest for entertainment that bordered on hedonism. The ritual dancing and drumming of African slaves were still remembered from the days when African-Americans gathered at Congo Square on Sundays to practice their indigenous music. Parades, funeral processions, advertising campaigns, and holiday festivals (of which Mardi Gras is an example) were memorable parts of New Orleans life, and they created a seemingly endless demand for band music. Riverboats, nightclubs, and the bordellos of the red-light district of Storyville needed dance music or music for easy relaxation.

In this milieu, small parade bands flourished. These forerunners of jazz bands played marches, popular tunes, and ragtimes. They were converted into dance bands as the demand for such music grew, and their style of playing had long since assimilated African-American qualities such as swinging rhythms, expressive vocal imitations, and group improvisation.

New Orleans jazz, which emerged as a distinct idiom shortly after the turn of the twentieth century, is a style of music rather than a particular genre or form. Most typically, the style is associated with a small band made up of five to seven players. This band is divided into two groups. One marks the beat and plays harmonies, and the other is entrusted with melodic ideas. A typical New Orleans jazz band has a melody group of cornet (often the leading melodic instrument), clarinet, and trombone; the rhythm section might consist of piano, drums, banjo, and string bass or tuba. In the early days of jazz, these bands were usually staffed along racial lines, made up entirely of black or of white musicians. The term **Dixieland** is used to refer to a New Orleans–style jazz band consisting of white players.

Such bands played primarily for dancing. Their music was varied in type. They played rags, marches, blues with or without a singer, popular songs, and, occasionally, newly composed music. The forms of these pieces were equally varied, but two prototypes are discernible, derived either from the rag or from the blues. Jazz pieces based on ragtime are multithematic. New themes are heard in each of several sections. Each theme may be immediately repeated to freely improvised variations (again called *choruses*). As in a

**449**

rag, some of the themes constitute a contrasting *trio* section in a key different from the opening strains. Jazz pieces based on blues, by contrast, tend to be monothematic. They consist of continuous variations on an unchanging harmonic formula and, melodically, on an initial melody that is itself often preexistent. They remain from beginning to end in the same key, typically F, B♭, or E♭.

The most characteristic aspect of early New Orleans jazz is group improvisation. All of the melody instruments in this style improvise on a known harmonic pattern or a basic melody. Often one instrument (typically the cornet) stands forth as the primary bearer of the tune, and the others add countermelodies. Sections of intricate polyphony stemming from group improvisation sometimes alternate with soloistic choruses in which one player improvises alone.

The best-known bands in the New Orleans style ironically became famous after leaving New Orleans for New York, Chicago, or other locations. The Original Dixieland Jazz Band came to New York in 1917 and garnered attention for its driving rhythm and elemental excitement. The Creole Jazz Band, led by the cornetist Joe "King" Oliver, was formed in 1922 in Chicago. This band's recordings, such as the much-admired "Dippermouth Blues," mix blues choruses in group improvisation with soloistic choruses. In such works, the blues is transformed from a folk song into an instrumental genre of dance music.

One of the most important musicians to emerge from the New Orleans style was the pianist and composer "Jelly Roll" Morton (1885–1941). His career is typical of the successful popular musician of his time. He was born in New Orleans, where he learned the skills of a ragtime pianist. As an adult, he traveled throughout the country, plying his trade as a pianist and composer. In Chicago around 1926 he founded a New Orleans–style jazz band, the Red Hot Peppers, with whom he made a series of important recordings. Morton was unusual for a New Orleans musician in the extent to which his music was composed and often written down in advance of performance. This aspect of his work clearly derives from his background in ragtime. Many of his pieces were first written for piano and later transcribed for jazz band. Toward the end of his life, he was interviewed by the American folklorist Alan Lomax, leaving a valuable record of his activities. At this time he made the claim, often repeated though certainly untenable, that he was the inventor of jazz.

His celebrated "Black Bottom Stomp" (Recording 13.4) shows both Morton's musical eclecticism and his profound originality. A *stomp* is a piece with a heavy pulse, and the *black bottom* is a dance akin to the Charleston, whose irregular pattern of accents is much in evidence in this recording. This composition was recorded in 1926 with the Red Hot Peppers, which represented a typical New Orleans ensemble: trumpet, clarinet, trombone, piano, banjo, string bass, and drums. The rhythm group is not, however, restricted to a secondary role, as its members often take prominent melodic passages.

"Black Bottom Stomp" is closest in conception to ragtime, the tradition from which Morton came. Much of it appears to have been composed and possibly even notated in advance of the recording session. It uses, by and large, the syncopated rhythms of ragtime, and its form is akin to the ragtime paradigm. But Morton also blends in aspects of blues by expanding the two basic themes of the work through a succession of chorus variations, each containing an element of improvisation.

**Jelly Roll Morton, "Black Bottom Stomp"**
Recording 13.4

**Introduction**   0.00   A brief passage featuring cornet, clarinet, and trombone.

**Part 1**

**Chorus 1a**   0.07   The cornet states a melody, accompanied by the other melody instruments in an improvised counterpoint:

**Chorus 1b**   0.22   This chorus features the cornet alternating with the full ensemble; fragments of the melody are preserved, as is its underlying harmonic progression.

**Chorus 1c**   0.37   This chorus is another variant of the basic harmonic progression, although the clarinet's melody is not closely related to that of chorus 1a.

**Interlude**   0.52   The interlude serves to produce a change of key from B♭ to E♭.

### Part 2 (Trio)

**Chorus 2a**   0.56   This section establishes a new harmonic progression that will be maintained in each of the variations that follow. At 1.01 the cornet and trombone play a **break,** an important feature of the New Orleans style, when they play freely for a few seconds as the accompaniment falls momentarily silent.

**Chorus 2b**   1.15   The clarinet is now featured in an improvised solo over the harmonies of chorus 2a. The melody is constructed from a **riff,** a short melodic motive that is repeated over and over with slight changes.

**Chorus 2c**   1.33   Morton now plays an unaccompanied chorus on the piano, very much in the style of ragtime.

**Chorus 2d**   1.51   The cornet's chorus returns to a variant of the melody of part 2, now in **stop time,** during which the accompaniment is silent except for punctuating notes.

**Chorus 2e**   2.10   A chorus featuring the banjo.

**Chorus 2f**   2.29   Now that the primary melody instruments have had their choruses, Morton returns to the entire ensemble, in which the drums have a short break.

**Chorus 2g**   2.48   The final rousing chorus features a "shouting" trombone break.

## Louis Armstrong and the Expansion of the New Orleans Style

In the decade following World War I, New Orleans jazz underwent remarkable stylistic growth as it spread literally throughout the world. It was embraced by people from all walks of life and all ethnic backgrounds and also by serious musicians and audiences. Musicians trained in New Orleans were increasingly in demand in the northern states for recordings and live performances, and the New Orleans style was thus transported to Chicago, New York, and Saint Louis, where regional versions took root.

One of the most basic transformations of the New Orleans style in the 1920s and 1930s was an increased prominence of virtuoso soloists, who came to include the trumpeters Louis Armstrong and Bix Beiderbecke, the clarinetist and saxophonist Sydney Bechet, and pianists including James P. Johnson and Fats Waller.

The innovations of Louis Armstrong (1900–1971) are especially important. Armstrong was born and raised in New Orleans and counted King Oliver among his early trumpet teachers. In 1922, like so many leading New Orleans musicians in the 1920s, he migrated to Chicago, in order to join Oliver's band. Later he worked in the big band of Fletcher Henderson in New York, returning to Chicago in 1925 to found his

*Louis Armstrong was a founder of jazz as an artistic genre. The expressivity and virtuosity of his playing continue to be imitated to this day.*

own band. In 1927 and 1928 he rose to unprecedented fame for a jazz musician through recordings with groups called the Hot Five and the Hot Seven. They performed music based on the New Orleans band concept, but with a greatly increased emphasis on solo playing.

From 1929 to 1947 he worked with a larger band that served to underscore his own virtuosic talents, in a radical departure from the collective New Orleans style. During these years he was increasingly known as a singer, with a distinctively gravelly and soulful voice. He was especially adept at "scat" singing, rhythmically animated vocalizing on nonsense syllables. From 1947 until his death in 1971, Armstrong toured with a group called the All Stars. During his later years, he played the trumpet sparingly and focused instead on singing and entertaining.

His rendition of "West End Blues" with the Hot Five in 1928 is one of his finest recordings (Recording 13.5). The six-member ensemble is clearly based on the New Orleans conception. It has a front-line melody group consisting of trombone, clarinet, and Armstrong's trumpet. The rhythm section consists of piano (played by the great Earl "Fatha" Hines), banjo, and drums. But the New Orleans style of group polyphony is entirely displaced by soloistic, virtuosic improvisations.

The melody of the work was composed earlier by Armstrong's mentor, King Oliver. It is supported by the standard 12-measure blues harmonic pattern, in the key of B♭, preceded in Armstrong's version by a stunning introduction played by Armstrong alone. The entire rendition consists of a series of solo choruses, in which Armstrong is featured. In some choruses,

**453**

Oliver's melody is entirely ignored, and at other times it is only hinted at.

Our attention is most drawn to Armstrong's expressive playing. He begins notes or note groups with an explosive attack, often continuing to display his ideas in cascades of sound covering the entire range of the instrument. His choice of notes in these imaginative improvisations is sometimes freed from the simple underlying harmonies of the key of B♭, and it emphasizes the blue notes A♭ and D♭. Armstrong was the first jazz trumpeter to emphasize the high register of the instrument, which has since become the jazz trumpeter's stock-in-trade.

*Listening Guide*

**Louis Armstrong/Joe Oliver, "West End Blues"**
Recording 13.5

| | | |
|---|---|---|
| **Introduction** | 0.00 | Solely devoted to a cascading solo by Armstrong. |
| **Chorus 1** | 0.15 | Armstrong is featured on this variation of Oliver's melody, which becomes increasingly remote from the original. The tune begins |
| **Chorus 2** | 0.50 | The trombone now improvises on the blues harmonies, generally ignoring the tune. |
| **Chorus 3** | 1.23 | The clarinet is featured in a repartee with Armstrong's scat singing. The clarinetist dwells on the head motive of Oliver's tune. |
| **Chorus 4** | 1.58 | This variation, taken by the pianist Earl "Fatha" Hines, almost steals Armstrong's thunder in its inventiveness and relaxed virtuosity. In the middle, Hines adds a touch of ragtime. |
| **Chorus 5** | 2.31 | Armstrong is again featured, and the 12-bar blues chorus is expanded toward the end to convey a sense of conclusion. |

## Swing and the Big Band Era

The 1930s witnessed a continued transformation of New Orleans jazz, leading to the emergence and ultimate dominance of a style called **swing.** Swing was encountered primarily in music for moderately large dance bands, with or without a singer. It represented a continuation of some aspects of New Orleans jazz, such as the frequent use of blues forms, but it was opposed to the spirit of early jazz in its simplified and unified texture and rhythm, reliance on precomposed music or musical arrangements, emphasis on soloistic playing rather than group polyphony, and a tendency to dwell on clichés.

Perhaps the most striking characteristic of music of the swing era is the prominence of large dance bands, which grew out of the smaller New Orleans jazz ensembles but eventually entirely replaced them. The typical big band of the late 1930s numbered about 13 players, sometimes augmented by a singer. It was constituted of three trumpets, two trombones, three or four saxophones, and a rhythm section of piano, guitar, drums, and string bass. Its sound was characterized by powerful volume and sharp attacks, and it provided the potential for alternation among the basic brass and woodwind subgroups. It was not at all geared to the intricate polyphony of the New Orleans jazz band. The leading bands contained outstanding soloists, who were featured in alternation with passages for the full ensemble.

The big bands came to rely on written arrangements and original compositions. This was a complete departure from the New Orleans spirit, where players often could not read music and had to rely almost exclusively on their improvisatory abilities. The big band arrangements allowed for improvisation in soloistic choruses, but they sometimes tended toward predictable melodic and orchestrational patterns.

The music played by these bands was still primarily intended to accompany dancing, although certain bands, notably that of Duke Ellington, also played nonfunctional music intended solely for listening. The works they performed were in part reminiscent of the 1920s: instrumental blues and multithematic works moving through several keys. But their repertory increasingly came to contain music based on popular songs, which was vital to a band's success because such songs were well known and in demand. Popular songs of this time had varying forms, the simplest and most common of which consisted of two short melodic ideas arranged in the pattern *aaba.* Popular songs were integrated into big band dance pieces in several ways. The simplest was to let the tune and its underlying harmonic progression constitute a chorus, which could then be continuously varied by the full band or by quasi-improvised solos. In other works, a version of the song began the band

**455**

arrangement, which was then augmented by new music and by a free return of subsections. Big bands of the 1930s and 1940s also relied on original compositions, of which those of Duke Ellington are outstanding.

The prototype of the swing band of the 1930s and 1940s was an orchestra led by Fletcher Henderson in New York in the late 1920s. His group had the instrumentation of the later big band, and he and his arranger, Don Redman, used it to alternate soloistic and group choruses. In the full sections, Henderson often pitted the brass and woodwinds in an antiphonal dialogue. These features later became clichés of the swing band of the 1930s and 1940s. Henderson's conception was taken over and developed by bands led by Jimmie Lunceford, William "Count" Basie, and the "King of Swing," Benny Goodman, for whom Henderson served as arranger in the 1930s.

The big bands of Duke Ellington were also influenced by Henderson and by the onset of swing, although Ellington's brilliance as a composer led his ensemble in a new direction. Edward "Duke" Ellington (1899–1974) was born in Washington, D.C., and he taught himself musical rudiments and piano playing. He moved to New York in 1923, leading a band that played at a Broadway nightclub. The size of his group had increased by the late 1920s to big band proportions, and he played at the Cotton Club in Harlem from 1927 until 1932, garnering wide recognition. He became increasingly active as a composer for his group, using the forms of the popular song, blues, and other short instrumental pieces. Beginning in 1935 he began to compose lengthy, often multimovement works in the swing idiom. During the war years, he gave jazz concerts at Carnegie Hall, and after the war, he toured with his band and worked as a composer for film and for the stage.

Although no single work can illustrate all aspects of Ellington's fertile imagination, his composition "Ko Ko" (1940, Recording 13.6) is one of his most celebrated and shows his daring expansion of the blues form. His medium for this recording is the classic big band: three trumpets, three trombones, four saxophones, piano (played by Ellington himself), guitar, drums, and string bass. The overall form is conventional. It is a blues consisting of successive choruslike variations on a main theme and a traditional harmonic progression. But virtually

*Duke Ellington transformed jazz into a genre that was not solely improvisational. He produced jazz works of many types, including lengthy and highly structured compositions.*

**Listening Guide**

**Duke Ellington, "Ko Ko"**
Recording 13.6

**Introduction**    0.00    The baritone saxophone reiterates the keynote E♭ and the basic short-short-short-long rhythmic motive, above which the trombones play syncopated chords.

**Chorus 1**    0.12    A valve trombone states the basic melody, made up of repeated statements of the riff shown below. The saxophones create an accompanimental dialogue.

**Choruses 2–3**    0.31    A slide trombone now takes over the melody, accompanied by other trombones. The intense quality of the trombonist's sound is enhanced by his use of a mute, giving it an urgent and vocal quality that is increased by Ellington's orchestration and by the driving rhythm.

**Chorus 4**    1.07    The saxophones have the main melodic material, varying the riff of the first chorus. They are accompanied in a highly intricate fashion by the ostinato of the trumpets and the dissonant chords of the piano.

**Chorus 5**    1.25    The excitement and complication continue to grow as the trumpets take up the riff melody in the low register, pitted against a frantic saxophone figure.

**Chorus 6**    1.44    The entire band takes up the riff, alternating with the swinging rhythm of breaks played by the string bass.

**Chorus 7**    2.02    The steadily growing excitement of the work now reaches its climax as the trumpets soar into their highest register while the saxophones pick up the melody.

**Coda**    2.21    An elongated return to the introduction.

## Music Today

### Wynton Marsalis

Virtually never in the history of music has a leading jazz instrumentalist also achieved genuine prominence as a performer of serious music. The two types of playing require different techniques. Different modes of attack (initiating a sound) are needed, as are different types of vibrato, different qualities of sound, and different ways of phrasing. The classical way of playing not only differs from jazz but, for most players, is inimical to it. To be sure, many have tried to bridge the gap between the two worlds. The clarinetist Benny Goodman, the great swing band leader and soloist, often played Mozart, and he commissioned a work by Béla Bartók. But it cannot be said that Goodman's classical playing measured up to his jazz.

Around 1980 there appeared a trumpeter on the American musical scene whose gifts and inspiration were so great as to make the barriers between jazz and serious playing seem insig-

nificant. His name is Wynton Marsalis. Born in 1961 in New Orleans, Marsalis received a thorough grounding in music of all types. He had a natural and intense affinity for jazz and a prodigious talent as a classical player. At the age of 17, he attended the Berkshire Music Center at Tanglewood, in Lenox, Massachusetts, where he pursued training as a classical soloist and orchestral musician. This interest was further developed during his study at the Juilliard School in New York.

But at the same time he also studied the music of the great masters of jazz, and he thoroughly assimilated the idiom of Louis Armstrong, King Oliver, and other trumpet greats. After graduating from Juilliard, he toured with the Jazz Messengers, led by drummer Art Blakey, and he quickly established himself as a leading young jazz artist. His work as a classical trumpet soloist was undiminished, as shown by his many recordings of the treacherously difficult trumpet literature from the baroque period. In 1983 he received the unique honor of winning Grammy awards for recordings in both classical and jazz divisions.

Marsalis now plays jazz with his own band, sometimes collaborating with his brother, Branford, a gifted jazz saxophonist. He is regularly seen on television as an enthusiastic and articulate spokesperson for jazz, which he holds to be a pure expression of spiritual values of African-American culture.

nothing else about the piece is predictable. It is in the minor mode (on the keynote E♭), which allows Ellington to achieve more complicated harmonic combinations. The work is unified, like many classical compositions, by recurrent motives, especially the rhythmic figure consisting of three short notes followed by a long value. This motive appears in the baritone saxophone in the introduction, and it is then cast as a riff from which the main theme is constructed in the first chorus. The riffs that are heard in choruses 4 and 5 are also made from this rhythm.

Typical of big band arrangements, the choruses feature either a soloist or the full ensemble. The solo choruses are probably improvised, although most of the work is written out in advance. The use of breaks in the sixth chorus is notable, and there is much of the typical antiphonal dialogue between the various subgroups of the band. Ellington goes far beyond most big band arrangements, however, by melding the instruments into unusual combinations, creating intricate polyrhythmic interactions (especially in the fourth chorus), and constructing unusual and highly expressive chords.

## Developments After World War II

Shortly after the end of World War II, the popularity of big bands began to wane. From then to the present, the development of jazz followed many of the same lines as the development of serious music of the same period. It was a time of rapid innovation interspersed with revivals of earlier styles. Some of the stylistic innovations of the 1950s and 1960s associated with serious music, including atonality, free rhythm and beat, and chance, were used on an experimental basis by jazz musicians. In this discussion, we shall touch on only a few major developments that mark the postwar decades: bebop, cool jazz, and free jazz.

### Bebop

The style of **bebop** (an onomatopoetic term imitating a characteristic rhythmic sound) was the major alternative to the music of the big swing bands during the decade following the war. By this time, the big bands seemed dated, given their tendency toward a sameness of sound and orchestration, predictable melodic ideas, and a limited range of expression. Progressive jazz musicians were increasingly dissatisfied with the artistic restrictions of a medium devoted primarily to dance music.

Around 1945, musicians who worked in Harlem jazz clubs—including Charlie Parker, Dizzy Gillespie, Max Roach, Bud Powell, and Thelonious Monk—began to experiment with a new style that was aggressively modern and intentionally rejected both the swing band idiom and older forms of jazz such as the New Orleans style. Their rebellious artistic spirit is clearly akin to that of contemporary serious composers, such as Pierre Boulez, who wished to overturn the old order in music and start anew in a manner attuned to the new spirit of the postwar period.

Their music, which came to be called bebop (also *bop* or sometimes *rebop*), was played by small instrumental ensembles, usually numbering four or five and typically containing saxophone, trumpet, piano, bass, and drums. They rejected the sonorous image of the big band, its powerful volume, and the predictable alternation between woodwind and brass subgroups with occasional improvised solos. Instead, their music was primarily soloistic and homophonic. When more than one melody instrument played at the same time, they typically played in unison. The piano and drums added harmonies and pulse and sometimes emerged as soloists.

The music of bebop often used variation forms based on recurrent and preexistent harmonic progressions derived from blues or from certain well-known popular songs. But it typically ignored preexistent melodic ideas or formulas and relied instead on improvised melodies of great complexity. Perhaps the most striking stylistic feature of bebop is its rhythm and sense of beat. The tempos of bebop are often extremely fast—so fast, in fact, that the pulse is difficult to follow and seems little in evidence. The virtuosic melodies spun out above this type of rhythm are also very fast and impelled relentlessly forward. They often outline chords that are remote to the underlying key, they contain many chromatic tones, and they project irregular accents that further obscure a clear pulse. Given the experimental nature of the music and its rhythmic complications, it is not intended to accompany dancing. Bebop is instead a nonfunctional art form.

The musician most closely connected with this new style was the saxophonist and composer Charlie "Bird" Parker (1920–1955). Parker's influence on progressive jazz of the postwar decades was immense, and his liberating originality—which asserted that jazz must not remain stylistically inert—initiated a crucial period of growth and development in jazz history. Parker was born in Kansas City, a city with a long and distinguished tradition of jazz, where he was first active as a professional jazz saxophonist. In 1945 he formed his own ensemble, which performed in New York and

*The saxophonist Charlie "Bird" Parker was central to the emergence of modern jazz of the 1950s. His style helped to establish bebop as the preeminent jazz development in the decades following World War II.*

460

elsewhere. From 1947 to 1951 he performed primarily in New York, where he recorded many works with a band that also enlisted the trumpeter Miles Davis. He died tragically at the age of 35.

Parker's music is a remarkably original mixture of preexistent musical elements and new, improvisatory additions. Many of his pieces use the underlying harmonies of the blues or the well-known harmonic progressions of popular songs (Gershwin's "I Got Rhythm" was a particular favorite). But the melodies that he and his cohorts improvised to these harmonic structures were wholly new in their freedom from underlying chords, their remarkable sense of rhythm, and the brilliant virtuosity of playing.

"KoKo" (Recording 13.7) is a celebrated example of his early bebop style. (The piece has no connection with Ellington's "Ko Ko" beyond the common title.) It was recorded in 1945 in New York, where Parker was joined by trumpeter Dizzy Gillespie (who also plays piano on the recording), drummer Max Roach, and bassist Curley Russell. The music has little connection to any jazz style we have seen so far. Our attention is drawn at first to the breakneck speed at which the music passes and to the virtuosic melodic improvisations of Parker and Gillespie. Their unison playing is nothing less than stunning in its precision.

**Charlie Parker, "KoKo"**
Recording 13.7

| | | |
|---|---|---|
| **Prelude** | 0.00 | The saxophone and muted trumpet set the mood of the work by playing in alternation or in precise unison. |
| **Improvisation** | 0.25 | Parker now takes over with a breathless, headlong bebop improvisation. It spans two statements (choruses) of the underlying harmonic progression. |
| **Interlude** | 2.05 | The drums add a solo that entirely dispenses with regular beat, creating, instead, a flurry of sound and motion. |
| **Postlude** | 2.27 | The prelude is repeated. |

The drums establish the beat, but, given its high speed and irregular accents, the pulse does not become a restrictive element. The underlying chords, similarly, are far in the background, played sparsely and dimly by the piano. These chords, drawn from the popular song "Cherokee," still guide the melodic motions, but less strictly so than in traditional jazz. Even the bass, an instrument that normally functions to clarify the harmonies, plays in a steadily walking (or, better, running) rhythm with notes that establish lines rather than chords.

The work is clearly oriented toward Parker's improvisation, which is a technical tour de force. It is very free of the underlying harmonies, and its structure is not dictated by balanced phrases or by any regularly placed cadences. But despite his bypassing these conventional guides, his melody achieves a clear shape and direction.

### Cool and Free Jazz

The aggressive modernism of bebop of the 1940s and early 1950s was moderated by a widespread development in instrumental jazz around 1950 called *cool jazz*. Its main practitioners were the bands led by the pianist Lennie Tristano, saxophonists Lee Konitz and Gerry Mulligan, and trumpeter Miles Davis. Cool jazz has certain elements in common with bebop but none of its fire, daunting virtuosity, or incisive dissonance. The tempos of cool jazz are typically moderate, and the beat is clearly kept by the drummer playing smoothly with brushes. The listener's attention is drawn to the improvised solos of the melody instruments, which are relaxed, tuneful, and rather conventional in harmonic implications.

The conventional character of cool jazz was in turn totally altered in the 1960s by the advent of what is often called *free jazz*. As the name implies, this is a blatantly experimental style that eliminates most or all structural aspects of earlier jazz. Underlying harmonic progressions are sometimes set aside entirely or replaced by freely dissonant chords. Improvisation (done both soloistically and in groups) becomes unguided by either regular beat or by harmonies. Works in this style are typically elongated to beyond an hour, and the traditional structure of jazz—continuous improvised variations on preexistent melodies or harmonic patterns—is replaced by irregular phrases and unpredictable formal plans.

One of the leaders of this new approach to jazz in the 1960s was the saxophonist Ornette Coleman (b. 1930). Born in Texas, Coleman traveled widely in his early years, playing in conventional styles and also following up the modernistic implications of Charlie Parker's work. By the late 1950s, his experiments had attracted a large following, and he recorded works of great originality. His "Free Jazz" of 1960 is a very lengthy study in unpremeditated improvisation by a group of players. They have no common theme, no recurrent harmonic pattern, and rarely a stable beat to lead them, only their intuition and sensitivity to ideas of the other musicians. The style has certain similarities to the concept of chance music put forth in the 1950s by John Cage. Coleman, however, was never dogmatic. He also experimented with serialized jazz and taught himself a number of instruments.

"Lonely Woman" (1959) (Recording 13.8), though not as radical as "Free Jazz," illustrates aspects of his experimental mode in its early stages. Four instruments are heard on the record. Coleman plays saxophone, Donald Cherry plays trumpet, and a rhythm group of string bass and drums provides a background. The style of playing is almost a caricature of bebop. The trumpet and saxophone often play in unison, but the virtuosic precision of a

**Listening Guide**

**Ornette Coleman, "Lonely Woman"**
Recording 13.8

| | | |
|---|---|---|
| **Introduction** | 0.00 | The drums establish a fast bebop tempo while the bass plays a recurrent melodic figure in the home key of D minor. |
| **A** | 0.18 | The saxophone and trumpet play, roughly in unison, a melody in D minor. It has the standard form of a popular song chorus, *aaba*. Note the saxophone breaks in the *a* sections. The bass plays an accompaniment that slides between tones. |
| **B** | 1.47 | The saxophone now states a new improvisation, sometimes accompanied by a chromatic line in the trumpet. |
| **A'** | 2.54 | The unison duet of section A returns. |
| **Coda** | 4.31 | After a conclusion of the duet, the drums and bass bring the work to an end. |

duo such as Parker and Gillespie is totally missing. Coleman and Cherry play out of tune, with only an approximation of coordination. Their intention seems to be expressivity rather than adherence to conventional musical values. Occasionally, Coleman's sound becomes distorted, which only enhances the melancholy sentiments suggested by the title.

Coleman's experiments with new jazz ideas were extended by several other artists of the 1960s and later. The saxophonist John Coltrane (1926–1967) combined a distinctively robust sound with improvisations that are freed from standard harmonic progressions. His melodies often become virtuosic cascades of notes that have been described as "sheets of sound" and are to an extent inspired by the style of Charlie Parker. Albert Ayler (1936–1970) went even further than Coltrane and Coleman in renouncing the basic jazz concept of improvisation above recurrent harmonic progressions. His intensely expressive improvised soliloquies make distant references to preexistent melodic ideas, but they convey the impression of expressive streams of consciousness. The pianist Cecil Taylor (b. 1933) brought his study of modernism in serious music to his jazz compositions. These use experimental devices such as chance, tone clusters, atonality, and pointillistic textures, and the results resemble the style of Webern as much as they do conventional jazz.

Jazz in the present day exhibits no single or dominant style. Virtually every major idiom from ragtime to free jazz is practiced by a number of contemporary professional artists, and many combine styles freely. Throughout its history, jazz has had a close relationship with other forms of popular music. In the 1920s and 1930s, as noted earlier, jazz successfully assimilated the popular song idiom by bringing popular tunes, harmonic progressions, and forms into its own improvised, variational musical domain. In the 1960s and 1970s, the great increase of interest in rock 'n' roll posed a similar challenge. Were jazz artists to ignore rock or to embrace it, as they had earlier embraced Tin Pan Alley? This is a crucial and still unanswered question as jazz approaches a new century. Miles Davis was the leading jazz figure who most sought a fusion of the two styles. In his recording *Bitches' Brew* (1970) and in later works, he used amplified instruments in a manner reminiscent of rock, and he also experimented with repetitive and simplified rock rhythms.

## TOPICS FOR DISCUSSION AND WRITING

**1.** Are ragtime and early blues examples of jazz? Or are they separate forms of popular music? Argue on both sides of this question, using evidence from the recorded examples in this chapter. In the music by Jelly Roll Morton, Louis Armstrong, Duke

Ellington, Charlie Parker, and Ornette Coleman, isolate elements that hark back to ragtime and early blues. Would jazz have attained its greatness as an art form if these two genres had not existed?

**2.** The art of the female blues singer has continued from the time of Ma Rainey and Bessie Smith continuously to the present day. One of the greatest contemporary blues singers is Ella Fitzgerald. Compare a blues piece from one of her many albums (such as *These Are the Blues,* Verve 829536-2) with the singing of Bessie Smith in "Lost Your Head Blues." How are their techniques of enunciation, swing, and expression similar and different? Keep in mind that Ella Fitzgerald is not exclusively a blues singer; she is in fact more active as a popular singer.

**3.** Research the origins of the term *jazz.* Use your findings to hypothesize what music should and should not be covered by the word, and be prepared to support your position. A useful starting place for your research would be the articles by Alan P. Merriam and Fradley H. Garner, "Jazz: The Word," *Ethnomusicology* 12 (1968), 373–396; and by Mark Gridley, Robert Maxham, and Robert Hoff, "Three Approaches to Defining Jazz," *Musical Quarterly* 73 (1989), 513–531.

**4.** The term *fusion* was commonly used in the 1970s and 1980s to refer to a style, associated at first with Miles Davis, that combines elements of jazz and rock. Pick an appropriate work by the groups Weather Report or the Mahavishnu Orchestra, and try to isolate elements that belong to traditional jazz and others stemming from rock.

## ADDITIONAL LISTENING

A good way to become acquainted with the classics of jazz and related styles is to listen to works contained in recorded anthologies. Some that are currently available are listed here.

*Atlantic Jazz.* Twelve LPs, Atlantic 81712-4. A reissue of recordings made by Atlantic Records from 1947, organized by style.

*Blue Note 50th Anniversary Collection.* Five LPs, Blue Note 92547-1. A reissue of recordings made by Blue Note from 1936. Arranged chronologically.

*The Great Band Era: Thirty-seven Top Bands Play Ten Years of Pop Tunes (1936–1945).* Reader's Digest special recordings. Eleven discs.

*History of Jazz: New York Scene, 1914–1945.* Folkways RF-3. One LP containing historical recordings made from 1914 to 1945.

*The Smithsonian Collection of Classic Jazz.* Columbia Special Products P6 11891 (1973). Twelve LPs containing historical recordings and piano rolls, 1916–1966. Selection made by jazz historian Martin Williams.

## BIBLIOGRAPHY

Berlin, Edward A. *Ragtime: A Musical and Cultural History.* Berkeley: University of California Press, 1980.

Blesh, Rudi. *Shining Trumpets: A History of Jazz.* Second edition, revised and enlarged. New York: Knopf, 1958. Blesh was a pioneering jazz historian, but extremely restrictive in what he considers to be jazz.

————. *They All Played Ragtime.* Fourth edition. New York: Oak Publications, 1971.

Feather, Leonard. *The Encyclopedia of Jazz.* Revised edition. New York: Horizon Press, 1960. A standard reference volume.

————. *Inside Bebop.* New York: Da Capo Press, 1977. (Originally published in 1949.)

Evans, David. *Big Road Blues: Tradition and Creativity in the Folk Blues.* Berkeley: University of California Press, 1982.

Gridley, Mark. *Jazz Styles.* Second edition. London: Macmillan, 1985.

Hodeir, André. *Jazz: Evolution and Essence.* Translated by David Noakes. New York: Grove Press, 1956.

————. *Toward Jazz.* Revised edition. New York: Grove Press, 1976.

Mellers, Wilfrid. *Music in a New Found Land.* London: Barrie & Rockliff, 1964. Half of Mellers's coverage of American music centers on jazz.

Oliver, Paul. *The Story of the Blues.* Harmondsworth, England: Penguin, 1972.

Schuller, Gunther. *Early Jazz: Its Roots and Musical Development.* New York: Oxford University Press, 1968. Schuller argues strongly for the connection between African folk music and jazz.

————. *The Swing Era: The Development of Jazz, 1930–1945.* New York: Oxford University Press, 1989.

Shafer, William, and Johannes Riedel. *The Art of Ragtime.* Baton Rouge: Louisiana State University Press, 1973.

Shapiro, Nat, and Nat Hentoff, eds. *Hear Me Talkin' to Ya.* New York: Dover, 1966. (Originally published in 1955.)

Southern, Eileen. *The Music of Black Americans.* Second edition. New York: Norton, 1983.

Stearns, Michael. *The Story of Jazz.* Revised edition. New York: Oxford University Press, 1970.

Williams, Martin. *Jazz Panorama: From the Pages of the Jazz Review.* New York: Da Capo Press, 1979. (Originally published in 1962.)

# 14

The Music of
Selected World Cultures

## The Great Wave

*Off the east coast of Japan, boats founder under the force of gigantic waves. The sacred Mount Fuji lies calmly in the distance, suggesting rest and permanence, but the foreground boils with the fury of wind and water at their most menacing. The crests seem to take on the form of a great monster with a thousand fingers, leaving the helpless sailors little hope of survival.*

*But this is no familiar landscape picture in the European sense. It has little realism, no convincing perspective, no logical source of light, and the great storm that whips the waves is apparently accompanied by few clouds. Its impact relies instead on the subtlety of its colors, its fantastic rhythms of line and shape, and the virtuosity by which the design is printed. This masterpiece,* **The Hollow of the Deep-Sea Wave,** *is the work of the great nineteenth-century Japanese artist Hokusai, from a collection of landscapes called* **Thirty-Six Views of Fuji.**

*Hokusai (1760–1849) was not born into the aristocratic society from which most successful artists in Japan had earlier come. Instead, he learned the crafts of design, calligraphy, and printing from a master of the* **Ukiyo-e** *school, a group of artists who appealed to lower levels of Tokyo society. He made his reputation by illustrating books with colored wood-cut prints and by printing broad sheets. At first his works bypassed the highly refined and symbolic images of classical courtly design in favor of themes sure to please a larger bourgeois public. These often depicted popular actors of the day or— even more in demand—images of people engaged in various forms of pleasure or entertainment.*

*But the* **Ukiyo-e** *artists such as Hokusai eventually refined the art of print making to a level that has never been exceeded. After conceiving of and drawing the design, the artist transferred the image to a flat wood block. The block was inked and multiple images were printed. Then the block was again inked, now in color, and the same papers were printed. The process could be repeated over ten times, until the exact colored tones, mixtures, and densities were obtained.*

*Hokusai's* Thirty-Six Views of Fuji *was a collection of broadsheets published over the years from 1823 to 1829. Here the former* Ukiyo-e *designer aspired to the most tradition-bound of all genres of Japanese art: the landscape. He betrays his bourgeois background by localizing his images. All contain views of Japan's sacred mountain, and these are made from various well-known vantage points. But, true to classical Japanese landscapes, they otherwise avoid the mundane or realistic, projecting instead fantastic images, perfectly balanced forms, and ravishing colors. It is little wonder that following the opening of communication between Japan and the West in the later nineteenth century, Western artists would find inspiration in these prints. Turner, Van Gogh, and the French impressionists repeatedly tried to capture their charm and technical perfection. The composer Claude Debussy was especially delighted by Hokusai's prints, and he proudly displayed* The Hollow of the Deep-Sea Wave *in his own apartment. He and Hokusai shared many of the same insights into nature, its profound beauty, and its essential musicality.*

In our survey of classical and popular music of our own Western culture, we have encountered works of considerable sophistication. These pieces have endured for centuries by virtue of their profound beauty and continuing relevance to our inner life and mind. Music possessing these same qualities also exists in distant regions of the world, far removed from our own culture. We shall conclude our survey of the art of music by touching on some of the most distinguished of these distant musical traditions.

Music the world over has much in common with our own Western variety. It can be divided into classical, folk, and popular categories, using the same criteria for this subdivision that were mentioned in the Prelude of this book. The basic components of music, such as melody, harmony, and rhythm, apply equally well to music in India, Africa, and the Orient as to music in Europe and America. Non-Western music has many of the same goals and functions as our own. It can impart spiritual enlightenment, aesthetic delight, and pure entertainment. It can embody poetic or emotional ideas, and it plays a powerful role in religious or social gatherings and ceremonies.

But there are also important differences. The instruments of music, until relatively recent times, have taken on different shapes in the non-European traditions, lending them, to our ears, unusual and fascinating sonorities. Musical notation has played a much smaller role outside of the West. To be sure, many classical non-Western musics, as in Japan and Indonesia, have been preserved by being written down, but these written sources are usually not crucial to musical practice. The singers and instrumentalists of these regions, by long-standing tradition, learn their art and specific works by rote in an oral process. Perhaps due to the secondary importance of written music, musical style outside of the European tradition has progressed and changed at a much slower pace than in the West.

The musical cultures of the world have not been entirely isolated from one another, either at present or in the past. Certain African tribal instruments show the influence of those from Indonesia, and Indonesian culture at a very ancient time was shaped by the fine arts of India. In the present day, one can hear Beethoven symphonies excellently performed in Tokyo by Japanese orchestras, and English and American popular music is now available literally around the world. Beginning in the late nineteenth century, classical European and American composers came under the influence of non-Western music. Mahler's late symphonies and songs, for example, use the scales of Oriental music. The Japanese instrument called the **koto** has been featured in concertos by the American Henry Cowell.

At the 1889 World's Fair in Paris, Claude Debussy was captivated by Indonesian **gamelan** music, which was performed by native musicians at the

Dutch pavilion. Six years later, he wrote to his friend Pierre Louÿs: "Do you not remember the Javanese music, able to express every shade of meaning, even indescribable shades, that make our tonic and dominant seem like ghosts?" Debussy recorded his recollections in several of his own pieces, our understanding of which is certainly enhanced by knowledge of the model on which they are based. Even in the present day, serious composers derive inspiration from the traditional musics of the world. Steve Reich's music echoes his study of African drumming, and the structures of Hindustani music are evident in works by Philip Glass. The Japanese composer Toru Takemitsu similarly bases his music on a mixture of traditional Japanese courtly elements and Western avant-garde techniques. Now at the end of the twentieth century, as peoples and cultures come closer together, it is imperative that musicians everywhere acquire a closer familiarity with the music of the whole world.

In this chapter, we shall investigate aspects of the traditional music of five flourishing cultures outside of the European orbit. These are intended to give a taste of a much larger and richer artistic diversity. Three of these cultures—India, Japan, and Indonesia—possess classical music of an artistic refinement and complexity that rivals our own. The other two—African and Native American—are tribal cultures. Art in these domains plays a role that is often different from that in the West, but the attainments of its musical practitioners are nonetheless sophisticated and important.

## The Classical Music of India

India has fostered one of the world's great musical cultures. Its music includes a diverse folk art that is carried on in an oral tradition by people untrained in music. An increasingly Westernized popular music is also heard, performed by professional musicians for the entertainment of a large audience. Our main focus will be on India's remarkably rich classical music. Like its Western counterpart, it is based on an ancient and elaborate written theory, it is practiced by intensely trained professional singers and instrumentalists, and it is intended for the enjoyment and enlightenment of a knowledgeable audience.

The geographic scope of our inquiry extends beyond the modern state of India to its northern neighbors of Pakistan, parts of Afghanistan, and Bangladesh and to the southern island of Sri Lanka. These collectively form the region called South Asia, whose musical traditions are sufficiently similar to be studied as a unit. The region has an illustrious cultural history. In

472

ancient times, it was the site of one of the greatest early civilizations, in which there arose the religion of Hinduism and the social structure of castes. The culture of North India was transformed in the eighth to tenth centuries A.D. by waves of Muslim invaders, who established kingdoms centered around a lavish courtly life. By the fifteenth century, Indian classical music in its modern shape was formulated in these regal circumstances, primarily by Muslim musicians.

By the sixteenth century, the Muslim Mogul Empire ruled most of northern India. Under the ruler Akbar (1542–1605), musicians such as the renowned Miya Tansen were supported. From about this time, the music of South India began to evolve in a distinctive manner, leading to the present situation where the music of North India (called the Hindustan) is to an extent distinct from that of South India (the Carnatic regions). The decline of the Mogul Empire in the eighteenth century allowed the furthering of European economic interests, and by the second half of that century, India had come under the economic and political control of Great Britain. Following World War II, India was granted independence from Britain, and the largely Muslim regions in the northwest and the northeast were split off as the state of Pakistan. In 1971, East Pakistan achieved independence and was renamed Bangladesh.

Modern Indian classical music is a continuation of the aristocratic court tradition of the fifteenth and sixteenth centuries. It consists mainly of vocal music, whose words may be either sacred or secular. It also includes instrumental pieces, which in recent times have grown in importance. Indian music embodies an art that is carried on in separate but related theoretical and practical traditions.

*This eighteenth-century Indian painting shows musicians improvising on a raga. The instruments include lutes, drums, cymbals, and the bin (stick zither). In the middle is the Hindu god Krishna, who plays the flute.*

The vocalists and instrumentalists who practice Indian music learn their art primarily by direct study from and imitation of a master, often from members of their own families. These musicians do not always make their works conform to written theories or notated music, and accordingly, the theoretical tradition is not always a reliable reflection of the practical one.

## Music of the Hindustan (North India)

The classical music of both North and South India stems from a single musical tradition, which over the course of the past 400 years has split apart in certain details. Let us begin our investigation of North Indian music by studying a sample work and by applying to it the analytical procedures developed in connection with Western music. We can then generalize about its constructive and stylistic properties and compare it to other works in both the northern and southern styles.

Recording 14.1 contains a short, unnamed instrumental piece performed by three North Indian musicians. It is relatively simple in its construction, thus all the more appropriate to our intuitive approach to its analysis. We cannot call it a composition per se because it is largely improvised. Our attention in this music is first drawn to its fascinating and distinctively "Indian" sound, as well as to its almost jazzy rhythms. Let us begin by assessing the former.

The bell-like melody instrument in this piece is the **jaltarang,** a minor Indian instrument consisting of a set of porcelain bowls. These are tuned to different pitches by partially filling them with water, and the rims of the bowls are then struck by wooden sticks. We also hear a drum, called a **tabla,** which is frequently encountered in North India. It consists actually of two small drums placed in front of the player, who sits cross-legged on the floor or on a stage. The percussionist plays with the fingers and heels of both hands, and he is able to produce different pitches and a variety of sounds. The remaining instrument is the **tambura,** which sounds a continuous drone on the pitches F♯ and C♯. It is a large lutelike instrument usually having four strings, which the player plucks or strums in order to approximate a continuous tone. The instrument usually stands upright in front of the player. The tabla and tambura are depicted in Figure 14.1.

Each of the three instruments on the recording plays a very distinct musical role. The jaltarang carries a melody, the tabla creates rhythmic interest, and the tambura sustains a drone. The texture that results, essentially homophonic, is characteristic of most Indian classical music. Harmony in the Western sense is not an important factor, nor is polyphony. The form of the

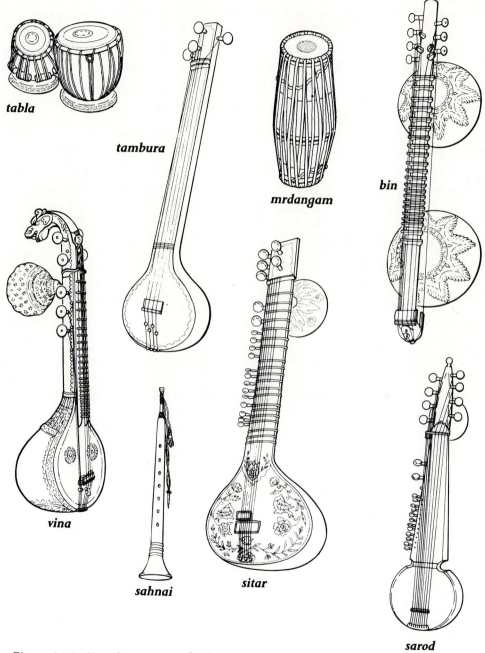

**Figure 14.1** *Musical instruments of India*

music in Recording 14.1 is fairly clear. It begins with a short introduction in which the drone first establishes its notes F♯ and C♯, followed by improvised playing by the jaltarang. There is no sense of regular beat or meter in this introduction, and the drums do not play. The jaltarang player begins in a middle register and then moves upward, as though to expose the pitches that will be available to him later and to forecast certain motivic figures.

After the introduction, the jaltarang player signals the beginning of the body of the work by a passage that establishes a clear beat in a very fast tempo. The drums now enter with a driving, intricate rhythm in the same quick tempo. The jaltarang then sounds a short melodic phrase, illustrated in Figure 14.2. The remainder of the piece consists of improvisation on this phrase, with ever-greater virtuosity and increasing speed. The basic passage reappears periodically, creating a rondolike form, and toward the end, the jaltarang player gives way briefly to the tabla's improvisation as the center of attention.

**Figure 14.2**

The form of the piece, in which an unmetered introduction leads to a rhythmically strict melodic phrase, followed by improvisations on that melody, is encountered in virtually all Indian instrumental works. The diversity of form and genre present in Western instrumental music is absent, although the variety of interpretations of the Indian three-part pattern is infinite. Often the introduction will be long and multipartite. In some works, it is connected to the statement of the basic melody by passages in which regular rhythm and pulse gradually become evident.

The melodic content of the work in Recording 4.1 is not based only on improvisations on a fundamental melody. It is guided more generally by a particular **raga.** This Sanskrit word denotes a system of melodic organization that is central to Indian music. In addition to its general meaning, there are hundreds of individual ragas, each of which suggests distinctive melodic principles. At least in theory, a specific raga has its own pitch collection or scale, its own distinctive ascending and descending melodic shapes and characteristic motives, and its own focal pitches and ornaments. Ragas are also associated with certain times of day that are best suited to them, certain optimal seasons of the year, and specific emotional states.

The melody contained on Recording 14.1 is based on a raga called *Bhupali.* Its most distinctive feature is its pitch content, which is pentatonic. Scales of this type (touched on in Chapter 11) have five notes per octave; these notes are synonymous with an ascending major scale whose fourth and seventh notes are omitted. Most Indian ragas have seven notes per octave, but pentatonic ones, as here, are also common. In the tuning used on this recording, the underlying scale consists of the notes F♯, G♯, A♯, C♯, and D♯. *Bhupali* uses these same five notes whether the melody ascends or descends (not always the case in Indian ragas). In theory, *Bhupali* should have the third note of its scale (here A♯) as a central tone, but, as treated by the musicians on this recording, F♯ appears to be the point of focus. Only at the very end of the improvisation does A♯ emerge as important.

As raga controls the melodic dimension of an Indian classical work, **tala** guides the element of rhythm and meter, thus affecting both the improvisation of the melody instrument and the accompaniment of the drummer. The tala that is chosen for a piece establishes a recurrent cycle of pulses or counts. The tala heard in Recording 14.1 is the very common one called *tintal.* It has a cycle of 16 counts. Since the tempo of the music is very fast, these are not necessarily heard as beats but rather as divisions of a beat. In *tintal,* the first, fifth, and thirteenth counts are emphasized, thus creating a regular pulse and meter that are clearly in evidence in the music. The ninth beat of the cycle is, in theory, unemphasized and thus called "empty" *(khali),* although the distinction between the emphasized and empty beats is not always clear from the music as performed on the recording. The basic melodic phrase following the introduction spans one cycle of the tala. In fact, this central musical phrase is closely identified with and tends to incorporate both the underlying raga and tala.

The tabla player accompanies the melodic improvisations primarily by a very simple pattern of drum strokes called a *theka.* These strokes represent, in a basic way, the underlying pulses and stresses of *tintal.* In our sample piece, the *theka* amounts to a continuous string of very short notes, with emphasis on every fourth note (except for the empty pulse). The percussionist makes some simple elaborations of the *theka* by subdividing some of the pulses, and toward the end, he improvises on the *theka* by temporarily changing its characteristic pattern of accentuation. The very end of the improvisation is marked by a device called *tihai.* This is the introduction of a brief rhythmic-melodic motive that is repeated three times in succession and concludes on the first count of the tala cycle, thus giving the piece a clear ending.

In other pieces of Hindustani music, the melody is carried by a singer. Often the tune is shadowed by an instrument. Some of the most common melodic instruments are the *sitar, bin, sarod,* and *vina* (the last prevalent in Carnatic regions). Flutes and reed instruments (such as the oboelike *sahnai*) are also used for melodies. The tabla is the preeminent drum of North India, as is the *mrdangam* in the south. These instruments are shown in Figure 14.1.

## Carnatic Music

The Carnatic regions of India are those south of an imaginary line connecting the coastal cities of Bombay and Calcutta. Their culture, unlike that of the north, has been relatively unaffected by Islam, and their music today is perhaps less well known in the West than the music of the Hindustan. In general, the classical music of South India is similar to that of North India. Both share the same three-part medium consisting of melodic line, drum, and drone, and they use a similar conception of raga and tala. But the instruments of the south are different and more likely to include Western instruments such as the violin. Dance pieces are more common in the south, and improvisation is more often displaced by the use of compositions learned and preserved by rote. Carnatic vocal music tends to use religious texts addressed to the Hindu god Krishna or Rama.

Many of these features are exemplified by the composition "Banturiti" (Recording 14.2). This is an example of the most common genre of Carnatic music, called *kriti,* and its composition and poetry are attributed to the greatest of South Indian composers, Tyagaraja (1759–1847). The words are a devotional petition to the god Rama:

> Please take me as a guard in your court, O Rama.
> Endow me with the will to control worldly desires, lust, anger and
> pride.
> With awe of your shield, with an emblem inscribed "devotee of
> Rama," and with the name of Rama as a weapon, Tyagaraja,
> whom you protect, asks, please take me as a guard in your
> court.

We hear immediately that the basic texture consists of the same combination of melody, drumming, and drone that characterizes Hindustani music, although the melody here is vocal, and it is shadowed by the playing of a violin. The primary drum is the mrdangam, which is later joined by a tambourinelike drum called a *kanjira.* The mrdangam, shown in Figure 14.1, is barrel-shaped, with membrane heads on opposite ends that are laced down under tension. The drone is produced by a tambura.

*Figure 14.3*

The work begins with a setting of the drone (here to the pitches C and G), without the unmetered introduction. The singer begins straightaway with a musical phrase, called the *pallavi,* that sets the first sentence of the text and later returns as a refrain. It is based melodically on the raga *Hamsanadam,* although the melody of the *pallavi* touches primarily on only four of its notes (C, the central pitch; D; G; and B). Other notes are suggested by ornaments and slides between tones. The basic structure of the *pallavi* phrase is shown in Figure 14.3. In the first section of the piece, the *pallavi* phrase is repeated again and again, increasingly with variations.

The rhythm of this first section is based on the common tala *Adi.* This pattern has a cycle of eight pulses, with emphasis on pulses 1, 5, and 7. The actual rhythm of the opening passage, however, exhibits a complicated structure having little connection with the tala, where the rhythms of the vocal melody and the drum do not coincide.

After the repetitions of the first section, the second sentence of text is set to a new melodic phrase. Like the first, it is repeated several times with variations. Here the voice explores a higher register in a more recitational manner while the drum rhythm becomes more animated and virtuosic. Next is a return to the music and text of the first section, with certain variants. The third and final sentence is set to the music of the second, and the entire work is concluded by a final return to the *pallavi* music.

## *Traditional Music in Japan and the Far East*

The musical cultures of China, Japan, and their neighboring countries are closely intertwined. Throughout the extensive artistic history of these lands, which extends back to the second millennium B.C., music has been used for rituals, for political indoctrination, and for educational purposes. Increasingly in modern history, it has also provided entertainment, often connected with dance or with the narration of tales, and it has acquired an especially close relationship with theater. The melodic element of Far Eastern music is usually based on scales with seven notes per octave, with emphasis on a pentatonic subgroup. These melodies, with or without singing, are clearly the central elements, since Western-type harmony or counterpoint has little importance.

**479**

## *Music Today*

### Ravi Shankar

The artistry of Indian musicians would have remained relatively unknown to Western audiences, were it not for the work of one individual, Ravi Shankar. Almost singlehandedly, he has brought the sounds and virtuosity of the Hindustan to the awareness of Europe and America, and his music has found devoted followers here equally among fans of rock 'n' roll and with classical audiences.

Shankar was born in 1920 in the North Indian city of Benares. He came from a family of musicians and artists, from whom he received his early training. His brother Uday also excelled in the arts, becoming one of the most esteemed classical dancers of his era. Shankar specialized in the lutelike **sitar,** with which he has amazed audiences around the world since the 1950s. During this decade he first traveled and performed in the West, whose music—both popular and classical—he also relishes.

He has collaborated with numerous Western musicians. With the concert violinist Yehudi Menuhin he made several recordings, and Shankar shares with Menuhin a great interest in music as a means to political and social betterment of all humanity. His music was much esteemed by the Beatles, especially by his friend George Harrison, and the Beatles imitated Shankar's idiom in their song "Within You Without You" from the album *Sgt. Pepper's Lonely Hearts Club Band.*

Shankar has significantly enriched the ancient art of the sitar, achieving recognition in his homeland as a *pandit,* a wise and learned person. He has also sought to unite Eastern and Western musical cultures. He often composes for film, and he has worked in the Western genres of ballet and concerto.

His influence on modern Western composers continues undiminished. In the mid-1960s he collaborated with Philip Glass on the preparation of a film score. As Glass later recounted, his new awareness of the repetitive structure of Indian rhythm was his guide in the creation of his own distinctively repetitive or "minimalist" idiom.

Many musical instruments, including flutes, **zithers,** and lutes, are found in similar forms throughout the region.

In China, the **pipa** and the **qin** are basic to instrumental music (see Figure 14.4). The pipa resembles the lute. It performs soloistic (often descriptive) music, or it can accompany singing. The qin is a very ancient zither whose strings are plucked with the fingers. It is traditionally used for courtly functions.

As is the case in all cultures of the Far East, Chinese music is closely associated with theater. There exist numerous regional types of theater, in

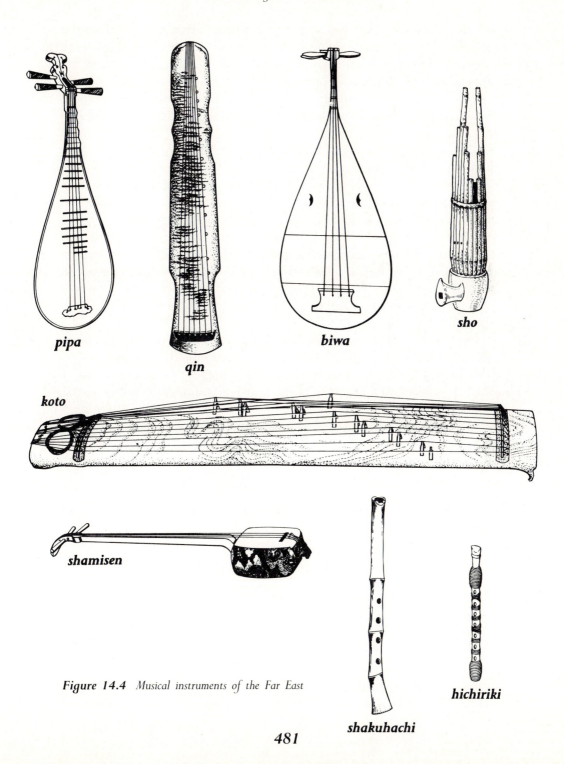

**pipa**

**qin**

**biwa**

**sho**

**koto**

**shamisen**

**shakuhachi**

**hichiriki**

*Figure 14.4* *Musical instruments of the Far East*

which the importance of music is so great as to warrant applying to them the term *opera*. The *Peking opera,* for example, maintains the same popularity throughout China that it has enjoyed since the nineteenth century. It consists of singing, dialogue, acting, and often acrobatics, with the musical accompaniment of melodic instruments (mainly strings) and percussion. The music is essentially monodic, based on a small number of standard tunes with differing texts.

Music in Japan is based on a continuous tradition extending back at least to the sixth century A.D., when leaders of a powerful regional clan established an empire whose center was first at Nara, then at Kyoto. The imperial Japanese court was modeled on that of the Tang dynasty, then the ruling family in China. Courtly music was largely based on foreign models, especially those imported from China and Korea. Later, from the twelfth century to well into the nineteenth, Japan was ruled by military figures called *shoguns,* who led a feudal society centered in various cities. At their courts, the traditional music of the Nara emperors continued to flourish and its genres were expanded, especially when music was brought into the flourishing forms of theatrical entertainment.

In 1867, in part due to powerful Western interests, the shoguns were overthrown and the ancient line of emperors was restored. This event led to the creation of a modern, nonfeudal, and increasingly Westernized society and political structure and to the permanent establishment of Tokyo as the capital of Japan.

The oldest and most tradition-bound genre of music in Japan is called **gagaku** (literally, "elegant music"). It was putatively brought to Japan in the fifth century by court musicians from Korea, and it developed in imitation of courtly Chinese music. It has existed in the courts of Japanese rulers continuously to the present, and it also plays a role in Shinto religious ceremonies. *Gagaku* is a generic term designating many different types of courtly music. It includes purely instrumental works, a limited repertory of ancient folk songs in which a singer is accompanied by instruments, and songs and dances associated with Shinto ceremonies. The most important *gagaku* music is the instrumental type, which can be used to accompany dancing (called *bugaku*) or as an independent genre (called *kangen*).

The music of both *kangen* and *bugaku* falls into two types, depending on whether the pieces originally stemmed from China and India or from Korea and Manchuria. The difference now between these two is found primarily in the instruments used (see Figure 14.4). In all types, the primary melody instrument is the **hichiriki,** a small, oboelike reed instrument. Its melody is usually duplicated or shadowed by small wooden flutes such as the *ryuteki* or

**Part of a larger gagaku ensemble at the Imperial Palace in Tokyo is assembled in this picture.**

*komabue.* In some orchestrational styles, there is also a zither called the *koto,* a lute called a *biwa,* and a mouth-organ called the *sho.* This last instrument has 17 small vertical pipes extending from a wind-chest into which the player blows. It produces chords of five or six notes, and it is used to shadow and partially duplicate a melody.

All of the *gagaku* ensembles include a variety of percussion instruments. The *taiko* is ever-present. This is a colorfully painted drum played with beaters. In *bugaku* a huge version is used. The gong called the *shoko* is also used in all ensembles, as is a form of small drum, usually played with sticks. The rhythms played by the percussionists can be isolated strokes or a distinctive pattern in which drum beats seem to accelerate without reference to a regular beat.

A typical *kangen* performance brings together a large ensemble with two to four of each woodwind and string instrument playing in unison. A work usually begins with a brief passage for solo flute in a free rhythm, which touches on notes of the underlying scale. The full ensemble then enters with a loud and, to Western ears, rather strident sound. The melodic motion is very slow and deliberate. Works are now performed from memory by musicians on the staff of the imperial court. These artists generally learn their craft and specific pieces by rote, although much of their music is also preserved in musical notation.

*A performance of a Japanese Kabuki drama.*

Many basic genres of traditional Japanese music are also associated with three types of theater: *No, Bunraku,* and *Kabuki.* No was established in the late fourteenth century. In its present manner of performance, it is a highly stylized, symbolic form of theater that conveys a refined and elegant idea through storytelling, song, dance, and visual symbolism. It combines entertainment with a decidedly ritualistic ceremony.

No is performed by a few lavishly costumed actors on a special stage. Musicians sit at the back of the stage, and a chorus of singers is assembled at the right. The stories are generally drawn from history. The music of No includes singing by the main actor (in either recitational or lyrical style), unison singing by the chorus, and instrumental music that accompanies dancing. The instruments in modern No drama are a flute (the *nohkan*) and three drums. Their playing, like all gestures in this idiom, is understated and sparing.

Bunraku is the famous Japanese puppet theater. Stories are acted out by puppets controlled by three men, all fully in view of the audience. The stories are narrated by a singer, accompanied by the banjolike *shamisen,* also in full view. This narrative music is called *gidayu,* named after a seventeenth-century singer in Osaka, and it consists of an alternation of passages solely for the shamisen with lyrical or recitational singing. The Kabuki theater is of more recent origin, more eclectic in its makeup, and more popular in spirit. Stories may be taken from No, from Bunraku, or from other sources. Music is played both onstage and off, and the ensembles usually have flutes, several shamisen, and percussion. The music may be narrational, in the manner of *gidayu,* it may accompany dancing, describe scenery or moods, or accompany singing.

The most important melodic instruments of Japanese music—the biwa, koto, shamisen, and shakuhachi—each have their own genres and repertories. All except the shakuhachi are used primarily in ensembles. Let us examine this last instrument and its traditional music. The shakuhachi is an end-blown flute made of bamboo. It somewhat resembles the recorder. Its sound and playing techniques have made it almost synonymous with Japanese music (it is shown in Figure 14.4). Ancestors of such end-blown bamboo flutes were found in *gagaku* ensembles even in the Nara period, and later it was traditionally played by wandering Buddhist priests.

In the present day, the shakuhachi plays either in ensembles or, more typically, as a highly refined and expressive solo instrument. The modern instrument has five finger holes tuned to a pentatonic scale, but it can also play other tones by adjusting the angle at which the instrument touches the lips or by covering the finger holes only partially. The centerpiece of its literature consists of "original music," a repertory of about 60 soloistic works from the seventeenth and eighteenth centuries. It also plays so-called borrowed pieces, generally transcriptions from the traditional koto repertory, and also new works composed from the nineteenth century to the present.

**A performance of a Japanese No drama is seen in this photograph.**

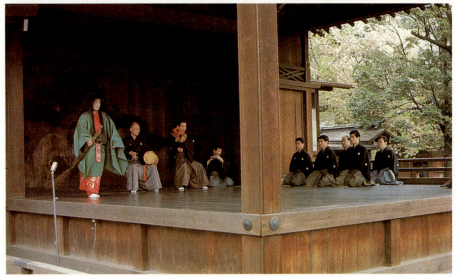

"Shokaku-Reibo" ("Depicting the Cranes in Their Nest," Recording 14.3) was composed by the shakuhachi virtuoso Kinko Kurosawa (1710–1771). Kurosawa's music for his instrument is the basis of the original repertory. This piece is descriptive in nature, as indicated by the title, and its effect depends perhaps more on the expressive interpretation of the notated music than on the notes themselves. The music, an excerpt of which is heard on Recording 14.3 performed by the virtuoso Coro Yamaguchi, has no specific form and no regular rhythm or meter. The player repeats certain motives and then moves on to others, generally moving from the low register of the instrument to a higher one. Like most Japanese music, this piece is slow in movement, understated in gesture, and highly refined. The nuances of the player—including sliding between tones, releasing notes with an expressive fall, a fluttering effect of the tongue, or a rapid trembling with the fingers—are characteristic of the instrument in the hands of a virtuoso. These effects aid the performer in making the music suggestive and clear in its power to represent images or ideas. The main pitches available to the instrument are found in the scale C-D-E♭-F-G-A♭-A-B♭.

## African Music

Of all the major traditional musical cultures of the world, that of Africa is perhaps the most complicated. This situation stems from many factors: the complexity of the music itself, its lack of a musical notation or of a written musical theory, the scarcity of documentation of its historical development, the size of the continent of Africa, its many languages, and its divergent cultural and artistic traditions. In a brief survey such as this, we can at most hope to arrive at some generalizations concerning African music and to study a specific work.

The earliest civilization in Africa was formed in Egypt in the fourth millennium B.C. Then and in the centuries following, music was a prominent aspect of courtly life among the pharaohs and subsequently had a decisive impact on the musical culture of ancient Greece. In the first four centuries A.D., northern Africa was largely controlled by Roman conquerors and then, from the seventh century, by Arab tribes unified by the religion of Islam. The history of sub-Saharan regions is little documented prior to the sixteenth century or later, but it is likely that this part of Africa was divided into regional kingdoms of which the most powerful and widespread were made up of Bantu-speaking peoples.

The sixteenth through nineteenth centuries in Africa were marked by steadily increasing colonialism. Economic and political control, especially in coastal regions, was exercised by European powers. The western areas of Africa were exploited for slaves, who, from the seventeenth century onward, were captured to be shipped primarily to the New World. By 1900 virtually all of Africa was subdivided into provinces controlled by France, England, Portugal, and other European nations. After 1950, these regions gradually achieved independence, and today the continent is divided into more than 50 sovereign nations.

The clearest cultural division of Africa is between the northern lands, stretching from Mauritania on the west coast to Egypt and Sudan in the northeast, and the southern or sub-Saharan parts of the continent. The North is unified culturally and historically by Islam, the dominant religion of this region since the seventh century. Arabic is the primary language among the peoples of this part of Africa, most of whom are Caucasians. The larger sub-Saharan part of the continent is inhabited primarily by Negroid peoples. They speak an amazing variety of languages—probably more than 800— although these can be classed into relatively few groups, of which the Bantu languages are dominant.

## Music of Arabic Africa

In the seventh century and thereafter, Arabic tribes in northern Africa embraced Islam and were unified into an empire that extended from Spain, through North Africa, around the eastern Mediterranean, and into modern-day Turkey. Three basic languages—Arabic, Persian, and Turkish—were spoken in the empire, which was ruled by one or more caliphs. As the Middle Ages progressed, the unity of the empire steadily declined, ending definitively with the dissolution of the Ottoman Empire in 1918. The culture and traditional music of the entire region, however, are closely related.

Music in Arabic Africa consists of folk and popular songs, chanting of religious texts, and a well-developed classical music. Despite the traditional skepticism with which Islam has viewed a worldly art such as music, the courts of the Islamic Empire fostered an artistic musical culture that still exists today among the higher social strata. During the Middle Ages, a period during which the learning and artistic traditions of classical antiquity were nearly extinguished in western Europe, the caliphs of the Near East eagerly patronized the arts and sciences and otherwise fostered a civilization that was probably the world's most distinguished. Modern artistic music of the Near East originated in this milieu.

The classical music of North Africa is now typically played and sung by an ensemble consisting of voice and stringed and percussion instruments. The most popular stringed instrument throughout the Arabic world is the ʿ**ud** (see Figure 14.5). This very ancient instrument was transported through Muslim Spain to Europe, where its name (*al-ʿud,* "the ʿud") was transformed into *lute* and where it flourished in the Renaissance and baroque periods. Other important string instruments include a zither called the **qanun** and a small instrument having one to three strings and played with a bow, called the **rabab.** The European violin is also found in modern Arabic music, as it is in the Carnatic regions of India. Wind instruments in the traditional music of North Africa include the long and slender end-blown flute called the *nay* and the oboelike *zurna.* Many types of drums are characteristic of this music, especially the *darabukka.* All of these are depicted in Figure 14.5.

The music of these ensembles is generally centered on a single melodic line that is accompanied by percussion. It may consist of composed pieces learned by rote, improvisations, or a combination of the two. The most basic genre of composition is the *nawba,* which consists of a succession of distinct sections of contrasting character. The melodic materials are based on one or more *maqamat,* which resemble Indian ragas. Each *maqam* limits the players to a particular scale of notes (often deviating entirely from the half-step-based intervals of Western music). It also establishes a keynote and registral boundaries, and it provides stock motivic figures. Like the Indian ragas, the *maqamat,* at least in theory, convey emotional content. The percussion play recurrent rhythmic figures based on patterns akin to the Indian talas.

### Music of Sub-Saharan Africa

Unlike the North, Africa south of the Sahara is not culturally unified, and its traditional music is so diverse as to defy generalization. It contains no distinctly classical music. There exists in this region primarily a type of folk music that can be called *tribal.* (The term *primitive* is also used to describe the music of Black Africa, although this word is misleading as to the high degree of complexity that the music exhibits.) Tribal music exists among illiterate people, and its materials and techniques are passed on purely by oral tradition. Tribal music plays an especially large role in social and religious gatherings.

Music that is played and sung in Africa is primarily functional. It is made both by professional and amateur musicians to celebrate rites of passage (such as weddings or funerals), in worship, at social gatherings, and to accompany work, storytelling, and dance. This music is also heard by its listeners as

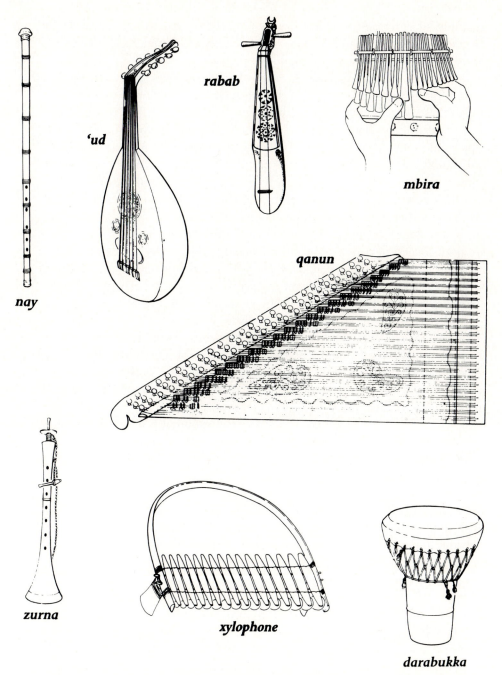

**rabab**

**'ud**

**mbira**

**nay**

**qanun**

**zurna**

**xylophone**

**darabukka**

**Figure 14.5**  *Musical instruments of the African continent*

a source of entertainment and beauty. Its genres and forms appear highly diverse, although call-and-response patterns, characteristic also of African-American folk music, are common.

African music (referring here to that of the sub-Saharan regions) is most typically played by ensembles of instruments with or without singers. Sometimes these groups will be heterogeneous in makeup, but at other times they consist of versions of a single instrument. Drum ensembles are especially important. Solo playing or singing is encountered as well. A great diversity of instruments, representing all basic types, can be found. Drums are especially numerous, although no single variety is identifiable. Versions of the xylophone (see Figure 14.5) are common, and this may be an indigenous African instrument. The *hand piano* (called the *mbira* or *kalimba* in some African languages) is almost certainly of African origin. Among the stringed instruments are bow-shaped devices whose sound is controlled by the player's mouth or by some resonating device, along with zithers, lyres or harps, and fiddles of various kinds. Flutes—end-blown, transverse, or collected as panpipes—are common, as are trumpets made from wood or from animal horn.

Perhaps the most distinctive stylistic aspect of African music is its emphasis on rhythm, whether produced by drum ensembles or by melodic instruments. Rhythmic lines containing very different figures are often superimposed to create intricately complicated patterns and polyrhythms. These may be loosely coordinated, coming together with a common beat only sparingly. The individual line is typically constructed from some repeated rhythmic figure. Melodic lines may be added contrapuntally to rhythmic ones. These melodies use a diversity of scales, ranging from those of only a few notes to more familiar pentatonic or seven-note types. Harmony can result in such contrapuntal works in fleeting pitch clusters or in parallel and coordinated movement among two or more lines.

A sample of drum and wind music from West Africa is found on Recording 14.4 This was recorded in northern Ghana, and the music was probably intended to accompany dancing. The instruments consist of three *gulu* drums (cylindrical drums played with sticks or the hands) and four *wiiks,* end-blown flutes of limited pitch. The music is typical in its contrapuntal texture. The drums play several patterns, which together clearly establish a beat and a fairly regular and motoric rhythm. Several flutes produce a repetitive melodic line that dwells on the alternation of only two pitches, roughly a semitone apart. Another flute is dimly heard in a higher register playing a more elaborate melodic figure. The music is expanded primarily by ostinato, and its form consists of a regular alternation of sections where all of the instruments play and other passages where only a few drums and flutes continue with variants on the basic materials.

## Music in Indonesia: Java and Bali

The modern-day republic of Indonesia consists of numerous islands in the Malay Archipelago, extending from Sumatra in the west to part of New Guinea in the east. The main economic and cultural centers are on the western islands of Sumatra, Java, and Bali. The region, which lies directly on the equator, is diverse in language and culture, reflecting its complicated history and diffuse geography. Throughout their history, the islands of Indonesia have absorbed wave after wave of outside cultural and religious influences. In the early centuries of the Common Era, Indian culture, together with the Hindu and Buddhist religions, became dominant. This influence is still felt in Indonesian theater, called *wayang,* which often portrays tales from the Indian epics, the *Mahabharata* and *Ramayana.* Hindu is still a dominant religion on the island of Bali, despite its having taken on many indigenous characteristics.

In the thirteenth century, Islam was brought to the islands by Arab traders. It became the principal religion by the sixteenth century, and, today, about 85 percent of the population of Indonesia is Muslim. From the sixteenth century, the many native kingdoms of Indonesia began to come under the economic and political sway of Europe. The Dutch were especially successful in colonizing the region, which by 1800 was known as the Dutch East Indies. The nineteenth and early twentieth centuries saw a steady increase in nationalistic and separatist sentiment among the Indonesians, leading to independence in 1945. After a devastating period of civil warfare in the 1960s, peace and relative prosperity have returned to this nation.

The closely related musical cultures of Java and Bali are the best known in all Indonesia. In the late nineteenth century, musicians from these islands traveled to Europe, where their music made a lasting impression, especially in France. Modern French composers from Debussy to Boulez have time and again evoked the pulsating, metallic sonorities of Indonesian music in their own compositions. Balinese and Javanese music is known and admired by Westerners for its vibrancy, color, and imagination.

The music of Java and Bali is highly artistic in its degree of sophistication but folklike in that it is practiced as much by amateur musicians in social circumstances as by professionals in formal settings. The traditional music of the islands functions as informal, communal entertainment and also in religious ceremonies. Music is also crucial to the famous *wayang* theater of Java and Bali, in which artfully crafted puppets act out stories in presentations that can last an entire night. The puppets' shapes are often exaggerated by lighting so as to cast fantastic shadows. The puppeteer chants the stories and directs the accompanying music. A related type of theater replaces the puppets with live actors and dancers.

## Media and Instruments

The generic term for an Indonesian musical ensemble is *gamelan*. It may include only a few instruments or as many as 80, it is diverse in its makeup, and it may include one or more voices. Instruments in a gamelan conform to either the *pelog* or *slendro* tunings (described below), but large ensembles may mix instruments of both types, allowing for greater musical flexibility. The large ensembles are characterized by their metallic percussion instruments, but smaller and softer gamelans using voice, flutes, and stringed instruments exist as well. A large gamelan is characteristic of courtly or aristocratic private circumstances, but gamelans of more modest proportions are common in villages, where they are staffed by amateurs who perform for religious ceremonies or festivals or informally for social occasions.

*A Balinese gamelan accompanying dancers.*

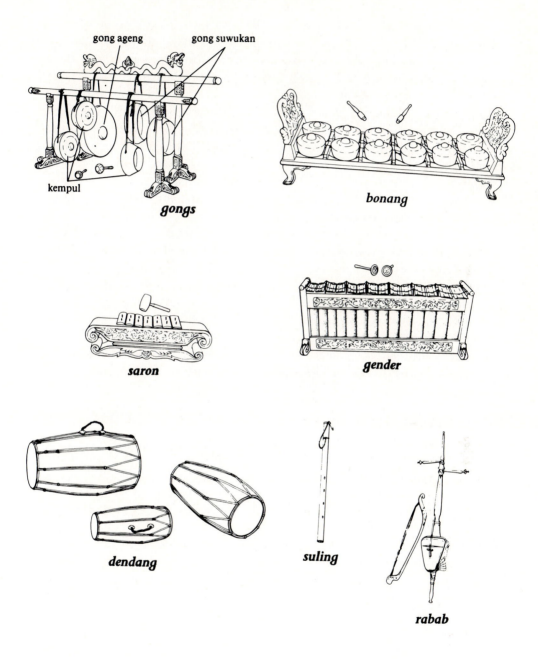

**Figure 14.6** *Indonesian musical instruments*

The instruments of the gamelan reflect the great artistry of the Indonesian people, not only in music but also in woodworking and metalworking, carving, and painting. They are usually beautiful in appearance, and their sounds are inherently attractive. The instruments themselves, as well as their music, have religious significance for most Indonesians. The most distinctive family is the metallic percussion instruments of the **gong** family. The term *gong,* like the names of most Indonesian metallophones, is onomatopoetic. The gongs (see Figure 14.6) are of various sizes, of which the largest, called *gong ageng* in Java, is sounded in order to mark off basic musical phrases. Related to the gongs are metallic kettles such as the large *kethuk,* the paired *kempyang* (intentionally left out of tune to produce a throbbing resonance), and the rows of smaller *bonang.*

Other percussion instruments include the **saron,** whose few bronze bars are strung over a box resonator; it plays a basic slow-moving melodic line. The *gender* is an instrument similar to the xylophone, with bars of bronze rather than of wood. Drums include the two-headed *dendang,* the smaller *ketipung,* and the large, suspended *bedug.* Some of these are shown in Figure 14.6. The main wind instrument is an end-blown bamboo flute (the *suling*), and the string family is represented by zithers of different sizes and a bowed lute called the *rabab.* This instrument is related to that of the same name in North Africa and to the medieval *rebec,* a predecessor of the violin.

## Musical Style

The music of a gamelan consists typically of a slow-moving melody played by sarons, which is simultaneously varied in faster motion by as many other melodic instruments as are present. Pairs of melody instruments often create the effect of a single melodic line by alternating notes in an interlocking manner. Gongs play at regular intervals, the lower instruments less frequently than the higher ones. Their sounds serve to mark off phrases and subphrases. The entire ensemble is usually led by one player, often a drummer if the group is large, who directs changes in tempo and coordinates large-scale form. Musical works are generally learned by rote or through rehearsal, although Indonesia now has a musical notational system.

The melodic element of the gamelan rests on either a pentatonic collection of notes (called *slendro*) or a seven-note scale similar to the Western major scale (called *pelog*). Different notes of either scale can be emphasized, a distinction that is associated with different emotional qualities.

## Music for the Balinese Theater

An example of the colorful music of Indonesia is heard in Recording 14.5. This is an excerpt from music used in Bali's *wayang kulit,* or shadow puppet theater. It is similar to the puppet theater of Java, although the gamelan is somewhat smaller. When presenting stories from the Indian *Mahabharata,* the music is typically provided solely by four gender. Each of these xylophonelike instruments is provided with about ten bronze bars strung above bamboo resonators. The instrument is played with mallets, and in this case, its notes are tuned to the pentatonic *slendro* scale. This is roughly equivalent to the Western scale E♭-F-A♭-B♭-C, although the intervals are not exactly the equally tempered intervals of Western music, and the four gender are not themselves at precisely the same level of pitch. Their small discrepancies of intonation create a shimmering, throbbing sound. The sound of the mallet hitting the metal bar is also very apparent, tending to produce a rhythmic series of clicks that enhances the musical effect.

The music clearly consists of two streams of sound combined polyphonically. One contains the melody, which regularly comes to a pause on an important pitch such as E♭, C, or F. The two players who create the melody interlock their notes so that an effect of a single melodic line is produced. The other two players create an accompaniment consisting of a rhythmical stream of notes that is almost mesmerizing in its regularity and colorful sonority. Indeed, this highly rhythmicized and repetitive music may remind us of the style of American minimalist composers such as Steve Reich.

**Balinese musicians.**

495

# The Music of Native North Americans

It is generally held that Native Americans (or American Indians) migrated in successive waves across the Bering land bridge during prehistoric times. They subsequently spread throughout North and South America, where they developed a large number of languages and cultures. In North America, distinct cultural and geographic groupings of tribes developed in the Eastern Woodlands, the Northeast, the Southeast, the Plains, the Plateau and Great Basin of the West, the Southwest, and the Northwest. Some of these areas saw the development of sophisticated tribal cultures, but others, especially those where the land was forbidding, remained artistically barren.

Music has traditionally played a very large role in the culture of Native Americans. Although their music is as diverse as other aspects of their art, there is also much common ground. Most music by Native Americans of whatever tribal allegiance is sung, either by a soloist or by a chorus, and the accompaniment is usually limited to percussion instruments. The music is normally monophonic and consists of songs passed on in an oral tradition. These are constructed by simple repetition of phrases or cells, sometimes based on a very limited number of notes. The words normally deal with matters of religion, prayer, or storytelling, and they often include nonsense syllables, shouting, and animal cries. They are usually sung in a robust, forceful manner. The melodies are based on many different scales, with the pentatonic scale common. The music is closely associated with religion, ritual, and dancing.

The instruments of music among these aboriginal peoples are limited primarily to drums, rattles, flutes, and whistles. The musical bow, akin to that found in African music, is seen, and among the wind instruments, the **bull roarer** is also found. This instrument consists of a flat noisemaking device tied to a string. When it is swung around, it produces a shrill sound.

## TOPICS FOR DISCUSSION AND WRITING

**1.** Aspects of Indian classical music first came to the attention of many Americans in the 1960s, when it was studied and imitated by the Beatles. Listen to their song "Within You Without You" (from the album *Sgt. Pepper's Lonely Hearts Club Band*), and isolate elements that are authentically Indian. What instruments are used? Does the texture of the accompaniment conform to the Indian norm? Why might the Beatles have used Indian musical elements for this song?

**2.** Listen to Steve Reich's lengthy minimalistic study *Drumming* (on DGG 427428-2 or Nonesuch/Elektra CD 79170-2), and seek to isolate aspects of African musical practices that it contains. The work was composed shortly after Reich returned from a study of African drumming in Ghana in 1970.

**3.** Debussy's character piece for piano "Pagodes," included in the collection *Estampes* in 1903, reflects his fascination for Indonesian and other Oriental music heard at the Paris World's Fair in 1889. Listen to this colorful and exotic piece, and isolate the authentically Eastern elements of its style.

**4.** In recent decades, leading Japanese composers have been inclined to mix Western avant-garde precepts of composition with traditional Oriental materials. A leader in this development is Toru Takemitsu (b. 1930). Listen to his lengthy work for *gagaku* titled *In an Autumn Garden* (Varèse Sarabande Records 47213). Focus on the fourth movement (whose subtitle is the same as that of the entire work), and identify the instruments. Isolate traditional features of Japanese court music, and also point to musical procedures that are typical of contemporary Western composers.

## ADDITIONAL LISTENING

### African Music

Many recordings are available on Folkways, Nonesuch/Elektra, and Lyrichord. See especially the Nonesuch "Explorer Series," the UNESCO Collection titled *Rhythm of the Manding* (Grem/Waira DSM 042), and the three-volume *African Rhythm and Instruments* (Lyrichord 7328, 7338, and 7339).

### Indian Classical Music

Ravi Shankar has recorded his sitar music for World Pacific and Columbia/CBS, and the sarod music of Ali Akbar Khan is heard on Connoisseur Society Records. The Nonesuch/Elektra "Explorer Series" has several recordings in this category, as do Monitor Records, Oriental Records, Nimbus Records, and Lyrichord Records.

### Japanese Traditional Music

The Nonesuch/Elektra "Explorer Series" has several recordings of Japanese music that are easily available. The UNESCO Collection, *A Musical Anthology of the Orient* (Musicaphon BM 30 L2012-2017) and the 13-volume anthology *Hogaku Taikei* (Nippon Victor UP 3006-3031) may be difficult to obtain.

### Javanese and Balinese Music

The Dutch company Philips has many recordings of gamelan music, as do Nonesuch/Elektra and Lyrichord.

### Native American Music

New World, Indian House, and Canyon Records specialize in the music of Native Americans.

# BIBLIOGRAPHY

## General Sources

*Ancient and Oriental Music* (Volume 1 of *The New Oxford History of Music*). London: Oxford University Press, 1957. Authoritative articles by different authors.

*Ethnomusicology.* This journal, published at Wesleyan University since 1953, is regularly consulted by specialists in non-Western music.

Kunst, Jaap. *Ethnomusicology*. The Hague: Nijhoff, 1959. Long a standard work.

Malm, William. *Musical Cultures of the Pacific, the Near East, and Asia*. Englewood Cliffs, N.J.: Prentice Hall, 1967.

May, Elizabeth, ed. *Music of Many Cultures: An Introduction*. Berkeley: University of California Press, 1980. Excellent articles by different authors, also with illustrative records.

Merriam, Alan P. *The Anthropology of Music*. Evanston, Ill.: Northwestern University Press, 1964.

Nettl, Paul. *Folk and Traditional Music of the Western Continents*. Englewood Cliffs, N.J.: Prentice Hall, 1965.

*The New Grove Dictionary of Musical Instruments*. New York: Grove's Dictionaries, 1984. An up-to-date source on instruments from all nations.

## Studies of Specific Musical Cultures

Jairazbhoy, Nazir. *The Rags of North Indian Music: Their Structure and Evolution*. London: Faber & Faber, 1971. A basic analytical study.

Jones, A. M. *Studies in African Music*. Two volumes. London: Oxford University Press, 1959. Jones's remarkably detailed study focuses on West African music.

Kishibe, Shigeo. *The Traditional Music of Japan*. Tokyo: Kokusai Bunka Shinkokai, 1966.

Kunst, Jaap. *Music of Java*. Two volumes. Second edition. The Hague: Nijhoff, 1949.

McPhee, Colin. *A House in Bali*. New York: John Day, 1946.

————. *Music in Bali*. New Haven, Conn.: Yale University Press, 1966. The definitive English-language study of its subject.

Malm, William. *Japanese Music and Musical Instruments*. Tokyo: Tuttle, 1959.

Merriam, Alan P. "Traditional Music of Black Africa." In *Africa,* edited by Phyllis Martin and Patrick O'Meara. Bloomington: Indiana University Press, 1977, pp. 243–258.

Nettl, Paul. *North American Indian Musical Styles*. Philadelphia: American Folklore Society, 1954.

Nketia, J. H. Kwabena. *The Music of Africa*. New York: Norton, 1974. Highly recommended survey.

Shankar, Ravi. *My Music, My Life*. New York: Simon & Schuster, 1968.

Wade, Bonnie. *Music in India: The Classical Traditions*. Englewood Cliffs, N.J.: Prentice Hall, 1979.

# *Appendix*

# Musical Notation

Learning to read music begins with an understanding of the notational signs and symbols that represent musical elements. The rules by which music is written down are reasonably simple. But to be able to apply this knowledge—to play, sing, or imagine music given in written form—is more difficult in that it requires lengthy practice and instruction. Here we will concentrate solely on the first step: understanding the meaning of basic musical notation.

## The Notation of Pitch

Let us first review aspects of musical tones that were discussed in Chapter 1. Pitches in music are designated by the first seven letters of the alphabet. In ascending order, these are A, B, C, D, E, F, and G. The note after G is again called A because it is an octave above the previous A. The sequence A through G can then be repeated indefinitely in ever-higher registers.

But there are also notes that fall between some of those with simple letter names. These in-between tones are named by using the pitch letter lying immediately above or immediately below them, plus the word *sharp* (if the note lies just above the lettered pitch) or *flat* (if it is just below the lettered pitch). The note between A and B, for example, is called equally A♯ or B♭ (read "A-sharp" and "B-flat"). There are no tones lying between B and C or between E and F. As illustrated in Figure A.1, the notes with regular letter names correspond to the white keys on the piano. The in-between tones are produced by black keys.

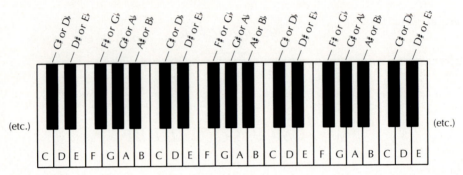

**Figure A.1**

    Pitch notation tells us the name of the tone and also the register in which it occurs. This is accomplished by the placement of a *note head* (a small open or solid circle or oval) on a *staff.* The staff consists of five parallel lines, which can temporarily be expanded to a larger number by so-called *ledger lines.* These are illustrated in Figure A.2. Note heads are situated either straddling a line or in the space between lines. Each note head represents a single tone, and these are read from left to right. Some examples are shown in Figure A.3.

**Figure A.2**

**Figure A.3**

    We now need only one more bit of information to tell us just which pitch the note head refers to. This is the *clef.* A clef is a sign placed at the left end of a staff. It informs us which lines and spaces of that staff refer to which pitch letters. There are three different types of clefs: G clef (𝄞), F clef (𝄢), and C clef (𝄡).

The G clef is so named because its coiled lower part straddles the staff line that represents the note G. Almost always, this will be the second line from the bottom of the staff, in which position the G clef is also called the *treble clef.* The pitch letters of the other lines and spaces can easily be computed once the second line is defined as G. In the following example, we see the notes represented by lines and spaces in treble clef (a few sharpened notes are also included):

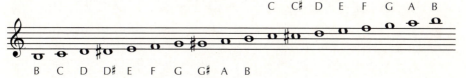

Notice how the in-between notes (D♯, G♯, and C♯ above) are indicated. The symbol for sharp (♯) or flat (♭) is entered just to the left of the note head. Also observe that the pitches placed on this staff could, by the use of more and more ledger lines, be extended further upward or downward.

An F clef is placed on the staff so that its two dots straddle a line representing the note F. Almost always, this will be the second line down, whereupon the F clef is called the *bass clef.* The notes represented by lines and spaces in bass clef are shown in the following example. Observe that a note on the second line down is defined by the bass clef as F.

The placement of the C clef is less standardized, but it is most commonly situated straddling either the second line from the top or the middle line of the staff. In either case, a note on this line is defined as C, and the pitch letters of the other lines and spaces can be computed from this point of orientation:

Next we need to learn the specific register in which these letter pitches occur. This can be done by locating *middle C* on the piano keyboard. Recall

**501**

where the note C occurs in the pattern of black and white keys (see Figure A.1). Now sit squarely in front of the middle of the piano keyboard. Middle C will be the note C that is closest to dead center of the keyboard (it will actually be slightly left of center). Middle C is a basic point of orientation in reading music. It is represented by these notes in the three basic clefs:

Notice that the line straddled by the C clef, whatever its position, always refers to middle C. We can now find the exact location of any notated pitch by figuring its position above or below middle C.

## The Notation of Rhythm and Meter

Rhythmic notation tells us how long a note is sustained before going on to the next note. These durations are communicated by note shapes, *time signatures,* and tempo. We have already seen examples of the open or solid note heads. Their placement on a staff helps to communicate pitch. Now we must learn the meaning of the rest of the note shape, which helps to communicate duration. The following are the main such shapes and their names:

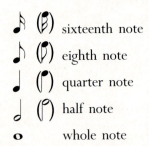

The rhythmic value of these shapes is the same, regardless of the direction of the stem. Notes with "flags" (the wavy shape at the opposite end of the stem from the note head) may be connected together with one or more "beams." Notes under a single beam are all eighth notes, and those under a double beam are all sixteenth notes, for example:

The duration of each of the five basic note values is permanently fixed relative to the others. Specifically, an eighth note is held twice as long as a sixteenth note; a quarter note, twice as long as an eighth; a half note, twice as long as a quarter; and a whole note, twice as long as a half note. Placing a dot to the right of a note head extends the duration of that note by 50 percent. Some of these fixed durational values are illustrated here:

𝅝 = ♩♩   ♩ = ♪♪♪♪   ♩ = 𝅘𝅥𝅯𝅘𝅥𝅯𝅘𝅥𝅯𝅘𝅥𝅯 𝅘𝅥𝅯𝅘𝅥𝅯𝅘𝅥𝅯𝅘𝅥𝅯

♩. = ♩♩♩   ♪. = ♪♪♪

The length of silences, called *rests,* is also precisely notated in a way that is similar to the basic note shapes. The shapes and names of the principal rests and their equivalencies to the basic note values are as follows:

𝄿    sixteenth rest (duration = ♬ )

𝄾    eighth rest (= ♪ )

𝄽    quarter rest (= ♩ )

▬    half rest (= ♩ )

▬    whole rest (= 𝅝 )

To determine precisely how long these note values and rests are sustained, two other factors must be taken into consideration: time signature and tempo. A time signature is placed just to the right of the clef at the beginning of the first staff. It consists of two numbers in tandem, the most important of which are $\frac{2}{4}$, $\frac{3}{4}$, $\frac{4}{4}$ (also abbreviated 𝄴), $\frac{2}{2}$ (also abbreviated 𝄵), and $\frac{6}{8}$.

Generally speaking, the lower of the two numbers tells us which note value is sustained for the duration from one beat to the next (which musicians, somewhat confusingly, describe as receiving the value "of one beat"). Let us illustrate with the time signatures $\frac{2}{4}$, $\frac{3}{4}$, or $\frac{4}{4}$. In each, the lower number is 4, implying that the quarter note "receives the beat." This means that in music with these signatures, the quarter note will be sustained for an amount of time equal to that from one beat until just before the next. By knowing that the quarter note receives the beat, we can easily compute the duration of the other note values and rests. Samples are given in Figure A.4. In $\frac{2}{2}$ signa-

**Figure A.4**

**Figure A.5**

**Figure A.6**

ture, the half note receives the beat, and in $\frac{6}{8}$ either the dotted quarter or (in very slow tempos) the eighth note receives the beat. A time signature thus relates the basic note values to the beat. Some typical rhythms are depicted in various signatures in Figure A.5.

From Chapter 2, recall that *meter* consists of a regular grouping of musical events and their underlying beats into cells usually having two, three, or four beats. This phenomenon in music is easily accounted for in notation by placing a vertical line (a *bar line*) through the staff every two, three, or four beats, thus marking off the metric cell. The small quantity of music between two consecutive bar lines is called a *measure*.

The prevailing meter of the music is reflected in the upper number of the time signature. In $\frac{2}{4}$, $\frac{2}{2}$, and $\frac{6}{8}$, a bar line occurs after every second beat; in $\frac{3}{4}$, after every third beat; and in $\frac{4}{4}$, after every fourth beat. Some typical rhythms and meters are depicted in Figure A.6.

## Miscellaneous Notational Signs and Practices

When a sharp or flat sign is introduced in a measure, it stays in effect for that note throughout the remainder of the measure. If the flat or sharp sign is to be canceled, a *natural sign* (♮) is entered just to the left of a note head. Sample appearances of these uses of flat, sharp, and natural signs are shown in the following:

At the beginning of a staff line, between the clef and the time signature, we will often see a group of flat signs or a group of sharp signs (the two are never mixed together). These are called *key signatures.* In essence, they tell the musician to perform a particular note either flat or sharp every time it occurs, unless a natural sign is entered to cancel that effect. The flats or sharps in a key signature occur in a fixed order: If there is one flat in a signature, it will always be situated on the B line or space, making all Bs into B♭s unless a natural sign is written. Flats occur in a signature in the order B♭, E♭, A♭, D♭, G♭, C♭, and F♭. In signatures with sharps, the first will always be found on the F line or space. Sharps occur in the order F♯, C♯, G♯, D♯, A♯, E♯, and B♯. The effect of a sample key signatures is shown in the following example:

*Figure A.7*

An indication of tempo (often using the Italian words surveyed in Chapter 2) is normally written once only, above a staff line near where the music begins. The loudness or **dynamic level** is usually entered beneath the staff, using abbreviations of Italian words:

> $pp$ (pianissimo), very soft
>
> $p$ (piano), soft
>
> $mf$ (mezzo forte), moderately loud
>
> $f$ (forte), loud
>
> $ff$ (fortissimo), very loud

Music for more than one performer is often printed in a *score* format. In this arrangement, all of the different lines of music that are heard at the same time are represented by staff lines that are displayed one above the other. A typical page of score is shown in Figure A.7 (from the finale of Beethoven's Symphony No. 9). We can see that no fewer than 19 staff lines are piled up vertically. In fact, Beethoven's symphony often has even more than 19 separate musical lines, since some of the staff lines carry the music of two different instruments. This page represents slightly more than three measures of music. The music is fast, as Beethoven tells us in the Italian words at the top, and the names of the required instruments and voices are listed (again in Italian) at the left margin.

# Glossary of Musical Terms

For other definitions and clarifications, see the *The New Harvard Dictionary of Music,* edited by Don Michael Randel (Cambridge, Mass.: Harvard University Press, 1986).

**Absolute music**  Instrumental music, such as a symphony, that lacks overt programmatic content.

**Academy**  In Renaissance Italy, a gathering for purposes of discussion. In the seventeenth and eighteenth centuries, a concert.

**Accompaniment**  A stratum in a musical composition, primarily consisting of harmonies, that enhances a melody.

**Aleatoric music**  Music in which basic compositional decisions are left to random or chance procedures. Also called *indeterminate* or *chance music.*

**Alto**  A female voice in a relatively low register. Also called *contralto.*

**Aphoristic style**  A twentieth-century musical style in which works take on extreme brevity and concentration of materials.

**Aria**  In the sixteenth century, an improvised strophic song, often based on preexistent harmonic or melodic patterns. After 1600, a musical number in an opera or related genre, sung by solo voice with orchestral accompaniment.

**Arioso**  A vocal style more expressive than recitative, but not so melodious and animated as aria.

**Artistic music**  Music written by trained composers for knowledgeable audiences, the object of which is to communicate meaning, to move the emotions, or to edify. Also known as *classical* or *serious music.*

**Atonal**   Written in a twentieth-century style in which a keynote or use of the system of tonality is not evident.

**Ballade**   A poetic-musical form in fourteenth- and fifteenth-century French songs.

**Ballata**   A poetic-musical form in fourteenth-century Italian songs. Similar to the French *virelai.*

**Balletto**   A madrigalesque composition of light character, often strophic, with "fa la la" refrains.

**Baritone**   The male voice range between tenor and bass.

**Baroque period**   In music history, the years from roughly 1600 to 1750.

**Bass**   A male voice in a relatively low register. Also, the lowest line of a musical work. Also, a large stringed instrument.

**Basso continuo**   An accompanimental stratum in a baroque work. Also called the *thorough bass.*

**Beat**   A regularly recurring pulse.

**Bebop**   A jazz style beginning in the 1940s for small ensembles, usually in very fast tempos.

**Binary form**   A musical form consisting of two distinct sections, each usually immediately repeated. A *rounded* binary form is one in which the opening melody of the first section returns midway through the second section.

**Blue note**   A note in a major scale lowered by a half step. Used in jazz performance and composition.

**Blues**   A strophic folk song originating among American blacks in the nineteenth century. It consists of variations on an established harmonic pattern. Later, any music that imitates the original blues.

**Boogie-woogie**   A type of blues in fast tempos with a recurrent bass line in a driving rhythm.

**Break**   In jazz, a very brief and often climactic solo for an instrument.

**Bridge**   See *Transition.*

**Broken chord**   A chord whose notes are played successively rather than simultaneously.

**Bull roarer**   A musical instrument consisting of a noisemaker attached to a string. It is made to sound by being swung in a rapid circular motion.

**BWV**   Abbreviation of *Bach-Werke-Verzeichnis,* a catalog by Wolfgang Schmieder of the complete works of Bach, whose numbers are commonly used to identify Bach's music.

**Cadence**   A point of conclusion in music.

**Cadenza**   An improvised passage for a soloist in a concerto or a vocalist in an aria.

**Cakewalk**   A nineteenth-century American plantation dance performed by slaves. Its syncopated rhythms made it a forerunner of *ragtime.*

**Canon**   A musical composition in which imitation in several lines is continuous and strict.

**Cantata**   A setting of a secular Italian text for small media, usually consisting of a succession of arias and recitatives. Also, a vocal composition for the Lutheran services of worship, consisting of arias, recitatives, choruses, and vocal ensembles.

**Cantus firmus**   A basic melody. Usually a preexistent melody used in some manner in the creation of an original composition.

**Canzona**   A genre of instrumental music of the sixteenth and seventeenth centuries. Normally a fugal work for instruments or keyboard.

**Canzonetta**   A madrigalesque composition of light character, usually strophic in form and homophonic in texture.

**Castrato**   A male singer, castrated as a child so as to preserve a voice of high pitch.

**Chamber music**   Music for small numbers of instruments in which only one player performs each line.

**Chance music**   See *Aleatoric music.*

**Chant**   A melody, normally with Latin religious words, sung in Roman Catholic services of worship. Also called *Gregorian chant* or *plainsong.*

**Character piece**   Instrumental music in one concise movement that establishes a definite character, emotion, or mood.

**Chiff**   A spitting sound occurring when an organ pipe first sounds.

**Chorale**   A Lutheran hymn, consisting of a melody and a strophic text.

**Chord**   A musical sound consisting of several notes, heard either simultaneously or in succession. See also *broken chord.*

**Chorus**   A medium consisting of a group of singers. Also, a passage of a jazz work consisting of a variation on a previous or preexistent melody or harmonic progression.

**Chromatic scale**   A scale in which consecutive notes are separated by half steps.

**Church cantata**   See *Cantata.*

**Classical music**   See *Artistic music.*

**Classicism**   A musical style, occurring especially from about 1750 to 1820, that emphasized simplicity, naturalness, and serenity. Works from these years form the *classical period* in music history.

**Closing theme**   A theme first appearing toward the end of the exposition of a movement in sonata form.

**Coda**   The concluding passage of a work or a movement.

**Concertmaster**   A member of an orchestra who is a leader or the assistant to a conductor—normally, the principal violinist.

**Concerto**   From the late baroque on, a work for one or more instrumental soloists accompanied by orchestra.

**Concerto grosso**   A concerto with more than one soloist.

**Contralto**   See *Alto.*

**Consonance**   A quality of chords or intervals suggesting stability and euphony.

**Counterpoint**   See *Polyphony.*

**510**

**Da capo aria**   A common aria form in baroque music, synonymous with ternary (A B A) form.

**Development**   A process in which motives are reiterated, varied, and paraphrased. Also, a passage in which development occurs, especially in a movement in sonata form.

**Dissonance**   A quality of chords or intervals suggesting instability and a lack of euphony.

**Dixieland**   Jazz played in the New Orleans style by bands normally consisting of white musicians.

**Dynamic level**   The degree of loudness.

**Electronic music**   Music whose sounds are generated, modified, or reproduced by electronic devices.

***Empfindsam* style**   A hyperemotional German musical style of the mid-eighteenth century. (*Empfindsam* means "sensitive.")

**English horn**   An instrument of the oboe family, lower in register than the oboe.

**Episode**   In a rondo form, a musical passage occurring between returns of the initial section. In a fugue, a passage not containing a complete statement of the subject.

**Estampie**   A medieval genre of instrumental music.

**Étude**   A practice piece. (*Étude* is French for "study.")

**Exposition**   A passage, especially in a movement in sonata form, in which principal themes are first stated. Also, the opening passage of a fugue, in which each line contains a statement of the subject.

**Expressionism**   A type of modernistic German art or theater of the early twentieth century. It suggests music having violent or decadent subjects, free and blatant dissonances, and bombastic dynamics.

**Field holler**   A solo sung by an American slave or field worker.

**Finale**   The last movement of a multimovement instrumental work. Also, the concluding section of an act of an opera, often emphasizing vocal ensembles.

**Flat**   A notational sign (♭) indicating the lowering of a tone by a half step. See also *Sharp*.

**Folk music**   Music performed by untrained musicians and transmitted orally.

**Form**   A plan governing the introduction and recurrence of themes, harmonies, or sections of a musical composition. Also called *structure*.

**Fortepiano**   An eighteenth-century piano.

**Fugue**   In general, music that exhibits an imitative texture. Specifically, a genre begun by imitation and continued in nonimitative polyphony.

**Fundamental**   The most prominent musical tone produced by an instrument's vibration.

***Gagaku***   Japanese traditional courtly music.

***Galant* style**   A style characteristic of mid-eighteenth-century music suggesting facility, tunefulness, and homophony.

**Gamelan**   An Indonesian instrumental ensemble.

**Genre**   A type of musical composition defined normally by a conventional medium and overall form.

**Glee**   A genre of music for male chorus on English texts.

**Gong**   A platelike metal percussion instrument struck by a beater.

**Graces**   Embellishments of a written melody added by performers. These normally take the form of notes added according to certain preestablished patterns.

**Grand opera**   Opera in nineteenth-century France having grandiose scale and resources.

**Gregorian chant**   See *Chant*.

**Half step**   The smallest interval of traditional music. All larger intervals are multiples of it. Also called a *semitone*.

**Harmonic**   An overtone that is a multiple of a fundamental frequency.

**Harmony**   In a specific sense, the accompanimental stratum of a musical work consisting of chords.

**Hichiriki**   An oboelike Japanese instrument.

**Homophony**   A musical texture consisting of one melodic line accompanied by other strata.

**Hymn**   A melody and text in strophic form sung in services of worship.

**Imitative polyphony**   A polyphonic texture in which a melody stated in one stratum is subsequently reiterated in other strata. See also *Fugue*.

**Impressionism**   A style of late-nineteenth-century French painting. In music, a style with pronounced evocativeness, delicacy, and fluidity. Often associated with the music of Claude Debussy.

**Improvisation**   Performing music extemporaneously, without written music.

**Indeterminate music**   See *Aleatoric music*.

**Interval**   The distance in pitch between two tones.

**Introduction**   A passage of a work, occurring at the beginning of a major section, that prepares the listener for more essential material to follow.

**Isorhythm**   An organizational device used especially in the late medieval motet in which a rhythmic phrase in one or more lines is repeated intact or with proportional extension or contraction.

**Jaltarang**   An Indian musical instrument consisting of water-filled porcelain bowls, played with wooden sticks.

**Jazz**   African-American popular music characterized by improvisation, swinging rhythms, syncopations, and expressive vocal or instrumental performances.

**Jubilus**   A melisma traditionally found in the Alleluia chant.

**Kapellmeister**   The musical director of an institution, such as a court, church, or theater.

**Kettledrum**   A tunable hemispheric drum. Also called *timpani*.

**Key**   See *Tonality*.

**Keynote**   The note (or its octave equivalents) that gives a melody its greatest sense of finality, completeness, or focus. Also called the *tonic*.

**512**

**Koto**   A Japanese zither.

**Leap**   Two notes sounded in succession that span an interval larger than a whole step.

**Leitmotif**   A musical motive, especially in an opera by Richard Wagner, that symbolizes a dramatic entity.

**Libretto**   The text of an opera.

**Lied**   German for *song.* (Plural is *lieder.*)

**Madrigal**   A genre of Italian or English vocal music, usually containing love poetry, for a small ensemble of unaccompanied singers.

**Madrigalism**   A musical illustration of the meaning of a word that is being sung. Also called *word painting.*

**Major scale**   A scale having the ascending order of intervals whole step, whole step, half step, whole step, whole step, whole step, half step. Music based on a major scale is said to be in the *major mode.*

**Mass**   The principal service of worship in the Roman Catholic church. Also, a musical genre consisting of a setting, usually for chorus and accompanying instruments, of texts of the ordinary.

**Mass of sound**   An element of modern composition characterized by a multiplicity of tone colors, pitches, and rhythms.

**Medium**   The instruments and voices called for in a specific musical work.

**Melisma**   An ornate passage in chant in which many notes are sung to a single syllable.

**Mélodie**   A French art song of the nineteenth and early twentieth centuries.

**Melody**   A succession of musical tones that belong together and convey a distinctive musical thought.

**Meter**   A regularly recurring emphasis or stress on beats that brings about a grouping of the intervening rhythms.

**Mezzo-soprano**   The female voice range between soprano and alto.

**Minimalism**   A musical style originating in America in the 1960s, characterized by repetition and gradual change.

**Minor scale**   A scale characterized by its first five ascending tones, which create the interval succession whole step, half step, whole step, whole step. Music based on a minor scale is in the *minor mode.*

**Minuet**   A seventeenth-century French courtly dance. Imitated in symphonic and chamber music of the late eighteenth century.

**Missa pro defunctis**   See *Requiem.*

**Mode**   The particular intervallic structure of a scale on which a work is based.

**Monody**   A song for solo voice and instrumental accompaniment from early-seventeenth-century Italy.

**Monophony**   A texture consisting solely of a melodic line.

**Motet**   A genre originating in the thirteenth century, consisting at first of one or more lines with texts added to a preexistent passage from chant. The characteristics of the genre changed radically in later usages.

**Motive**   A small, distinctive fragment of a melody.

**Movement**   A major subdivision of a lengthy work, characterized by a certain tempo.

**Music**   An organization of sounds and time capable of conveying meaning.

**Music drama**   Richard Wagner's term for his late operas.

**Musique concrète**   A type of electronic music in which basic sounds are recorded in an acoustic setting.

**Nationalism**   The quality of music that incorporates elements distinctively suggesting the culture or history of a nation or ethnic group.

**Neoclassicism**   The dominant style of European and American music between World War I and World War II. It emphasized traditional forms, genres, media, and styles.

**Neoromanticism**   An idiom reviving styles associated with nineteenth-century music.

**Nocturne**   A character work for piano in a dreamy or nocturnal mood.

**Note**   A musical sound having a certain pitch, volume, duration, and timbre. Also known as a *tone*.

**Octave**   An interval equivalent to 12 consecutive half steps.

**Opera**   A musical and dramatic genre in which most or all words of a play are sung.

**Opus**   Italian for "work." Opus numbers are traditionally assigned in chronological order by publishers to a composer's works.

**Oratorio**   A genre using biblical stories as texts and consisting musically of a succession of arias, recitatives, ensembles, and (especially) choruses.

**Orchestra**   A medium consisting usually of stringed, brass, woodwind, and percussion instruments.

**Orchestral concerto**   A three-movement orchestral work characterized by the rapid alternation of motivic material through different sections of the ensemble. Also known as a *concerto a4* or a *ripieno concerto*.

**Orchestration**   The art of distributing musical ideas to specific instruments of the orchestra.

**Ordinary**   Texts in the Roman Catholic Mass that recur in all or nearly all Masses.

**Organum**   An early type of polyphonic music, created by adding newly composed melodic lines to preexistent chants.

**Ostinato**   A brief, continuously repeated musical figure.

**Overtone**   A higher pitch produced simultaneously with a more prominent, or fundamental, pitch. Also called a *partial frequency*.

**Overture**   An orchestral prelude to a dramatic work, such as an opera, ballet, or spoken play. Also, a tone poem.

**Paraphrase**   A process of varying a preexistent melody by adding new rhythms and interpolating additional notes.

**Partial frequency**   See *Overtone*.

**Pentatonic scale**   A scale having five notes per octave.

**Period form**  A melodic pattern consisting of two symmetrical and related halves.

**Phrase**  A primary subdivision of a melody.

**Pipa**  A lutelike Chinese instrument. Also spelled *p'i-p'a.*

**Pitch**  The phenomenon of relative highness of a musical tone, produced by frequency of vibration.

**Pizzicato**  Playing a stringed instrument by plucking its strings.

**Plainsong.**  See *Chant.*

**Polyphony**  A texture consisting of more than one distinct melodic line. Polyphony may be imitative, as in canon or fugue, or free (nonimitative). Also called *counterpoint.*

**Polytonality**  The simultaneous use in music of two different keys.

**Popular music**  Music performed by professional musicians intended for the entertainment of a mass audience.

**Program music**  Instrumental music overtly containing literary or other nonmusical ideas or allusions.

**Proper**  Texts in the Roman Catholic Mass that are used on only a single occasion in the church year. These are identified by genre (for example, Alleluia).

**Qanun**  An Arabic zither.

**Qin**  A Chinese zither. Also spelled *ch'in.*

**Quintet**  A medium of five instrumentalists or a work for such an ensemble.

**Rag**  A piano composition using the style of *ragtime.*

**Raga**  A principle of melodic organization in Indian classical music. Also, a particular set of pitches and motives that guide improvisation in Indian music.

**Ragtime.**  Popular American music, especially for piano, that has the form of a march and uses a syncopated melody.

**Rabab**  An Arabic bowed string instrument.

**Rebec**  A medieval and Renaissance predecessor of the violin.

**Recapitulation**  The last of three major sections of a movement in sonata form. In this section, the principal themes return, all in the home key.

**Recital**  A concert featuring a single performer.

**Recitative**  A declamatory vocal style associated with opera and related genres.

**Refrain**  A recurrent passage.

**Register**  A segment of the range in which an instrument plays or a voice sings.

**Renaissance**  In music history, period from roughly 1425 until 1600.

**Requiem**  The Roman Catholic funeral Mass. Also known as a *Requiem Mass* or *Missa pro defunctis.*

**Resolution**  The motion of a dissonant interval, chord, or note to a consonant sonority or to a stable position.

**Rest**  A musical silence of specific duration.

**Restatement**  A passage in a fugue in which the subject reappears.

**Rhythm**  Patterns created by the durations of musical tones.

**Riff**  In jazz, a repeated motive.

**Ritornello**  An instrumental refrain.

**Rococo**  A style of decoration and interior design of the early eighteenth century, characterized by curved lines and organic shapes. Also, an early classical style with comparable features.

**Romanticism**  In music history, a style prominent in the years from roughly 1820 until 1900.

**Rondeau**  A poetic-musical form in fourteenth- and fifteenth-century French songs.

**Rondo form**  A formal pattern in which the recurrences of an initial section are separated by contrasting materials.

**Round**  A type of canon that can be repeated indefinitely.

**Rubato**  A temporary slowing or speeding of the tempo.

**Sackbut**  An early trombone.

**Saron**  An Indonesian percussion instrument in which metallic bars are made to sound when struck by a mallet.

**Scale**  An ascending or descending arrangement of tones underlying a musical passage or work.

**Scherzo**  A label used in movements of symphonies and chamber music of the late eighteenth and nineteenth centuries, usually in fast tempos and triple meters. (*Scherzo* is Italian for "joke.")

**Semitone**  See *Half step*.

**Sequence**  A steadily ascending or descending repetition of a motive.

**Serenade**  A love song. Also, a genre of eighteenth-century instrumental music of light character, cast in several movements.

**Serialism**  An approach to twentieth-century composition in which the order of occurrence of elements such as pitch, duration, register, and dynamics is governed by an arrangement determined in advance of composition.

**Serious music**  See *Artistic music*.

**Sharp**  A notational sign indicating the raising of a tone by a half step. See also *Flat*.

**Shawm**  A predecessor of the oboe.

**Sinfonia**  See *Symphony*.

**Singspiel**  German comic or sentimental opera of the eighteenth and nineteenth centuries.

**Sitar**  A lutelike instrument of North India.

**Sonata**  A genre of instrumental music originating in the late Renaissance. In the classical period and later, it is a multimovement work for solo keyboard or keyboard with accompanying instrument.

**Sonata form**  A form pervasively encountered in the first movements of instrumental works after 1750. It consists of an initial section, or *exposition,* in which basic themes are introduced, followed by a *development* passage in which these themes are paraphrased, and concluded by a *recapitulation,* in which the themes are reiterated.

**Song**  A work for voice, usually with instrumental accompaniment.

**Song cycle**  A group of songs intended to be performed together and linked by common poetic ideas or by recurrent musical elements.

**Soprano**  A female voice in a relatively high register.

**Speech melody**  A type of recitation used by twentieth-century composers in which musical rhythms are observed but pitches are only approximated.

**Spinet**  A small harpsichord. Also, an upright piano.

**Spiritual**  An American religious folk song.

**Stop time**  A brief passage in a jazz piece in which the accompanimental instruments are silent except for punctuating notes.

**String quartet**  A medium having two violins, viola, and cello. Also, a multimovement genre calling for this medium.

**Strophic form**  A formal pattern in which an initial section of music returns repeatedly, usually with changing words.

**Structure**  See *Form*.

**Subject**  The principal melody in a fugue.

**Subsidiary theme**  A theme, as in a sonata-form movement, that is introduced subsequent to the main theme or themes. It is usually less important than the main theme.

**Suite**  A collection of short instrumental pieces, usually dancelike in character and all in the same key.

**Swing**  A style of popular dance music for big bands, related to jazz.

**Symbolism**  A literary style in late-nineteenth-century France that emphasized symbolic suggestion rather than straightforward narrative.

**Symphonie concertante**  A concerto with more than one soloist.

**Syncopation**  A rhythmic figure in which notes begin slightly before and end slightly after beats or regular subdivisions of beats.

**Symphonic poem**  See *Tone poem*.

**Symphony**  A genre of orchestral music having three or four movements. Also, an instrumental passage in an early opera or related genre. Also, an orchestral concerto. Also, an opera overture. Also called *sinfonia*.

**Synthesizer**  An electronic device that aids in the creation of electronic music.

**Tabla**  A drum pair used in North Indian music. Specifically, the drum of the pair played with the right hand.

**Tala**  A principle of rhythmic and metric organization in classical Indian music.

**Tambura**  A large lutelike instrument used in Indian music to sound a drone.

**Tempo**  The speed of the beat.

**Tenor**  In modern music, a male voice in a relatively high register.

**Ternary form**  A formal pattern consisting of three sections in which the first and last are identical or similar but different from the middle section.

**Texture**  A quality of sound created by special dispositions of musical strata.

**Theme**  A recurrent and important melody in a musical composition.

**Thorough bass**  See *Basso continuo*.

**517**

**Through composition**  A formal principle in which sections do not recur in regular patterns.

**Timbre**  The distinctive quality of sound produced by an instrument or a voice. Also known as *tone color.*

**Timpani**  See *Kettledrum.*

**Toccata**  A work for keyboard or plucked instruments of the late Renaissance and baroque periods with a brilliant, improvisatory character.

**Tonality**  A system by which a keynote is expressed and contributes to musical organization and coherence. Also known as *key.*

**Tone**  See *Note.*

**Tone color**  See *Timbre.*

**Tone poem**  A programmatic orchestral work, normally in one movement.

**Tonic**  See *Keynote.*

**Transition**  A passage that links together two more important passages. Also called a *bridge.*

**Triad**  A type of three-note chord.

**Tribal music**  The folk music of nonliterate cultures.

**Trio**  A contrasting section in a minuet, scherzo, march, or ragtime. Also, a genre of chamber music for three players.

**Trio sonata**  A baroque sonata for two melody instruments and accompaniment.

**Trope**  Sections of text and music interpolated into a preexistent chant.

**Troubadour**  Poet-singer of courtly love in Provence in the Middle Ages.

**Trouvère**  Poet-singer of courtly love in France in the Middle Ages.

**Twelve-tone music**  Music using a compositional method devised by Arnold Schoenberg around 1921. The order of occurrence of most or all notes is governed by a preliminary ordering of all 12 tones.

**ʿUd**  The Arabian forerunner of the lute.

**Value**  The duration of a tone.

**Variations form**  A formal plan or process in which an initial element (usually a theme) returns repeatedly with alterations.

**Verismo**  Realistic Italian opera of the late nineteenth and early twentieth centuries.

**Vibrato**  A slight wavering in tone and pitch by a singer or an instrumentalist. Also, vibrant playing.

**Villanesca**  A madrigalesque composition of light or rustic character, usually strophic in form.

**Virelai**  A poetic-musical form in fourteenth- and fifteenth-century French songs.

**Virginal**  A small harpsichord.

**Whole step**  An interval the equivalent of two consecutive half steps. Also called a *whole tone.*

**Word painting**  See *Madrigalism.*

**Zither**  An instrument in which strings run the length of the body. The strings are sounded by plucking, bowing, or striking.

# Acknowledgments

———

*Page 2:* Picasso, Pablo. *Three Musicians.* Fontainebleau, summer 1921. Oil on canvas, 6′7″ × 7′3¾″. Collection, The Museum of Modern Art, New York. Mrs. Simon Guggenheim Fund / *Page 5:* Alinari/Art Resource, N.Y. / *Page 9:* K. Vyhnalek/Photo Edit / *Page 11:* *Le Chahut* by Seurat, Rijksmuseum Kroller-Muller / *Page 18:* Kunstmuseum, Basel/Photo: Hans Hinz / *Page 36:* Louvre/Service Photographique de la Réunion des Musées Nationaux / *Page 39:* Offentliches Kunstmuseum/Hans Hinz / *Page 41:* The Bettmann Archive / *Page 43:* From *Jazz,* Paris, 1947. As seen in "Rhythms and Line" by Jacqueline and Maurice Guillaud. Clarkson N. Potter, Inc., 1987 / *Page 46:* Kunstsammlung Nordrhein-Westfalen / *Page 52:* Musée National D'Art Moderne © Centre G. Pompidou/Photo: P. Migeat / *Page 61:* Courtesy The Classical Symphony, Chicago / *Page 62:* Kunstmuseum, Bern / *Page 64:* Courtesy Northwestern University School of Music / *Page 65 top:* Courtesy The Classical Symphony, Chicago / *Page 65 bottom:* Courtesy Northwestern University School of Music / *Page 67 top left:* Courtesy Steinway and Sons / *Page 67 top right:* The Granger Collection, New York / *Page 67 bottom:* Courtesy Northwestern University School of Music / *Page 68 right:* McKinley Studios, Inc., Chicago / *Page 71:* Cameramann/The Image Works / *Page 72:* Harrison Fund/Philadelphia Museum of Art Collection / *Page 78:* Bibliothèque Nationale / *Page 85 left:* Ron Scherl/Peter Arnold, Inc. / *Page 85 right:* Art Resource, NY / *Page 96:* Trumpet from Marin Mersenne, *Harmonie universelle,* 1635–37; shawms from Michael Praetorius, *Syntagmatis musici. Tomus II de organographia, 1619;* flutes, bagpipe and rebec from Martin Agricola, *Musica Instrumentalis Deudsch, 1529;* vielle from The British Museum / *Page 97:* Bells, drums and harp from Michael Praetorius, *Syntagmatis musici. Tomus II de organographia, 1619;* hurdy-gurdy, psaltery and lute from Marin Mersenne, *Harmonie universelle,* 1635–1637 / *Page 99:* From Annals of the New York Academy of Sciences, Vol. 314 *Machaut's World: Science and Art in the 14th Century,* © 1978 / *Page 104:* Courtesy The Early Music Consort of London / *Page 112:* Encomium musices, Amsterdam Philip Galle, © 1590 / *Page 116:* Alinari / *Page 116:* Nationalgalerie SMPK, Berlin/Photo: Bildarchiv Preussischer Kulturbesitz / *Page 117:* Uffizi Gallery/Scala/Art Resource, N.Y. / *Page 124:* The Bettmann Archive / *Page 128:* Venice: Ottaviano dei Petrucci, 1504 / *Page 132:* Courtesy of the Trustees of the British Museum / *Page 134:* Photo Researchers / *Page 144:* Alte Pinakothek, Munich / *Page 148:* Courtesy of the Trustees of the British Museum / *Page 149:* AERO Photo / *Page 156:* Tiroler Landesmuseum Ferdinandeum, Innsbruck / *Pages 164, 170:* The Bettmann Archive / *Page 184:* The Royal College of Music / *Page 189:* Princeton University Libraries / *Page 194:* From *The Notation of Polyphonic Music,* Willi Apel, The Medieval Academy of America, Cambridge, MA / *Page 199:* National Portrait Gallery, London / *Page 214:* The National Gallery, London / *Page 218:* From *Die deutschen Alpen* © 1990 by I.P. Verlagsgesellschaft, München / *Page 219:* Culver Pictures / *Page 229:* Liceo Musicale, Bologna/Scala/Art Resource, N.Y. / *Page 233:* Louvre/Service Photographique de la Réunion des Musées Nationaux / *Page 234:* ICM Artists/Photo: P. Schaaf / *Page 235:* The Royal College of Music / *Page 236:* Haydnmusem in Eisenstadt / *Page 240:* Kunsthistorisches Museum, Vienna / *Page 255:* Courtesy of the Trustees of the British Museum / *Page 259:* The Dannie and Hettie Heineman Collection/Pierpont Morgan Library / *Page 266:* Library of Congress / *Page 274:* Historic Museum of the City of Vienna / *Pages 288, 294, 295:* Louvre/Service Photographique de la Réunion des Musées Nationaux / *Page 300:* The Bettmann Archive / *Page 301:* Museum of the City of Vienna / *Page 307:* Auerbach Collection/Hulton Deutsch Collection/The Bettmann Archive / *Page 309:* Louvre/Service Photographique de la Réunion des Musées Nationaux / *Page 322:* Richard Wagner Museum, Lucerne / *Page 328:* Deutsche Fotothek, Dresden / *Page 330:* Musée d'Orsay/Service Photographique de la Réunion des Musées Nationaux / *Page 334:* Copyrighted, Chicago Tribune Company, all rights reserved / *Page 337:* Paul Gerda/Leo de Wys / *Page 344:* Nationalgalerie/Staatliche Museen zu Berlin/Bildarchiv Preussischer Kulturbesitz / *Page 354:* Andrew W. Mellon Collection/National Gallery of Art, Washington, D.C. / *Page 355:* Nationalarchiv der Richard Wagner Syiftung/Richard Wagner-Gedenkstatte, Bayreuth / *Page 362:* Stadtische Galerie IM Lenbachhaus, Munich / *Page 367:* Picasso, Pablo. *Houses on the Hill,* 1909. Oil on canvas, 25⅝″ × 31⅞″. Collection, The Museum of Modern Art, New York. Nelson A. Rockefeller Bequest / *Page 368:* Kunstsaamlung Nordrhein-Westfalen, Düsseldorf / *Page 374:* Courtesy List Publishing / *Page 377:* © The Walt Disney Company, a cartoon of Igor Stravinsky by a Disney artist / *Page 387:* Reynolda House Museum of American Art, Winston-Salem, N.C. / *Page 390:* Grosz, George. *Fit for Active Service* (1916–17). Pen and brush and India ink, 20″ × 14⅜″. Collection, The Museum of Modern Art, New York. A. Conger Goodyear Fund / *Page 391:* Historical Museum of the City of Vienna / *Page 402:* The Metropolitan Museum of Art, George A. Hearn Fund, 1957 / *Page 407:* Purchase, with funds from the Friends of the Whitney Museum of American Art, Mr. and Mrs. Eugene M. Schwartz, Mrs. Samuel A. Seaver, and Charles Simon. Photo: Geoffrey Clements, N.Y. / *Page 412:* Universal Edition, Vienna / *Page 416:* Roger Gordy / *Page 417:* excerpt from score to John Cage, *Water Music,* New York: C.F. Peters, 1952 / *Page 421:* The Rowan Gallery, London / *Page 426:* Beatriz Schiller / *Page 434:* Mondrian, Piet. *Broadway Boogie-Woogie.* 1942–43. Oil on canvas, 50″ × 50″. Collection, The Museum of Modern Art, New York. Given anonymously / *Page 439:* 1967.195 Stuart Davis, *Blips and Ifs,* oil on canvas, 1964. Amon Carter Museum of Western Art, Fort Worth, Texas / *Pages 440, 447:* The Bettmann Archive / *Pages 453, 456:* AP/Wide World / *Pages 458, 460:* UPI/Bettmann / *Page 468:* The Metropolitan Museum of Art, Bequest of Mrs. H.O. Havemeyer, 1929, The H.O. Havemeyer Collection / *Page 473:* Dept. of Archeology and Museums, Bombay / *Pages 475, 481, 489, 493:* From *New Harvard Dictionary of Music,* edited by Don M. Randel. Copyright © 1986 Reprinted by permission by the President and Fellows of Harvard College / *Pages 483, 484, 485:* Milt & Joan Mann/Cameramann International, Ltd. / *Page 492:* F. Schreider/Photo Researchers / *Page 495:* Susan McCartney/Photo Researchers.

# Index